Philosophy of Language

BLOOMSBURY KEY THINKERS

The Key Thinkers series takes a central topic in philosophy and introduces you to the people behind the ideas. Each book brings to life the arguments of a group of influential individuals with potted biographies and sophisticated discussions of their work and reception. They explain why these figures still matter and reveal how their thinking has changed the direction of a subject and the course of philosophy.

Key Thinkers in Philosophy available now from Bloomsbury:

Aesthetics, edited by Alessandro Giovannelli
Epistemology, edited by Stephen Hetherington
Ethics, edited by Tom Angier
Philosophy of Language, edited by Barry Lee
Philosophy of Mind, edited by Andrew Bailey
Philosophy of Religion, edited by Jeffrey J. Jordan
Philosophy of Science, edited by James Robert Brown

Philosophy of Language

The Key Thinkers

Second Edition

Edited by

BARRY LEE

BLOOMSBURY ACADEMIC
LONDON • NEW YORK • OXFORD • NEW DELHI • SYDNEY

BLOOMSBURY ACADEMIC
Bloomsbury Publishing Plc
50 Bedford Square, London, WC1B 3DP, UK
1385 Broadway, New York, NY 10018, USA

BLOOMSBURY, BLOOMSBURY ACADEMIC and the Diana logo are trademarks
of Bloomsbury Publishing Plc

First published in Great Britain 2020

Cover design: Maria Rajka
Cover image: © wujekjery / Getty Images

A catalogue record for this book is available from the British Library.

A catalog record for this book is available from the Library of Congress.

ISBN: HB: 978-1-3500-8409-4
PB: 978-1-3500-8408-7
ePDF: 978-1-3500-8407-0
eBook: 978-1-3500-8406-3

Series: Key Thinkers

Typeset by Newgen KnowledgeWorks Pvt. Ltd., Chennai, India
Printed and bound in Great Britain

To find out more about our authors and books visit www.bloomsbury.com
and sign up for our newsletters.

CONTENTS

PREFACE

This second edition of *Philosophy of Language: The Key Thinkers* includes a revised and expanded introduction and two new chapters: one on L. Susan Stebbing (1885–1943) and the other on feminist philosophy of language. When the opportunity arose to increase the range of the book many possibilities presented themselves. It seemed right, however, to commission chapters on the work of women philosophers in philosophy of language. The chapter on Stebbing highlights a figure who has been largely overlooked until recently but whose thoughts on what is worth serious consideration in philosophy of language and how it should be approached seem to be particularly relevant to the circumstances in which we find ourselves in the twenty-first century. The chapter on feminist philosophy of language breaks with the strategy adopted in other entries, of focusing on individual philosophers, to introduce a range of lively debates in which many philosophers are making interesting contributions and, in several cases, challenging traditional ways of thinking about the relations between areas of philosophy. I am grateful to Bloomsbury for making it possible to add to the volume in this way.

ACKNOWLEDGEMENTS

I thank Tom Stoneham for advice and guidance on many aspects of this book project. I am grateful to Guy Longworth and Rachael Wiseman for very helpful comments on drafts of my introduction to this volume and for many enjoyable discussions on the philosophy of language. A number of undergraduate student readers made very useful comments on draft chapters: thanks here to Daniel Brigham, Madeleine Brown, Tim Inman, Tom Le Cocq, Sara Osborne, Ty Partridge and Rebecca Thorn. I am indebted to an anonymous reader for Bloomsbury who gave very helpful suggestions for revision and expansion of the first edition. I am grateful to my wife, Catherine, for her (apparently endless) patience and support. This book is dedicated to the memory of Ty Partridge, who died suddenly in the summer of 2010.

NOTES ON CONTRIBUTORS

Arif Ahmed is reader in philosophy at Cambridge University. His publications include *Saul Kripke* and – as editor – *Wittgenstein's Philosophical Investigations: A Critical Guide*.

Kent Bach is professor emeritus of philosophy at San Francisco State University. He has written extensively in philosophy of language, theory of knowledge and philosophy of mind. His books include *Thought and Reference* and – with Michael Harnish – *Linguistic Communication and Speech Acts*.

Thomas Baldwin is emeritus professor of philosophy at the University of York. His publications include *Contemporary Philosophy: Philosophy in English since 1945*, *The Cambridge History of Philosophy 1870–1945*, *Maurice Merleau-Ponty: Basic Writings*, *Reading Merleau-Ponty* and – as co-editor with Consuelo Preti – *G. E. Moore: Early Philosophical Writings*.

Michael Beaney is professor of history of analytic philosophy at the Humboldt University in Berlin and professor of philosophy at King's College London. His publications include *Frege: Making Sense*, *Analytic Philosophy: A Very Short Introduction* and – as editor – *The Frege Reader*, *Gottlob Frege: Critical Assessments of Leading Philosophers* (4 volumes, co-edited with Erich Reck) and *The Oxford Handbook of the History of Analytic Philosophy*.

Siobhan Chapman is professor of English at the University of Liverpool. Her publications include *Paul Grice, Philosopher and Linguist*, *Language and Empiricism*, *After the Vienna Circle* and *Susan Stebbing and the Language of Common Sense*.

John Collins is professor of philosophy at the University of East Anglia. He is the author of many articles in the philosophy of language and mind, and the monographs *Chomsky: A Guide for the Perplexed* and *The Unity of Linguistic Meaning*.

Bryan Frances is the research professor of theoretical philosophy at the University of Tartu. His publications include papers in philosophy of language, philosophy of mind, epistemology, philosophy of religion and metaphysics.

Gary Kemp is lecturer in philosophy at the University of Glasgow. His publications include *Quine: A Guide for the Perplexed*, *Critical Thinking: A Concise Guide* (with Tracy Bowell) and *Quine versus Davidson: Truth, Reference and Meaning*.

Barry Lee is lecturer in philosophy at the University of York. His research interests are in philosophy of language and metaphysics, particularly the metaphysics of time.

Guy Longworth is reader in philosophy at the University of Warwick. His interests include the history of analytic philosophy and philosophical issues arising from the communication of knowledge. He is the editor of *Proceedings of the Aristotelian Society*.

Kirk Ludwig is professor of philosophy and cognitive science at Indiana University, Bloomington. He works in the philosophy of language, philosophy of mind and action, epistemology and metaphysics. He is the editor of *Donald Davidson*, co-author with Ernest Lepore of *Donald Davidson: Meaning, Truth, Language, and Reality* and *Donald Davidson's Truth-Theoretic Semantics*, and co-editor with Ernest Lepore of *A Companion to Donald Davidson*. His most recent books are *From Individual to Plural Agency: Collective Action 1*, *From Individual to Plural Agency: Collective Action 2* and *The Routledge Handbook of Collective Intentionality*, ed. with Marija Jankovic.

Kenneth A. Taylor is Henry Waldgrave Stuart Professor of Philosophy at Stanford University. His publications include *Truth and Meaning: An Introduction to the Philosophy of Language*, *Reference and the Rational Mind* and *Meaning Diminished: Toward Metaphysically Modest Semantics*. He co-hosts the nationally syndicated public radio programme *Philosophy Talk* in the United States.

Maura Tumulty is associate professor of philosophy at Colgate University. Her publications include papers in the philosophy of language and philosophy of mind. Her book *Alien Experience* is forthcoming.

Pierre Wagner is a member of the faculty of the Philosophy Department, University Paris 1 Panthéon-Sorbonne, and of the IHPST (Institut d'histoire et de philosophie des sciences et des techniques). His publications include *La Machine en logique*, *La Logique* and – as editor – *Carnap's Logical Syntax of Language*.

Bernhard Weiss is professor of philosophy at the University of Cape Town. His publications include *Michael Dummett* and *How to Understand Language: A Philosophical Inquiry*.

Introduction

Barry Lee

1. Language and philosophy

We live in and through language. To speak less metaphorically, much of the business of our lives is carried out through linguistic means. It is largely with words that we organize our activities and attempt to construct representations and models of the world. It is largely through words that we express ourselves, both to others, and to ourselves – since much if not all of our thinking is conducted with words. Language use is a largely distinctive feature of human life. Although other animals communicate (in the sense of transmitting information) in something like the way we find in language-use, no other animal we know of has a resource with the expressive power and range found in humans' language-using capacities.

Philosophers are interested in language not just because it is so central to human life – though that alone would be good reason to subject it to some philosophical scrutiny. As already hinted, questions of the relationship between language and thought are important. (For instance, some philosophers argue that language is a necessary means for thought, so that without language we would be incapable of the thinking that seems to come so naturally to us.) And there are other motives. At least some philosophers hope that getting clearer about language and its fundamental structures will help them to get clearer about the structure of the world – about metaphysics. So, for instance, philosophers who are interested in the nature of time, and the status of past and future things, try to get clear about how tense works, and how we might account for the meaning of tensed claims. (Why one might think that the structure of language is a guide to the structure of reality is itself bound up with fundamental issues in the philosophy of language. Some key philosophers of language would question the claim: see the chapters on Carnap and the later Wittgenstein in this volume.) Another more general reason why philosophers are interested in language is that the business of philosophy – argument and conceptual clarification – is conducted using linguistic tools, and philosophers want to subject those tools to careful and critical examination, to try to ensure that they are up to the job, and that more or less subtle traps set by language don't lead us into making mistakes in argument, seeing things the wrong way, or pursuing questions that are in fact senseless (in that they arise from confusions).

2. A unified account of language?

When we begin to study language, what we first encounter is linguistic activity (speech in Japanese, correspondence in French, signing in BSL and so on). Despite the huge variety found in this activity – we use language to plan, joke, speculate, describe, theorize, soliloquize, question, command, beg, fictionalize, transmit knowledge and information, and to do a great many other things – it is plausible that language-use is in some significant sense a unified phenomenon. And where there are phenomena which are potentially unified, there is an impulse to seek a single theoretical account of them, an account which shows how they are connected and provides, where possible, explanations of what we observe. In physics, for example, atomic theory provides the basis of accounts of the relations between pressure, volume and temperature in gases, the proportions of materials consumed in chemical compounding, the phenomenon of Brownian motion and so on. That a theoretical claim helps to provide explanations and predictions across a wide range of phenomena in this way provides us with one reason to think it true. Where such a claim is part of an account which is unbettered, this is *inference to the best explanation.*[1]

It would be good, then, to have a unified and systematic account of central aspects of language-use, an account which showed what our varied linguistic activities have in common, and explained, where possible, what we observe. But what key concept or concepts might be at the centre of such a unified and systematic account?

There is one very obvious and tempting answer here: *meaning*. The phenomena of language use are unified, it seems, in that they exploit the meaningfulness of linguistic expressions. Now, of course, even if this proposal is correct, there is still a very long way to go. Having selected meaning as our key concept, we immediately face some very difficult questions concerning meaning and related issues, including:

- What is it for words to have meaning?

- How do words mean what they do?

- What is it for a speaker to understand an expression ('grasp its meaning'), or know a language?

- How is linguistic communication possible?

- How can it be that words have publicly accessible meanings?

Before we pursue such questions, however, we should pause and note two important cautionary points.

First, it may be that the phenomena of language-use are *not*, in fact, unified in a way amenable to a grand systematic theory, but are better viewed as arising in a range of activities loosely bonded by various relations of similarity. Such a view might not seem very plausible, once one is gripped by the appeal of the idea that meaning is the 'essence of language', but it's arguable that the Wittgenstein of the *Philosophical Investigations* held something like this radical 'no system' view (see the chapter on Wittgenstein and the *Investigations* below). In any case there is reason to maintain a certain critical distance from the notion of meaning. This brings us to our second point.

The term 'meaning' is drawn from what we might call 'talk about talk'. In our everyday activities, we make claims of various sorts which are 'about language', and about linguistic activities – for example, 'jongen' in Dutch *means* boy, Galileo *said that* the earth moves, Tom *understood* what David said, Ben *speaks* French, 'Everest' *names* a mountain in the Nepal–China border region. Focusing more closely on 'means' and related expressions, we say such things as: 'La neige est blanche' in French *means the same as* 'Snow is white' in English; when David said 'Coffee will keep me awake' *he meant* he'd decided not to have coffee. It is not obvious that the concept or concepts which are active in these sorts of everyday claims are suited to a role in a systematic and general theory. On the one hand, it may be that even if a concept, *meaning*, figures in a general and systematic account of language-use, it will need to be a revised and sharpened relative of the everyday concept/s (here we might draw an analogy with the way in which the concepts of theoretical physics, such as force or mass, are revised/ sharpened relatives of everyday concepts). On the other hand, and more radically, it may be that, though language-use *is* amenable to treatment in an overarching and systematic theoretical framework, the final theory will be one in which a notion of meaning plays *no significant role*. (Of the key figures studied in this volume, Quine argues for a general account of language-use which has no special place for a notion of meaning, and Chomsky holds that the features of language which are distinctive and pervasive, and amenable to systematic theoretical treatment, are primarily syntactic and grammatical – though his views on meaning are more nuanced.)

Now we are in a position to note a number of reasons why language deserves distinctively *philosophical* attention – why philosophers should mount a philosophical investigation of language, rather than simply waiting on linguistic science to return its results. First, as we have just noted, it seems likely that the key concepts to be deployed in a systematic account of language-use will be drawn from, or be descendants of, concepts in our everyday talk-about-talk. As such, care will be needed to clarify the content of those everyday concepts and to keep a watchful eye on perhaps otherwise unannounced and therefore potentially misleading revision, refinement or even conflation of those concepts. Secondly, as can be noted by looking back to the questions which arise if we pursue a general theory based on meaning, the kinds of questions which arise are *constitutive* questions ('What is it' questions) and questions of possibility: *What is it* for words to have meaning? *How* do words mean what they do? *How can it be* that words have publicly accessible meanings? *How* is linguistic communication *possible*? Such questions are, if not philosophy's exclusive preserve, at least ones which invite close philosophical attention. Thirdly, as suggested already, there are significant connections between the deepest questions about language-use and philosophical issues in other areas: connections with the philosophy of mind (e.g. with regard to beliefs and the way we report them; with regard to whether language is merely a means for expressing thoughts had independently of language, or something which enables us to have thoughts; and with regard to what it is to think about, say, a particular thing in the world), and at least potentially there are connections with metaphysics (e.g. with regard to the natures of types of entity we might consider positing in order to account for the meaning of expressions), and epistemology (e.g. with regard to how we might have knowledge of or access to the entities that some particular theories say are bound up with meaning).

Let's summarize what we've seen so far. Language-use is a pervasive and distinctive feature of human life. Language-use is of philosophical interest. It would be very good, from a theorist's point of view, to have a general and systematic theoretical account of language-use, though we should be prepared for the possibilities (a) that careful investigation of language will provide no unified 'deep' theory, and (b) that even if a general theory is forthcoming, it may look quite different from what we might initially expect, in terms of the precise nature of its key concepts or – more radically – in terms of its general nature.

Now, let's look further at how far we might get by following through on the idea that it is *meaning* which provides the key to a systematic account of language-use.

3. Two simple accounts of meaning

It's plausible that an account of language-use which makes a concept of meaning central cannot simply stop at that: we need some account of the nature of meaning, and how words mean what that they do.

We've already raised difficult-sounding questions about meaning, and meanings would seem to be an odd kind of thing. Compare the case of genetics. A geneticist can account for the patterns of transmission of characteristics from ancestor to descendant, but seems to owe us an account of what genes are, otherwise the explanation seems incomplete, and genes 'spooky' – that is, not properly related to the overall picture of the world which science reveals. The debt begins to be paid off when genes are related to DNA, and the mechanism of transmission begins to be explained. Now, it may be that meanings are not going to be explained in physical or biological terms, but the theorist who talks about language in terms of meaning will need to say something more about the nature of meaning, at least relating the content of the concept of meaning to other concepts. In this section we'll look at two simple outline proposals concerning the nature of meaning.

The first simple proposal aims to exploit connections between language and thought. In uttering a sentence I can express a thought, and in hearing and understanding my utterance you can come to entertain the thought too (and see it as the thought that I have expressed). Without considerable further work, this proposal too simply raises further questions. What are thoughts? (They would seem to be odd sorts of things. They do not seem to be found in public space. It is tempting to think of them as inner psychological occurrences, but this is problematic, as we'll see.) And how is it that a sentence – a mere string of sounds/marks/patterns of illumination/gestures – can express a thought? Further, if what it is for a sentence to have a meaning is for a speaker to associate a thought with it, then how can another person identify which thought a speaker associates with a particular sentence? And how is communication to be possible? (These last two questions seem particularly problematic if thoughts are inner psychological occurrences.)

The second proposal can be seen as trying to address, or perhaps sidestep, these sorts of difficulties. This proposal focuses instead on relations between words and things – things present in public space. Ordinary speakers don't usually have theories about what meaning is, in advance of studying philosophy or linguistics, but many ordinary speakers would endorse both the view that many proper nouns *stand for* or *refer to* particular things, and the view that these relations are very important to these words meaning what they do. Accounts of this second kind try to develop and expand this thought to provide a general account of meaning. And accounts of this type have proved popular, holding a prominent position in philosophical reflection on language for more than one hundred years. The proposal seems promising, in that both words and things are present in public space – at least, many things for which we have words are present there. Again, however, difficult questions arise when we try to develop the basic suggestion. How might we develop what looks like a reasonable proposal for proper nouns so that it applies to other kinds of expression? (It might seem very plausible that 'Barack Obama' stands for the man Barack Obama, but what does 'red' stand for, or 'and', or 'because'?) Further, what is it for a word to *stand for* a thing? What makes it the case that a word stands for a thing? And how are we to accommodate what seem to be the connections between language and thought – between the linguistic activities of speakers and their mental lives?

A further, broader and deeper difficulty can be raised at this stage – one which faces both thing theories and at least a great many thought theories. We'll raise it first with regard to thing-theories. Suppose for the sake of argument that we have managed to assign things to words. The difficulty arises when we note (i) that when we use language we typically use whole sentences, and (ii) that how a sentence is made up from its component words has an impact on what it means. For example, 'Reg loves Amy' and 'Amy loves Reg' are made up from the same words, but mean different things (and, tragically, one can be true when the other is false). The problem is that simply by associating things with words we will not have provided the means to deal with the dependence of sentence meaning on sentence structure. If our account relates words to things one by one, then for all our account says, a sentence is just a list.

Accounting for the way in which word meanings and sentence structure together determine sentence meanings – what we can call *the problem of the unity of the proposition* – is not a negotiable component of a theory of meaning. It is very plausible that this feature of human languages makes a vital contribution to their enormous expressive power, and is crucial to the ability of speakers with finite powers to use and understand sentences they have not encountered previously – what we can call the *productivity* of language.

An analogous problem afflicts at least many thought-theories: to deal with the problem of explaining how sentences are related to thoughts, we might posit connections between words and thought-elements. Again, without further work, it is far from clear how such an approach could count a sentence as any more than a list of such elements.

Note that the problems raised for simple thought and thing theories here are not presented as fatal to all thought- or thing-based accounts; rather, what is important to note is that these difficulties have to be faced. *Simple* thought or thing theories are unlikely to prove satisfactory, but more developed and sophisticated theories might deal with the problems. Indeed, it would be a sorry prospect if connections to thought or the world were barred, because it would seem that any viable theory must make connections of some kinds between language, thought and the world.

In these first three sections, I have sought both to indicate why we should be interested in an investigation into the nature of language, and to outline the large-scale questions and puzzles that arise when we begin such an inquiry. In the sections that follow, I sketch some of the main ideas put forward by the key thinkers discussed in individual chapters, in order to begin to relate them to one another, and show how they bear on the big questions. In the next section, I sketch truth-based accounts of meaning. In Section 5, I note some virtues of truth-based accounts, some problems that they face, and various responses to these problems offered by Frege, by Russell and by Wittgenstein (in his early work). In Section 6, I consider Logical Empiricist views (including the views of Carnap), and Quine's critical response to them. In Section 7, I look at various challenges to what I will call the 'mainstream' approach which aims to provide a systematic account of language use in terms of meaning, with meaning elucidated in terms of truth and reference.[2] Here I consider challenges raised against the mainstream approach by Wittgenstein (in his later work), Quine, Stebbing, Austin, Chomsky and Derrida.[3] (The ideas and arguments discussed in Bryan Frances's chapter on Kripke are highlighted in Section 5 – in relation to Frege – and in Section 7 – in relation to the later Wittgenstein.[4]) In Section 8, I sketch some ideas due to Grice which are important in their own right, and which may help defend the mainstream view against some of the challenges. In Sections 9 and 10, I turn to two major figures who have sought to clarify the nature of meaning by investigating how to construct systematic meaning theories for individual languages: Donald Davidson, who advocated a truth-based approach; and Michael Dummett, who raises significant further difficulties for truth-based accounts and presses for an alternative approach. In Section 11, I consider some criticisms which have been raised by feminist philosophers of language against approaches to language use implicit in much of the 'mainstream' work considered in this volume, and moves to correct the identified deficits. As we have noted, language is a social phenomenon. Linguistic interactions facilitate but are also potentially impacted by social relations. Much of the work in philosophy of language considered in this volume operates at a level at which significant social features of language-users are not considered: social status, power-relations, race, gender, sexuality do not figure, and instead users are primarily considered simply as idealized speakers and hearers (though it should be acknowledged that Austin pays attention to particular social roles such as court judge and marriage officiant). Further, there is in mainstream work a tendency to focus on *successful* communication, rather than on situations in which there are difficulties, distortions or abuses (Stebbing is an interesting early exception in her critical examination of public discourse). Feminist philosophers of language have subjected both of these features of 'mainstream' approaches to criticism and explored the ways in which ethically and politically loaded features of social relations between speakers can interact with broad and deep issues of meaning and communication.

I close this introduction with some brief summary remarks and suggestions on how to use the discussions presented in this book. Further detailed discussion of the issues raised in this introduction can be found in the excellent individual figure chapters which follow.

4. Truth-based accounts of meaning

A solution to the problem of the unity of the proposition is implicit in Frege's work. Frege's primary concern was not with everyday language; rather he wanted to show that arithmetic was a part of logic. In order to do this he needed to show how arithmetical claims could be derived from a small number of claims by purely logical means. (Along the way, Frege pretty much invented modern logic, and formulated powerful accounts of sentences and inferences which had previously resisted systematic treatment. See Mike Beaney's excellent account of Frege's work below.) Since Frege's concern was with relations of logical entailment between sentences – what follows from what, which further sentences would have to be true if particular sentences were true – he naturally focused upon the truth-relevant properties of sentences, and in turn on how individual expressions contributed to determining truth-involving properties of sentences.[5] This strategy promises a solution to the problem of unity: whereas it is difficult to see how assigning things or thought-elements to words can result in anything but sentences being viewed as lists, it is relatively easy to assign truth-relevant properties to expressions in a way which allows for the role of structure in determining the truth-relevant properties of sentences.[6]

In Frege's version of this general kind of theory, basic expressions are seen as being associated with an extra-linguistic entity, in virtue of which association they contribute to determining the truth-value[7] of the sentences in which they appear: this association is the expression's *reference*; and the item to which an expression refers is called its *referent*. Frege, then, can be seen as framing his account in terms of a refined and specific version of *standing for*. (Frege's mature theory of meaning involves a further key element, in addition to reference. We will consider this development in the next section.) On Frege's account, some complex expressions have reference, with the reference of specific complex expressions being determined by the references of their parts, and the way they are put together. This includes sentences, with true sentences referring to an object, the truth-value *True*, and false sentences referring to another object, the truth-value *False*. (This seems odd at first consideration, but sits quite naturally with seeing complex expressions as having reference, and with the fact that sentences can figure as parts of larger sentences.)

The promising aspects of truth-based accounts of word meaning are more easily illustrated in the kind of truth theory deployed by Davidson in his account of meaning and interpretation (see the chapter on Davidson for further details). In Davidsonian truth theories, expressions are assigned properties which contribute to determining the truth-*conditions* of the sentences in which they appear (the truth-conditions of a sentence are simply the conditions under which it is true) and there is no insistence on having a notion of reference which is applicable to complex expressions. For example, we might have

(R1) 'Barack' (noun phrase) refers to Barack
(S1) 'smokes' (verb phrase) is satisfied by a thing if and only if that thing smokes
(C1) A sentence made up from a noun phrase followed by a verb phrase is true if and only if the thing to which the noun phrase refers satisfies the verb phrase

These together determine the following:

'Barack smokes' is true iff Barack smokes

Theories of this general kind are so promising because they show how an important semantic property (i.e. a meaning-property) of sentences can be determined by assignments of semantic properties to their component expressions. We'll see why this is good shortly.

It's worth making a brief aside here. Those new to the philosophy of language are often surprised at the amount of time spent discussing what seem to be quite specific proposals concerning the semantics of particular kinds of expressions (e.g. proper names). What is, I hope, beginning to be apparent is that broad proposals about the nature of meaning need to be tested in the details of language, and we can only give a proper evaluation of such views by providing an account which plausibly extends to the whole of language: we do theory of meaning – in the sense of giving a general account of the *nature* of meaning – only by trying to construct systematic theories of meaning for specific languages – that is, theories which account systematically for the meaning of each of the sentences in the language. We'll return to these issues below.

5. Some benefits and costs of truth-based accounts

Truth-based accounts of meaning chime very well with our intuitions that language can be (and is) used to transmit information and pass on knowledge: typically, when a speaker utters a declarative sentence, she presents it as true; and a hearer who knows the truth-conditions of the sentence will see her as presenting herself as holding that that particular condition obtains.

The sorts of accounts we've sketched also seem to have another important virtue. They show how it can be possible for us to understand novel sentences – sentences we have not heard before; and they show how it can be possible for language to be learnable by finite creatures with finite capacities.

Accounts based on truth and reference do, however, face some significant problems.

First, there is a difficulty with 'empty' terms: expressions which don't have reference. According to a theory of the simple type we've sketched, the meaningfulness of a name consists in its referring to a particular thing: 'Barack' refers to Barack (that particular flesh-and-blood man). This adverts to a relation between an expression and a thing, and for this kind of expression, it is standing in that relation to a thing which is what makes it meaningful. But now, what about expressions which seem to be in this category, and seem to be meaningful (they are used in what seem to be meaningful ways), but which lack reference? What about 'Santa', 'Sherlock Holmes' and 'Vulcan'?[8] Our account says that 'Barack' refers to Barack, but there is no true statement (of the relevant form) beginning '"Santa" refers to ...'.

Secondly, there seem to be aspects of meaning which cannot be accounted for in terms of reference. The key semantic property of our theory is reference. The reference of an expression is just a matter of its relation to a particular object. The movie actor Cary Grant was born Archibald Leach. So 'Cary Grant' and 'Archibald Leach' are exactly alike in terms of reference. But it seems that anyone who understood 'Cary Grant is Cary Grant' (grasped its meaning) would recognize it as true on that basis, whereas it seems that someone might *understand* 'Cary Grant is Archibald Leach' (grasp *its* meaning) and yet not recognize its truth – suppose they knew Archie as a child, but learned the name 'Cary Grant' watching movies. ('Cary is Archibald' might come as *news* to someone who understood it, hence the usual name for this puzzle: *the problem of informative identities*.) The key point here is that our attributions of reference – and these are the only attributions of semantic properties to expressions we've made so far – seem unable to account for what seems to be a difference of meaning here.

There are other challenges too – particular variations on challenges which face any attempt to provide an account of meaning. In virtue of what does an expression refer? (What is it for a word to have meaning?) And what is it for a speaker to grasp the reference of an expression? (What is required for a speaker to understand – to be semantically competent with – an expression?)

Responses to these problems and challenges have been various.

Frege introduced an additional semantic property into his account: *sense*. The sense of an expression involves a *mode of presentation* or *mode of determination* – intuitively and roughly, a way in which the referent is presented (to the speaker), or a way of determining ('picking out') a referent. The sense of an expression is then the mode of presentation (or mode of determination) *obligatorily associated with the expression* – the mode of presentation (or determination) which a speaker *must* associate with the expression to qualify as understanding it.[9] How exactly we might fill out what Frege says about sense into a fully explicit and satisfying account is a contested issue, but one kind of account starts with the idea that a mode of presentation is a way in which the *referent* is presented to (the mind of) the speaker.

Introducing senses promises to deal with our problems and challenges in the following ways. The names 'Cary Grant' and 'Archibald Leach' can be seen as possessing different senses: the modes of presentation involved are modes of presentation of the same object, but this need not be apparent to a speaker who grasps both. And it may be (though this is controversial) that there can be sense without reference (without a referent), allowing for the possibility of meaningful but empty names. And, further, we can say that to understand an expression (and have a grasp of its reference sufficient for understanding) is to grasp its sense, and that expressions are meaningful in virtue of having sense assigned to them.

Theories which talk about senses face their own difficulties, however. As noted already, the precise nature of sense is contested. If senses are to be aspects of public, shared meanings, then senses will have to be sharable and accessible. Frege carefully distinguished senses from what he called *ideas* (private mental items such as mental images). We can perhaps see how a mode of presentation can be public property if it is something like a *perspective* on an object – for example, the familiar prospect of the White House onto its frontage, which can be enjoyed by anyone suitably placed. If there are to be senses *without* referents, however, senses threaten to be stranger, more rarefied and 'ghostly'. Seeing senses as (something like) perspectives on referents sees them simply as abstractions from our mind-involving dealings with the world. But it is difficult to see how there could be perspectives on *nothing*. For this reason it seems that, if there are to be senses without referents, senses will have to be abstract objects, existing independently in an abstract realm; and this raises difficulties – about how we have knowledge of them, how they are associated with words and how we come to know how others associate them with words.[10]

We can note as an aside that the case for sense faces further challenges. For one thing, our observations concerning informative identities might be explained in terms of modes of presentation but *without* having modes of presentation figure as aspects of objective meaning. It might be, for instance, that all there is to the public meaning of an ordinary proper name is its reference, with modes of presentation only being involved in individual speakers picking out the referent, so that different speakers might associate different modes of presentation with the same name (quite legitimately, and without any doubts being raised about their semantic competence with the name).[11] It is true that the advocate of Fregean sense can present a further argument for sense, relating to occurrences of co-referring names in the context of propositional attitude reports – including reports of beliefs, like 'George believes that Cary Grant is a film star', 'George does not believe that Archibald Leach is a film star' (see Section 9 of the chapter on Frege). It may be that this argument provides stronger support than is provided by the puzzle of informative identities, as in these cases the truth-conditions of the sentences seem to be involved, but a forceful objection has been raised against this argument by Saul Kripke (see the chapter on Kripke, Sections 1–3, for detailed discussion).

Frege classed definite descriptions (phrases such as 'the mother of Barack Obama') as referring expressions.[12] He saw the reference of complex expression as determined by the references of their parts: with, for example, the reference of 'the mother of Barack Obama' being determined by the reference of 'Barack Obama' and the function associated with 'the mother of', which takes us from Barack to Ann Dunham. This is problematic when it comes to empty descriptions, such as 'the greatest prime number'. There seem to be meaningful sentences (possessing truth-values) which contain empty descriptions, but how are we to see a reference being determined for such a sentence if one of its significant parts lacks reference altogether?[13]

Russell proposed that definite descriptions be dealt with differently. He suggested that they are not referring expressions, but rather devices of quantification: instead of making a claim directly about a particular object (like 'Everest is a mountain', which says of a particular thing – Everest – that it has a particular characteristic – being a mountain), a sentence involving a definite description makes a quantificational (a 'how many') claim, about the numbers of things having particular characteristics. For example 'the man skiing down Everest is French' is true, according to Russell's view, if and only if it is the case that there is *exactly one* man skiing down Everest, and that *all* men skiing down Everest are French. This gets round the problem of empty descriptions: definite description phrases just do a very different job from referring expressions; they don't have to have a reference determined for them in order for them to be meaningful; and intuitively, it's clear how we can understand descriptions on the basis of understanding the predicates which feature in them (characterizing expressions like 'is a man', 'is skiing down Everest' and so on), together with quantifying expressions like 'there is exactly one', without any need to pick out a particular object as being related to the description.

Russell's theory of descriptions deals nicely with the problem of empty descriptions. It can also deal with the problem of informative identities involving two definite descriptions (such as 'The inventor of ball-wheeled wheelbarrows is the inventor of cyclonic vacuum cleaners'). But it does not deal in any obvious way with the analogous difficulties for proper names. If we want to avoid having to say that proper names have senses, a different solution must be sought. Russell suggested that proper names in everyday language (natural language) were in fact *disguised* definite descriptions.[14] (Very much later, however, Saul Kripke showed that there were severe difficulties to be faced in trying to account for the meaning of proper names by seeing them as disguised definite descriptions.[15])

Accounting for the meaning of apparently simple expressions in terms of definite descriptions cannot go on forever. It seems that the process must stop somewhere, with expressions which are attributed fundamental semantic properties. This brings us back to fundamental issues. What are the fundamental semantic properties? How is it that expressions have these properties? What is it for a speaker to grasp these properties?

For Russell, at the fundamental level there are 'logically proper names' which really do function by referring. To understand such a name, one has to be *acquainted* with its referent, in a special sense: one has to be in direct cognitive contact with the referent. Since the meaningfulness of such a name consists in its referring, the meaningfulness of such a name demands the existence of its referent.

In his earlier work, Wittgenstein held views with significant points of similarity to those of Russell. (See the chapter on Wittgenstein and the *Tractatus Logico-Philosophicus* in this volume.) He held that at a fundamental level linguistic meaning must be a matter of expressions standing in the (genuine) naming relation to elements of reality, with arrangements of these names *picturing* the facts they represented.

The views of Russell and Wittgenstein here seem problematic. Acquaintance is very demanding, and it is far from clear that we stand in any such relation to anything. Russell's suggestion, that what we are acquainted with are 'sense data' – basic items of sensory experience – makes serious difficulties for the publicity of meaning: if the meaning of my words is grounded in connections with *my* sense data, it's difficult to see how you can know what my words mean. Wittgenstein's view in the *Tractatus* comes at a heavy metaphysical cost – it requires the existence of indestructible simples – and its view of the basis of meaning in projection (a mental act of correlating a name with a simple) seems obscure; and there are other points at which significant objections may be raised against the account.

We have been looking at attempts to account for linguistic meaning in terms of truth and reference. We have noted some of the pressures which come to bear on such accounts, including the difficulties in spelling out the notion of sense faced by Fregean accounts, and the various metaphysical and epistemological worries which arise with regard to the views of Russell and Wittgenstein. We'll turn now to the next major trend in the development of theories of meaning: Logical Empiricism. Logical empiricist views can be seen as offering potential solutions to at least some of the difficulties encountered so far.

6. Logical empiricism and Quinean holism

The Vienna Circle was a group of philosophers and scientists who met regularly to discuss philosophical issues between 1924 and 1936. Key figures in the group included Moritz Schlick, Otto Neurath and Rudolph Carnap. The broad outlook of the group was empiricist and anti-metaphysical: they held that knowledge was grounded in experience of the world, and were suspicious of claims about realms allegedly beyond such experience. They held that natural science was a model for genuine knowledge. And they proposed a criterion of meaningfulness: roughly, that for a sentence to be meaningful is for there to be ways of supporting or undermining its claim to truth by appeals to the contents of experience. The outline criterion was filled out in various different ways, at the extreme in the *principle of verification*: the claim that to understand a sentence is to know its method of verification/falsification (to know how it might be demonstrated to be true or false on the basis of experience).

The approach of the Vienna Circle was reformist, rather than descriptive: they were open to the idea that some linguistic practices might be modified, or even abandoned as not properly meaningful. This outlook opened up the possibility that in some cases where it proved difficult to give accounts of meaning, the problems could be shrugged off as due to defects in language and our practices of language-use, rather than shortcomings in the theoretical approach applied.

One aim of Vienna Circle thinkers was to construct a language suitable for empirical science. In very rough outline, the typical strategy was to frame accounts of the vocabulary figuring in observational sentences in such a way that the meaning of those sentences was accounted for in terms of the observations which would confirm or infirm (verify or falsify) each sentence. The significance of more theoretical sentences was then to be accounted for by seeing them as (equivalent to) logical constructions of observation sentences. This sort of view has quite a lot of intuitive appeal at first glance: we learn to use words like 'cat' in situations in which the word is associated with characteristic experiences, and it seems that the idea might generalize.

The Logical Empiricist programme faces problems in two key areas: logic and mathematics. Logical knowledge does not seem to be empirical, so what is its status? A typical response was that the sentences expressing the principles of logic are *analytic* (i.e. determined as true simply in virtue of the meanings of their component expressions and the way those expressions are put together in the sentence).

Mathematics was another matter. Mathematics seems to be required for modern science, but mathematics seems to talk about strange objects, namely numbers. (When we say 'There is a prime number between 12 and 16' we seem to speak truly, and the truth of this claim seems to require that there exists some thing which is a number and prime.) What are these objects? And how do we have knowledge of them? We don't seem to encounter them in the world available to experience. We might be tempted to say that they exist in a special realm, and that we intuit their properties by a special faculty, but this would seem to be highly dubious by empiricist standards. One response to this difficulty is to try to show that the truths of mathematics follow from truths of logic. This is logicism. Frege had attempted to push through the logicist programme (with somewhat different motivations), but his attempt had been shown to fail by Russell, who pointed out that a key principle used by Frege generated a contradiction, and so could not be true. A significant part of the Logical Empiricist project is taken up with trying to resolve these difficulties concerning mathematics.

Logical Empiricism faces key objections in more easily graspable regards. First, the criterion of meaningfulness is difficult to articulate in a precise and satisfying way. And further, it seems self-undermining: What might confirm/infirm *it*? And if it's not open to *empirical* evaluation, on what basis might it be held to be analytic?[16] Secondly, the picture of meaning presented by Logical Empiricism can be seen as dubious. To what do the basic observational sentences relate – sense experience or objective matters? If the former, we face the sorts of difficulties noted above relating to the views of Russell and Wittgenstein. If the latter, then other problems arise, problems noted by Quine. The key point here is that it is dubious that any 'observational' sentence can be conclusively established as true or false on the basis of observations alone. For example, an experience as of a pink swan does not verify 'There is a pink swan'; such an experience might be reasonably *discounted* on any one of a large range of grounds, for example on the basis of a belief that lighting conditions were deceptive. Thirdly, appeals to analyticity can appear dubious from an empiricist perspective. Notoriously, Quine argued that attempts to explain analyticity were unsatisfying, and that sharp and determinate attributions of meaning to linguistic expressions were not supportable by empirical investigation of language-use. In Quine's naturalistic view of language, our linguistic activities are expressions of complex dispositions, and 'our statements about the external world face the tribunal of sense experience not individually but only as a corporate body' (Quine, 1961 [1951], p. 41); and indeed, as Quine holds that an (epistemologically significant) analytic/synthetic distinction cannot be maintained, our evaluations of even logical and mathematical claims are open to revision in the light of experience – though very serious and specific pressures would be required to force changes at such levels.

It's worth noting here that Carnap's views don't obviously fit the rather simple caricature of Vienna Circle orthodoxy sketched above: he held that we could specify a wide range of languages, each with their own rules, and choose between them on the basis of various considerations. This makes the question of whether Quine's criticisms apply to his views a difficult one (see the chapters on Carnap and Quine, this volume).

7. Challenges to the mainstream approach: Wittgenstein and the *Philosophical Investigations*, Quine (again), Stebbing, Austin, Chomsky and Derrida

The attempts to provide a satisfying theoretical account of language that we have looked at so far have some broad features in common. They attempt to provide an account of meaning which is systematic, in the sense that sentence meanings are to be accounted for on the basis of attributions of abiding semantic properties to their component words. They give a key role to the notions of reference and truth in attempts to specify these abiding properties. And they target very broad and general features of language, focusing on successful communication of information between speakers. These common features have been subjected to criticism on a variety of counts.

In his *Philosophical Investigations*, Wittgenstein presents a number of criticisms of attempts at systematic accounts of meaning. Some of these are primarily applicable to views similar to Russell's and those he himself expressed in the *Tractatus* – for instance where he attacks the idea that proper names in natural language should be analysed in terms of complex expressions – but others cut much deeper and have potentially much wider application. Among other things, Wittgenstein emphasizes the vast range of activities in which language figures, going far beyond the giving of descriptions of how things stand; he presses the idea that one and the same sentence may be used to do very different things on different occasions (e.g. at PI 79, where he lists a number of things that might be meant by saying 'Moses did not exist'); and he questions the extent to which an account of language use in terms of associations between expressions and meanings can be genuinely explanatory. He suggests that the use of language is woven into non-linguistic activities in many different ways – so that it may be that there is no underlying 'essence' of linguistic activity to be captured by an overarching theory – with the various complexes of linguistic and non-linguistic activity counting as language in virtue of a network of overlapping dimensions of similarity ('family resemblance'). Crucially, he subjects the idea that (some kind of *grasp* of) meaning *guides* use to severe critical scrutiny in his consideration of 'following a rule' (see the chapter on Wittgenstein and the *Investigations*, and the chapter on Kripke, which contains an interesting discussion of Kripke's important and much-discussed reading of Wittgenstein's remarks in this area). The extent to which Wittgenstein's arguments support what seem to be his radically anti-systematic conclusions is a matter for careful investigation. Some attempts at systematic accounts of language-use and meaning coming after Wittgenstein can be seen as paying careful attention to the *use* of language by creatures engaged in activities in a shared world, in ways which might provide responses to at least some of the worries he raises (see the chapter on Davidson – especially the discussion of 'radical interpretation' – and the chapter on Grice). It is clear, however, that the concerns voiced by Wittgenstein in his later work cannot simply be disregarded.

Quine can also be seen as a severe critic of what I've characterized as 'the mainstream'. He suggested that we consider to what degree assignments of meaning to expressions in a language not previously encountered by the investigators might be supported by empirical data about the use of that language plausibly available prior to its translation – so-called *radical translation*. He argued that, at the very least, the results would be insufficient to make out anything like our pre-theoretical notion of meaning as scientifically respectable, because too many different and incompatible hypotheses about the meanings of the expressions of the language to be translated would be equally well supported by the evidence. He also argued that, contrary to initial appearances, establishing unique assignments of reference to expressions was not a basic task to be completed in giving an account of our linguistic capacities. (See the chapters on Quine and Davidson.[17])

In comparison with the grand sweep of the views of Quine and the later Wittgenstein, the work of Susan Stebbing and J. L. Austin on the philosophy of language can seem quite modest; but their contributions, and their more or less implicit critiques of the character and direction of 'mainstream' investigations, should not be underestimated.

Stebbing's work has until recently been largely overlooked and, where noticed at all, undervalued, but it deserves serious consideration, especially since some key elements of it can now be seen to have been significantly ahead of their time and, more importantly, relevant to issues that are of pressing concern today.

In one sense, Stebbing was not a revolutionary. She was in agreement with Frege, Russell, the early Wittgenstein, and the Logical Empiricists, at least in the broader and more moderate aspects of their thinking: like them, she believed that it is appropriate to approach the everyday use of language critically, and also appropriate to apply the systematic techniques of formal reasoning in thinking about and trying to clarify language-use; and she was (in her 1930) an early advocate of the new logic developed by Frege and Russell. (Though she was suspicious of the idea that reform and systematization of language might solve all philosophical problems, this might be seen as, relatively speaking, a matter of detail.)

Stebbing's approach can be seen as more radical and ground-breaking, however, in relation to two further factors: first, the attention she pays 'ordinary language' – the details of the ways in which words are used in our everyday talk – and secondly, her concern with the use of language in thinking about and discussing practical issues, including politics and ideals. Stebbing's work in this second area seems particularly relevant to issues we face in the twenty-first century. In her later work (particularly her 1939), Stebbing applied sustained critical scrutiny to the use of language in public discourse – about politics, ethics and social issues. She paid particular attention to ways in which poor reasoning could be disguised in persuasive language, and appeals to emotive responses coded into apparently reasoned talk. (Her examination of what might be called pathological or non-ideal linguistic exchanges anticipates some work in feminist philosophy of language – see below.) Through her writing – aimed at readers outside professional philosophy – she sought to equip people with tools which would enable them to clarify their own thinking about important issues and, perhaps even more importantly, critically evaluate the speech of politicians, scientists, advertisers and religious figures. Her advocacy of the application of careful, critical and systematic thinking to the public discussion of political, social and ethical issues is timely and worthy of further consideration.

Like Stebbing, Austin was concerned with the variety of ways in which speakers *use* meaningful sentences. He laid out a careful account of linguistic acts, on which one and the same utterance could be seen as the execution of various different kinds of action. He also made some interesting and provoking observations on the evaluation of utterances with regard to truth. Austin's work on linguistic acts is significant, and his distinctions remain widely accepted. His work on truth has until recently been largely disregarded. As Guy Longworth argues in his chapter on Austin, this may be a significant oversight, since it may well pose a serious problem for truth-conditional accounts of meaning.

In terms of linguistic acts, Austin distinguished between: *locutionary acts* (roughly, acts of uttering a sentence with a particular meaning, for example, uttering the words 'Barry would like some cake' with the content *Barry would like some cake*); *illocutionary acts* (roughly, acts of making an utterance with a particular content and a particular *force*, for example, uttering 'Barry would like some cake' with the force of a request, as when ordering in a café); and *perlocutionary acts* (acts consequential on locutionary and illocutionary acts, such as incidentally reminding a hearer of the deliciousness of cake, causing them to want some). His account of linguistic acts raises one significant challenge for advocates of truth-based accounts of meaning. Some illocutionary acts are evaluable in ways which are not directly connected with truth: for example, if I say 'I will give you £10 tomorrow' to someone in the right sort of context, I incur an obligation to give them £10 the following day. Here the truth of the utterance does not seem to be an issue.[18]

There does seem to be a question here for the advocate of truth-based theories, but it may not be fatal: the sentence just mentioned does have truth-conditions, and it seems open to the theorist to tell a story as to how these figure in its use in particular contexts. More difficult are the considerations Austin raised concerning the evaluation of utterances in terms of truth.

In outline, Austin presented examples in which one and the same sentence could be used on one occasion to make a statement (an illocutionary act) which would be rightly judged true, and on another occasion to make a statement rightly judged false, in such a way that it seems implausible that there should be a constant truth-condition associated with the sentence as (the basis of) its meaning. Now, there are cases in which there are variations of this kind which are attributable to constant aspects of sentence meaning which relate to context. A statement utterance of 'I am hungry' by a particular speaker at a particular time is true if that speaker is hungry at that time, so that variations in the truth evaluation of particular utterances of the sentence are traceable to elements making a constant contribution to determining truth-conditions in context. Similarly, an utterance of 'Barry is tall' made in a philosophy department may be true, whereas one made at a basketball game may be false, and this attributed to a tacit specification of a relevant comparison group in each particular case. These sorts of ideas probably led to this aspect of Austin's work being largely overlooked for a considerable time, but it may be that some at least of his examples cannot be dismissed so easily – in these it is arguable that hidden references to contextual factors cannot accommodate the variations in truth evaluation in a way compatible with word-meaning being accounted for in terms of constant contributions to truth-conditions. This case is pressed in the chapter on Austin.

Chomsky holds a radical position on what aspects of language are amenable to systematic theoretical treatment. In outline, his view is that the stable linguistic phenomena which can be explained by a unified theory are matters of grammar (generalizations concerning syntactic structures displayed in individuals' linguistic behaviour), rather than mastery of externally specified public languages. Significantly, for our present concerns, he doubts the cogency of mainstream semantics, which tries to specify constant-contribution meanings in terms of relations between expressions and particular entities. He presents a number of arguments in favour of this view; for example, in relation to standard reference-specification treatments of names ('Barack' refers to Barack), he points out the apparent inability of this strategy to address our use of empty names, and its limited use in accounting for occurrences of names as mass terms ('After the jet engine accident, there was Simon Cowell all over the runway') or general nouns ('What this team needs is a Beckham').

The final challenge to the 'mainstream' I want to note at this point in the discussion comes from outside the philosophical tradition within which all of the other key figures considered in this volume can be seen as having worked (however uncomfortably, at times, in the case of the later Wittgenstein). The writings of Jacques Derrida are apt to seem difficult (and difficult in unfamiliar ways) to philosophers in that 'analytic', largely Anglophone, tradition. In his chapter, Thomas Baldwin attempts to present Derrida's key ideas on language in ways that will be accessible to analytic philosophers, and subjects those ideas to critical scrutiny. Derrida holds that linguistic meaning arises in the 'play of differance' – 'differance' is Derrida's invented term covering both networks of *differences* between different expressions (in which, it's suggested, they have significance partly in virtue of these relations of difference), and *deferral* (the dependence of meaning upon *repeated* uses of expressions on different occasions). Derrida sees this view as having significant philosophical consequences – for example, in undermining the '*myth of presence*', according to which meanings are taken to be available to thinkers directly, and in turn undermining what he calls 'the philosophy of the West'. Crucially, for our purposes, Derrida suggests that the view determines that no systematic and objective account can be given of the workings of language; because (roughly) any such account would itself depend upon the play of differance. Baldwin criticizes these suggestions (in what is a rich and significant evaluation of Derrida's work in this area), arguing that the view *cannot* be used to condemn systematic inquiries which do not depend upon the assumption that meanings are 'present'. Examples of inquiries which do not depend on the suspect assumption include Kant's philosophy, and Kripke's investigation of claims concerning existence and essence in his *Naming and Necessity* (Kripke, 1980), which pays careful attention to the workings of language. Baldwin concludes that Derrida's insights should lead us to look to 'transcendental' investigations into what grounds the *possibility* of meaning, and that Derrida's own *Of Grammatology* (Derrida,

1974) should be seen 'as an enquiry which aims to vindicate the conception of language as "movement of differance" by showing how this explains the possibility of meaningful language' (Baldwin, this volume).

8. Grice and the semantics/ pragmatics distinction

Paul Grice is famous within philosophy for two major contributions to thought about language. The first is a contribution to pragmatics (roughly, what speakers can achieve with the use of meaningful sentences through broadly linguistic means). This contribution was his account of conversational implicature and maxims of conversation. The second is a proposal in the theory of meaning: his account of speaker meaning in terms of reflexive intentions. In this introduction I will focus on the first contribution.

Suppose we're at a football match. Our team is losing. You say, 'Should we go?' and I respond with 'I am very cold'. Intuitively, there's a sense in which I've said 'Yes, we should go', but there's no temptation to suppose that the *sentence* I uttered has that meaning: the proposition (claim) *expressed* by the sentence I used – that I'm very cold – is different to the proposition *conveyed* by my using it – that we should go. It seems that here we can distinguish between *semantics* (in the sense of the systematic determination of sentence meaning by constant word-meanings) and *pragmatics* (roughly, how speakers exploit word- and sentence-meanings in more or less systematic ways in their linguistic activities). Grice highlighted effects of this general sort, and provided an account of how they work. (In outline, the account depends upon the idea that conversation is a cooperative activity, governed by certain tacit guidelines. Speakers can exploit these guidelines: when an utterance seems to breach them, this triggers a search for an explanation of why the speaker said what she did, and this can lead to identification of a conveyed – 'implicated' – proposition.)

Phenomena of this sort are intriguing, but Grice's treatment of them has wider significance. In our football example, the difference between the proposition expressed and the proposition conveyed is marked – no one is likely to suppose that the *sentence* 'I am very cold' must mean 'Let's go' on this occasion. But there are more subtle cases: cases in which the difference between the proposition expressed (by the sentence) and the proposition conveyed is not so marked, so that we might be tempted into thinking that the sentence, on that occasion at least, has that proposition as its meaning. So we might mistake a merely conveyed proposition for a sentence meaning. This is potentially very important. For instance, one form of argument against attempts to give systematic accounts of language use in terms of assignments of constant meanings to words depends on citing apparent variations in the meaning of expressions – some of the considerations raised by Wittgenstein, Austin and Chomsky against specifically truth-and-reference-based semantics can be seen in this light. Grice's distinction may provide a defence, if the variations can be understood as variations in what is *conveyed*, rather than what is expressed in terms of the semantically determined meanings of the sentences used. (It's a very interesting question whether Grice's machinery can form the basis of a satisfactory response to all considerations of this broad sort. See the chapters on Austin and Chomsky in this volume and, as a useful and entertaining outline of some of the issues, Sainsbury, 2001.)

9. Davidson, truth theories and 'radical interpretation'

The idea that an account of meaning could be framed in terms of truth is implicit in Frege's work, and in much that followed, but the suggestion was developed in an exciting, original and powerfully systematic way by Donald Davidson, starting in the mid-1960s. Davidson's version of the view introduced two main novel elements. First, Davidson applied work on truth in formal languages (artificial logical languages) to the study of natural language and the elucidation of meaning. Secondly, he investigated how a theory of truth might be applied in interpreting the speech of a group speaking an unknown language on the basis of evidence concerning their behaviour – what he termed *radical interpretation*. This second element introduces the possibility that Davidson might solve some of the deepest and most pressing puzzles concerning language-use and meaning. If it could be shown how facts about meaning are determined by facts about behaviour (in a way that could be discerned by observers of that behaviour), then we would have gone a long way towards showing how it is that words mean what they do, what it is for a speaker to mean what they do by the words that they use, and how linguistic communication is possible.

In the 1930s, Alfred Tarski had shown how to construct theories of truth for formal languages. Tarski showed how semantic properties could be assigned to basic expressions in such a way that the conditions of application of an expression 'is true (in language L)' to all of the sentences of language L were clearly defined. (A sketch of how this kind of theory can begin to deal with simple subject–predicate sentences is given in Section 4 – see the chapter on Davidson for more detail. One of Tarski's great achievements was to show how complex quantified sentences like 'Someone dances and laughs' can be accommodated.) The outputs of Tarski-style theories were 'T–sentences', sentences analogous to: ' "Calais est une ville" is true (in French) if and only if Calais is a town.' Tarski's truth definitions relied on a notion of meaning: confidence that it was *truth* that had been defined was secured by requiring that the sentence used to state the condition of the application of the truth predicate is a *translation* of the mentioned sentence in the target language (the 'object language'), in each of the T-sentences.

Davidson turns Tarski's procedure on its head. He assumes that we have a grip on the concept of truth, and then attempts to show how evidence available *before* successful interpretation of a language might be brought to bear on selection of a Tarski-style truth theory for that language, in such a way that the theory would serve to provide interpretations of sentences in that language – that is, assignments of meaning.[19] Davidson's investigation of radical interpretation followed on from Quine's radical translation. Davidson was deeply influenced by Quine: both philosophers are concerned with the way in which assignments of meaning might be determined by evidence available prior to successful interpretation; but there are more and less subtle differences between their views, and difficult questions concerning the fundamental characters of their accounts of language. Here I can give only a brief indication of what some of the significant differences and points of comparison might be. First, Quine's preference is for evidence that, so far as is possible, is in line with the outlook of physical science: he talks in terms of patterns of stimulation prompting assent behaviour, for instance. Davidson, on the other hand, is content with evidence concerning speakers *holding true* specific sentences in particular kinds of environmental circumstances, and *holding true* is both a *mental* attitude and one with semantical content. Davidson holds that evidence concerning holding true doesn't just *include* facts about meaning (we can, he hopes, have good reason to believe a particular speaker holds a particular sentence true without already knowing ourselves what that sentence means) but in depending upon holding true we have not escaped from the range of psychological and content-involving concepts (*thought, meaning, belief, desire, intention, truth* and so on), concepts which can seem puzzling and mysterious from the perspective of physical science. Secondly, Quine emphasizes both the possibility that a range of intuitively different meaning-assignments might be compatible with his behavioural evidence on all objective measures, and how more or less practical considerations might affect choice of translation theory (thus making selection of one theory over another non-objective); whereas Davidson emphasizes the role of what he claims are a priori principles in constraining determination of truth-theory in radical interpretation.

Davidson did not, it seems, provide a *reductive* account of meaning – he does not give, and did not intend to give, an analysis or explanation of meaning in terms acceptable to physical science – instead he hoped to use his investigation of radical interpretation to illuminate and clarify the concepts involved – *meaning, truth, belief, desire, intention* – by showing how they are related to one another in a larger structure. Whether he succeeded in giving a genuinely illuminating account of the relations between these concepts is contested (as we have noted already, the idea that meaning can be accounted for in terms of truth faces objections from a number of sources), but Davidson's project is bold and ingenious, and uncovers a great deal concerning the problems to be faced in providing an account of language and meaning.

10. Dummett on theories of meaning

Like Davidson, Dummett aims to provide a satisfying philosophical account of meaning (a theory of meaning) by investigating how we might construct a *meaning theory* for a language – a systematic specification of the meanings of the expressions in the language (including its sentences). Unlike Davidson, Dummett does not think that specifications of truth-conditions can play a central role in such a meaning theory. Dummett's arguments for this position are subtle and complex, depending on a number of constraints on what can be considered a satisfactory meaning theory. (Bernard Weiss's detailed discussion of Dummett's work is perhaps the most challenging in this book.) But we can begin with the following rough sketch. Knowledge of a language consists in knowledge of a meaning theory for that language – speakers must be somehow rationally sensitive to the meanings of their words, otherwise language-use could not be guided by meaning – but this knowledge must be implicit, rather than explicit. (Explicit knowledge is knowledge that possessors can put into words, and ordinary speakers cannot articulate meaning theories for their languages in explicit terms.) We can make sense of *implicit* knowledge in terms of *abilities*: speakers must be able to *manifest* their knowledge of the theory through their abilities. Moreover, since language can be *acquired* by those who do not already possess it, the specification of the theory must not merely presuppose conceptual expertise equivalent to understanding. (So, for example, reference-specifying clauses like '"Obama" refers to Obama', which might be found in a Davidson-style truth-theory for a language, would not be counted satisfactory by Dummett's standards.) Clear manifestation of grasp of the semantic properties of a sentence assigned by a truth-theoretic account would require recognition of the obtaining of the truth-conditions of the sentence. But now comes the nub of the argument: there are many sentences such that their truth/falsity is not open to recognition (e.g. 'Every even number is the sum of two primes', 'Alexander the Great had a mole in his right armpit', and, perhaps, some what-if claims in which the 'if' is never a reality – say, 'If I had practised really hard for the last ten years, I would be able to sing like Adele'). Grasp of the semantic property which is meant to be assigned to such sentences by truth-theoretic accounts is thus not manifestable, and so, Dummett concludes, the property cannot be assigned as the key semantic property in a tenable theory. Dummett's argument constitutes a serious challenge to truth-theoretic approaches. Dummett has proposed an alternative approach to systematic semantics, based in assertability conditions, but this alternative has itself been seen to face serious obstacles.

11. Language, the social, and feminist philosophy of language

I began this introduction by saying that we live in and through language. It is language which makes possible the complex *social* lives that we lead, allowing us, among other things, to coordinate our activities, accumulate and share knowledge and understanding, and – in our better moments – attempt to understand and care for one another. The development of the philosophy of language over the past one hundred and forty years has been marked by moments of insight into the social aspects of language, and the ways that language and meaning interact with the social. Wittgenstein in the *Investigations* put great weight on the ways in which language is integrated into and dependent upon shared activities and ways of life. Grice highlighted the ways in which conversations are cooperative activities. Davidson stressed the extent to which understanding an individual's words is inseparable from a broader project of making sense of them as a thinking agent with beliefs and desires and intentions. Even Frege, who saw understanding as an individualistic act – associating a sense with an expression – emphasized the public nature of meaning and the role of language in articulating and transmitting shared knowledge. There are further examples of the recognition of links between meaning and the social. Kripke famously presented a view of the functioning of names on which the reference of a name is determined by the history of its use, placing a key aspect of meaning 'outside of the head' of the individual language-user and dependent upon the broader life of a linguistic community.[20] Hilary Putnam and Tyler Burge both argued that the determination of reference of terms like 'gold' and 'arthritis' is a matter of 'shared linguistic labour' in a linguistic community.[21]

Although these advances have paid attention to the social dimension of language, they have typically not considered the ethically and politically loaded dimensions of social structures; in particular, the class, race, gender, age, social status and power-relations of speaker and audience have typically been put to one side in attempts to understand the broadest and most general features of language and meaning. But, in an increasingly varied and lively range of exchanges and debates beginning around the mid-1970s, feminist philosophers of language have questioned this general approach and explored the ways in which gender is relevant to a philosophical understanding of language.[22]

The topics covered by feminist philosophy of language include (but are not restricted to) the way that (stereotypically) male viewpoints can be coded into ordinary language, the erasing effect that allegedly gender-neutral uses of 'he' can have, and the possibility of *silencing* – the idea that social circumstances (such as widespread stereotypical views of women) might make it impossible for women to perform certain linguistic acts, such as refusing unwanted sexual advances. Proposals of this kind are striking and engaging in their own terms, but they also mark an important movement in philosophy, in challenging the traditional division between 'theoretical' philosophy (where the concern is with 'broad features of reality', pursued in metaphysics, logic, the philosophy of language and epistemology) and 'value theory' (ethics and aesthetics). In the phenomena of silencing, for instance, we see a way in which evaluative attitudes can be intimately involved in something as fundamental as the possibility of communication.

In her chapter on feminist philosophy of language, Maura Tumulty considers two key issues in feminist philosophy of language: the debate over silencing, already mentioned; and the understanding of generics (as found in claims such as 'Sharks attack bathers', 'Cats are cunning' and 'Women are sensitive' in which a common noun, such as 'shark', appears without an expression, such as 'all', 'most' or 'some', indicating the number or proportion of such things are involved). Tumulty shows how these live debates can both inform our responses to pressing social issues and enrich our broader philosophical understanding of language. Her discussion gives a vivid sense of the way in which philosophy of language continues to grow and develop as a discipline, responding to contemporary concerns by building on its heritage and applying careful and patient reasoning to highly contested and potentially divisive issues.

12. Closing remarks

The philosophers whose work is examined in this book raise high-level questions about language. To what extent, if at all, is language-use amenable to treatment in terms of detailed and systematic theory? If it is amenable, should the theory make use of a concept of meaning? And if it should make use of such a concept, what account can be given of it, and what other concepts should figure centrally in its analysis or elucidation? (Truth? Reference? Sense? Or other concepts?) To what extent, and how, does everyday language encode particular viewpoints and biases? To what extent do speakers' attitudes, values and social circumstances impact upon the fundamental expression of meaning and the business of communication? The views of the philosophers considered take up various positions on these questions, and on questions of the relations between language, mind, the world, and the social and political circumstances in which we find ourselves – questions, for example, concerning how things must stand with a speaker's individual psychology when they understand a linguistic expression of a particular kind, how any semantic relations between words and objects are set up and maintained, or what is required for a speaker to be able to perform a linguistic act of a particular kind (and what might disrupt or frustrate such an ability).[23] In this introduction I have sought to give an overview of the debates concerning these questions, and how the views of the philosophers discussed in the individual chapters that follow bear upon them. I hope I have conveyed some sense of both the intellectual excitement of philosophy of language – in which difficult questions relating to epistemology, metaphysics, the philosophy of mind and the philosophy of value converge – and the degree to which – now, more than one hundred and twenty years after Frege began to lay out materials and tools with which we might attempt to construct a systematic account of language use – the deep and central questions remain open and fiercely contested.

    A note on the nature of this book, and how to use it: The chapters which follow are not 'arm's length', general surveys of the views of the figures they consider. Chapter authors have selected what they see as the most important ideas and arguments put forward by the philosophers they discuss, and have engaged with these critically. The chapters do not attempt to be complete surveys of thinkers' views, or entirely non-partisan in their approach. Chapter authors have advocated particular interpretations and evaluations of the work of their subjects, themselves taking up positions in ongoing debates.[24] The focus and partiality of the chapters will, I hope, help to bring you into close and critical engagement with the views presented. The nature of the book means that you should view it as an entry-point to the debates it introduces. To arrive at a considered view of the issues, you will need to read and think further – exploring primary texts, following up on suggestions for further secondary reading, and reflecting carefully on the arguments.

Further reading

Good general introductions to the philosophy of language include: Kemp (2018); Lycan (2018); Miller, A. (2007); Morris, M. (2007); and Taylor (1998). (Both Kemp and Lycan provide concise, lively and highly accessible introductions to a range of core issues.) An interesting introduction to some central issues through selections from important primary sources together with carefully constructed commentaries and reading notes is given by *Reading Philosophy of Language*, ed. Jennifer Hornsby and Guy Longworth (Oxford: Blackwell, 2005). More traditional collections of classic papers include the generously proportioned *Readings in the Philosophy of Language*, ed. Peter Ludlow (Cambridge, MA: MIT Press, 1997) and the somewhat more handily sized *Arguing about Language*, ed. Darragh Byrne and Max Kölbel (Abingdon: Routledge, 2010). Two very useful collections containing 'state of the art' overview essays on particular aspects of the philosophy of language are *A Companion to the Philosophy of Language*, ed. Bob Hale, Crispin Wright and Alexander Miller, 2nd edn (Oxford: Blackwell, 2017) and *The Oxford Handbook of Philosophy of Language*, ed. Ernest Lepore and Barry C. Smith (Oxford: Clarendon, 2006). Two very interesting books which explore the relations between language, mind and world primarily through investigations into proper names and related expressions are McCulloch (1989), and Sainsbury (2005) (chapters 1 and 2 of Sainsbury's book give a concise and elegant introduction to the issues). For advice on additional reading on the individual key figures mentioned in this introduction, see the further reading recommendations and bibliographies attached to the relevant chapters.

Notes

1 The drive for unified accounts or theories is not restricted to 'hard' science: an account of Shakespeare's plays which found in them a

substantive and distinctive view of human nature and the human condition would deserve our attention and, if it fitted the texts and was not outdone by an alternative view, earn a degree of credence.

2   The division of views and figures into 'mainstream' and critical or 'anti-mainstream' camps is rough and ready, and largely intended as a presentational and organizational device. It provides an initial way of placing views, and should be refined in further study.

3   The order in which figures are discussed in this introduction does not perfectly replicate the historical order in which those figures began to make their key contributions, for thematic and presentational reasons. The greatest distortion, perhaps, in terms of simple chronology is in placing discussion of Derrida before discussion of Grice and Davidson.

4   Introductions to Kripke's work with regard to the philosophy of language typically emphasize his views on naming and necessity. In this volume the concentration is on his views on arguments for Fregean sense, the role of intuitions in philosophy of language, and his interpretation/development of Wittgenstein's remarks on following a rule.

5   More precisely, a set of sentences $\{S_1, S_2, ..., S_i\}$ *entails* a sentence S_n if and only if it is not possible both for all of S_1 to S_i to be true and S_n not true.

6   It is relatively easy, it should be said, only following in the wake of the brilliant and ingenious work of Frege and Tarski. (More on Tarski later.) And the ease *is* only relative: providing an account of the truth-relevant properties of all of the sentences in a language like English requires providing an account of the contributions of all the various kinds of expressions we find in such a language to determining such truth-relevant properties; and that is a very challenging enterprise.

7   The truth-value of a sentence is just its status with regard to truth and falsity: its being true or its being false.

8   In the nineteenth century it was thought that, because of variations in the orbit of the planet Mercury not otherwise predicted by Newtonian physics, there must be a planet orbiting even closer to the Sun, and 'Vulcan' was introduced as a name for it. It turned out that there is no such planet. The behaviour of Mercury is explained by Einsteinian physics. It's this example of a serious use in science of a name which *turned out* to be empty which I have in mind here (rather than the explicitly fictional home planet of Spock in *Star Trek*). The case is particularly interesting as it can't simply be put to one side for special treatment as consciously playful uses of empty names in fiction might be.

9 The point about *obligatory* association is glossed over surprisingly often. See Evans (1982, section 1.4, esp. pp. 15–16), for a nice account of sense which emphasizes the point.

10 The notion of an abstraction here can be illustrated by an account of sense suggested by Gareth Evans (1982, esp. section 1.5): modes of presentation are picked out in terms of *ways of succeeding in thinking about* a particular object, so that two thinkers entertain the same MoP when they think about the same object in the same way. On this type of account, concerns about the peculiar status of senses as abstract objects, and about how we are able to grasp/access them, appear to become less pressing.

11 This is a controversial proposal, but it deserves some consideration. It might be objected that the suggested idiosyncratic-modes-of-presentation view would fail to account for the way in which informative identities can be used to communicate quite specific information; but speakers can be confident that they are deploying the same or similar modes of presentation in particular situations for reasons other than that these are components of name meaning. It is striking that many of the most plausible examples in this area feature definite descriptions (e.g. 'The point of intersection of *a* and *b* is then the same as the point of intersection of *b* and *c*' in relation to the triangle example noted in the chapter on Frege). More on definite descriptions shortly.

12 A definite description, as we are concerned with them here, is a phrase starting with the definite article (in English, 'the') followed by a singular count-noun phrase (such as 'cat with blue eyes').

13 Frege has a response to this problem (see Section 8 of the chapter on Frege), but that response itself faces difficulties.

14 Frege quite often sketched attributions of sense to proper names using definite descriptions. As a result it has been suggested that he simply held a view similar to Russell's, or that he *had* to hold such a view in order to cash out the notion of sense. It is not obvious that either of these suggestions is correct (see Evans (1982), section 1.5, and McDowell (1977)).

15 See Kripke (1980), esp. Lecture II. See also section 4 of the chapter on Kripke, and Sainsbury (2005, section 1.4), for sketches of Kripke's objections.

16 It might be responded that the principle is methodological, and embodies a challenge to those who would claim meaningfulness for sentences that lack empirical content of the relevant kind to explain how it is that these sentences are meaningful.

17 It is an open question whether Quine establishes a degree of indeterminacy concerning meaning which is sufficiently high to

completely undermine any claim to theoretical respectability, particularly when we take into account the connections made between the truth-conditions of sentences by the repeated appearance of words in different combinations. For an interesting discussion see Wright (2017).

18 If the person I speak to comes to me after two days and points out that I haven't come up with the cash, my saying 'It seems what I said has turned out false; but that happens with quite a lot of the things I say' isn't likely to satisfy them.

19 This is a rough characterization of Davidson's aim. See Kirk Ludwig's important remarks on the exact nature of the Davidson's project in his chapter.

20 For a sketch of Kripke's picture of the determination of name reference, see Section 5 of the chapter on Kripke. For Kripke's exposition, see the last third of Lecture 2 in Kripke (1980). For a helpful introductory discussion, see Lycan (2018, chapter 4).

21 See Putnam (1975a), and Burge (1979; 1986).

22 These feminist critiques and positive proposals are important in their own right but they also provide a useful model for work in relation to other underrepresented and disadvantaged groups, though it is likely that the exact nature of the issues which arise for other groups – and what corrective approaches are appropriate – will differ from case to case.

23 The question of the relations between understanding of (or what we might call semantic competence with) expressions of particular kinds and matters of broader individual psychology is a fascinating one. The idea that the connections are relatively simple and direct has been seriously questioned. For example, where it once seemed that semantic competence with a name must consist in some kind of extra-linguistic, mental or cognitive connection with its referent, the possibility of more complex pictures have opened up, including pictures on which semantic competence is a matter of being a participant in a public linguistic *practice* of use of the name. For further discussion of the latter sort of view, see Section 5 of the chapter on Kripke, and Sainsbury (2005, chapter 3, esp. sections 5–7).

24 You will find disagreements between chapter authors both on points of interpretation and on substantive philosophical issues.

Bibliography

Byrne, Darragh and Kölbel, Max (2010), *Arguing about Language*. Abingdon: Routledge.

Derrida, J. (1974), *Of Grammatology*, trans. G. Spivak. Baltimore, MD: Johns Hopkins University Press.

Evans, Gareth (1982), *The Varieties of Reference*. Oxford: Clarendon.

Kemp, Gary (2018), *What Is This Thing Called Philosophy of Language?* 2nd edn. Abingdon: Routledge.

Kripke, Saul (1980), *Naming and Necessity*. Oxford: Blackwell.

Lepore, Ernest and Smith, Barry C. (eds) (2006), *The Oxford Handbook of Philosophy of Language*. Oxford: Clarendon.

Ludlow, Peter (ed.) (1997), *Readings in the Philosophy of Language*. Cambridge, MA: MIT Press.

Lycan, William G. (2018), *Philosophy of Language: A Contemporary Introduction*, 3rd edn. Abingdon: Routledge.

McCulloch, G. (1989), *The Game of the Name: Introducing Logic, Language and Mind*. Oxford: Oxford University Press.

McDowell, J. (1977), 'On the Sense and Reference of a Proper Name', *Mind*, 86, pp. 159–85. Reprinted in *Reference, Truth and Reality*, ed. M. Platts. London: Routledge and Kegan Paul, 1980, pp. 141–66.

Miller, A. (2007), *Philosophy of Language*, 2nd edn. London: Routledge.

Morris, M. (2007), *An Introduction to the Philosophy of Language*. Cambridge: Cambridge University Press.

Quine, W. V. (1961 [1951]), 'Two Dogmas of Empiricism', in his *From a Logical Point of View*, 2nd edn. Cambridge, MA: Harvard University Press, pp. 20–46. Originally published in *Philosophical Review*, 60 (1951), 20–43.

Sainsbury, R. M. (2001), 'Two Ways to Smoke a Cigarette', in his *Departing from Frege: Essays in the Philosophy of Language*. London: Routledge, 2002, pp. 192–203. Originally published in *Ratio*, 14, 386–406.

Sainsbury, R. M. (2005), *Reference without Referents*. Oxford: Clarendon.

Stebbing, Susan (1930), *A Modern Introduction to Logic*. London: Methuen (2nd edn. revised, 1933).

Stebbing, Susan (1939), *Thinking to Some Purpose*. Harmondsworth: Penguin.

Taylor, K. (1998), *Truth & Meaning: An Introduction to the Philosophy of Language*. Oxford: Blackwell.

Wittgenstein, L. (1953 – cited as PI), *Philosophical Investigations*, trans. G. E. M. Anscombe, ed. G. E. M. Anscombe and R. Rhees. Oxford: Blackwell.

Wright, C. (2017), 'The Indeterminacy of Translation', in B. Hale, C. Wright and A Miller (eds), *A Companion to the Philosophy of Language*, 2nd edn. Oxford: Blackwell, 2017, pp. 670–702.

CHAPTER ONE

FREGE

Michael Beaney

Gottlob Frege (1848–1925) was primarily a mathematician, logician and philosopher of mathematics rather than a philosopher of language as that might be understood today. However, in inventing modern logic and pursuing his main goal – the demonstration that arithmetic can be reduced to logic – he was led to reflect on how language works, and the ideas he introduced in doing so laid the foundations for the development of philosophy of language, especially within the analytic tradition, in the twentieth century.

1. Life and works

Frege was born in Wismar, on the Baltic coast in northern Germany, in 1848, and he studied mathematics, physics, chemistry and philosophy at the Universities of Jena and Göttingen from 1869 to 1873. In 1874 he was appointed to teach mathematics at Jena, where he remained for the rest of his academic career. He retired in 1918 and moved back to the Baltic coast, where he died in 1925.[1]

Frege published three books in his lifetime: *Begriffsschrift* (*Conceptual Notation*) in 1879, *Die Grundlagen der Arithmetik* (*The Foundations of Arithmetic*) in 1884 and *Grundgesetze der Arithmetik* (*Basic Laws of Arithmetic*) in 1893 (Volume I) and 1903 (Volume II). Frege's main aim in these books was to demonstrate the logicist thesis that arithmetic is reducible to logic. To do so, Frege realized that he needed to develop a better logical theory than was then available: he gave his first exposition of this in *Begriffsschrift*, 'Begriffsschrift' (literally, 'concept-script' or 'conceptual notation') being the name he gave to his logical system. (In what follows, I shall use 'Begriffsschrift' in italics to refer to the book and without italics to refer to Frege's logical system.) In *Grundlagen* he criticized other views about arithmetic, such as those of Kant and Mill, and offered an informal account of his logicist project. In *Grundgesetze* he refined his logical system and attempted to provide a formal demonstration of his logicist thesis. In 1902, however, as the second volume was in press, he received a letter from Russell informing him of a contradiction in his system – the contradiction we know now as Russell's paradox. Although Frege hastily wrote an appendix attempting to respond to this, he soon realized that the response failed and was led to abandon his logicism. He continued to develop and defend his philosophical ideas, however, writing papers and corresponding with other mathematicians and philosophers. It is these philosophical writings, and his four most important papers, in particular, which have established his status as one of the founders of modern philosophy of language. These papers are 'Function and Concept' (1891), 'On Sense and Reference' (1892a), 'On Concept and Object' (1892b) and 'Thought' (1918). The main ideas in these four papers form the subject of the present chapter. We start with the idea that lay at the heart of his new logical system.

2. Frege's use of function–argument analysis

The key to understanding Frege's work is his use of function–argument analysis, which he extended from mathematics to logic. Indeed, it is no exaggeration to say that all Frege's main doctrines follow from his thinking through the implications of this use.[2] We can begin with a simple example from mathematics. In analytic geometry, the equation for a line is $y = ax + b$: this exhibits y as a function of x, with a and b here being constants (a being the gradient of the line and b the point where the line cuts the y-axis on a graph). Let $a = 2$ and $b = 3$. If $x = 4$, then $y = 11$: we say that 11 is the value of the function $2x + 3$ for argument 4. We call x and y the variables here: as x varies, so too does y, in the systematic way reflected in the function. By taking different numerical values for x, we get different numerical values for y, enabling us to draw the relevant line on a graph. Frege thought of sentences – and what those sentences express or represent – in the same way: they can be analysed in function–argument terms. Sentences, too, have a 'value' which can be seen as the result of an appropriate function for an appropriate argument or arguments. If we think of this value as in some sense its 'meaning', then we can regard this meaning, too, as a function of the 'meanings' of what we might loosely call its 'parts', that is, of what function–argument analysis yields as the constituent elements of the sentence. What are these 'meanings' and 'parts'? This is the question that Frege attempted to answer in his philosophical work, and it is the main aim of the present chapter to explain his answer.

Let us see how Frege applied function–argument analysis in the case of sentences, starting with simple sentences such as 'Gottlob is human'. In traditional (Aristotelian) logic, such sentences were regarded as having subject–predicate form, represented by 'S is P', with 'S' symbolizing the subject ('Gottlob') and 'P' the predicate ('human'), joined together by the copula ('is'). According to Frege, however, they should be seen as having function–argument form, represented by 'Fa', with 'a' symbolizing the argument ('Gottlob') and 'Fx' the function ('x is human'), the variable x here indicating where the argument term goes to complete the sentence. The sentence 'Gottlob is human' is thus viewed as the value of the functional expression 'x is human' for the argument term 'Gottlob'. Besides the terminological change, though, there might seem little to choose between the two analyses, the only difference being the absorption of the copula ('is') into the functional expression ('x is human').[3]

The advantages of function–argument analysis begin to emerge when we consider relational sentences, which are analysed as functions of two or more arguments. In 'Gottlob is shorter than Bertrand', for example, 'Gottlob' and 'Bertrand' are taken as the argument terms and 'x is shorter than y' as the relational expression, formalized as 'Rxy' or 'xRy'. This allows a unified treatment of a wide range of sentences which traditional logic had had difficulties in dealing with in a single theory.

The superior power of function–argument analysis only fully comes out, though, when we turn to sentences involving quantifier terms such as 'all' and 'some'. Take the sentence 'All logicians are human'. In traditional logic, this was also seen as having subject–predicate form, 'All logicians' in this case being the subject, with 'human' once again the predicate, joined together by the plural copula 'are'. According to Frege, however, such a sentence has a quite different and more complex (quantificational) form: in modern notation, symbolized as '$(\forall x)(Lx \rightarrow Hx)$',[4] read as 'For all x, if x is a logician, then x is human'. Here there is nothing corresponding to the subject; instead, what we have are two functional expressions ('x is a logician' and 'x is human') linked together by means of the propositional connective 'if ... then ...' and bound by a quantifier ('for all x'). In developing his Begriffsschrift, Frege's most significant innovation was the introduction of a notation for quantification, allowing him to formalize – and hence represent the logical relations between – sentences not just with one quantifier term but with multiple quantifier terms.

Traditional logic had had great difficulty in formalizing sentences with more than one quantifier term. Such sentences are prevalent in mathematics, so it was important for Frege to be able to deal with them. Consider, for example, the sentence 'Every natural number has a successor'. This can be formalized as follows, 'Nx' symbolizing 'x is a natural number' and 'Syx' symbolizing 'y is a successor of x':

(S) $(\forall x)(Nx \rightarrow (\exists y)(Ny \;\&\; Syx))$.[5]

This can be read as 'For all x, if x is a natural number, then there is some natural number which is its successor'. This shows that there is a much more complex (quantificational) structure involved here than the original sentence might suggest. Since what inferences can be drawn from such complex sentences depend on their quantificational structure, it is only when we have an adequate way to represent this structure that we can properly exhibit the relevant logical relations.

For a good illustration of this, consider the sentence 'Every philosopher respects some logician', which is ambiguous. It can mean either (1) that whatever philosopher we take, there is some (at least one) logician whom they respect (not necessarily the same one) or (2) that there is indeed some one (at least one) logician whom every philosopher respects. Quantificational logic provides us with a succinct way of exhibiting this ambiguity:

(1) $(\forall x)(Px \rightarrow (\exists y)(Ly \ \& \ Rxy))$.

(2) $(\exists y)(Ly \ \& \ (\forall x)(Px \rightarrow Rxy))$.

The first can be read as 'For all x, if x is a philosopher, then there is some y such that y is a logician and x respects y'; the second can be read as 'There is some y such that y is a logician and for all x, if x is a philosopher, then x respects y'. The formalization makes clear that the difference lies in the order of the quantifiers – $\forall\exists$ versus $\exists\forall$. While the second implies the first, the first does not imply the second: mistakenly reasoning from the first to the second is known as the quantifier shift fallacy. Quantificational logic allows us to diagnose the error and avoid making it in our own reasoning.

3. Some key distinctions

Quantificational logic has proved itself to be far more powerful than any of the logical systems that existed prior to Frege's Begriffsschrift. As far as the development of philosophy of language is concerned, its significance lies, at the most general level, in the gap it opened up between grammatical form and logical form. The grammatical structure of a sentence is not necessarily a good guide to its logical structure, in other words, to the inferential relations it has with other sentences. Take the example of 'All logicians are human' again. This might look as if it has a similar structure to 'Gottlob is human', a view reflected in the treatment of both as having subject–predicate form, 'All logicians' and 'Gottlob' being the subjects. On Frege's view, however, there are two quite different relations here: subordination and subsumption, respectively. To say that all logicians are human is to assert a relationship between being a logician and being human, namely, that the first implies the second: the concept of being a logician is subordinate to the concept of being human. To say that Gottlob is human, on the other hand, is to say that the object Gottlob falls under the concept of being human: the object is subsumed under the concept. When we say that 'All logicians are human', we do not mean that the collection or set of logicians is human (the set is not being subsumed under the concept of being human); rather, we mean that any member of this collection is human, that is, that anything that is a logician is also human. This is what is captured in its formalization in quantificational logic, which makes clear that from it, together with any sentence 'A is a logician', we can infer 'A is human'. Frege stresses the distinction between subordination (which holds between two concepts) and subsumption (which holds between an object and a concept) throughout his work.[6] For him, this is a fundamental logical distinction which is obscured by focus merely on the subject–predicate structure of sentences.

Presupposed by this distinction is the most fundamental distinction of all for Frege: that between object and concept. This distinction follows directly from Frege's use of function–argument analysis. Take 'Gottlob is human' again. Analysing this in function-argument terms yields 'Gottlob' as the argument term and 'x is human' as the functional expression. Frege takes 'Gottlob' as the name of an object and 'x is human' as the name of a concept. On Frege's view, in other words, concepts *are* functions. Furthermore, just as functions are different from objects, so concepts are different from objects. Indeed, this distinction is absolute for Frege, which he expresses by saying that while objects are 'saturated', concepts (and functions) are 'unsaturated'. What he means by this is that while names of objects are 'complete', concept-words (functional expressions) contain 'gaps' to indicate where the argument terms go. This gap is indicated by the use of the variable x in, for example, 'x is human'. This seems reasonable at the linguistic level: the expression for a concept must show where the argument term goes to produce a well-formed sentence. It is more problematic at the level of what the words refer to. Frege talks of concepts themselves being 'unsaturated', mirroring the unsaturatedness at the linguistic level. He admits that this talk is metaphorical, but the ontological status of concepts has proved controversial.[7]

The final distinction to be explained here is the distinction between first-level and second-level concepts. To illustrate this, let us consider the central idea of Frege's logicism, the claim that a number statement involves an assertion about a concept.[8] To say that Jupiter has four moons, for example, is to say that the concept *moon of Jupiter* has four instances. More precisely, it is to say that the first-level concept *moon of Jupiter* (under which fall the four objects that are the individual moons of Jupiter) itself falls within the second-level concept *has four instances*. So first-level concepts are concepts under which objects fall, and second-level concepts are concepts within which first-level concepts fall.[9]

This construal of number statements is important in Frege's logicist project because the concept *is instantiated* can be defined purely logically, thus setting Frege on the path of providing logical definitions of all numerical concepts. To say that a concept *F* is instantiated is to say that there is some *x* such that *x* is *F*, symbolized logically as:

(EQ) $(\exists x)Fx$.

The concept *is instantiated* is thus represented by means of the existential quantifier, which thus turns out to be a second-level concept. The same is true of the universal quantifier, since to say that everything is F is to say that the concept F is universally instantiated:

(UQ) $(\forall x)Fx$.

Frege's construal also has significance outside the context of logicism. Consider negative existential statements such as 'Unicorns do not exist'. We might be tempted to construe this as attributing to unicorns the property of non-existence. But if there are no unicorns, then how is this possible? On Frege's view, however, the statement is to be interpreted as 'The concept *unicorn* is not instantiated', which can be readily formalized as follows, 'U*x*' symbolizing '*x* is a unicorn':

(U) $\sim(\exists x)Ux$.

This makes clear that there is no mysterious reference to unicorns, only to the *concept* of a unicorn. What the statement says is that there is nothing that instantiates this concept. We have here another example of how the subject–predicate form of a sentence can be misleading. Representing it in quantificational theory reveals that its logical form is quite different.

Frege was well aware of the philosophical significance of this construal. As he points out, it offers a diagnosis of what is wrong with the traditional ontological argument for the existence of God.[10] On his account, to say that something exists is not to attribute a property to something, in other words, it is not to say that an object falls under a first-level concept (the concept of existence, so supposed), but to say that a first-level concept falls within a second-level concept, namely, the concept of being instantiated. The concept of existence thus turns out to be a second-level rather than a first-level concept, although, strictly speaking, what we should say is that talk of existence is to be analysed in terms of the second-level concept of being instantiated. The general strategy here – reformulating a potentially misleading sentence to reveal its 'real' logical form – was to become a central idea of analytic philosophy.[11] It also illustrates why philosophy of language became so fundamental to analytic philosophy. Careful attention to the meaning and logical structure of sentences opens the way to successful resolution of philosophical problems.

4. Conceptual content

We have seen how Frege interprets 'All logicians are human' as 'For all x, if x is a logician, then x is human', for example, and 'Jupiter has four moons' as 'The concept *moon of Jupiter* has four instances'. But what justifies these interpretations? A traditional logician might object to them by saying that they *change the subject*: 'All logicians are human' is about all logicians, not about the relationship of subordination between two concepts; and 'Jupiter has four moons' is about the planet Jupiter, not about the concept *moon of Jupiter*. According to Frege, however, subject–predicate analysis is of no logical significance: all that is relevant is what he calls – in his early work – 'conceptual content'. It is this that determines the inferential relations between sentences, which is what is logically important.

The example Frege gives to introduce the idea is the following pair of sentences:[12]

(GP) At Plataea the Greeks defeated the Persians.
(PG) At Plataea the Persians were defeated by the Greeks.

Although there is a grammatical difference here, 'the Greeks' being the subject in (GP) and 'the Persians' being the subject in (PG), there is clearly something that they have in common, which Frege calls their 'conceptual content'. Two sentences have the same conceptual content, on Frege's view, if and only if whatever we can infer from one, together with any additional assumptions, can also be inferred from the other, together with those same assumptions. In effect, this is to say that two sentences have the same conceptual content if and only if they are logically equivalent. If (GP) is true, then (PG) is true, and vice versa.

What Frege is suggesting, then, is that for logical purposes, we do not need to take into account all those aspects of our use and understanding of sentences that might be called their 'meaning' in the widest sense of the term: we need only concentrate on their 'conceptual content', which we can think of as constituting the logical core of their meaning.[13] But what exactly *is* this content? In his early work, Frege seems to have thought of it as something like the 'circumstance' or 'state of affairs' represented.[14] In the case of (GP) and (PG) above, this seems plausible: what they have in common is that they both refer to the same battle: the battle at Plataea between the Greeks and the Persians which the former won and the latter lost. Whether we describe this battle as the Greeks defeating the Persians or the Persians being defeated by the Greeks seems irrelevant: it is one and the same event to which we are referring.

Returning to Frege's use of function–argument analysis, we can now state what Frege saw – at any rate, in his early work[15] – as the 'value' of a sentence when construed in function–argument terms: its conceptual content. We have also noted that functional expressions are taken to represent concepts or relations, and names to represent objects. So we have one answer to the question posed at the beginning of Section 2. The value or logical meaning of a sentence is its conceptual content, regarded as the result of an appropriate function (a concept or relation) for an appropriate argument or arguments (object or objects). Unfortunately, however, the notion of conceptual content was to prove problematic, as Frege realized when he reconsidered his earlier views about identity statements.

5. The problem of identity statements

Consider the example Frege gives at the beginning of his paper 'On Sense and Reference' (see Diagram 1): 'Let *a*, *b*, *c* be the lines connecting the vertices of a triangle [PQR] with the midpoints of the opposite sides. The point of intersection of *a* and *b* is then the same as the point of intersection of *b* and *c*.'[16]

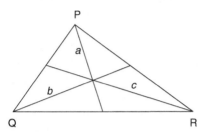

Diagram 1

What we have here is an identity statement:

(AB) The point of intersection of *a* and *b* = the point of intersection of *b* and *c*.

At the time of *Begriffsschrift*, Frege regarded the 'content' of a name as the entity designated. But what is the content of (AB)? If the conceptual content of a sentence is the circumstance or state of affairs represented, then what is this in the case of an identity statement? It would seem to be more than just the entity designated by the two names, which would not distinguish between the sentence and the name. Another possibility is the self-identity of the entity designated, but this does not seem plausible, either. One reason why both of these possible answers are unsatisfactory is that neither would distinguish (AB) from the following identity statement:

(AA) The point of intersection of *a* and *b* = the point of intersection of *a* and *b*.

This identity statement is trivially true, while (AB) tells us something. (AA) is an instance of a logical truth, namely, $a = a$, while (AB) is not. So there is a logical difference, which means that there must be a difference in conceptual content, according to Frege's criterion for sameness of conceptual content.

In §8 of the *Begriffsschrift*, where he discusses the matter, Frege states that the content of an identity statement is 'the circumstance that two names have the same content'.[17] This allows us to distinguish between (AB) and (AA), for in the first case, the content is the circumstance that the names 'the point of intersection of a and b' and 'the point of intersection of b and c' have the same content, while in the second case, the content is the circumstance that 'the point of intersection of a and b' and 'the point of intersection of a and b' have the same content. However, this still seems not to capture the real difference here, for it is not just the mere fact that two names have the same content that is significant. As Frege puts the objection at the beginning of 'On Sense and Reference', where he criticizes his earlier view, names can be arbitrary. I could arbitrarily give something the names 'm' and 'n', for example, but then saying '$m = n$' is not to express any 'proper knowledge', as Frege puts it.[18] What is important is what the names tell us about the object designated. What (AB) tells us, for example, is that the point designated in one way, namely, as the point of intersection of a and b, turns out to be the same point designated in another way, namely, as the point of intersection of b and c.

In fact, Frege recognized this at the time of the *Begriffsschrift*, too, when he considers a similar geometrical example. Here he distinguishes between content and mode of determination of content and writes that 'different names for the same content are not always merely a trivial matter of formulation, but touch the very heart of the matter if they are connected with different modes of determination'.[19] The name 'point of intersection of a and b' determines the same point as the name 'point of intersection of b and c', for example, but in a different way. Despite recognizing the relevance of modes of determination, however, Frege continues to maintain that the content of an identity statement is the circumstance that two names have the same content, which does no justice to the role that modes of determination play in our use and understanding of identity statements.

As we have noted, (AB) tells us something whereas (AA) does not: both are true, but while (AB) is informative, (AA) is trivial. Since the same point is determined (twice) in both cases, the difference must clearly lie in the fact that (AB) involves two different modes of determination – and this must be reflected in the 'content' of (AB), at least in some sense of 'content'. What Frege comes to see is that *two* notions of content are needed, and from 1891 onwards he distinguishes between 'sense' ('*Sinn*') and 'reference' ('*Bedeutung*').[20] In the case of names, the reference of a name is the object designated, while the sense of a name is what contains the mode of determination of the object designated – or its 'mode of presentation', as Frege also calls it in 'On Sense and Reference'.[21]

Armed with this distinction, Frege can then give an account of why (AB) can be informatively true while (AA) is only trivially true. The two names 'point of intersection of a and b' and 'point of intersection of b and c' have the same reference, which is why both identity statements are true, but they express different senses, which is why (AB) can tell us something – namely, that determining a point in one way gives the same result as determining a point in another way. So, too, in the other – and more famous – example that Frege gives at the beginning of 'On Sense and Reference': 'the Morning Star' and 'the Evening Star' have the same reference, but express different senses, which is why we can learn something in being told that the Morning Star is the Evening Star. In general, identity statements of the form '$a = b$' are true if and only if 'a' and 'b' have the same reference, and are informative only if 'a' and 'b' express different senses.

6. The sense and reference of sentences

Frege's distinction between sense and reference seems well motivated in the case of names. (We will turn to some problems in Section 8.) But Frege also applied the distinction to sentences. On Frege's early view, as suggested above, the content of a sentence is the 'circumstance' represented; on his later view, with content split into sense and reference, the sense of a sentence is the thought expressed, and the reference of a sentence is its truth-value (if any). It seems plausible to identify the sense of a sentence with the thought it expresses – at any rate, if we consider grammatically well-formed sentences in the indicative mood, which are used correctly in an appropriate context.[22] In uttering (AB), for example, we express the thought that the point of intersection of a and b is the same as the point of intersection of b and c. In general, in uttering an indicative sentence 'p' (correctly, in an appropriate context), we express the thought that p.

Frege's claim that the reference of a sentence is its truth-value seems far less plausible, especially when we take into account Frege's view that the truth-values are *objects*, which he calls 'the True' and 'the False'. All true sentences, according to Frege, refer to the True, while all false sentences refer to the False. Once again, though, the key to understanding Frege's claim is his use of function–argument analysis, and identity statements remain at the heart of his concern. Consider the functional expression 'x = the point of intersection of b and c', which yields the following identity statements when 'x' is replaced by the respective names (see Diagram 1):

(AB) The point of intersection of a and b = the point of intersection of b and c.

(BB) The point of intersection of b and c = the point of intersection of b and c.

(CB) The point of intersection of c and a = the point of intersection of b and c.

(PB) Vertex P = the point of intersection of b and c.

(QB) Vertex Q = the point of intersection of b and c.

(RB) Vertex R = the point of intersection of b and c.

Of these, (AB), (BB) and (CB) are true, while (PB), (QB) and (RB) are false. It thus seems natural to take the 'value' of (AB), (BB) and (CB), which results from applying the function to the respective arguments, as their truth, and the 'value' of (PB), (QB) and (RB) as their falsity.[23] Indeed, this makes talk of *truth-value* seem entirely appropriate.

Why does Frege think that the truth-values are objects? Here the answer hinges on his distinction between concept and object: concepts are represented by 'unsaturated' expressions, objects by 'saturated' expressions. Sentences, like names, are saturated expressions, so they must represent objects. On Frege's view, then, sentences refer to either the True or the False just as names such as 'the point of intersection of b and c' refer to the objects they stand for.[24]

What we have in these considerations, though, is not so much an argument as merely a motivation for identifying the reference of a sentence (understood as the value that results from applying a function to an argument or arguments) with its truth-value. Frege does not consider other possibilities. Why should we not take the reference of true identity statements as the self-identity of the relevant object, for example, and the reference of false identity statements as the non-identity of the relevant objects? (This still allows us to regard their sense as the thought expressed.) There may be objections to such a suggestion, but Frege does not present them.[25] With his new view in place, however, Frege was able to streamline his ontology and offer a simple account of concepts. In Frege's ontology, there are just objects and functions, of which one important type is concepts. Concepts are functions whose value is always a truth-value.[26] Concepts, in other words, map objects (the references of names) onto one of two particular objects, the True and the False (the references of sentences).

7. The sense and reference of concept-words

According to Frege, the distinction between sense and reference applies to both names and sentences (which turn out to be a type of name). In none of his three published papers of the early 1890s, however, does Frege discuss its application to concept-words – or to functional expressions in general. This led to much dispute in the early secondary literature, which was only resolved when other writings from the period were published in 1969 and 1976.[27] It then became clear that Frege did indeed regard concept-words as having both a sense and a reference, at least when properly used in logic and science: the reference of a concept-word is the concept itself and the sense contains the mode of determination of the concept.

Traditional logicians had distinguished two features of concepts: their extension and their intension. The extension of a concept is the set of objects that fall under the concept, while the intension (roughly) is what we understand in grasping the concept: the condition that must be met for something to fall under the concept (which might be exhibited in a set of properties). It would be tempting to interpret Frege as lining up the sense/reference distinction with the intension/extension distinction. But while, as a first approximation, sense corresponds to intension, the reference of a concept-word is not its extension, on Frege's view, but the concept itself, understood as a function – an unsaturated entity. Frege does indeed see concepts as having extensions, but since these are sets, they count as objects, not concepts, and must be distinguished from the concepts themselves.

Frege's view of the sense and reference of the three types of expression – sentences, names and concept-words – is schematically summarized in a letter he wrote to Edmund Husserl in 1891:[28]

sentence	proper name	concept-word	
↓	↓	↓	
sense of the sentence (thought)	sense of the proper name	sense of the concept-word	
↓	↓	↓	
reference of the sentence (truth-value)	reference of the proper name (object)	(reference of the concept-word (concept)) →	object falling under the concept

Frege never changed his views on sense and reference after he had formulated them in 1891. The diagram above thus represents his final and considered position.

8. Two problems about names

Frege's views on sense and reference set much of the agenda for the development of philosophy of language in the twentieth century. In the remaining two sections of this chapter, we briefly look at some of the problems raised by these views, the debates about which have fuelled this development. In this section we consider two problems about the sense and reference of names, the first concerning whether names can have a sense without a reference, and the second concerning whether names can have a reference without a sense.

According to Frege, the sense of a name contains the 'mode of determination' – or as he also sometimes puts it, the 'mode of presentation' – of its reference. But if there is no reference, then how can there be a mode of presentation of it? Does sense, therefore, not require reference? Yet Frege himself admits that there can be names that have sense but lack reference. Fictional names such as 'Odysseus' provide one set of examples, and there are other examples such as 'the greatest number' which have a sense that *entails* a lack of reference.[29] Frege's views might look inconsistent if we think of senses solely as 'modes of presentation', but Frege rarely uses this term himself; he talks far more often of 'modes of determination', and this is the better term to use because it carries no implication of reference. If we were to think, say, of a mode of determination as a specification of a condition that something must meet (in order to be the reference of a name whose sense contains that mode of determination), then it may turn out that nothing meets that condition, even though the condition itself is perfectly coherent. On Frege's view, for example, 'the present King of France' has a sense even though it lacks a reference.

A qualification needs to be made here, however. For Frege nevertheless insisted that in an ideal language, that is, in a logical language suitable for scientific purposes (where truth is the goal), all names must have a reference (since otherwise sentences that contain them would lack a truth-value). What we can do here, though, Frege suggested, is *stipulate* a reference for terms that might otherwise be thought to lack a reference – for example, we can stipulate that they refer to the number 0 (seen as itself a kind of object).[30] On Frege's view, then, names can indeed have a sense without a reference, although this is to be avoided in an ideal language.

Can there be names that have reference but not sense? By 'name' Frege understood any expression referring – or purporting to refer – to an object. It is customary now to distinguish between proper names, such as 'Aristotle', and definite descriptions, such as 'the present King of France'. The conception of sense just suggested – the sense of a (Fregean) name being specified as a condition that something must meet in order to be the reference of the name – clearly applies to definite descriptions: this is what enables them to have sense but lack reference. But does it apply equally well to proper names? What is the sense of 'Aristotle', for example? In a notorious footnote in 'On Sense and Reference', Frege writes that opinions may differ here, depending on what we take as the relevant condition. One person may take 'Aristotle' to have the same sense as 'the pupil of Plato and teacher of Alexander the Great', for example, while another may take it to have the same sense as 'the teacher of Alexander the Great who was born in Stagira'.[31]

There are objections, however, to such a 'description theory' of proper names. One problem is the threat of infinite regress or circularity, since any definite description contains names whose sense must in turn be specified. A second problem, which Kripke was to highlight, is that such a view fails to do justice to certain modal considerations.[32] One response is simply to deny that proper names have a sense at all. This was Russell's view: genuine (or logically) proper names merely refer.[33] According to Frege, however, to deny that proper names have sense is to deny that sentences that contain those names have sense. (Russell needed his theory of descriptions to avoid this implication.) Frege's own response was to stress again the differences between our use of language in everyday life and the demands of an ideal logical language. In the latter we must indeed specify a unique sense for each name, definition or demonstration being required wherever two names have the same reference. On Frege's own view, then, all names – whether proper names or definite descriptions – have both a sense and a reference, or at least should have in an ideal language; in other words, they do so wherever sentences containing them both express thoughts and have a truth-value.

9. Two problems about contexts

Fundamental to Frege's application of function–argument analysis to language is the idea that the 'value' of a sentence is determined by the 'value' of its (logically significant) parts. In his early work, Frege called this value 'content'. With content later split into sense and reference, however, this yields two principles of determination (sometimes also called principles of compositionality):

(PDS)   The sense of a sentence is determined by the sense of its (logically significant) parts.
(PDR)   The reference of a sentence is determined by the reference of its (logically significant) parts.

These principles have motivated a great deal of work in subsequent philosophy of language, but they are not unproblematic. In this final section we briefly consider two problems.[34]

The first concerns their application in so-called intensional contexts, that is, in contexts where there are attributions of propositional attitudes, such as saying of someone that they believe that p. Consider, for example, the following two sentences:

(GAA) Gottlob believes that Aristotle is Aristotle.
(GAP) Gottlob believes that Aristotle is the author of the
       Prior Analytics.

'Aristotle' and 'the author of the *Prior Analytics*' have the same reference, so by the principle (PDR), (GAA) should have the same reference, that is, truth-value, as (GAP). But (GAA) can clearly be true without (GAP) being true. Frege recognized the problem here and argued that in these cases, the reference of the embedded sentence, that is, what follows the 'that', is not its customary or direct reference but its indirect reference, where this is taken as its customary sense.[35] In other words, in intensional contexts, the reference of the embedded sentence is the sense, that is, thought, that the sentence (normally) expresses. This is plausible in itself, for what determines whether (GAP), say, is true is the *thought* that Gottlob takes to be true (not the truth-value of the embedded sentence). The principles of determination can thus be preserved, albeit at the cost of complicating the account of sense and reference. There are further complications when we consider cases of multiply embedded sentences (such as 'Bertrand hopes that Gottlob believes that Aristotle is Aristotle'); and the issue continues to be debated in philosophy of language today.[36]

There is a general message suggested here: that what counts as the sense and reference of an expression depends on the context. This message is reinforced when we consider the problem of indexicality. Indexicals are expressions such as 'I', 'you', 'here', 'there', 'now' and 'then', whose reference depends systematically on the context; and they pose a serious problem for Frege's conception of sense. For if the reference changes, then so too must the sense. Consider the following:

(TS) Today is sunny.

Uttered today, this expresses a different thought from that which would be expressed if uttered tomorrow; so the sense of 'today' – as partly determining the thought, in accord with (PDS) – must differ on the two occasions. But then what is it?

Here is one suggestion as to how (TS) might be understood:

(DS) Monday 3 December 2018 is sunny.

But it is clearly possible to hold (TS) as true but (DS) as false, and vice versa, in which case they cannot be taken to express the same thought; and the same will apply to any attempt to 'cash out' the indexical in terms of a definite description.[37] The only response might seem to be to take the sense of any indexical as used on a given occasion as primitive and irreducible. It is clear, however, that Frege allowed that the thought expressed by (TS) uttered today could be expressed on other occasions.[38] To express tomorrow what I said today, I would have to utter:

(Y₁S) Yesterday was sunny.

But how far can this go on? Next Monday, I might say:

(Y₇S) The day before the day before the day before the day before the day before the day before yesterday was sunny.

Yet there is obviously a better sentence:

(LMS) Last Monday was sunny.

This introduces the concept *day of the week*, so arguably goes beyond what is expressed in uttering (TS). And if we consider what I would say in a few years' time, then it seems that I am going to end up using (DS) to express the thought, and we are back with the dilemma. In trying to capture the same thought through time, we seem to have been led to an arguably *different* thought.

Frege never provided a satisfactory solution to the problem of indexicality. As far as he was concerned, this was a problem that affected our use of ordinary language – and once again, was to be avoided in an ideal logical language (in which all indexicality is to be cashed out, as we might put it). Nevertheless, indexicality – and contextuality generally – is a pervasive feature of ordinary language, and the problems cannot be brushed aside if we want to apply Frege's ideas.[39] They do suggest that the principles of determination and the account of sense and reference need, at the very least, to be qualified in important ways. This task was one of the many things that Frege bequeathed to his successors.

Further reading

The Frege Reader (1997) contains the four key papers discussed in this chapter, as well as substantial selections from Frege's three books and other works. For elaboration of the account given in this chapter, see Beaney's *Frege: Making Sense* (1996). Mark Textor's *Frege on Sense and Reference* (2010) also offers a useful book-length guide to many of the ideas covered in this chapter. The four-volume collection of papers edited by Beaney and Reck (2005) contains the most influential papers, on all aspects of Frege's philosophy, published between 1986 and 2005. Volume 4 is on Frege's philosophy of thought and language. A more recent collection, *The Cambridge Companion to Frege* (2010), edited by Potter and Ricketts, contains further papers. There is an entry on Frege in the online Oxford Bibliographies (Beaney, 2014b), which provides a more detailed guide to reading. Finally, for an introduction to analytic philosophy generally, in which Frege's ideas play a key role, see Beaney's *Analytic Philosophy* (2017).

Notes

1   For a detailed chronology of Frege's life, see Thiel and Beaney (2005), where further references to biographical accounts can be found.
2   Although written 12 years after the completion of the *Begriffsschrift*, the clearest account of this can be found in Frege (1891).
3   On this, see, for example, Frege's letter to Marty of 1882, reprinted in Frege (1997, p. 81).
4   Here, and in what follows, I use modern notation rather than Frege's own two-dimensional Begriffsschrift. For an explanation of Frege's symbolism, see App. 2 of Frege (1997).
5   It should be noted that Frege does not himself use a separate symbol for the existential quantifier, relying on the equivalence, as we now write it, of '$(\forall x)Fx$' and '$\sim(\exists x)\sim Fx$' (cf. 1879, §12), nor for conjunction, which he defines in terms of conditionality and negation (1879, §7).
6   See, for example, Frege (1882/1997, pp. 80–1); (1892b/1997, pp. 189–90).
7   See, for example, the papers in Beaney and Reck (2005, IV, Part 12); Oliver (2010); Ricketts (2010); Heck and May (2013).

8 See esp. Frege (1884, §§53, 57/1997, pp. 103, 106–7). For further discussion, see Beaney, 2005, §4, and Beaney (2017, chapter 1).

9 Since Frege thinks that the relation between objects and first-level concepts (subsumption) is different from, though analogous to, the relation between first-level and second-level concepts, he talks of objects 'falling under' first-level concepts and first-level concepts 'falling within' second-level concepts; see Frege (1892b/1997, p. 189). Both relations are different from subordination, which is a relation between concepts of the same level.

10 See, for example, Frege (1882/1997, p. 82); (1884, §53/1997, p. 103).

11 I have called this 'interpretive analysis', which I see as characteristic of the Fregean strand in analytic philosophy. Cf. for example, Beaney (2014a, §6: 2016; 2017, chapter 3).

12 Frege (1879, §3/1997, pp. 53–4).

13 In his later work, Frege calls those aspects of meaning that lie outside this logical core 'shading' or 'colouring' (see, e.g., 1892a, p. 31/1997, p. 155; 1892b, p. 196, fn./1997, p. 184, fn. G; cf. 1918, p. 63/1997, pp. 330–1; and esp. 1897, pp. 150–5/1997, pp. 239–44). These aspects have also been called 'tone'.

14 See, for example, Frege (1879, §§3, 9). Cf. Beaney (2007).

15 By Frege's 'early work', I mean his work up to and including the *Grundlagen* of 1884, when the notion of conceptual content was operative. From 1891 onwards, this notion is split into the dual notions of sense and reference, as we will shortly see.

16 Frege (1892a, pp. 25–6/1997, p. 152). Frege does not provide the diagram himself, but it has been added here for illustration (as in *The Frege Reader*).

17 Frege (1879, p. 14/1997, p. 64).

18 Frege (1892a, p. 26/1997, p. 152).

19 Frege (1879, p. 15/1997, p. 65).

20 The distinction is first drawn in Frege (1891), but receives its fullest explanation in Frege (1892a). The translation of '*Bedeutung*' has generated enormous controversy. In *The Frege Reader* (Frege, 1997) I left it untranslated, for the reasons I give in §4 of my introduction. For detailed discussion of the problem of translating Frege's use of 'Bedeutung', see Beaney (2019).

21 Frege (1892a, pp. 26–7/1997, p. 152).

22 It is common to see the indicative (declarative) mood as basic and other moods, such as the imperative and interrogative, as derivative. If so, then the sense of a non-indicative sentence can be taken as the sense of the corresponding indicative sentence. For discussion of the issues raised here, see, for example, Boisvert and Ludwig (2006).

23 Cf. Frege (1891, p. 13/1997, p. 137). Frege gives the example of the function $x^2 = 1$ and considers the four identity statements (equations) that result from taking −1, 0, 1 and 2 as arguments: −1 and 1 yield true identity statements, while 0 and 2 yield false identity statements.

24 Cf. ibid. I discuss Frege's introduction of truth-values as objects in more detail in Beaney (2007).

25 A further possibility is to develop Frege's earlier idea of the 'circumstance' or 'state of affairs' represented. It may be harder to think what this might be in the case of identity statements (which may be one reason why Frege offered a metalinguistic construal of their 'content' in his early work), but it looks attractive in the case of simple sentences such as 'Gottlob is human' and is arguably what Frege needs to fill the gap that opens up between sense and reference. I discuss some of the issues raised here in Beaney (1996, esp. §8.1).

26 Cf. Frege (1891, p. 15/1997, p. 139).

27 See Frege (1969), and in particular his '[Comments on *Sinn* and *Bedeutung*]', trans. in Frege (1997, pp. 172–80); and Frege (1976), and in particular his letter to Husserl of 24 May 1891, partly trans. in Frege (1997, p. 149).

28 See Frege (1976, pp. 96–7); trans. in Frege (1997, p. 149).

29 Cf. for example, Frege (1892a, pp. 28, 32–3/1997, pp. 153, 157).

30 See, for example, Frege (1892a, p. 41/1997, p. 163).

31 Frege (1892a, p. 27, fn./1997, p. 153, fn. B).

32 See, for example, Kripke (1980), esp. Lecture 1. See the chapter on Kripke in this volume.

33 See the chapter on Russell in this volume.

34 For a fuller account of these problems, see my introduction to Frege (1997, pp. 29–35), on which I draw here.

35 See Frege (1892a, p. 37/1997, p. 160).

36 For a brief recent account of the issue, see Textor (2010, pp. 182–91).

37 This has been called 'the problem of the essential indexical' (Perry, 1979). It is similar to the problem that arises if we identify the sense of a proper name with the sense of some corresponding definite description, as discussed in the previous section.

38 Cf. Frege (1918, p. 64/1997, p. 332).

39 For an introduction to these problems, see Beaney (1996, §7.4), and Textor (2010, pp. 154–70).

Bibliography

Beaney, Michael (1996), *Frege: Making Sense*. London: Duckworth.
Beaney, Michael (1997), 'Introduction', in Frege, 1997, pp. 1–46.

Beaney, Michael (2005), 'Frege, Russell and Logicism', in Beaney and Reck, 2005, vol. I, pp. 213–40.

Beaney, Michael (2007), 'Frege's Use of Function-Argument Analysis and His Introduction of Truth-Values as Objects', in Dirk Greimann (ed.), *Essays on Frege's Conception of Truth, Grazer Philosophische Studien*, 75, pp. 93–123.

Beaney, Michael (ed.) (2013), *The Oxford Handbook of the History of Analytic Philosophy*. Oxford: Oxford University Press.

Beaney, Michael (2014a), 'Analysis', in *The Stanford Encyclopedia of Philosophy* (Summer 2018 Edition), ed. Edward N Zalta, https://plato.stanford.edu/archives/sum2018/entries/analysis/ (accessed June 2018).

Beaney, Michael (2014b), 'Gottlob Frege', in D. Pritchard (ed.), *Oxford Bibliographies in Philosophy*. New York: Oxford University Press, online at: www.oxford bibliographies.com (accessed June 2018).

Beaney, Michael (2016), 'The Analytic Revolution', in Anthony O'Hear (ed.), *History of Philosophy*. Cambridge: Cambridge University Press, pp. 227–49.

Beaney, Michael (2017), *Analytic Philosophy: A Very Short Introduction*. Oxford: Oxford University Press.

Beaney, Michael (2019), 'Translating "Bedeutung" in Frege's Writings: A Case Study and Cautionary Tale in the History and Philosophy of Translation', in P. Ebert and M. Rossberg (eds), *Essays on Frege's Basic Laws of Arithmetic*. Oxford: Oxford University Press, pp. 603–51.

Beaney, Michael and Reck, Erich H. (eds) (2005), *Gottlob Frege: Critical Assessments*, 4 vols. London: Routledge.

Boisvert, Daniel and Ludwig, Kirk (2006), 'Semantics for Nondeclaratives', in Ernest Lepore and Barry C. Smith (eds), *The Oxford Handbook of Philosophy of Language*. Oxford: Oxford University Press, pp. 864–92.

Dummett, Michael (1973), *Frege: Philosophy of Language*. London: Duckworth; 2nd edn, 1981.

Frege, Gottlob (1879), *Begriffsschrift*. Halle: L. Nebert; Preface and most of part I (§§1–12) trans. in Frege, 1997, pp. 47–78.

Frege, Gottlob (1882), 'Letter to Marty, 29.8.1882', trans. in Frege, 1997, pp. 79–83.

Frege, Gottlob (1884), *Die Grundlagen der Arithmetik*. Breslau: W. Koebner; selections trans. in Frege, 1997, pp. 84–129.

Frege, Gottlob (1891), 'Funktion und Begriff', Jena: H. Pohle; trans. as 'Function and Concept' in Frege, 1997, pp. 130–48.

Frege, Gottlob (1892a), 'Über Sinn und Bedeutung'. *Zeitschrift für Philosophie und philosophische Kritik*, 100, 25–50; trans. as 'On *Sinn* and *Bedeutung*' in Frege, 1997, pp. 151–71.

Frege, Gottlob (1892b), 'Über Begriff und Gegenstand'. *Vierteljahrsschrift für wissenschaftliche Philosophie*, 16, 192–205; trans. as 'On Concept and Object' in Frege, 1997, pp. 181–93.

Frege, Gottlob (1893/1903), *Grundgesetze der Arithmetik* (vol. I 1893, vol. II 1903). Jena: H. Pohle. Selections trans. in Frege, 1997, pp. 194–223, 258–89.

Frege, Gottlob (1918), 'Der Gedanke'. *Beiträge zur Philosophie des deutschen Idealismus*, 1, 58–77; trans. as 'Thought' in Frege, 1997, pp. 325–45.

Frege, Gottlob (1969), *Nachgelassene Schriften*, ed. H. Hermes, F. Kambartel and F. Kaulbach. Hamburg: Felix Meiner; trans. as Frege, 1979.

Frege, Gottlob (1976), *Wissenschaftlicher Briefwechsel*, ed. G. Gabriel, H. Hermes, F. Kambartel, C. Thiel and A. Veraart. Hamburg: Felix Meiner; abridged and trans. as Frege, 1980.

Frege, Gottlob (1979), *Posthumous Writings* (translation of Frege, 1969 by P. Long and R. White). Oxford: Blackwell.

Frege, Gottlob (1980), *Philosophical and Mathematical Correspondence* (translation of Frege, 1976, ed. B. McGuinness, trans. H. Kaal). Oxford: Blackwell.

Frege, Gottlob (1997), *The Frege Reader*, ed. and with an introduction by M. Beaney. Oxford: Blackwell.

Heck, Richard G. and May, Robert (2013), 'The Function is Unsaturated', in Beaney, 2013, pp. 825–50.

Kripke, Saul (1980), *Naming and Necessity*. Oxford: Blackwell.

Oliver, Alex (2010), 'What Is a Predicate?' in Potter and Ricketts, 2010, pp. 118–48.

Perry, John (1979), 'The Problem of the Essential Indexical', *Noûs*, 13, pp. 3–21.

Potter, Michael and Ricketts, Tom (eds) (2010), *The Cambridge Companion to Frege*. Cambridge: Cambridge University Press.

Ricketts, Thomas (2010), 'Concepts, Objects and the Context Principle', in Potter and Ricketts, 2010, pp. 149–219.

Textor, Mark (2010), *Frege on Sense and Reference*. London: Routledge.

Thiel, Christian and Beaney, Michael (2005), 'Frege's Life and Work: Chronology and Bibliography', in Beaney and Reck, 2005, Vol. I, pp. 23–39.

CHAPTER TWO

RUSSELL

Kenneth A. Taylor

In this chapter, I focus on two distinctions made by Russell and a thesis that he rested on those distinctions. The two distinctions are (i) a semantic distinction between (logically) proper names and definite descriptions and (ii) an epistemic distinction between knowledge by acquaintance and knowledge by description. On that pair of distinctions, Russell rested the thesis that every proposition that we are capable of understanding must be wholly composed of constituents with which we are directly acquainted. Though Russell's theory of descriptions has been subject to a variety of objections, his fundamental insight about the difference between names and descriptions retains much of its validity. By contrast, the epistemic distinction between knowledge by acquaintance and knowledge by description fares less well. There is probably not anything at all with which we are directly acquainted in Russell's intended sense: hence strictly speaking, Russellian acquaintance may be an empty notion that corresponds to no cognitive state that we are ever actually in with respect to any object of thought. Still, many philosophers who agree there is nothing with which we are directly acquainted have thought that some less demanding version of Russell's thesis must be correct. So I close this chapter with a brief examination of various attenuated versions of the principle of acquaintance.

1. Russell's theory of descriptions

Definite descriptions are expressions like 'the king of France', 'the tallest mountain on earth' or 'the most populous state of the USA'. Such phrases are formed from 'the' followed by a singular count-noun phrase. According to Russell, descriptions must be sharply distinguished from what he called logically proper names. Genuine, or *logically proper*, names are, in a sense to be explained below, bona fide logical constituents of the sentences in which they occur. The sole semantic function of a genuine name, on Russell's view, is to stand for an object, and to do so, as it were, directly, without the mediation of anything like a Fregean sense. By contrast, Russell took definite descriptions to be what he called 'denoting complexes'. Although Russell took denoting complexes to be 'meaningless in isolation', he allowed that they have what he called 'definitions in use'. What Russell means by this combination of views is (i) that no description is meaningful in virtue of being associated with a meaning, in the sense of something the description stands for, and (ii) that the correct theory of definite descriptions works by accounting for whole sentences containing definite descriptions, rather than by saying something about definite descriptions in isolation from their occurrences in whole sentences. Or to put the point differently, definite descriptions are neither free-standing grammatical constituents nor independently meaning-bearing semantic units of the sentences in which they occur. Any appearance to the contrary is a sort of grammatical illusion. Indeed, Russell held that upon proper logical analysis definite descriptions, in effect, 'disappear'.

No one now would agree with every last detail of Russell's views on descriptions (for instance, modern semantic theories can treat descriptions as in some sense genuine grammatical constituents of the sentences in which they appear), but the core of his view remains very plausible, and – perhaps more importantly – it would be difficult to overstate the power and enduring philosophical influence of the underlying thought that seeing past the superficial and often misleading surface grammar of the sentences of our language to the hidden logical forms of those sentences is the key to resolving or dissolving certain otherwise intractable philosophical puzzles. Indeed, it is because of the power of this idea that Russell's theory of descriptions has been called a paradigm of philosophy.

The core of Russell's theory is deceptively simple. Russell effectively suggests that any sentence of the form

The F is G

(where 'F' is a singular noun phrase like 'dog', 'present king of France' or 'Swiss surfer', and 'is G' is a normal predicate like 'is bald', 'is a man' or 'is running') will have truth-conditions as follows:

There is at least one thing which is an F,
and there is at most one thing which is an F, and
every F is G

(or, somewhat more concisely, there is exactly one F and every F is G).

Thus stated, Russell's theory may seem neither startling nor obviously deserving of its status as a paradigm of philosophy. We may begin to appreciate the true significance of Russell's philosophical achievement, however, if we note that the natural and default assumption about definite descriptions is that they are indeed meaning-bearing semantic units, grammatically and semantically on a par with logically proper names. Until Russell came along, no one imagined otherwise. But this natural and tempting assumption quickly lands us with a variety of puzzles. What Russell shows is that the only way to resolve those puzzles is to abandon that natural and tempting default assumption. And he offers what purports to be an explicit and systematic analysis of the true semantic character of sentences containing definite descriptions that solves or dissolves the puzzles generated by the default assumption that definite descriptions are meaning-bearing semantic units.

Three puzzles motivate Russell's theory of descriptions. The first concerns apparent violations of Leibniz' law concerning the indiscernibility of identicals. The second concerns apparent counterexamples to the law of excluded middle. The third concerns true statements of non-existence. And we will see that the key to resolving the puzzles is precisely to surrender our perhaps natural and default assumptions about how definite descriptions function. Let's consider each puzzle in turn.

According to Leibniz' Law, if a is identical with b – that is, if a is *one and the same thing as* b – then whatever is true of a must also be true of *b*. By Leibniz' Law, every instance of the following inference scheme is valid:

(1) *a* is F
(2) *a* = *b*
(3) *b* is F

But now consider the following triad of sentences:

(4) George wants to know whether Obama is the 2009 Nobel Peace Prize laureate
(5) Obama is the 2009 Nobel Peace Prize laureate
(6) George wants to know whether Obama is Obama

Sentence (6) seems not to follow from the conjunction (4) and (5). To paraphrase Russell, it would seem odd to ascribe an interest in the law of identity to George, in the scenario described. Yet (4)–(6) would seem to be an instance of our scheme. To see this, take 'George wants to know whether Obama is ___' as a complex predicate and take both the expression 'Obama' and the expression 'the winner of the 2009 Nobel Peace Prize' as singular referring terms capable of occupying the argument place of that predicate. This problem is related to the problem of informative identities: if we see, for example, 'Obama' and 'the winner of the 2009 Nobel Peace Prize' as genuine singular terms (logically proper names), there seems to be no way to account for the apparent difference in meaning between 'Obama is Obama' and 'Obama is the 2009 Nobel Peace Prize laureate'.

Russell's second puzzle involves apparent violations of the law of excluded middle. That law implies that there is no middle ground between truth and falsity. Exactly one of a sentence and its negation will be true and exactly one false. If φ is true then its negation $\sim\varphi$ is false; if φ is false then $\sim\varphi$ is true. It may seem to follow by the law of excluded middle that exactly one of the following should be true and exactly one of the following should be false:

(7) The present king of France is bald.
(8) The present king of France is not bald.

Suppose we enumerate all the things in the world that are bald. There will not be among them anyone who is presently king of France. On the other hand, if we enumerate all the things in the world that fail to be bald, there will not be among them anyone who is presently king of France. Are we to conclude, in apparent violation of the law of excluded middle, both that it is false that the present king of France is not bald and false that the present king of France is bald? 'Hegelians, who love a synthesis', says Russell (1905), 'will probably conclude he wears a wig'. Note that even if one is suspicious of this way of generating a puzzle, it remains the case that most competent speakers of English who consider pairs like (7) and (8) do not think that exactly one of the pair is true, and that is sufficient to generate *a* puzzle at this point.

The third puzzle concerns claims of non-existence. Consider the following sentence:

(9) The round square does not exist.

This will strike many as straightforwardly true. But now suppose that we take (9) to be grammatically on a par with 'Obama is not a fool'. That sentence is true if and only if a certain object – namely, Obama – fails to have a certain property – namely, the property of being a fool. By parity of reasoning, it may be tempting to say that (9) is true if and only if a certain object – namely, the round square – fails to have a certain property – namely, the property of existence. But, as Whitehead and Russell (1927) put it, 'If there were such an object, it would exist. We cannot first assume that there is a certain object and then proceed to deny that there is such an object.' If a putative 'object' lacks the supposed property of existence, there is no object to be the bearer or non-bearer of any property in the first place. So (9) cannot after all be construed as denying of a certain object that it has a certain property. Another way to come at what is puzzling here is to note that if 'The round square' is viewed exclusively as a candidate genuine singular term, in Russell's sense, then if it stands for nothing, it will be semantically flawed – it will lack the association with an object which makes such terms meaningful: so, if we try to make the negative existential claim come out true, we seem bound to deprive it of meaning; and if we try to secure its meaningfulness, we seem bound to have it being false. On either way of coming at the issue, our puzzle is to say just what truth (9) expresses and how it manages to express that truth.

According to Russell, the key to solving our puzzles is to appreciate that definite descriptions are not genuine referring terms at all. Russell thinks that once we give a proper logical analysis of the relevant sentences – and recognize them as complex quantificational or 'how many' claims – the puzzles dissolve.

Take (9) again, for example. Superficial grammar suggests that the definite description 'the round square' is a referring expression – a sort of complex singular term – and thus a genuine constituent of (9). Indeed, one might even think that the expression 'the round square' occupies the subject place in the relevant sentence. That is not a silly view. Frege, for example, treated descriptions as complex proper names. According to Russell, however, his paraphrase of (9) reveals its true, but hidden, logical form. In that logically revealing paraphrase, there occurs neither the expression 'the round square' itself nor any other single expression that counts as a direct logical paraphrase of that expression. Where the original contains a single, syntactically complex term, the paraphrase contains a distributed collection of quantificational claims, no part or parts of which can be regarded, either jointly or severally, as occupying the position of the grammatical subject in the paraphrase. Indeed, the true logical form of (9) is not given by a sentence in subject–predicate form at all. And once we see this, solutions to each of our puzzles will be more or less immediately forthcoming.

Consider the following example:

(10)   The Swiss surfer is a redhead.

Imagine three different scenarios with respect to Switzerland and its surfer or surfers (here and throughout we'll take it that 'Swiss surfer' applies to habitual surfers with Swiss nationality). First, suppose that Switzerland has one and only one surfer. In that case, it would say something true if and only if the one and only Swiss surfer is a redhead and it will say something false if and only if the one and only Swiss surfer is not a redhead. This fact may appear to lend initial support to the thought that the phrase, 'the Swiss surfer' has the semantic function of standing for a certain object. When there is a unique Swiss surfer, the truth or falsity of (10) depends on how things stand with that very thing.

But this isn't the entire story. Consider a scenario in which Switzerland has many surfers. In such a scenario, 'the Swiss surfer' does not pick out some one definite object on which the truth of falsity of (10) directly depends: (10) is false in the imagined scenario – or so Russell thought – but not because some one definite object fails to be a redhead. On Russell's view, (10) as it stands would be false even if *all* of Switzerland's many surfers were redheads. For according to Russell, part of what (10) says is that Switzerland has a unique surfer (i.e. has exactly one (current) surfer). And so the bare fact that Switzerland fails to have a unique surfer itself suffices to render (10) false. But Switzerland can fail to have a unique surfer either by having more than one or by being entirely devoid of surfers. In sum total, then, there are at three ways in all for (10) to be false. It is false if there is exactly one Swiss surfer, who fails to be a redhead. And it is false if Switzerland has either no surfers or many surfers. And only when Switzerland has exactly one surfer, does the truth or falsity of (10) even appear to depend on how things are by some one definite object.

There is a paraphrase of (10) that, in contradistinction to (10) itself, wears its truth-conditions fully on its sleeve. That paraphrase is manifestly true in all and only the circumstances in which, according to Russell, (10) is true and manifestly false in all and only the circumstances in which, according to Russell, (10) is false:

(11)   There is exactly one Swiss surfer, and every Swiss surfer is a redhead.

We are now in a position to understand Russell's solutions to our three puzzles.

Consider (9) again. Going by superficial grammatical appearances, (9) appears to entail that a certain object lacks a certain property. At first glance, (9) would appear to be on a grammatical par with the sentence 'Obama is not a fool'. But we can now see why that appearance is misleading. Looked at in Russell's way, we see that (9) does not deny the property of existence to some one definite object. Sentence (9) really says that no object in the universe has the property of being uniquely both round and square. It isn't about some one particular (non-existent) object, in other words, but about the universe itself or the set of objects that happen to exist in the universe. It denies that that set contains an object which is uniquely both round and square. Sentence (9) has the true form:

(12)   It is not the case that there is exactly one thing which is both round and square.

Notice that (12) is compatible with the existence of many round squares. To deny that there are *any* such objects, we need something like:

(13)   It is not the case that there exists something which is both round and square.

It is worth noting here that not only does Russell not treat the description 'the round square' as referring expression, but he also doesn't treat 'exists' as a predicate. Existence isn't, on Russell's view, a property that individual objects may either have or fail to have. We express existence or non-existence through a combination of quantifier or 'how many' words, predicates, variables and the identity sign. To say that Obama exists, for example, is not to ascribe the property of existence to Obama, but to say there exists something that is identical with Obama as follows:

(14)   There exists an x such that x = Obama.

Our second puzzle arose from that fact that it does not seem to be the case that exactly one of

(7) The present king of France is bald.

and

(8) The present king of France is not bald.

is true – in apparent contradiction of the law of excluded middle. But it turns out that on a Russellian analysis (7) and (8) are not contradictory opposites at all. In terms of Russell's theory, (7) and (8) can be glossed as (15) and (16) below:

(15)   There is exactly one thing which is a present king of France and everything that is a present king of France is bald.

(16) There is exactly one thing which is a present king of France and it's not the case that everything that is a present king of France is bald.

Obviously, (15) and (16) will both be false if it's not the case that there is exactly one thing which is a present king of France. Further, once we have Russell's spelling out of the form of 'The present king of France is bald', we can see that 'The present king of France is not bald' is ambiguous, and admits of at least two readings. One of these is given by (16), the other is

(17) It is not the case that there is exactly one thing which is a present king of France and everything that is a present king of France is bald.

It is (17) which is the proper negation of (7)/(15). In any particular situation, exactly one of (15) and (17) will be true, and there is no breach of the law of the excluded middle.

Now, consider our first puzzle. The following gives a rough initial intuitive feel for the Russellian logical form of (4):

(20) George wants to know whether it is the case both that one and only one thing is a 2009 Nobel Peace Prize laureate and that every 2009 Nobel Peace Prize laureate is identical with Obama.

And (21) represents a gloss of the Russellian logical form of (5):

(21) One and only one person is a 2009 Nobel Peace Prize laureate and every 2009 Nobel Peace Prize laureate is identical with Obama.

Intuitively, it seems evident that (6) above does not follow from (20) and (21). More importantly, logical analysis reveals that the failure of (6) to follow from (20) and (21) in no way violates Leibniz' law. (20) is not a sentence of the form 'a is F' and (21) is not a sentence of the form 'a = b'. The denoting complex 'the 2009 Nobel Peace Prize laureate' disappears upon logical analysis and thus is not a bona fide term for which 'Scott' can be substituted.

2. Proper names

The full significance of Russell's theory of descriptions cannot be appreciated without considering the sharp contrast that Russell sees between descriptions and what he calls logically proper names. Logically proper names are genuine grammatical constituents of the sentences in which they occur. Such expressions function not as mere 'denoting complexes', but refer 'directly' to an object. Russell's central example of a logically proper name is actually not really a name in ordinary parlance but the demonstrative 'this'. The word 'this', he says, 'is always a proper name, in the sense that it applies directly to just one object, and does not in any way describe the object to which it applies' (Russell, 1918, p. 201).

Using a more contemporary idiom, we can put the stark semantic distinction between genuinely referring expressions and denoting complexes envisioned by Russell by saying that sentences containing genuinely referring expressions express so-called *singular* or *object-dependent* propositions, while sentences containing definite descriptions or other denoting complexes (but no genuinely referring expressions) express *non-singular*, *general* or *object-independent* propositions. A singular or object-dependent proposition is a proposition the very existence of which depends, and depends essentially, on the existence of a certain object.[1] If *p* is an object-dependent proposition, then there is a certain object *o* such that *p* would not exist at all (and thus would not be thinkable or expressible), if *o* failed to exist. Object-dependent propositions may be contrasted with what are variously called non-singular, general or object-independent propositions. The identity of a general proposition is not dependent on the existence of any particular object. What one expresses when one says, for example, that a cat is coming down the street, does not depend for its existence upon any particular cat. Its truth or falsity does not depend on whether Willard (or Ludwig, or Bertie ...) is coming down the street. Even if there were no cats at all in existence, we could still both think and assert – albeit falsely – that a cat is coming down the street. That very content – the content that a cat is coming down the street – would still exist and still be the content of a possible assertion even if there were no cats at all in the world.

Influenced by the work of Saul Kripke and David Kaplan, many contemporary thinkers hold that sentences containing what we ordinarily think of proper names – names like 'Barack Obama' or 'George Bush' – express genuinely singular or object-dependent propositions. We will come back to this point, but first we should note that Russell does not share that view. On *his* view, such expressions are not really proper names at all, at least not logically speaking: rather, such putative names are really definite descriptions in disguise. Sentences containing ordinary proper names express general rather than singular or object-dependent propositions.

Russell's grounds for denying that ordinary proper names are genuinely referring expressions are parallel to his reasons for thinking that explicit definite descriptions are not genuinely referring expressions. Recall that he holds that the sole semantic function of a genuine proper name is to stand for a bearer. For Russell, it follows directly, therefore, that a proper name cannot simultaneously both lack a bearer and be semantically significant (genuinely meaningful). But consider the (apparent) name 'Santa Claus' as it occurs in:

(22)   Santa Claus lives at the North Pole.

Despite the fact that there is no Santa Claus, it is plausible that (22) expresses a determinate proposition. On Russell's view, there is such a proposition, and that proposition is strictly literally false. If 'Santa Claus' were a genuine or logically proper name, according to Russell, (22) would fail to express a proposition. Since (22) expresses a determinate proposition, even though there is no object for 'Santa Claus' to refer to, the proposition expressed by (22) cannot be a singular or object-dependent proposition, but must be a descriptive or general proposition. Sentence (22) does not say (falsely) of some one definite object that it lives at the North Pole. Rather, it expresses a proposition more like (23) below:

(23)   The jolly, white-bearded, red-suited, fat man, who brings toys to good children at Christmas-time, lives at the North Pole.

Thus we see that on Russell's view, the expression 'Santa Claus' is an abbreviated or disguised form of the definite description 'the jolly, white-bearded, red-suited, fat man, who brings toys to good children at Christmas-time'.

It is worth briefly comparing and contrasting Russell's views both with the views of Frege and with views of those in the more recent direct reference tradition. On Frege's views, no sentence whatsoever expresses an object-dependent proposition.[2] Frege held: (i) that no referring expression ever contributes *just* its referent to the proposition expressed by any sentence in which it occurs; (ii) that names typically have two distinct semantic roles – that of referring (to a referent) and that of expressing a sense; and (iii) that a name could have the role of expressing a sense, even when it failed to refer to any object. Frege thus has the resources to deny Russell's view that a genuine name that fails to stand for a referent is *ipso facto* meaningless. A name always contributes its sense and never its reference to what is expressed by any sentence containing it. And because senses can exist and be the very senses that they are whether or not they determine a reference, sentences containing non-referring proper names express object-*in*dependent, rather than object-dependent propositions, at least on the reading of Frege that I have offered here.

Russell rejects the distinction between sense and reference. But when it comes to what we ordinarily think of as proper names, Russell and Frege have considerable commonality. They both think, for example, that definite descriptions and ordinary proper names have a great deal in common. Russell, of course, thinks that ordinary proper names are definite descriptions in disguise and that, as such, they are not proper grammatical constituents of the sentences in which they apparently occur. Frege, by contrast, thinks that definite descriptions are just complex proper names and are, as such, proper constituents of the sentences in which they occur. On either way of thinking about it, ordinary proper names and definite descriptions turn out to have much the same semantic and syntactic characters. In particular, both Frege and Russell held that both sentences containing explicit definite descriptions and sentences containing ordinary proper names express object-independent rather than object-dependent propositions – again, at least on the reading of Frege we're considering here.

Many contemporary philosophers of language hold that even ordinary proper names are what Kripke (1980) called rigid designators and what Kaplan (1989) called devices of direct reference. Rigid designators denote the same object in all possible worlds. Devices of direct reference refer without the mediation of any Fregean sense or Russellian descriptive content. Many definite descriptions are not rigid designators, and no definite description is a device of direct reference, not even those which do (like 'the positive square root of 4') designate rigidly. If that is right, Russell was simply wrong to suppose that ordinary proper names are nothing but definite descriptions in disguise – though this is not the place to discuss in detail the grounds for thinking that even ordinary proper names are rigidly designating devices of direct reference.[3]

3. Knowledge by description versus knowledge by acquaintance

Russell holds that we can refer to an object directly – in the *semantic* sense of 'direct' we have effectively been using so far – only if we are directly *acquainted* with that object – here 'direct' is used in a cognitive/epistemological sense. To be directly acquainted with an object is to cognize it 'without the intermediary of any process of inference, or any knowledge of truths' (Russell, 1912, p. 46). Objects with which we are directly acquainted are, in a sense, immediately present to the mind. And Russell is claiming that it is only when an object is immediately present to the mind that it is possible for us to refer to it and to talk and think about it 'directly'. Now, Russellian direct acquaintance with an object requires an extraordinarily tight cognitive hold on that object. One who is directly acquainted with an object, cannot, for example, intelligibly doubt its existence. Moreover, when a thinker is directly acquainted with an object, it is not possible that she be presented with that very object twice over, without recognizing that she is presented with the very same object again. Hence when we are directly acquainted with an object, informative statements of identity, of the sort that motivated Frege's distinction between sense and reference, are simply not possible with respect to that object.

By Russell's own admission, there are precious few objects with which we are directly acquainted. Though he does equivocate on this issue, he seems to hold that only what he called absolute simples are possible objects of acquaintance. Among the absolute simples, he counted only sense data, certain universals, and one's own inner states. He took it to be an open question whether one could be directly acquainted with an enduring self. When this relatively meagre inventory of absolute simples is conjoined with his views about genuine names, it follows that objects to which we can directly refer are few and far between. Since, for example, an object like Socrates is decidedly not the possible object of immediate of awareness for any person currently living, we cannot refer to or think about Socrates *directly* – indeed, by Russell's lights we probably can't even refer to or think about directly Obama or people we take ourselves to encounter 'in person'.

But Russell's severe epistemic strictures on direct reference are not intended to banish Socrates or Obama entirely from the realm of that about which we can think or speak. First, Russell allowed for the possibility that Socrates was immediately acquainted with himself. So at a minimum, Socrates may have been able to refer directly to himself. But, more importantly for our present purposes, Russell allows that the rest of us can at least know Socrates *by description*. And this allows us to think and talk about him – or at least various 'logical complexes' intimately associated with him – indirectly. Now the view that we cannot think or talk about Socrates directly is connected to Russell's view, briefly examined above, that ordinary proper names are really definite descriptions in disguise. For on Russell's view, a sentence like 'Socrates was put to death at the hands of the Athenians' – which apparently makes a claim about the individual Socrates – is really a short-hand way of saying something like (24) or (25) below:

(24) The teacher of Plato and husband of Xanthippe was put to death at the hands of the Athenians.

(25) The philosopher accused of corrupting the young was put to death at the hands of the Athenians.

Each of (24) and (25) makes a claim not directly about some one definite individual, but about what we might call a structure of properties. In effect, (24) says that the property of being a teacher of Plato and husband of Xanthippe, on the one hand, and the property of having been put to death at the hands of the Athenians, on the other, have exactly one common instance.[4] It is not entirely wrong to think of Socrates – who is perhaps present to himself as a simple, but was known to others only via various logical complexes with which he was somehow intimately associated, but not identical – as the common bearer of these two properties, but he neither was nor is identical with either property. Nor was/is he identical with the combination of those properties. Indeed, without change of meaning, (24) could be true even if Socrates had never existed, or if he had had existed but never taught Plato and married Xanthippe. Another way to appreciate that Socrates is not, as such, directly semantically implicated in the semantic content of (24) is to note that (24) can be rephrased as (26) below:

(26)   The teacher of Plato and husband of Xanthippe, *whoever he was*, was put to death at the hands of the Athenians.

And (26) is explicitly non-committal about the identity of the teacher of Plato and husband of Xanthippe. Notice, moreover, that although Socrates, in fact, both taught Plato and was accused of corrupting the young, (24) and (25) make different assertions about different structures of properties. Sentence (25) says, in effect, that the property of being uniquely a philosopher accused of corrupting the young and the property of being put to death at the hands of the Athenians have one instance in common. For all the contents of (24) and (25) require in order to be true, the person that makes (24) true could simply be distinct from the person that makes (25) true. At a minimum, this helps us to see another sense in which neither (24) and (25) can be said to be *directly* about a certain individual – one with which only a certain long-dead Greek philosopher could be directly acquainted. That individual is not, as such, the direct subject matter of either (24) or (25).

4. Whither acquaintance?

Few now think that either direct reference or so-called singular, object-dependent thought requires anything so strong as Russellian direct acquaintance. But many contemporary thinkers do believe that Russell was right to impose an epistemic constraint on the thinkability of an object as such. So many contemporary philosophers remain somewhat Russellian in spirit, in this regard at least. It is frequently claimed, for example, that if one is to have thoughts 'about' an object, then one must 'know which' object one is thinking or talking about. And knowing which object one is thinking or talking about is taken to be a matter of being able to recognize that object as the same again when one is presented with it again, at least over some range of circumstances.

This said, there has been little post-Russellian consensus on just how tight one's epistemic hold on an object must be if one is to be able to think and talk about it by use of a (directly) referring expression like a name. In a justly famous and classic article, David Kaplan (1968), for example, argued that an object as such is thinkable only if the thinker is *en rapport* with the object. One is *en rapport* with an object, roughly, if one has the sort of cognitive commerce with the object that renders one's use of a name *of* that object what he called *vivid*, where vividness has to do, roughly, with the fulsomeness and accuracy of the descriptive contents one associates with the relevant name. Roughly, a name was supposed to be vivid for a speaker if a speaker has lots of accurate descriptive information about the bearer of that name. If one has a vivid name of an object, one will, presumably, be able to recognize that object as the same again in a variety of different circumstances and as it appears under a variety of different guises. Kaplan's other criterion of *of-ness* had to do with the kind of role the object itself played in the genesis of a speaker's use of the name. The idea is that it's not enough that one know a lot of truths about the relevant object. The object itself has to have played a decisive and central role in generating one's knowledge of those truths, where having a 'decisive and central role' is somehow a matter of one's causal and or perceptual encounters with the relevant object. Though Kaplan-style rapport is intended to be a strong constraint on what we might call the thinkability of an object, it isn't as strong as Russellian direct acquaintance. An object with which one is en rapport is not, for example, immediately present to the mind. Even if one has a vivid name of an object, there can still be scenarios in which the object is present in a surprising or unrevealing guise. On such occasions, one might fail to recognize that one is presented with the same object again.

Weaker than Kaplan's *rapport* is ordinary 'knowledge wh' – that is, ordinary knowledge who, what, when or where. In a quite ordinary and intuitive sense, I *know who* my wife Claire is, *know when* I am writing this sentence, *know which* computer I am writing it on and *know where* I am now sitting. But with the exception of my wife, it is unlikely that I stand even in a relation as strong as

Kaplanian rapport with respect to these objects. What exactly is ordinary knowledge who, what, when or where? I won't attempt to answer that question here. I will just say that it is clearly necessary, though just as clearly not sufficient for ordinary knowledge-who, what, when or where concerning ordinary concrete objects that one have some causal and or perceptual commerce with the relevant object. On the other hand, it is clearly sufficient, but perhaps not necessary, for ordinary knowledge-which that an agent have frequent enough perceptual contact with the object or is able reliably enough to recognize the object as the same object again under various circumstances. How much perceptual contact is enough? How reliably is reliably enough? There may be no satisfactory and stable answer to these questions sufficient to yield a fixed and determinate criterion of what it takes to grasp the reference of a name or to use a name competently to refer to an object. One important consideration is that our workaday conception of knowledge-who would seem to be highly context-sensitive and interest-relative: what we require, in order to count a claim that *b knows wh- c is* as correct, varies with what we're up to and what we're interested in. For instance, it's plausible that in some contexts, I count as knowing who Smith is only if I can visually discriminate between her and others. In other contexts, even if I cannot recognize Smith as Smith when I see her, I may nonetheless count as knowing who she is merely on the basis of having read the collected works of Smith and thinking of her as author of those works. Suppose I know little more about Smith than that she is the author of such-and-such important works of philosophy. At a philosophical conference, someone asks me, 'Do you know who Smith is?' And I respond, 'Yes I do; she is the noted author of *The World as Representation and Represented*'. Even if that is the sum total of my knowledge of Smith, it would seem that here I speak truly. Indeed, suppose that I am attending a crowded reception at the conference and that I know that Smith is in attendance too. Dying to make the acquaintance of the renown Smith, I ask my friend to point Smith out to me. 'Which one is, Smith?' I ask. Suppose my friend does point Smith out. And that I now come to know what Smith looks like. Despite my newly acquired capacity to recognize Smith when I see her, there is a sense in which I knew who Smith was all along. I may have gained some additional recognitional abilities with respect to Smith, but it seems wrong to say that I have for the first time come to know who Smith is and to think singular thoughts about her. All along, even before I could visually discriminate Smith, my knowledge of Smith was sufficient to enable me to have Smith in mind in such a way that I was thereby able both to understand singular propositions about Smith and to use the name 'Smith' competently to think and talk about her.

Now, it would be an interesting and challenging task to work out the weakest possible cognitive hold on an object that suffices for rendering that object thinkable in a singular or *de re* sense, but I won't attempt that challenging task here. Instead, I will close by suggesting that acquaintance and its progressively more attenuated successor notions may have been oversold as necessary constraints on the thinkability of an object in the first place. The search for the cognitive relation, whatever it is, that would suffice to render an object as such, rather than a mere one-sided presentation of that object, available to thought is rooted in the philosophical worries about what we might call the epistemic one-sidedness of all reference. Many philosophers have noted that in any presentation of an object to either perception or thought, it is possible to distinguish what object is being presented from the way that objected is being presented. It is equally widely noted that the same object may be presented to the mind in different ways, in different presentations. Consider the perceptual presentation of a chair. When a perceiver views a chair from underneath, in bad lighting, with its upward facing surfaces occluded from view, the chair is presented in one way. When the very same chair is viewed under good lighting, from above, with its downward facing surfaces occluded from view, it is presented in a different way. In the two different perceptual episodes, we have the very same chair presented again, but in different ways, via two different clusters of what we might call presentational properties. Now the phenomenon of one-sidedness has tempted many philosophers to believe that the contents of our thoughts are given by the one-sided presentational properties by which we always (indirectly) apprehend objects, that we cannot be said to entertain an object *directly* unless all one-sidedness is drained out of our cognition of it. It was something like this thought that lay behind both Russell's original notion of acquaintance and behind Frege's introduction of the distinction between sense and reference. In our own time, David Kaplan has claimed that there could be a pure, natural and primitive notion of *de re* or singular belief only if we were able to make 'perfectly good sense of the claim that George IV has a belief about Sir Walter Scott independently of the way in which he is represented to George'. Though I lack the space to argue the point here, I close by suggesting that the epistemic one-sidedness of all reference need not cause us to despair about the very possibility that an object as such, rather than a merely one-sided presentation of that object, might be available to thought. In order for us to be able to think and talk about an object there must be causal and informational links sufficient to render our words and our thoughts semantically answerable to how things stand with that very object. But there is no reason to suppose that conditions sufficient to accomplish such semantic linking must *ipso facto* be sufficient to give us the kind of very tight cognitive hold on the object that Russell demanded. And if that thought could be sustained, there would be no reason to insist that direct reference to an object, in either thought or talk, requires that we stand in the kind of intimate cognitive relation to it that Russell imagined we must.

Further reading

Stephen Neale's *Descriptions* (Cambridge University Press, 1990) offers an up-to-date defence of Russell's theory of descriptions that deploys many of the resources of contemporary logic and linguistics.

Mark Sainsbury's *Russell* (Routledge, 1979) gives a wide-ranging critical analysis of the entirety of Russell's philosophical outlook.

Peter Strawson's 'On Referring' (*Mind*, 1950) contains important early criticisms of Russell's views.

Keith Donnellan's 'Reference and Definite Descriptions' (*Philosophical Review*, 1966) introduces a philosophically important distinction between the referential use of definite descriptions and the attributive use of such descriptions.

For an up-to-date discussion of the entire range of issues raised by the notion of a singular thought, see the essays in *New Essays on Singular Thought*, ed. Robin Jeshion (Oxford University Press, 2010).

Notes

1 Although I use the expressions 'singular' and 'object-dependent'
   as if they were synonymous here, I note that in the hands of some
   contemporary thinkers, these two concepts come apart. They maintain
   that even sentences containing empty names may express contents that
   are in some sense singular, even though they do not express any object-
   dependent proposition. See, for example, Jeshion (2002); Sainsbury
   (2005); Taylor (2010).
2 This account of Frege's views has been challenged by some. Evans
   (1985) argued that Frege wavered on whether there could be genuine
   singular terms which had sense but lacked reference, and concluded
   that Frege should not have allowed that there could be genuine
   singular terms with sense but not reference. Evans' reading of Frege
   brings Frege much closer to Russell on this score. The interpretive
   issues raised by Evans are complex, delicate and important. I have
   largely ignored them here and have taken Frege's stated view that there
   can be sense without reference at face value.
3 See the chapter on Kripke in this volume for a brief account of some
   of the arguments against taking ordinary proper names to be disguised
   definite descriptions. The connection between direct reference and
   rigid designation is complex. Some descriptions are rigid, but no
   descriptions are devices of direct reference.
4 Of course, in the final and complete analysis 'Xanthippe', 'Plato'
   and 'Athenians' would have to have been analysed away in terms of
   descriptions too.

Bibliography

Evans, G. (1985), *The Collected Papers*. Oxford: Clarendon Press.
Kaplan, D. (1968), 'Quantifying in', *Synthese*, 19, pp. 178–214.
Kaplan, D. (1989), 'Demonstratives', in J. Almog, H. Wettstein and J.
   Perry (eds), *Themes from Kaplan*. New York: Oxford University Press,
   pp. 481–564.
Kripke, S. (1980), *Naming and Necessity*. Oxford: Basil Blackwell.
Jeshion, R. (2002), 'Acquaintanceless De Re Belief', in J. Campbell, M.
   O'Rourke and D. Shier (eds), *Meaning and Truth: Investigations
   in Philosophical Semantics (Topics in Contemporary Philosophy)*.
   New York: Seven Bridges Press, pp. 53–74.
Russell, B. (1905), 'On Denoting', *Mind*, 14, pp. 479–93.

Russell, B. (1912), *The Problems of Philosophy*. Oxford: Oxford
University Press.
Russell, B. (1918), 'The Philosophy of Logical Atomism', in R. C. Marsh
(ed.), *Logic and Knowledge*. London: George Allen and Unwin.
Sainsbury, R. (2005), *Reference without Referents*.
Oxford: Clarendon Press.
Taylor, K. (2010), 'On Singularity', in R. Jeshion (ed.), *New Essays on
Singular Thought*. Oxford: Oxford University Press, pp. 77–102.
Whitehead, A. and Russell, B. (1927), *Principia Mathematica*, Vol. 1, 2nd
edn. Cambridge: Cambridge University Press.

CHAPTER THREE

WITTGENSTEIN: *TRACTATUS LOGICO-PHILOSOPHICUS*

Arif Ahmed

1. Introduction

'Napoleon invaded Russia in 1812' says something true; 'Napoleon *didn't* invade Russia in 1812' says something false; but 'Napoleon Russia 1812' doesn't say anything true *or* false. What explains this difference between what you *can* and *can't* say? Slightly more pretentiously:

(1) How do bits of a symbolism get to say something true or say something false about the extra-linguistic world?

When he wrote the *Tractatus*, Wittgenstein thought that it is just this feature of languages that distinguishes them from non-languages. For him therefore, the philosophy of language just *is* the attempt to answer question (1). And that is what the *Tractatus* is supposed to be doing.

2. Logical space

We must first grasp what *sort* of thing a sentence or other symbolic item says: what sort of thing is its *content*.

Think of all the ways that the world might have been; call these ways 'possible worlds'. There are possible worlds at which Napoleon invaded Russia in 1812 (and the *actual* world is among them). And there are possible worlds at which he did *not* invade Russia in 1812. There are many more possible worlds than you could hope to describe, for there are worlds corresponding to every way in which things might have gone differently, however minutely, from how they actually went. (For instance there is a possible world that is just like this one except that in it you had one fewer hair on your head on your fifteenth birthday.) But there *aren't* any possible worlds at which Napoleon both did and didn't invade Russia in 1812, or at which some bachelors are married, or at which 2 + 2 = 5. Such 'worlds' are impossible: they do not correspond to any way that *our* world *might* have been.

Now Wittgenstein thought that the content of a sentence, the proposition it expresses, is a *set of possible worlds*, namely those worlds that it describes truly. That is: imagine the actual world set in a 'logical space' of all possible worlds. Then each proposition divides that space into two regions: the worlds that make it true and the worlds that make it false. For instance the proposition *That Napoleon invaded Russia in 1812* rules in all those worlds where he took that drastic step in that fateful year; it rules out all those where he didn't. So question (1) becomes: how can a sentence *effect* such a partition?

Explaining Wittgenstein's answer involves distinguishing two levels: that of 'elementary' propositions and that of 'ordinary language' – for he gave different answers at each level. Let us turn to that distinction.

3. Elementary propositions

Wittgenstein thought at this time that the fundamental connection between language and reality was that of reference: sentences are composed from referring expressions that get meaning by *naming* bits of reality.

But he agreed with Russell (Russell, 1985, pp. 62–3) that most 'names' of ordinary language were not really referring expressions at all. Rather they could be analysed into definite descriptions – 'The capital of France' for 'Paris'; 'The victor of Austerlitz' for

'Napoleon' – and then contextually eliminated via Russell's well-known procedure (Russell, 1985, pp. 117–23). For instance 'Vulcan is hotter than Mercury' gets explained as 'The planet that lies in Mercury's orbit is hotter than Mercury'; this in turn becomes: 'There is at most, and at least, one planet in Mercury's orbit, and whatever is a planet in Mercury's orbit is hotter than it.' The name 'Vulcan' has vanished altogether; further analysis eliminates 'Mercury'. This also illustrates the further consequence of that procedure that '[a] proposition that mentions a complex will not be nonsensical, if the complex does not exist, but simply false' (*TLP*, 3.24).

Let me now introduce the fundamental thesis of the *Tractatus*, that in which its author claimed to encapsulate 'the whole sense of the book': 'what can be said at all can be said clearly, and what we cannot talk about we must consign to silence' (*TLP*, p. 3). In the present context we can interpret that as follows: what a sentence says, that is, what it takes for that sentence to be true, can be *explicitly spelt out*.

Now consider an everyday proposition of ordinary language, say that expressed by:

(2) The broom is in the corner.

Let that broom be composed of a broomstick and a brush. Then if the broomstick had not been connected to the brush then the broom would not have existed; so (2) would have been not nonsensical but false. So the connection of broomstick and brush is part of what it takes for (2) to be true. But (2) does not mention broomstick or brush; *it* therefore does not explicitly spell out what it says. So by the fundamental thesis, what (2) says must be analysable into propositions that do. The following represents a start on that analysis:

(3) The broomstick is in the corner, and so is the brush, and the broomstick is fixed in the brush.

This says more clearly – that is, more explicitly – what (2) says less clearly; for the sentential components of (3) correspond to what, by the preceding argument, must be propositional components of (2) and (3)'s common content.

If this argument works anywhere then it works everywhere; hence any proposition that mentions composite objects is going to fall short of saying clearly what it nonetheless says. But if what can be said at all *can* be said clearly, then that proposition must be analysable into propositions that *do* say clearly what they say at all; that is – by the foregoing argument – propositions that mention not composite but only *simple* objects (which are what Wittgenstein calls 'objects': *TLP*, 2.02). And among these propositions the logically atomic ones are the *elementary propositions* (*TLP*, 4.21). And it is at *these* propositions that Wittgenstein's answer to (1) is directed in the first instance.

That completes our sketch of the distinction between complex and elementary propositions. Wittgenstein's answer to question (1) is going to be that elementary propositions mean what they do by *picturing* reality; and complex propositions mean what they do because they are logical syntheses of elementary ones. That, on his view, is the *essence* of linguistic meaning. Let us now consider this answer in more detail.[1]

4. The picture theory

The key idea is that an elementary proposition means in something like the way a picture represents. Taken flat-footedly this is obviously false: the elements of a decent picture *resemble* whatever they depict, but the elements of an elementary proposition *don't* resemble whatever they denote.

But for Wittgenstein what makes something a picture is its being a *fact*: the fact that its elements are related in a certain way (*TLP*, 2.14–2.141). *What* it represents is that the worldly items corresponding to these elements are related in the *same* way (*TLP*, 2.15).

Now there is more than one way to conceive the elements of a picture and hence more than one way to conceive their relation. The most obvious conception of the elements of a painting is as *blobs of paint*; so the painting itself is the fact that they are *spatially arranged* in some way. Thus we might conceive three blobs of paint for the eyes and nose to be among the elements of *Mona Lisa*; and then the painting itself is (in part) the fact that the nose-blob lies between the eye-blobs. And that is why the painting *says that* the corresponding elements of reality stand in the same relation of betweenness, that is, that a certain Italian lady has a nose between her eyes.

The natural application of this point to a sentence expressing an elementary proposition would treat its *words* as its elements and the sentence as the fact of their *spatial* arrangement. But this is no good: if 'Fa' expresses an elementary proposition then 'a' denotes the simple object *a*, 'F' denotes the universal F-ness (which is also a simple object), and 'Fa' is the fact that 'a' is to the right of 'F'. But *TLP* 2.15 says that 'Fa' says that these worldly correlates of its elements are related in the *same* way as those elements. That is, that *a* is *to the right of* F-ness. But 'Fa' *doesn't* say that *a* is *to the right* of F-ness. It says that *a has* F-ness.

But there is *another* way to conceive the elements of a painting that applies better to sentences. Conceive of *Mona Lisa*'s elements as: the nasal blob, and the *property* of *being between two ocular blobs*. Then these *two* elements stand in the following relation: the nasal blob *has* the property. And so by *TLP* 2.15 the painting says that the two worldly correlates of *these* elements – Mona Lisa's nose, and the property of being between her eyes – stand in the *very same* relation, that is, that her nose *has* that property.

So too for sentences: don't think of 'Fa''s elements as the *words* 'a' and 'F' but rather as the word 'a' and the *property* of *being to the right of* 'F'. Then 'Fa' is the fact that these elements stand in the relation that one *has* the other; thus by 2.15 it says that their worldly correlates – *a* and F-ness – stand in *the very same* relation, that is, that *a has* F-ness. The fact that we can apply *TLP* 2.15 to *Mona Lisa* on *both* conceptions of its elements explains why Wittgenstein would have called it a 'spatial' as well as a 'logical' picture (*TLP*, 2.171–2.19). But sentences of the sorts of languages that philosophers usually investigate or imagine are not spatial pictures; but the ones that express elementary propositions *are* still *logical* pictures.

All this leaves it unexplained how the names that figure in elementary propositions get *their* references, that is, how they get to denote simple objects. In the *Tractatus* Wittgenstein's answer is that the *thinking language user* achieves this by using propositional signs *and meaning them* in one way rather than in another. By doing so she correlates the names of her language with simple objects. This is the 'method of projection' of *TLP* 3.11. Even by Wittgenstein's own high standards his discussion of this point is obscure; and the whole idea, that some psychic act of projection or 'meaning it' must accompany overt linguistic use in order to make it meaningful, became an important target of *Philosophical Investigations*.[2]

The question of how language and other methods of depiction *say* something about reality is really a perplexity about how sentences, paintings, maps and so on can present something *other than* themselves. The essence of the picture theory is that it is *not* wholly other: the relation between the elements of a picture is *the very same* as that between the corresponding elements of reality in the possible situation that it depicts. What remains of the lacuna between picture and what it depicts is that between the elements and what they denote; and what fills *that* gap is the method of projection. These are the central points of Wittgenstein's theory of symbolic representation.

5. Complex propositions

So much for elementary propositions. What about the *non*-elementary ones that predominate in natural language? Wittgenstein's answer was that every non-elementary proposition is a *truth-function of elementary ones*. What does this mean?

A proposition p is a truth-*function* of propositions $q_1, q_2, ..., q_n$ just in case the truth-*values* of the latter settle the truth-*value* of the former in all possible circumstances. For instance, if p says that it is raining or it is snowing, q_1 says that it is raining and q_2 says that it is snowing, then p is a truth-function of q_1 and q_2: no two possible worlds that agree over q_1 and q_2 are going to disagree over p. So Wittgenstein thought that the truth-value of *every* proposition is settled by the truth-values of the elementary ones.

Now take all the distributions of truth-values among elementary propositions that make a given p true: these are its *truth-grounds* (*TLP*, 5.101). Then the possible worlds where p's truth-grounds obtain are exactly those worlds where p is true, that is, those among which p claims that the actual world lies. So the truth-grounds of p settle what p *says* in that modal sense of 'what p says' introduced at Section 2. Hence to account for the truth-grounds of a proposition is to account for its content. That completes Wittgenstein's answer to (1).

6. Consequences

Here are two consequences of the view we've outlined – one for metaphysics and one for logic.

The first follows from the picture theory's generality. Wittgenstein thought (*TLP*, 3–3.001) that *thoughts* are pictures: what we can and cannot picture is just what we can and cannot think. It is no use trying to 'get outside' thought: if a thought is really about anything – that is, if it is a *thought* at all – then it must conform to the constraints on meaningful discourse that the picture theory imposes.

This means that any general formal constraints on symbolism mirror literally unthinkable features of the universe. They belong to its 'logical form'. Thus consider the distinction between particular and universal. We have an obscure sense – which does not qualify as a thought – that components of monadic facts somehow 'fit together'. We cannot *describe* this incomparable thing in language or thought; but language and thought *illustrate* it. For the essence of the picture theory is that the elements of meaningful subject–predicate sentences *share* just that 'fitting together' of their elements with the reality that they depict. Or consider the number of simple objects: language cannot tell us that the world contains these and these objects; but the multiplicity of its names reflects this (*TLP*, 4.1272, 5.5561). The *Tractatus* puts it in terms of a famous distinction: these metaphysical things cannot be *said*; but our language *shows* them to us (*TLP*, 4.12–4.121; cf. 6.36).

The second consequence concerns *logical* consequence. Russell considered logic a science, its job being to discover truths about actuality of the kind 'which can be made concerning everything without mentioning any one thing or predicate or relation' (Russell, 2004, p. 86). For instance the logical truth of 'If, if Mary is fat then Tom is bald, and Mary is fat, then Tom is bald' is explained by its belonging to the generally true schema: $((p \supset q) \wedge p) \supset q$.

But for Wittgenstein logic is about what follows from what (*TLP*, 6.1264); and it doesn't say *anything at all* about the world. That one proposition follows from others is not a truth distinct from those of the non-logical sciences; it is rather an inevitable by-product of the representational mechanism that those sciences already employ, that is, that described in Section 5. More particularly, *q* follows from $p_1, p_2, ..., p_n$ iff the truth-grounds that are common to the p_i are among the truth-grounds of q. Logic 'is not a field in which *we* express what we wish with the help of signs, but rather one in which the nature of the natural and inevitable signs speaks for itself' (*TLP*, 6.124).

7. Conclusion

This very brief account has been necessarily both lacunary and dogmatic. Some of the power of the *Tractatus* resides in its cosmic sweep but most of its value resides in the detailed working out of Wittgenstein's theory of symbolism and its application to issues that I have not touched upon: the Theory of Types (*TLP*, 3.33–3.333), solipsism and the self (*TLP*, 5.541–5.5423, 5.6–5.641), the nature of mathematics (*TLP*, 6.01–6.031, 6.2–6.241), and of rational mechanics (*TLP*, 6.3–6.3751), the theory of value (*TLP*, 6.4–6.45) and the nature of philosophy (*TLP*, 6.5–7).

Further reading

The best short introductions to the *Tractatus* are still those by Anscombe (1959) and Mounce (1981). Among more demanding discussions, the best short one is Ramsey's critical notice (1923). Two other classics are: Black (1964) and Pears (1987).

According to a tradition that I have not discussed, the *Tractatus* is not supposed to say anything. Rather it is supposed (as Pears puts it) to be a kind of emetic that purges you of itself as well as of philosophy. For more on, and by, those 'New Wittgensteinians' who believe this, see Crary and Read (2000).

Notes

1 Sections 1–3 of this exposition qualify it as a realist interpretation of the *Tractatus*, according to which the structure of possibilities is the independent guarantor of linguistic meaning. This point is controversial: for an excellent discussion of both it and the alternative,

on which the real possibilities of our world merely shadow the
expressive possibilities of our language, see Pears (1987, chapter 5).

2 This interpretation of *TLP* 3.11 is controversial; for an alternative
reading, see Mounce (1981, pp. 31–3). For further discussion, see
Hacker (1999).

Bibliography

Anscombe, G. E. M. (1959), *An Introduction to Wittgenstein's* Tractatus.
London: Hutchinson.

Black, M. (1964), *A Companion to Wittgenstein's* Tractatus.
Cambridge: Cambridge University Press.

Crary, A. and Read, R. (eds) (2000), *The New Wittgenstein*.
London: Routledge.

Hacker, P. M. S. (1999), 'Naming, Thinking and Meaning in the
Tractatus', *Philosophical Investigations*, 22 (2), pp. 119–35.

Mounce, H. O. (1981), *Wittgenstein's* Tractatus: *An Introduction*.
Oxford: Blackwell.

Pears, D. (1987), *The False Prison: A Study of the Development of
Wittgenstein's Philosophy*, Vol. I. Oxford: Clarendon Press.

Ramsey, F. P. (1923), 'Critical Notice of the *Tractatus*'. *Mind*, 32, pp.
465–78.

Russell, B. (1985 [1918]), *The Philosophy of Logical Atomism*. Chicago
and La Salle, IL: Open Court.

Russell, B. (2004 [1912]), 'On Scientific Method in Philosophy', in his
Mysticism and Logic. Mineola, NY: Dover, pp. 75–96.

Wittgenstein, L. (1961 [1921]), *Tractatus Logico-Philosopicus*, trans. D. F.
Pears and B. F. McGuinness. London: Routledge.

CHAPTER FOUR

CARNAP

Pierre Wagner

1. Language planning and its practical motivations

In his 'Intellectual Autobiography', Carnap makes the following comments about language: 'Throughout my life, I have been fascinated by the phenomenon of language .... In school I was interested in languages, especially Latin. I often thought of becoming a linguist' (Carnap, 1963a, p. 67). Many of his writings bear witness to this major interest. If we want to understand in what precise sense language has been central for him, however, we have to keep in mind that Carnap's primary aim is not, for example, to give a theoretical account of linguistic competence or of language as a natural phenomenon: 'I was more inclined toward theoretical construction and systematization than toward description of fact. Therefore I had more interest in those problems of language which involved *planning* and *construction*' (Carnap, 1963a, p. 67, emphasis added). Of course, far from focusing exclusively on artificial symbolic and logical languages, he often refers to the analysis of sentences and terms of natural languages ('untamed' languages like ordinary German or English). But studying language as it is commonly used, and answering the related issues of today's philosophy of language are certainly not the main points of his philosophical agenda.

The most well known aspects of Carnap's work on language are, on the one hand, the use of logical methods for the analysis of sentences and terms in metaphysics and science, and, on the other hand, the definition of language systems for the reconstruction of scientific theories. Less well known is Carnap's interest in the construction of an auxiliary language for international communication. His 'Intellectual Autobiography' (Carnap, 1963a, §11) and his unpublished papers give evidence of his interest in international languages, such as Esperanto. One of his motivations here was 'the humanitarian ideal of improving the understanding between nations' (Carnap, 1963a, p. 69).

Practical motivations are also at the basis of the general philosophical programme on which Carnap worked throughout his life, and which is the key to understanding what he has to say about language: the clarification and re-shaping of our conceptual system through the use of logical methods applied to the analysis and the construction of languages. Carnap and Neurath, along with other logical empiricists, emphasized the importance of the analysis of language, both for the scientific, anti-metaphysical attitude they wanted to promote, and for the unity of science. The authors of the 'Vienna Circle Manifesto' (Carnap, Hahn, Neurath, 1929) were also convinced of the connections between a reform of language and the defence of their political and social ideals. But whereas Neurath thought that we should start with the language given to us and proceed in reforming and improving it from within, eliminating step by step 'dangerous (e.g. metaphysical) terms' without trying to find a perfectly clear and exact basis on which to build it (see Neurath, 1941/1983), Carnap insisted on making an extensive use of the tools of modern logic to build new linguistic frameworks defined by explicit rules.

More generally, what Carnap has to say about language is informed by the overall long-lasting philosophical project just mentioned and by the reconstruction of our knowledge implied by it. In his hands, the analysis of sentences, the explication of concepts, and the construction of languages are nothing but means towards this end. It is crucial to be aware that for him, language is a tool, not a natural phenomenon that one should merely study, or a sacred entity that one should leave untouched: 'In my view, a language, whether natural or artificial, is an instrument that may be replaced or modified according to our needs, like any other instrument'

(Carnap, 1963b, p. 938). This view is connected with Carnap's programme of explication in a way which shall be clarified below.

2. The (meta)-linguistic turn

Carnap's conception of language was deeply influenced by Frege. In 1910 and 1913 he attended Frege's courses on *Conceptual notation* (*Begriffsschrift*), and later studied Frege's other works. Carnap followed Frege in wanting to devise a purified logical language to be used as a sharp analytical tool. But whereas Frege's main concern was with the foundations of mathematics (although his reflections on language are by no means restricted to the language of mathematics), Carnap would soon understand the significance of such an instrument for the analysis of philosophical problems and work on the possibility of its application to the propositions of science in general. Before 1931, however, Carnap did not articulate any systematic theory of language. Language was to be used as a universal notation, but not regarded as an object of study in its own right. In *The Logical Structure of the World* (1928), for example, no systematic account of what a language is, or method of studying languages, was provided. Indeed, Carnap and other members of the Vienna Circle were deeply influenced by Wittgenstein's claim that the form of a proposition, as well as many other properties of language and linguistic expressions, cannot be meaningfully *stated*, although they can be *shown* (Wittgenstein, 1921/1922, §§4.121, 4.1212, 6.36), and for some time they were not even sure that it was possible to talk *about* language – to describe its syntax, for example – in a meaningful way.

Things changed radically in the early 1930s: Carnap rejected Wittgenstein's assessment of any metalinguistic discourse as meaningless, and he decided to apply the distinction between an object-language and a metalanguage to the analysis of the language of science as a whole. The idea was to distinguish between a language regarded as an object of study (the 'object language') and a (possibly different) language in which the study itself was conducted (the 'metalanguage').[1] Three authors had been instrumental in this methodological turn. First, in the 1920s, Hilbert had introduced the method of metamathematics, in which the sentences and proofs of mathematics were first codified in a formally defined language and then taken as an object of study in their own right. This was one of the basic ideas of Hilbert's programme, which aimed at proving *(meta)mathematically* some properties (completeness, consistency, decidability etc.) *of* mathematical (formalized) theories. Secondly, Carnap had learned from Tarski about the use of metalogic in the Polish school of logic: taking a metalinguistic viewpoint in order to formulate statements and give *logical* proofs *about* logic. Thirdly, as early as 1930, Carnap heard of Gödel's method for the arithmetization of syntax. This offered a clear way of expressing statements *about* some language L *in* L itself. The idea of a metalinguistic method suitable not only for logic or mathematics but for the whole language of science occurred to Carnap in 1931, while he was working both on the foundations of mathematics and on the reconstruction of the system of our knowledge. Carnap relates this event in a colourful passage of his 'Intellectual Autobiography':

> After thinking about these problems for several years, the whole theory of language structure and its possible applications in philosophy came to me like a vision during a sleepless night in January 1931, when I was ill. On the following day, still in bed with a fever, I wrote down my ideas on forty-four pages under the title 'Attempt at a metalogic'. These shorthand notes were the first version of my book *Logical Syntax of Language*. (Carnap, 1963a, p. 53)

The Logical Syntax of Language was published in 1934 in German, and an augmented version was translated into English and published in 1937. It contains Carnap's first systematic exposition of a method for studying languages, what he called the *syntactical* method. This excluded any use of the concepts of meaning, reference and truth. Shortly after the publication of the German edition, however, Carnap heard from Tarski about his method for providing exact definitions of truth for deductive language systems. He acknowledged that Tarski's semantic metalanguage offered an important and precise way of explicating many logical concepts (such as logical consequence or logical truth) and he soon complemented his syntactical method with a semantic one. In the late 1930s, he also borrowed distinctions from Charles Morris, dividing the theory of language into syntax, semantics and pragmatics (Carnap, 1939). Whereas syntax restricts its investigations to the formal properties of expressions and the formal relations between them, semantics (at least as it is envisaged by Carnap) takes into consideration the relationships between the expressions of a language and their *designata* (i.e. what they stand for or refer to). As for pragmatics, it considers also the speaker and her linguistic activities, not only the expressions themselves and their designata. With hindsight, the restriction of any metalinguistic talk about language to *syntactical* properties of linguistic entities and *syntactical* relations between them may be interpreted as an overreaction to the difficulties raised by various semantic paradoxes and theories of meaning.[2]

With the introduction of the syntactical method, Carnap thus makes two different moves – moves intertwined in *Logical Syntax*, but clearly distinguished in later works, after his acceptance of semantics. The first move is the adoption of a metalinguistic viewpoint for the study of languages which are then taken as objects of study. Against some of Wittgenstein's claims in the *Tractatus*, and in particular his contention that there are no (meaningful) sentences about the form of sentences, Carnap maintains that we should stop talking about *Language*, as if there were just one logical structure common to all languages, and consider instead the possibility of defining *varieties* of languages.[3] In addition, Carnap shows that there is a correct and acceptable way of formulating sentences *about* the sentences of a language. The second move consists in restricting the method used in the metalanguage to a syntactical one, excluding any talk about correspondences between linguistic expressions and objects of the world, and any consideration of meaning or reference.

The 'vision' Carnap had during the sleepless night of January 1931 brought a new conception of language, to which we shall return below; but this 'vision' also includes a new approach to philosophical problems *through language*. In the foreword to *Logical Syntax*, Carnap articulates a new understanding of the relationships between science, philosophy and the logical analysis of language:

> Philosophy is to be replaced by the logic of science – that is to say by the logical analysis of the concepts and sentences of the sciences, for the logic of science is nothing other than the logical syntax of the language of science. (Carnap, 1934/1937, p. xiii)

In a sense, logical analysis had already been applied to the concepts and sentences of the sciences in *The Logical Structure of the World* of 1928. What is new in 1931 is the recognition that many philosophical problems result from a lack of clear distinction between *object-questions*, which concern some specific domain of objects, and *logical questions*, which are about terms, sentences and other linguistic elements which *refer* to objects. According to Carnap, traditional philosophy tends to treat what are actually logical questions as if they were object-questions, thus making use of what Carnap calls the 'material mode of speech'; and consequently traditional philosophers can be (and often were) misled into thinking they are talking about *things*, when the problems they are trying to solve should really be thought of as problems about *language* (Carnap, 1934/1937, §72). In order to get rid of the pseudo-problems which result from this confusion, philosophy is to be replaced by the logical analysis of the *language of science*. This is Carnap's version of the so-called *linguistic turn*, taken by him in the early 1930s when he distinguished object-languages from metalanguages, and object-questions from logical ones. This is the basis of Carnap's ontological deflationism, which he often illustrates with the case of numbers. Asking about the 'essence of numbers' in an absolute way amounts to posing a typical pseudo-problem. The 'essence' question simply overlooks the relativity of number-talk to language: a formulation such as '5 is a number' (typical of the material mode of speech) is misleading and should be replaced by '"5" is a number-sign in language L' (which amounts to a translation of the former sentence into what Carnap calls the 'formal mode of speech'). Consequently, instead of asking about the 'essence' of numbers, what numbers 'really are', Carnap suggests that philosophers discuss and make decisions about the kind of *number-signs* which it would be most convenient to introduce (for some particular purpose) in the language we want to use. Another significant consequence of Carnap's view is that philosophical theses lose the absolutist character they have in traditional philosophy and are then relativized to some language – for example, one should not try to talk about the unity of science without mentioning the language in which this unity is supposed to be realized (see, for example, Carnap, 1935a/1996, p. 78).[4]

Although the linguistic turn was taken at the time Carnap advocated a purely *syntactical* method, he never renounced the linguistic turn itself, even when he embraced semantics. For him, language analysis remained 'the most important tool in philosophy' (Carnap, 1963a, p. 60).

3. Languages as systems of rules

In the context of the *Logical Syntax*, complicated issues arise about Carnap's use of the term 'language' and about the relations between natural languages and formal constructed ones. Carnap's exposition of the syntactical method makes it clear that it applies to languages conceived as formal systems completely defined by rules formulated in a metalanguage. These rules are of two different kinds: *formation rules* and *transformation rules*.

The *formation* rules of language L are meant to define the set of sentences of L in a purely formal way, that is, simply in terms of how signs may be put together to form sentences. The rules determine which strings of signs are sentences, and specify a (possibly infinitely large) set of sentences. The definition is purely formal in that it does not make any reference to the meaning and designata of the signs and expressions of the language. Signs and expressions of L may have meanings and designata, but these are disregarded when the syntactical method is applied.

On Carnap's understanding of the term, a 'language' also includes a *consequence* relation, defined by *transformation* rules. These rules may include axioms (also called 'primitive sentences'), inference rules (e.g. Modus Ponens: from B and B→C, infer C), as well as rules with an infinite number of premises (e.g. from $P(0)$, $P(1)$, $P(2)$, ... $P(i)$ ..., infer 'for all n, $P(n)$', where 'P' is a one-place arithmetical predicate and 'i' an index for positive integers). Axioms of L and their consequences in L are said to be *valid* in L. 'Validity' here does not have any absolute meaning: the set of valid sentences depends on the transformation rules. For example, in *Logical Syntax*, Carnap gives two specific systems, Language I and Language II – in the latter, the valid sentences include all the sentences of classical logic and mathematics; in the former, validity has a more restricted extension.

After considering at length the application of the syntactical method to these two calculuses (Language I and Language II), Carnap gives an exposition of 'general syntax', a method which is supposed to apply to *any* language.[5] The exposition is based on the following definition:

> By a language we mean here in general any sort of calculus, that is to say, a system of formation and transformation rules concerning what are called *expressions*, i.e. finite, ordered series of elements of any kinds, namely, what are called *symbols* ... In pure syntax, only syntactical properties of expressions, in other words, those that are dependent only upon the kind and order of the symbols of the expression, are dealt with. (Carnap, 1937, pp. 167–8)

This is a very special definition of 'language', to say the least, which seems to restrict the applicability of the syntactical method to very special kinds of languages, although Carnap does not exclude the possibility of applying his method to natural word-languages such as German or Latin.[6] In this respect, the limitations he mentions are of a *practical* character, concerning the great complexity of these languages and their 'unsystematic and logically imperfect structure' (Carnap, 1934/1937, p. 2).

Carnap's concept of a 'language' as a system of formation and transformation rules may seem extremely peculiar: we may think that this is not really language but mathematical knowledge formulated in a formally defined system. The answer to this objection lies in Carnap's philosophy of logic and mathematics.

Very roughly, the main point is that Carnap does not see the sentences of logic and mathematics as expressing any kind of *knowledge*, but as useful tools for deducing or transforming other sentences:

> *formal science* has no independent significance, but is an auxiliary component introduced for technical reasons in order to facilitate linguistic transformations in the *factual science* ... The *formal sciences do not have any objects at all*; they are systems of auxiliary statements without objects and without contents. (Carnap, 1935b/1953, pp. 127–8)

Carnap maintains that the sentences of mathematics, which are of the same nature as the sentences of logic, are not *about* anything – they do not have any objects. And precisely because logical and mathematical sentences are empty and do not express any knowledge, they can be regarded simply as part of the linguistic framework.[7] No wonder that Carnap is mainly interested in language systems in which logical and mathematical sentences are *analytic*, and that an explication of analyticity is such a fundamental issue for him.

The axiomatic approach to language that Carnap adopts in *Logical Syntax* is clearly inspired by Hilbert's metamathematics: a language is completely defined by rules formulated in the metalanguage, and these rules include both formation rules for the definition of sentences and transformation rules which determine a consequence relation and a set of *logically valid sentences*. There is, however, a major difference with Hilbert's methodology: whereas the metamathematics used in the Hilbert school has the *epistemological* goal of providing a solution to the problem of the foundations of mathematics,[8] Carnap's use of the metalinguistic standpoint for the definition of linguistic frameworks does not aim at giving any *justification* of mathematical sentences. Here again, to understand Carnap's conception of language we need to say a little bit more about his philosophy of logic and mathematics.

In the late 1920s, while searching for a foundation for mathematics, he tried to combine the views of logicians who had very different conceptions not only of mathematics but also – and maybe more importantly – of language (Hilbert, Frege, Brouwer, Wittgenstein, ...); but from *Logical Syntax* onward, he took a completely different position on this issue, giving up any search for a solution to foundational questions in mathematics, and adopting instead logical pluralism and the famous *principle of tolerance*:

> the view will be maintained that we have in every respect complete liberty with regard to the forms of language; that both the forms of construction for sentences and the rules of transformation (the latter are usually designated as 'postulates' and 'rules of inference') may be chosen quite arbitrarily ... By this method, also, the conflict between the divergent points of view on the problem of the foundations of mathematics disappears. For language, in its mathematical form, can be constructed according to the preferences of any one of the points of view represented;

so that no questions of justification arises at all, but only the question of the syntactical consequences to which one or other of the choices leads, including the question of non-contradiction. (Carnap, 1934/1937, p. xv)

Now, because logic and mathematics do not have any domain of objects, there is nothing for the sentences of these sciences to be *true of* – no matter of fact – and so here there is no absolute question of right or wrong, and no question of what the 'essence of numbers' might be. As a consequence, the adoption of a logical and linguistic framework is not a question of truth or correctness, but a question of expedience or convenience: 'Everyone is at liberty to build up his own logic, i.e. his own form of language, as he wishes' (Carnap, 1934/1937, p. 52). Indeed, any question of justification presupposes that some linguistic framework – including a consequence relation – is already in place. In Carnap's hands, the construction of language systems (including a consequence relation and a set of mathematical valid sentences) becomes a problem of engineering and planning. One language may be simpler, more expressive, more powerful, more convenient and so forth than another, and our choice may follow our needs. Comparison of linguistic frameworks may be made in a metalanguage, and if someone wants to adopt a linguistic framework, 'all that is required of her is that, if she wishes to discuss it, she must state her methods clearly, and give syntactical rules instead of philosophical arguments' (ibid.).[9]

In the late 1930s, after hearing about Tarski's use of a *semantic* metalanguage, Carnap complemented his syntactical method with a semantic one. Two kinds of languages defined by rules are then distinguished: on the one hand, non-interpreted languages (calculuses, with a relation of derivability defined by transformation rules), and on the other hand, semantic systems. In a semantic system, the set of sentences is also defined by formation rules but it is then *interpreted* by two kinds of semantic rules: *rules of designation* and *rules of truth* (see Carnap, 1939). For example, if 'a' is a name and 'B' a one-place predicate of the object-language L, the following sentences of the semantic metalanguage ML may be taken as *rules of designation*:

'a' designates the planet Venus
'B' designates the property of being blue

If '*non*' is a logical sign of L, we might have the following sentence of ML as a *rule of truth*:

> A sentence of the form '*non* ...' is true if and only if the sentence '...' is not true

On the basis of this kind of rule, Carnap shows how to define semantic concepts such as truth, L-truth and L-implication. The definition of L-truth (which is meant to *explicate* the familiar, imprecise notion of logical truth) is such that a sentence is said to be L-true if its truth is determined by the semantic rules alone, without taking into consideration the states of affairs which actually obtain in the world.[10] And a sentence B is said to be an *L-implicate* of sentence A if and only if, according to the semantic rules of S alone, if A is true, B is true.

Given a calculus K and a semantic system S, if they have the same set of sentences (typically, this is the case if they have the same formation rules), S is regarded as an *interpretation* of K; if all the valid sentences of K are true (respectively L-true) in S, S is a *true* (respectively *L-true*) *interpretation* of K.

After Carnap's semantic turn, new kinds of rules are added, but the basic conception of language remains: a language is defined by a system of explicit and precisely formulated rules which are stipulated.

4. Constructed languages, natural languages and explication

At this point, two questions arise, first concerning the relationships between natural languages (such as Italian and French) and constructed languages (defined by syntactical or semantic rules in a metalanguage), and secondly concerning the philosophical point of defining language systems by sets of rules. Notice that Carnap seems to suggest the possibility of representing even natural languages by systems of rules, and of applying the syntactical method to them (Carnap, 1934/1937, pp. 8, 228). A number of apparently competing answers to these two questions have been given.

Tom Ricketts, for example, argues that in *Logical Syntax*, Carnap proposes to regard natural languages as *instances* of calculuses: here, this means that the expressions of the calculus are coordinated with *types of expressions* of a natural language (inscription-types or utterance-types, rather than tokens of expressions), so that the syntactical terms ('analytic', 'consequence' etc.) initially defined for the calculus may after all be applied to the natural language: 'Modulo such a coordination of the sentences of a language with the formulas of a calculus, the syntactic classifications of those formulas can be projected onto utterances of sentences of the language' (Ricketts, 2004, p. 191). Without such coordination, a language such as English is nothing but 'a system of activities or, rather, habits, i.e., dispositions to certain activities, serving mainly for the purpose of communication and of co-ordination of activities among the members of a group' (Carnap, 1939, p. 3). 'Linguistic behaviour is, so to speak, in itself logically amorphous' (Ricketts, 2004, p. 193). This relation of coordination has peculiarities that Ricketts discusses in depth, but the general idea is that coordinating a natural language to a calculus amounts to imposing a grid on it. With such a grid in place, 'an utterance of such and so sentence can, for example, be redescribed as the utterance of such and so L-valid formula' (Ricketts, 2004, p. 191), and the acceptance or rejection of a sentence, given as an observed fact can also be regarded as the result of the testing of a hypothesis. More generally, with the grid in place, the terms which have been defined in pure syntax for calculuses can then be applied to the used language under consideration.

The analysis developed by Ricketts can be usefully contrasted with the answer proposed by A. W. Carus (Carus, 2007). According to Carus, there is no suggestion in Carnap's writings that a calculus should be regarded as a grid imposed on the behaviouristic description of the otherwise 'logically amorphous' natural languages. Quite the contrary: Carus insists on the continuity between constructed languages and evolved ones, and on the essential idea of a gradual *replacement* of less constructed languages by more precise and more constructed ones. He takes for granted that there are degrees of construction in human languages – the language of mathematical physics, for example, is more constructed than that of medicine or accounting (Carus, 2007, pp. 275–6). According to Carus, Carnap's constructed languages are not meant to *describe* or *interpret* the linguistic behaviour of a community but to *replace* imprecise concepts by more precisely defined ones, in other words to *explicate* the former by the latter; and in order to understand why Carnap takes pains to explore so many different possibilities of constructing languages in so many of his writings, we have to recognize that this kind of work takes place in the context of both the principle of tolerance and his programme of explication (see Carus, 2007, chapter 11). It is not clear, however, that Ricketts's interpretation excludes (as Carus seems to think it does) the reading of language systems as explications. On the other hand, whereas Carus compares *evolved* languages with *constructed* ones, Ricketts's point is about the relationships between *used* languages and *calculuses*, so that his point is a slightly different one. (On these issues, see Wagner, 2012.)

To clarify the debate, more needs to be said about explication. As Carnap understands it, an *explication* consists of the replacement of a concept already in use (the *explicandum*) by a more precisely defined one (the *explicatum*). This procedure begins with the informal clarification of the explicandum, before the definition of an exact concept, the explicatum, is given (see Carnap, 1950b, chapter 1). In this way, we can arrive at a more precise conceptual framework, and perhaps solve philosophical problems caused by the misuse of expressions of ordinary language. Although the method of explication is not formulated before 1945, it does not seem unreasonable to regard the formally defined languages of *Logical Syntax* as early forms of explication (although Carus, 2007, pp. 256–7, has slightly different and more cautious views on that point). But why, one wants to ask, should *language-systems* be regarded as *explications*, if an explication is the replacement of a *concept* by a *concept*? And what do systems such as Language I and Language II actually explicate?

Constructed language systems may be regarded as explications – or means for providing explications – simply because in many cases, the replacement of a term by another term cannot be effected at a local scale – it requires a revision of the structure of the whole language and a modification of its general rules. In such cases, as Carus points out, the point of a constructed language system is not the wholesale replacement of a language in use by a system of rules, but the explication of basic concepts which have significance in every part of the language. It should be added, however, that what

Carnap casually calls 'languages' or 'constructed language systems' actually are language *schemas*, that is, sets of rules which apply to a whole range of (actual or potential) languages and show in an exact way how to implement in them concepts that can be defined by these rules. Language I and Language II, for example, are not meant to replace a language of communication: the rules which define them give nothing more than the general features of a class of languages. Just as a logical, constructed language for arithmetic may serve the purpose of explicating the concept of a number, Carnap's point, in *Logical Syntax*, is to propose explications for some general concepts such as *logical consequence, validity, logical equivalence* and *analyticity*.

One final issue: Carnap spent a great part of his life searching for an explication of analyticity, and 'analytic' is central for most of his work on language construction. Carnap thinks that a correct understanding of analyticity is required by the methodology of science, and in particular by any explication of the basic distinction between formal science (logic, mathematics etc.) and factual science (including, among other disciplines, physics, chemistry and psychology).[11] Notoriously, Carnap's work on analyticity was challenged by Quine, who demanded an empirical characterization of analyticity, although he was convinced that the concept is too obscure to be scientifically acceptable and that no definition will clarify it.[12] Carnap basically gives two kinds of response: on the one hand, he takes up Quine's challenge, trying to show how an empirical (he uses the word 'pragmatic') characterization of analyticity could actually be provided (Carnap, 1955/1956); on the other hand, he argues that Quine does not correctly understand his project of providing an *explication* of analyticity through constructed languages. For Carnap, the point is neither to characterize (by a system of rules) some *existing* concept of analyticity given in ordinary language nor to regiment it in a logical notation, but to *explicate* the imprecise given concept, that is, to *replace* it by a more precisely defined concept, and Carnap's method for achieving this is the construction of languages defined by systems of rules having the specific features and properties he is looking for – typically, having a precisely defined concept of analyticity – (see Carnap, 1952/1990, p. 427). In the debate on analyticity, as in many other philosophical discussions about language, Carnap's position has often been misinterpreted as descriptive talk about facts, whereas what he has to say needs to be understood in terms of explication, replacement and language planning.

Further reading

A good place to start further exploration of Carnap's ideas on language is with sections 8, 10, 11 and 13 of Carnap's intellectual autobiography (Carnap, 1963a), Carnap's replies to critical essays by Quine, Beth, Strawson and Bar-Hillel (Carnap, 1963b), and the appendices to Carnap (1956). You might then explore more specialized areas, such as the idea of logical syntax (Wagner, 2009a), the debate over analyticity (Awodey, 2007) or the connections between evolved and constructed languages (Carus, 2007, chapters 9–10).

The titles mentioned here only include those which are not already listed in the bibliography of references given in the chapter.

Awodey, S. (2007), 'Carnap's Quest for Analyticity: the *Studies in Semantics*', in M. Friedman and R. Creath (eds), *The Cambridge Companion to Carnap*. Cambridge: Cambridge University Press, pp. 226–47.

Bar-Hillel, Y. (1963), 'Remarks on Carnap's Logical Syntax of Language', in Schilpp, 1963, pp. 519–43.

Beth, E. W. (1963), 'Carnap's Views on the Advantages of Constructed Systems over Natural Languages in the Philosophy of Science', in Schilpp, 1963, pp. 469–502.

Carnap, R. (1932), 'Die physikalische Sprache als Universalsprache der Wissenschaft', *Erkenntnis*, 2, 432–65. Translated as *The Unity of Science*. London: Kegan Paul, Trench, Trubner, 1934.

Carnap, R. (1932), 'Über Protokollsätze', *Erkenntnis*, 3, 204–14. Translated as 'On Protocol Sentences', *Noûs*, 21, 1987, 457–70.

Carnap, R. (1936–7), 'Testability and Meaning', *Philosophy of Science*, 3, 419–71; 4, 1–40.

Carnap, R. (1952), 'Meaning Postulates', *Philosophical Studies*, 3, 65–73. Reprinted in Carnap, 1956.

Carnap, R. (1958), 'Beobachtungssprache und theoretische Sprache', *Dialectica*, 12, 236–48. Translated as 'Observation Language and Theoretical Language', in J. Hintikka (ed.), *Rudolf Carnap, Logical Empiricist*. Dordrecht: D. Reidel, pp. 75–85.

Kazemier, B. H. and Vuysie, D. (eds) (1962), *Logic and Language: Studies Dedicated to Professor Rudolf Carnap on the Occasion of his Seventieth Birthday*. Dordrecht: D. Reidel.

Ricketts, T. (2003), 'Languages and Calculi', in G. Hardcastle and
    A. Richardson (eds), *Logical Empiricism in North America*.
    Minneapolis: University of Minnesota Press, pp. 257–80.
Ricketts, T. (2009), 'From Tolerance to Reciprocal Containment', in
    Wagner, 2009a, pp. 217–35.
Schilpp, P. A. (ed.) (1963), *The Philosophy of Rudolf Carnap*. Chicago,
    IL: Open Court.
Strawson, P. F. (1963), 'Carnap's Views on Constructed Systems versus
    Natural Languages in Analytic Philosophy', in Schilpp, 1963, pp.
    503–18.

Notes

1 This also implied a departure from Frege's conception of conceptual
   notation (*Begriffsschrift*). For a comparison, see Ricketts (2004). See
   the chapter on Frege in this volume.
2 On Carnap's motivations for adopting a purely *syntactical* method, see
   Awodey and Carus (2009).
3 In the context of a discussion of extensional versus intensional
   languages, Carnap writes: 'we all overlooked the fact that there is
   a multiplicity of possible languages. Wittgenstein, especially, speaks
   continually of "the" language' (Carnap, 1934/1937, p. 245). See
   what Wittgenstein writes in the *Tractatus*: 'Definitions are rules for
   translating from one language into another. Any correct sign-language
   must be translatable into any other in accordance with such rules: it is
   this that they all have in common' (3.343).
4 On Carnap's analysis of language as a basis of his critique of
   philosophy, see Wagner (2009b). On the elimination of metaphysics
   through logical analysis of language, Carnap (1931) is the most
   well-known paper, but it has also often been (rightly) criticized,
   and it actually develops views that Carnap maintained only for a
   short period of time, such as some version of the all-too-famous
   verificationist criterion of meaning, soon replaced by a variety of other
   possible criterions (testability, confirmability etc.). For these reasons,
   this 1931 paper should not be regarded as a general exposition of
   Carnap's views about language. On Carnap's deflationist later views
   on ontology and linguistic frameworks, see Carnap (1950a/1956).
5 Note that this particular approach by no means excludes other
   methods of investigation of languages, even in *Logical Syntax*:

   > When we maintain that logical syntax treats language as a calculus,
   > we do not mean by that statement that language is nothing more

than a calculus. [...] any particular language has, apart from that [syntactical] aspect, others which may be investigated by other methods. For instance, its words have meaning; this is the object of investigation and study for semasiology. Then again, the words and expressions of a language have a close relation to actions and perceptions, and in that connection they are the objects of psychological study. Again, language constitutes an historically given method of communication, and thus of mutual influence, within a particular group of human beings, and as such is the object of sociology.' (Carnap, 1934/1937, p. 5)

6 A word-language is a language in which the sentences are built out of words (e.g. the word 'Blue') rather than signs (e.g. the predicate 'B').

7 In *Logical Syntax*, things are actually slightly more complicated because in addition to *logical* rules of transformation, Carnap considers the possibility of defining languages with P-rules (physical rules) which do have empirical content. In this case, it is necessary to divide the valid sentences of the given language into L-valid and P-valid sentences. What Carnap has in mind are languages in which the logical and mathematical sentences are L-valid (i.e. analytical) sentences. We shall not consider the case of languages with P-rules here.

8 The foundation of mathematics was a much disputed issue, especially in the 1920s. Formalism, intuitionism and logicism were the main tentative (families of) solutions. For background on the foundations of mathematics, and the proposed solutions to the problem, see Horsten (2008, esp. sections 1, 2.1–2.3 and 3).

9 For such a discussion to take place, those who want to take part in it have to agree on a metalanguage ML, and this may be problematic because ML also includes a consequence relation and a set of logical and mathematical sentences regarded as valid. A discussion about ML itself is also possible, but this requires one further step in the hierarchy of languages, to a meta-metalanguage MML, about which disagreements may equally occur.

10 In a language with descriptive (i.e. non-logical) constants, a sentence may be true *simpliciter* without being L-true (see Carnap, 1939). A truth which is not an L-truth depends on the states of affairs which obtain in the world; an L-truth depends only on the rules of the semantic system under consideration.

11 Many aspects of Carnap's views on language are fundamental for his philosophy of science. This is the case of the explication of analyticity, but also of his research for a criterion of meaning and of the distinction he makes between an observational language and a theoretical language in his discussion of the reconstruction of

scientific theories in the 1950s. For more on the distinction between formal and factual science, see Carnap (1935b).

12 For lack of space, we have to leave aside the evolution of Carnap's and Quine's positions on this issue. See the chapter on Quine in this volume for some discussion of Quine's views on analyticity.

Bibliography

Awodey, S. and Carus, A. W. (2009), 'From Wittgenstein's Prison to the Boundless Ocean: Carnap's Dream of Logical Syntax', in Wagner, 2009a, pp. 79–106.

Carnap, R. (1928), *Der logische Aufbau der Welt*. Berlin-Schlachtensee: Weltkreis; 2nd edn, 1961, Hamburg: Meiner. Trans. from the 2nd edn by R. George as *The Logical Structure of the World*. Berkeley: University of California Press, 1967.

Carnap, R. (1931), 'Überwindung der Metaphysik durch logische Analyse der Sprache', *Erkenntnis*, 2, pp. 219–42. Trans. by A. Pap as 'The Elimination of Metaphysics through Logical Analysis of Language', in A. J. Ayer (ed.), *Logical Positivism*. Glencoe, IL: Free Press, 1959, pp. 60–81.

Carnap, R. (1934), *Logische Syntax der Sprache*. Vienna: Springer (trans. as Carnap, 1937, with additions).

Carnap, R. (1935a), *Philosophy and Logical Syntax*. London: Kegan Paul, Trench, Trubner. Reprint, Bristol: Thoemmes Press, 1996.

Carnap, R. (1935b), 'Formalwissenschaft und Realwissenschaft', *Erkenntnis*, 5, pp. 30–7. Trans. by H. Feigl and M. Brodbeck as 'Formal and Factual Science', in H. Feigl and M. Brodbeck (eds), *Readings in the Philosophy of Science*. New York: Appleton-Century-Crofts, 1953, pp. 123–8.

Carnap, R. (1937), *The Logical Syntax of Language* (augmented translation of Carnap, 1934). London: Kegan Paul, Trench, Trubner. and New York: Harcourt, Brace.

Carnap, R. (1939), 'Foundations of Logic and Mathematics'. *International Encyclopedia of Unified Science*, Vol. 1, No. 3. Chicago, IL: University of Chicago Press.

Carnap, R. (1950a), 'Empiricism, Semantics, and Ontology'. *Revue internationale de philosophie*, 4, 20–40 (reprinted with corrections in Carnap, 1956, pp. 205–21).

Carnap, R. (1950b), *Logical Foundations of Probability*. Chicago: University of Chicago Press; 2nd edn, 1962.

Carnap, R. (1952), 'Quine on Analyticity', in R. Creath (ed.), *Dear Carnap, Dear Van: The Quine–Carnap Correspondence and Related Work*. Los Angeles: University of California Press, 1990, pp. 427–32.

Carnap, R. (1955), 'Meaning and Synonymy in Natural Languages', *Philosophical Studies*, 6, 33–47 (reprinted in Carnap, 1956, pp. 233–47).

Carnap, R. (1956), *Meaning and Necessity*, 2nd edn. Chicago: University of Chicago Press.

Carnap, R. (1963a), 'Intellectual Autobiography', in Schilpp, 1963, pp. 1–84.

Carnap, R. (1963b), 'Replies and Systematic Expositions', in Schilpp, 1963, pp. 859–1013.

Carnap, R., Hahn, H. and Neurath, O. (1929), *Wissenschaftliche Weltauffassung. Der Wiener Kreis*. Vienna: Gerold. Trans. by P. Foulkes and M. Neurath as 'The Scientific World Conception: The Vienna Circle', in O. Neurath, *Empiricism and Sociology*, ed. M. Neurath and R. S. Cohen. Reidel: Dordrecht, 1973, pp. 299–318.

Carus, A. W. (2007), *Carnap and Twentieth-Century Thought. Explication as Enlightenment*. Cambridge: Cambridge University Press.

Horsten, Leon (2008), 'Philosophy of Mathematics', *The Stanford Encyclopedia of Philosophy* (Fall 2008 Edition), ed. Edward N. Zalta, available online at http://plato.stanford.edu/archives/fall2008/entries/philosophy-mathematics/.

Neurath, O. (1941), 'Universal Jargon and Terminology', *Proceedings of the Aristotelian Society*, 41, pp. 127–48. Reprinted in O. Neurath, *Philosophical Papers 1913–1946*, ed. R. S. Cohen and M. Neurath. Dordrecht: Reidel, 1983, pp. 213–29.

Ricketts, T. (2004), 'Frege, Carnap, and Quine: Continuities and Discontinuities', in S. Awodey and C. Klein (eds), *Carnap Brought Home: The View From Jena*. Chicago and LaSalle, IL: Open Court, pp. 181–202.

Schilpp, P. A. (ed.) (1963), *The Philosophy of Rudolf Carnap*. LaSalle, IL: Open Court.

Wagner, P. (ed.) (2009a), *Carnap's Logical Syntax of Language*. Basingstoke: Palgrave Macmillan.

Wagner, P. (2009b), 'The Analysis of Philosophy in *Logical Syntax*: Carnap's Critique and His Attempt at a Reconstruction', in Wagner, 2009a, pp. 184–202.

Wagner, P. (2012), 'Natural Languages, Formal Languages, and Explication', in P. Wagner (ed.), *Carnap's Ideal of Explication and Naturalism*. Basingstoke: Palgrave Macmillan, pp. 175–89.

Wittgenstein, L. (1921), 'Logisch-philosophische Abhandlung'. *Annalen der Naturphilosophie*, 14, 185–262. Trans. by C. K. Ogden as *Tractatus Logico-Philosophicus*. London: Kegan Paul, Trench, Trubner, 1922.

CHAPTER FIVE

STEBBING

Siobhan Chapman

L. Susan Stebbing (1885–1943) was at the forefront of developments
in analytic philosophy in the interwar period of the twentieth century.
She rose to prominence as the author of an important textbook
which discussed both logic in the Aristotelian tradition and the
new mathematical logic pioneered by Bertrand Russell and Alfred
Whitehead. She went on to become a leading proponent in what
was known as the 'Cambridge School of Analysis'. But, unusually
for an analytic philosopher of this period, she was also interested
in the ways in which language works in everyday situations, and
committed to the importance of logic in critical thinking and in
practical problem-solving. In her work, she increasingly emphasized
the importance of attending to how language is used, or misused,
by those intent on persuading or manipulating others. Her later
publications were largely aimed at a general readership and were
concerned with the real-life linguistic choices made by a variety
of influential figures, including scientists, clergymen, advertisers,
journalists and politicians, and with the ideological implications
of those choices. Her work prefigures subsequent developments in
thinking about language, both in philosophy and in some branches
of present-day linguistics. Her concern that ordinary people should
be equipped with a capacity to identify and critique ways in which
language can be used as a tool of illegitimate persuasion seems
prescient. Stebbing has been relatively neglected in recent decades

but deserves to be re-evaluated as a significant thinker in the philosophy of language.

1. Introduction: Life and work

Stebbing is an important figure in the study of language, but also an unusual one because it is difficult to place her in a specific category. Her work on logic and analysis would seem to align her with what might be described as 'formal' or even 'ideal language' analytic philosophy, which emphasizes the positive features of constructed logical languages and views ordinary language as flawed and in need of reform or replacement. But her interest in actual everyday communication would seem to give her more in common with the later development of 'ordinary language philosophy', which is often seen as distinct from or even incompatible with the formal tradition. She was an early British interpreter of and commentator on the work of the logical positivists. But her own views on analysis were incompatible with the exclusively linguistic focus of logical positivism and left open the possibility of metaphysical discussion, to which logical positivism was implacably opposed. Further, although she worked exclusively in philosophy and in some ways foreshadowed later developments in that discipline, approaches to the study of language similar to those she adopted are also evident in recent work in the separate academic field of linguistics.

Stebbing followed a largely conventional academic career path throughout her adult life. What is remarkable is that she did so with determination and ultimately with success at a time when the British academic establishment was generally unwelcoming and often overtly hostile to women.

Stebbing was born at the end of 1885 in Finchley, North London, the sixth and youngest child of Alfred Stebbing, a merchant, and his wife Elizabeth, née Elstob, who had been a music teacher before her marriage. Her given names were 'Lizzie Susan' but, disliking her first name, she chose to be known as 'Susan' throughout her life. She went up to Girton College in Cambridge in 1904. At the time the University of Cambridge did not award degrees or full University membership to women; indeed, it was not to do so during Stebbing's lifetime.

Philosophy was not Stebbing's first choice of subject. She was apparently interested in studying science but, under pressure from her family not to attempt a subject that was considered too taxing, she enrolled at Girton to study history. While at Cambridge, however, she began by chance to read some recently published philosophical work, which changed the course of her thinking. She completed her studies in history and then switched subjects to philosophy, or 'moral science' as it was then known in many British universities. In order to gain an official qualification she needed to register at a university that would award degrees to women, and in 1908 she moved to King's College London to take an MA in moral science. After graduating in 1912, she worked in a number of different short-term and part-time teaching posts in both schools and universities. Eventually, in 1920, she was appointed to a lectureship in philosophy at Bedford College for women, in the University of London, and she was to stay at that institution for the rest of her life. Throughout her career, particularly in the 1930s and early 1940s, Stebbing corresponded with or knew many of the leading figures in Western philosophy of the day. Her personal philosophical influences included Bertrand Russell, A. N. Whitehead and, especially, G. E. Moore. She also interacted with many philosophers who were her contemporaries or juniors; she worked with, disagreed with or influenced, among others, Rudolf Carnap, Ludwig Wittgenstein, Moritz Schlick, Karl Popper, Otto Neurath, John Wisdom, C. E. M. Joad, Max Black, Gilbert Ryle and A. J. Ayer.

In 1933, Stebbing was promoted to professor, thereby becoming the first woman to hold a full professorship in philosophy at a British university. She continued to teach and to write about philosophy in London and, after her college was evacuated at the start of the Second World War, in Cambridge. She also became increasingly involved in work with refugees from central Europe. She offered professional and often financial assistance to exiled scholars and she also devoted considerable time and resources to orphaned or fugitive children from Germany and Nazi-occupied countries. Stebbing suffered from periods of ill health throughout her life, and these often left her bedridden. In her later years, she experienced both impaired mobility and severe loss of hearing. These problems were caused by a disorder of the inner ear known as Menière's disease, which resulted in attacks of vertigo. The condition became progressively worse throughout her life. In the late 1930s, Stebbing was diagnosed with cancer and, although she initially appeared to respond well to treatment, the cancer returned and spread and she died in 1943 at the age of 57.

Stebbing's published output was prolific and wide ranging. She produced numerous book reviews, short notes and colloquium contributions alongside a number of major philosophical papers and seven books. In her lifetime she was lauded chiefly for her contribution to logic and to formal analytic method, particularly for her discipline-defining textbook *A Modern Introduction to Logic* (1930) and for her work in the Cambridge School of Analysis. She was also recognized for introducing the ideas of logical positivism to an English-speaking audience, addressing them in a lecture she gave to the British Academy in 1933, before the publication of A. J. Ayer's more famous and more provocative account of them in *Language, Truth and Logic* (1936). In a number of important papers in the early 1930s she focused on the nature of philosophical analysis, drawing attention to the different conceptions of it in the Cambridge School on the one hand and in logical positivism on the other.

From her early work onwards, Stebbing's understanding of logic was informed by considerations of how it might be applied in practical thinking and reasoning, and was illustrated in relation to the ways in which language is used in everyday communication. In her later work, her discussion of logic was focused more frequently and more specifically on instances of language in use. She also developed a conviction that as a professional philosopher, she had a duty to engage with a wider public audience and to confront practical issues of her day. As a result, her work became increasingly socially and politically directed. For instance, in *Philosophy and the Physicists* (1937), she criticized the way in which some contemporary writers were presenting recent scientific developments to a popular audience; she engaged in close analysis of the language they were using to reveal the misleading and potentially dangerous assumptions introduced. In her most widely read book, *Thinking to Some Purpose* (1939), she broadened her focus to consider the ideological implications of actual language use in a variety of everyday communicative interactions. In doing so she did not abandon her training in logic. For Stebbing, a commitment to rigorous logical argument was entirely consistent with the requirements of practical problem-solving and the need for clarity in all forms of communication.

As indicated above, a reading of Stebbing's work raises questions about any reductive division of analytic philosophy into 'ideal language' and 'ordinary language' approaches. 'Ordinary Language Philosophy' as a distinct school of thought in analytic philosophy is generally associated with the work of Oxford philosophers such as J. L. Austin and Gilbert Ryle and with the years immediately following the Second World War. Yet at least a decade earlier Stebbing was affirming her belief in the philosophical importance of attention to ordinary language. More than this, she was putting that belief into action, identifying and analysing a variety of different types of actual language use. Stebbing's work suggests an alternative to any view of analytic philosophy that sees it as split into two factions on the basis of differences over the role of language in philosophy. Rather, attention and sensitivity to language use can be seen as a recurring theme, an asset to philosophical analysis in both its more formal and its more discursive forms.

Stebbing dealt increasingly not just with language in use, but with its moral, political and ideological implications. In this, her work foreshadows much more recent developments in the study of language both within analytic philosophy and also outside philosophy in present-day linguistics. Critical Discourse Analysis (CDA), in particular, is specifically concerned with the ways in which language may be used to convey unquestioned, often hidden, ideological assumptions and has much in common with Stebbing's work in terms of its aims and its approach. This chapter offers an overview of Stebbing's work as a whole, but concentrates on the work in which she engaged most closely with everyday language and in particular on her later, more socially orientated writings. It is arguably in relation to this aspect of her work that Stebbing's chief intellectual contribution, and the philosophical and linguistic implications of her thinking, can best be appreciated.

2. Logic and ordinary language

Stebbing's early work was influenced by some of the major figures in contemporary analytic philosophy, including G. E. Moore, Bertrand Russell and Alfred Whitehead. She was particularly impressed by Moore's philosophical approach, which involved careful consideration of the language in which philosophical statements, and beliefs about the world more generally, are expressed. Moore argued that it could be demonstrated that there is an external world of objects independent of our experience, simply on the basis of personal knowledge of the certain truth of everyday sorts of claims, such as 'Here is a hand'. Stebbing's earliest writings were concerned with the nature of the physical world and our knowledge of it, and she advocated a broadly realist approach, as opposed to the idealism that had been in the ascendency at the turn of the century. But her thinking in the early decades of the twentieth century was also influenced by recent developments in logic and in particular by her careful reading of Whitehead and Russell's mammoth work, *Principia Mathematica* (1910).

Whitehead and Russell proposed a major development of traditional, Aristotelian logic. Traditional logic included provision for the analysis of the structure of some key forms of proposition and for some formal processes of deduction, for instance, in syllogistic reasoning. The new logic proposed in *Principia Mathematica* was more powerful and dealt with a greater range of propositions and arguments. It dealt with truth-functional sentence connectives (such as 'and', 'or' and 'it is not the case that'), relational expressions (such as 'is larger than') and a wider range of quantified claims (including multiply quantified claims such as 'For every number there is a number which is larger'). Whitehead and Russell aimed to show that mathematical statements could be explained within the same system, by showing that the truths of mathematics could be understood as purely logical tautologies. During the late 1920s Stebbing saw that undergraduate students were increasingly being expected to be familiar with this new logic for their university examinations, while the available textbooks dealt only with the then traditional, Aristotelian logic. Stebbing's *A Modern Introduction to Logic*, first published in 1930 and released in a slightly revised and extended second edition in 1933, was designed to bridge this gap. It introduced students to the foundations of traditional logic and to recent developments in the new mathematical logic. It also offered a discussion of scientific method, including problems and current debates concerning deduction and induction. The book was well received by Stebbing's philosophical contemporaries and was for many years a standard textbook on university reading lists. This section concentrates on Stebbing's perhaps surprising use of many examples of practical reasoning and of ordinary ways of talking in a book concerned with one of the most abstract and formal types of philosophy. The next section considers the traces it contains of the early stages of her thinking about analysis, which would lead to her contribution to the Cambridge School.

Stebbing's contemporaries in analytic philosophy were generally of the opinion that – although philosophy might be largely concerned with analysis – ordinary language, or the language used for everyday interactions, was of little use or interest to the philosopher. On the contrary, they thought, it was likely to mislead, trick or deceive with its inconsistencies and vagueness. *Principia Mathematica* itself is prefaced by a solo-authored piece by Russell in which he maintained that grammatical structure must be distinguished from logical structure. 'Ordinary language yields no help' in logical philosophy, he argues; '[i]ts grammatical structure does not represent uniquely the relations between the ideas involved' (Whitehead and Russell, 1910, p. 2).

A Modern Introduction to Logic is explicitly presented in this tradition. In her own preface, for instance, Stebbing explains that: '[t]he conception of logic as essentially formal, which results in the identity of pure logic and abstract mathematics … is the conception that underlies this book' (Stebbing, 1930, p. ix). Nevertheless, Stebbing encourages her readers to think about mathematical logic in relation to the familiar problems that they routinely solve, decisions that they make and, most of all, language that they use. That is, she argues that the principles explained and clarified in logic are principles we can and should use in our everyday lives.

Like other analytic philosophers, Stebbing alerts her readers to the differences between logic and natural language. But she does so not in order to demonstrate that natural language is faulty or deficient, but instead to show that it operates in a distinct manner. The use of 'some' in logic and in language is a case in point: 'The sign of quantity "some" is interpreted [in logic] to mean "some at least, it may be all". In ordinary speech we usually, though not always, use "some" to mean "some only", i.e. "some but not all", e.g. "Some men are fools"' (Stebbing, 1930, p. 48). Some decades later, discrepancies such as this between logic and natural language would form a major focus of interest, and indeed disagreement, for philosophers of ordinary language. Peter Strawson (1950), for instance, argued that the regularities of formal logic were not an appropriate measure for natural language: natural language was not misleading or imperfect; it simply had no logic. Paul Grice (1975), on the other hand, argued that a closer understanding of the regularities and norms of language use would explain how everyday interpretations are derived in context from what are in fact perfectly logical and regular features of natural language (see Grice, 1975 and the chapter on Grice in the present volume for further details). But in 1930, Stebbing's underlying claim, that the similarities and differences between the uses of logical expressions and their apparent counterparts in natural language were worth serious philosophical attention, was a novel one.

In *A Modern Introduction to Logic*, Stebbing also demonstrates the relationship between logical principles and everyday problem-solving, and here her examples sometimes hint towards political, or at least social, commentary. In the following example, she illustrates the importance to the understanding of particular facts of relating them to general facts; a principle that holds in science holds also in more everyday experience.

> For example, a new young voter may ask why a given politician has devoted most of his election speeches to decrying his opponents. She may be satisfied with the reply that politicians always behave like that. In so far as this answer appears satisfactory it is because it relates the given fact to the general fact of the characteristics possessed by politicians. The fact is no longer isolated and, as such, unintelligible; it is now recognized as an instance of a uniform connexion. If the questioner were to pursue the inquiries demanding why politicians so behave, she would be answered if it were pointed out that the effect of such behaviour is to decrease the hearer's confidence in the speaker's opponents and thus to secure votes for himself. Such an explanation takes the form of a reference to purpose. If the questioner understands the nature of this purpose and is familiar with the mental characteristics of the electorate, the explanation will be complete. We are so familiar with purposive action that an explanation in terms of purpose is always acceptable, whilst the appeal to the value implicit in the purpose is recognized as final. (Stebbing, 1930, pp. 390–1)

The reference to a voter who is new, young and female was extremely topical. Suffrage had been extended to women under the age of 30 only in 1928, and many young women were getting used to the idea of voting for the first time in the forthcoming general election of 1931. Stebbing was always reluctant to draw a direct link between philosophy and action, or to intervene personally in political or social affairs. But the conviction that purposeful, philosophically informed thinking could result in clearer and more honest decision making and action in everyday life stayed with her throughout her career. As the contemporary social and political situation moved towards crisis, this conviction became stronger.

3. Analysis and logical positivism

A Modern Introduction to Logic offers an early indication of Stebbing's thinking about analysis. Here, the influence of Russell's work on definitions is clear, but so too are the beginnings of a distinct analytic approach of her own. Russell, the principal author of the account of definitions in *Principia Mathematica*, argued that in the sentence 'Scott is the author of Waverley', for instance, the definite description 'the author of Waverley' is not an expression which refers to an individual, but is an 'incomplete symbol'. It might occupy the same grammatical position as a proper name and seem to perform a similar referring function, but logical analysis reveals this to be a misleading feature of the 'surface' structure of language. (See the chapter on Russell in this volume.) For Russell, then, the purpose of logical analysis was to clarify the underlying logical structure of our claims, and therefore the structure of our thoughts, which might otherwise be obscured by the language in which they are conveyed. Stebbing points out that words and other symbols express concepts, making it easy to confuse the clarification of symbols with the analysis of the concepts which they express. Concepts are abstract or universal notions such as those of time and causation, and their analysis 'consists in determining precisely what are the properties present in objects which fall under these concepts' (Stebbing, 1930, p. 439). Stebbing argues that Russell was sometimes guilty of confusing the definition of symbols with the analysis of the concepts that those symbols express. His account of definite descriptions, for instance, had involved a contradiction 'because he wanted to do two things at once, viz. to define *definition* as concerned with symbols, and to point out that *the analysis of a concept*, which may be most suitably *expressed* in a definition, constitutes an advance in knowledge' (Stebbing, 1930, pp. 440–1). It was a mistake to conflate the clarification of an expression through definition or logical analysis with the clarification of what is expressed, which should properly be the subject of conceptual analysis.

The possibility and implications of conceptual, as opposed to logical, analysis were fundamental to the Cambridge School of Analysis during the early 1930s. Building on work on logical atomism by Russell and by Wittgenstein, the Cambridge School was pioneered by Stebbing, although it was developed more fully by other philosophers, most notably John Wisdom. According to the Cambridge School, logical analysis was best understood as 'same-level analysis'; it could reveal much about the structure of a proposition and therefore the thoughts it could be used to express. Metaphysical analysis, on the other hand, aimed to take the analyst to a 'new-level' understanding of the actual facts expressed by the proposition. It consisted of a progressive decomposition of facts into simpler elements, with the ultimate aim of reaching simple objects of immediate experience. The analysis proceeded to a particular desired endpoint and could therefore be defined as 'directional'. Same-level analysis was concerned with the clarification of potentially misleading linguistic expressions by translating them into logically acceptable equivalent expressions. New-level analysis could be seen as more ambitious, aiming to establish how facts are made up from our actual, individual, experiences of the world.

Stebbing's published work in this field is tentative and exploratory rather than dogmatic, and she in fact offers little in the way of clear examples of what directional analysis might look like. In a paper entitled 'Substances, Events, and Facts' she argues that the ultimate purpose of directional analysis should be to reach what she calls 'basic facts', because 'these are the facts that together constitute the world, in the sense that all other facts are based upon them' (Stebbing, 1932a, p. 314). A sentence in ordinary language such as 'This desk is brown' expresses a fact, but that fact must undergo a process of directional analysis in order to establish the basic facts, or basic objects of experience, of which it is constituted. Stebbing argues that, because 'metaphysics is primarily concerned with the analysis of facts', directional analysis might offer a suitable method for 'metaphysical analysis' (Stebbing, 1932a, p. 310). In a slightly later article, 'The Method of Analysis in Metaphysics', she considers further the controversial implications of this claim. She draws on Moore's argument that the purpose of philosophical analysis is to explain how we know certain 'common sense' statements about the world to be true. Directional analysis might be able to reveal how the facts corresponding to complex ordinary language expressions such as Moore's 'Here is a hand' are composed of more basic facts which ultimately relate to basic objects of experience. Stebbing is non-committal as to whether such basic objects actually exist; her main purpose is to establish that they are necessary prerequisites for the success of directional analysis. But she does suggest that the philosophical notion of 'sense data' might offer the required notion: 'It seems to be that an absolutely specific shade of colour, or taste, or sound, may be simple in the required sense' (Stebbing, 1932b, p. 91). Stebbing's aim in this paper is to establish the issues and possible problems that would be involved in directional analysis, rather than explicitly to endorse it as a philosophical method. Nevertheless, her sensitivity to these issues was to prove fundamental to her subsequent response to logical positivism.

Logical positivism, associated most closely with the group of philosophers known as the Vienna Circle, is nowadays seen as one of the leading schools of thought and major developments in mid-twentieth-century analytic philosophy. In the early 1930s, it was little known outside of Continental Europe. Stebbing, however, was fluent in German and so was able to read the then relatively obscure journals such as *Erkenntnis* in which the logical positivists were publishing. She had met the Vienna Circle's acknowledged leader Moritz Schlick and had got on well with him, when he caused a stir at a conference in Oxford in 1930 by claiming that metaphysics was meaningless. The following dogmatic statement from a paper published a couple of years later is typical of Schlick and of the philosophical movement for which he was spokesman: 'The empiricist does not say to the metaphysician "what you say is false", but, "what you say asserts nothing at all!" He does not contradict him, but says "I don't understand you"' (Schlick, 1932, p. 107). The 'empiricist' of Schlick's comment was, for the logical positivists, the true philosopher. The only statements which the philosopher could accept as meaningful were those for which a definite truth-value could be determined. Analytic statements, such as 'All triangles have three sides', were determined as true simply by virtue of the meanings of the words they contained. Synthetic statements which could be established as true or false by empirical investigation were also meaningful; comparison with the world could be used to establish whether statements such as 'snow is white' or 'grass is pink' were true or false. All other statements, including metaphysical speculation, and also expressions belonging to ethics, aesthetics and religion, were unverifiable and therefore meaningless.

Stebbing was impressed by the rigour of the logical positivists' scientific approach and agreed with their insistence on clarity and transparency in philosophical discussion. But she did not follow them in their belief that philosophical analysis consisted essentially in the explanation of the meaning of statements in terms of evidence that would show them to be true or false, and the identification of statements which did not meet their criterion of meaningfulness. As she had explained in her own recent, carefully measured, comments on analysis, British philosophy of the time, including the Cambridge School, seemed to rely on certain metaphysical commitments. These included most importantly the existence of simple facts and basic experiences, which were the ultimate ends of analysis. For philosophers of this tradition, metaphysics had the potential to play an important role in philosophical analysis. It allowed for the close study of everyday beliefs and the language in which they were expressed, with the ultimate purpose of learning something about what there is in the world. For the logical positivists, metaphysical statements, including for instance any formulation of the claim that the world is composed of basic facts, were prescribed as unverifiable and therefore meaningless.

In 1933, Stebbing was invited to give the prestigious annual British Academy philosophy lecture and she chose to talk about logical positivism. In the published version of this lecture, she praises the clarity of its proponents, particularly Schlick, but she also criticizes some of their assumptions. In particular, she accuses them of ignoring or being oblivious to the existence of different types of philosophical analysis. As a result, they assumed that all analysis must be linguistic.

What we ordinarily say, we say unclearly. We speak unclearly because we think unclearly. It is the task of philosophy to render our thoughts clear. Hence, it is not incorrect to say that the 'object of philosophy is the logical clarification of thoughts'. But, though not incorrect, this statement is not itself a clear statement. We cannot clarify our thoughts by thinking about thinking, nor by thinking about logic. We have to think about what we were thinking about. The philosopher considers a given expression, and analyses it in order to find another expression which says more clearly what the original expression said less clearly. This investigation is not linguistic. We must first know what facts are the case before we can fruitfully employ analysis for the purpose of clarifying our thoughts about the world. (Stebbing, 1933, p. 86)

For Stebbing, logical positivism was in danger of becoming trapped in a closed loop, in which the analysis of language and the re-expression of thought became both philosophical method and end in itself. A major aim of the logical positivists was to develop a new, scientifically precise and empirically justified language to replace the irregularities and confusions of natural language. Analytic philosophers of the British tradition, however, aimed to arrive at a more precise picture of the facts of the world, which serve to explain our knowledge of the truth of certain natural language statements. Philosophers from the two schools of thought were in regular and frequently amicable discussion during the 1930s, not least in forums which Stebbing herself organized or to which she contributed. She was a founding board member, for instance, of the journal *Analysis* and the only British member of the organizing committee for the first Congress for the Unity of Science, held in Paris in 1935. The British and the logical positivist traditions were ultimately irreconcilable, but their discussions kept the nature of analysis at the heart of philosophical debate in the middle part of the twentieth century.

4. Critical thinking and ideology

During the 1930s, Stebbing was central to technical developments and debates in academic philosophy concerning analysis and logic. But she also played an increasingly prominent role as a public commentator on and critic of the language used by figures of the social and political establishment. For Stebbing, there was no contradiction or even tension between these two elements in her work. She saw the laws of logic as essentially applicable to actual arguments and practical processes of decision making, and an understanding of the underlying commitments of language as just as important in everyday as in philosophical communication. This much had been apparent in *A Modern Introduction to Logic*, where she argued that thinking directed to a particular practical purpose must be driven by sound logical principles. These views were expressed more forcefully in *Logic in Practice*, a shorter and more accessible book on logic published in 1934. In the preface she makes explicit the link she sees between formal logic and practical thinking. She argues that 'the study of logic does not in itself suffice to enable us to reason correctly, still less to think clearly where our passionate beliefs are concerned', but that nevertheless it is possible to develop the habit of sound reasoning in order to avoid certain mistakes: 'This habit may be acquired by consciously attending to the logical principles of sound reasoning, in order to apply them to test the soundness of particular arguments' (Stebbing, 1934, p. viii).

Logic in Practice offers a series of imagined scenarios in which a particular question must be answered or problem solved. It also includes analyses of extracts from actual textual presentations of reasoning or argument, which Stebbing uses to illustrate how thinking can work successfully and how it can fail to do so. For instance, she draws on extracts from political speeches quoted in newspaper reports on the General Strike of 1926 and looks at the shifting and inconsistent usage of particular words such as 'community', 'the people', 'public' and even 'strike'. Stebbing argues that when feelings are running high, as they were in relation to this socially and politically divisive issue, it is easy to 'be misled through a failure to recognize that a word is being used ambiguously' (Stebbing, 1934, p. 73).

An interest in the language of news reporting and of politics, and particularly the concern about how it might mislead individual thinking and public opinion, remained with Stebbing for the rest of her life. The next focus of her attention, however, was the language used by contemporary scientists to explain their ideas: particularly by scientists who proposed to present these ideas in a way that was accessible to a popular audience. There was a tremendous public appetite in the mid-1930s for books on current scientific advances that were written with the twin aims of edifying and entertaining their readership. Stebbing was concerned that the deliberately sensational language that such books often employed was in danger of misrepresenting rather than clarifying scientific developments. She was worried, too, that such language might encourage readers to believe that certain conclusions could be drawn from scientific discoveries which were not in fact justified. This was the topic of *Philosophy and the Physicists*, published in 1937. In this, she is particularly critical of Sir Arthur Eddington, a prominent and popular scientist whose writing style was designed to appeal to his readers' emotions and imaginations, often by purporting to show how scientific discoveries related to their own everyday experiences of the world. His 1935 book *The Nature of the Physical World* provides Stebbing with a number of examples of the type of writing which troubles her, including this passage in which he discusses the apparent implications of the atomic theory of matter for the everyday experience of stepping on to a floorboard:

> The plank has no solidity of substance. To step on it is like stepping on a swarm of flies. Shall I not slip through? No, if I make the venture one of the flies hits me and gives a boost up again; I fall again and am knocked upwards by another fly; and so on. I may hope that the net result will be that I remain about steady; but if unfortunately I should slip through the floor or be boosted too violently up to the ceiling, the occurrence would be, not a violation of the laws of Nature, but a rare coincidence. (Eddington, 1935, p. 328)

This is exactly the type of imprecise, impressionistic way of explaining physics to which Stebbing objects. She argues that rather than using everyday language to explain complex ideas, as Eddington apparently intended, he actually misuses that language. Much of Eddington's writing is simply nonsensical. For instance, the statement that 'the plank has no solidity of substance' makes no sense. The word 'solid' is used to denote certain properties, such as those demonstrated by a plank. So a plank with no solidity is not a novel scientific discovery but a simple contradiction in terms (Stebbing, 1937, p. 45). Using everyday language to describe scientific knowledge, which was in fact often at odds with everyday experience, was designed to engage readers' sentiment rather than their intellect and could only lead to confusion.

For Stebbing, the danger in Eddington's style of writing goes beyond the possibility of misleading, confusing or perhaps frightening his readership. The use of everyday language allows Eddington to manipulate his readers' understanding of scientific developments so as to introduce unjustified conclusions. For instance, he explains that the predictability that we perceive in the world around us is based only on our usual experience, not on any guaranteed stability. The laws of physics do not preclude apparently fantastical events such as a man falling though the floorboards; it is only in a version of the world filtered by our perceptions, not in the actual physical world, that these things are impossible. He goes on to argue that this means that the new scientific understanding of the world opens up a more general possibility that other types of truth, or other realities, exist despite our everyday failure to perceive them clearly. In this way he argues that advances in physics such as the atomic theory of matter give scientific credibility to the existence of spiritual and even divine versions of reality. For Stebbing, this final step in his argument is unsound, disingenuous and potentially dangerous.

Stebbing's next major publication was *Thinking to Some Purpose*, published in 1939. As in *Philosophy and the Physicists*, Stebbing's main aim was to raise awareness in her readership of imprecise or misleading uses of language and the unjustified conclusions to which they could give rise. Whereas her target in the earlier book had been the popular writings of contemporary scientists, her aim in this new book was more generally to expose the ways in which various forces in contemporary society sought to persuade and to manipulate. The world was on the brink of a war which Stebbing saw as having been brought about at least in part through propaganda and rhetoric, and it seemed to her imperative that the general electorate should be critically attuned to language use: 'Citizens must be able to think relevantly, that is, to think to some purpose. Thus to think is difficult. Accordingly, it is not surprising, however saddening it may be, that many of our statesmen do not trust the citizens to think, but rely instead upon the arts of persuasion' (Stebbing, 1939, p. 10).

Thinking to Some Purpose is stocked with examples of actual language use by contemporary figures such as advertisers, journalists, clergymen and politicians. Stebbing repeatedly demonstrates how language may be used to introduce assumptions which are not explicitly stated and how conclusions may be drawn from it which are not in fact justified. Some of her examples draw on specific principles of logic. She argues that the same rigour should be applied to interpreting everyday discourse as is needed in logic, where all parts of an argument need to be made explicit: 'people untrained in logic can detect a formal fallacy in a syllogistic argument once it is clearly set out' (Stebbing, 1939, p. 159). The following argument is valid; the truth of a consequent follows from the truth of an antecedent.

> If P, then Q
> P
> Therefore Q

It is also the case that the denial of the antecedent follows from the denial of the consequent:

> If P, then Q
> Not Q
> Therefore, not P

However, the denial of the consequent does not follow from the denial of the antecedent. Although it is less obvious, practice in logical reasoning can enable people to recognize that the following form of argument is not valid.

> If P, then Q,
> Not P,
> Therefore, not Q.

Stebbing argues that this sort of familiarity with logical reasoning should be at the forefront of people's minds when they are presented with everyday arguments:

> To assert that *if we prepare for war, then we shall preserve peace*, and that *we have not prepared for war* does not justify us in asserting that *we have not preserved peace*. To establish this conclusion we should have to maintain that *only if we*

have prepared for war, shall we preserve peace. Whether this latter statement be true or not, it was not what was asserted as a premise in the argument, which, as it is given, involves the 'fallacy of denying the antecedent'. (Stebbing, 1939, p. 163)

Stebbing also analyses longer extracts of language use in order to demonstrate how suggestion and persuasion may subtly be presented as reasoned argument. For instance, she considers this extract from a speech by Sir Stanley Baldwin during the general election of 1931. Baldwin was Conservative prime minister several times; in 1931 he was campaigning on behalf of the National Government and was arguing that a government made up of both Liberals and Conservatives could be successful:

> There must undoubtedly be some difficulty over the question of tariffs. Liberals would approach the problem with a Free Trade bias but with an open mind to examine and decide whether there were measures of dealing with the problem apart from tariffs. Conservatives would start with an open mind but with a favour for tariffs. They would start with an open mind to examine alternative methods, and the Cabinet as a whole would sit down with prefect honesty and sincerity to come to a decision on the matter.

Stebbing focuses on some of the word choices made by Baldwin in his speech:

> You will notice that Baldwin speaks of a Liberal bias for Free Trade and of a Conservative favour for tariffs. The word 'bias' carries with in an emotional significance of having prejudged the matter in a way that could hardly be regarded as consistent with having an 'open mind'. The word 'favour' does not, I think, have this significance. (Stebbing, 1939, pp. 66–7)

Stebbing also identifies general tendencies in everyday thinking which can be dangerous if they are not fully examined and which can be used either unwittingly or unscrupulously to mislead and persuade. Two examples considered briefly here are what she calls 'potted thinking' and what is more widely referred to as the 'argument from analogy'. In the former case, Stebbing draws attention to what she sees as the cognitive equivalent of potted meat (a cooked and tinned meat product, in many cases of dubious quality): 'potted thinking is easily accepted, is concentrated in form, and has lost the vitamins essential to mental nourishment' (Stebbing, 1939, p. 68). We want to be able to hold confident views on potentially complicated matters and so have a tendency to accept simple or concise statements of belief without inquiring too deeply into the details of the issue in question. To do so is often convenient, but it can lead us to simplify complex matters or to close our minds to the possibilities of revising our opinions in the light of new evidence. Political slogans are often a case in point, and so too are tendencies to identify simplistic oppositions between political systems which are 'good' (e.g. democracy) and those which are 'bad' (e.g. Communism).

In relation to linguistic usage, potted thinking can manifest itself in the currency of phrases such as 'lily-livered pacifists', 'bloated capitalists' and 'our magnificent police force'. Stebbing points out that 'such emotional language compresses into a phrase a personal reaction and an implicit judgement about a class of persons', and their repeated use may mean that people are unable to think about the group of people in question without the quality attributed to them (Stebbing, 1939, p. 75). She offers the following illustration. The *News Chronicle* had recently published a letter signed '"A Britisher", and Proud of it', which took exception to the use of the phrase 'British cowardice' in a recent leading article. The letter writer objected that 'the combination of these two word, together, is unknown in the English language, or in the tongue of any country in the world' and suggested 'British Diplomacy' as a more suitable alternative. For Stebbing, this letter 'reveals very clearly the way in which our admiration (or, in other cases, our contempt) for a certain class makes us unable to contemplate the possibility that we might be mistaken' (Stebbing, 1939, p. 77).

Stebbing notes a number of uses of analogies. They can be used to explain the unfamiliar in familiar terms and to suggest possible conclusions by a process of analogical thinking (Stebbing, 1939, p. 126). But people sometimes use analogies not just to suggest but actually to (try to) establish conclusions, and Stebbing is critical of this use. As she explains, the logical form of argument by analogy is as follows:

X has the properties p_1, p_2, p_3 ... and f;

Y has the properties $p_1, p_2, p_3 \ldots$
Therefore, Y also has the property f.

In everyday discourse, people often use apparent analogies to draw conclusions which are not sound. This is because they fail to consider the precise nature of the properties demonstrated by the entities being compared (the instances of p in the logical form). In addition to the properties they have in common, X and Y may also have other, independent properties. It is crucial that Y must not have any property which is incompatible with the property f; 'In such a case the argument that Y has f because X has and X and Y are alike in respect of the p's is fallacious, no matter how much we may extend the number of p's which both X and Y posses' (Stebbing, 1939, p. 113).

Stebbing provides many examples from political speeches in which analogies are suggested which do not stand up to logical scrutiny and from which persuasive but unsound conclusions are drawn. She notes, for instance, the many different uses which politicians had recently made of the analogy implicit in the figure of speech 'the Ship of State'. Here is just one example, from a broadcast speech in November 1935 by former Prime Minister Ramsay MacDonald:

> I began with a reference to the contrast between the state of the country in 1931 and its state to-day. The ship then near the rocks is again floating, and has been made seaworthy. There is rough and trying water ahead. How can it most wisely be encountered?

Stebbing points out that Ramsay MacDonald's argument and his call for support for the National Government which had been in power since 1931 were based on the implied analogy between a ship in danger and a nation in a time of crisis, an analogy which she argued was not logically sound. Stebbing concludes that even good analogies will eventually break down and that 'our tendency to forget this is exploited by those who aim at persuading us to accept their views without offering us any grounds that would be acceptable to a reasonable thinker' (Stebbing, 1939, p. 126).

The two related themes of the importance of logical thinking in everyday life and the implications and perils of the use and misuse of language were central to the publications of Stebbing's final years. In *Ideals and Illusions*, a short book published in 1941, Stebbing calls for a careful assessment of what ends are worth living for, maintaining a clear distinction between definite and explicit ideals on the one hand and comforting but misleading illusions on the other. Stebbing identifies a failure to make this distinction in many examples of contemporary writing on political, social and religious matters. In *A Modern Elementary Logic* (1943), Stebbing provides a shorter and simpler introduction to logic than *A Modern Introduction to Logic*, with an increased emphasis on the relationship between logical terms and the use of their apparent equivalents in natural language. Context and other specific characteristics of speech may have an important effect on what is conveyed, but they are ignored in discussing logical relations: 'To ignore them is justifiable in an elementary textbook, but this does not mean that they do not need investigation' (Stebbing, 1943, p. 35).

5. Legacy: Philosophy and linguistics

During Stebbing's lifetime, it was unusual for an analytic philosopher to pay serious attention to ordinary language. Soon after her death, 'Ordinary Language Philosophy' rose to prominence, particularly in Oxford. In this, sensitivity to everyday language was championed as a philosophical methodology in its own right, and the differences and similarities between logical expressions and their counterparts in natural language became a serious focus of study. The philosophers of ordinary language themselves paid little attention to Stebbing's work, although J. O. Urmson did pick up on some of the similarities between their method and hers. He praised her argument in *Philosophy and the Physicists* that attention to how people ordinarily use the word 'solid' demonstrates that it is simply nonsensical to describe a plank as having no solidity (Urmson, 1953, pp. 121–2).

Stebbing's conviction that analytic philosophers should engage with the social and political issues of the day, and that the tools of logic had practical as well as theoretical applications, was also unusual in her own time. Much more recently, some analytic philosophers have returned to this way of thinking about their discipline. Jason Stanley sums the situation up as follows:

For much of its history, analytic philosophy has appeared to endorse the artificial German split between 'theoretical' philosophy and 'practical', or normative, philosophy. But analytic philosophers working within feminist philosophy and philosophy of race have showed the value of the tools of so-called theoretical philosophy in the analysis of the central political concepts of power and oppression, suggesting that to divide philosophy in that way is incorrect. (Stanley, 2015, p. xix)

Stanley cites *Thinking to Some Purpose* as an early example of this type of practical application of analytic philosophy, and he uses Stebbing's notion of ideological beliefs as 'cherished beliefs', which are particularly hard to challenge, in his own account of the language of propaganda. Further, some recent publications have advocated the use of formal logical principles and rules in the analysis of beliefs, arguments and decisions in real-life present-day issues, although without citing Stebbing (see, for instance, Cheng, 2018; Sinnott-Armstrong, 2018).

Various branches of present-day linguistics are premised on ways of thinking about language which can also be found in Stebbing's work. Pragmatics owes much to work on the relationship between logic and natural language, particularly by philosophers of ordinary language. In pragmatics, the relationship between meaning and context, which Stebbing identified in *A Modern Elementary Logic* as crucial but at the time understudied, is a major focus of attention. Critical Discourse Analysis (CDA), a relatively recent development in linguistics, also has some striking resonances with Stebbing's work, particularly her later writings. CDA is concerned with the close analysis of the use of language in order to establish how ideological assumptions can be introduced into spoken or written texts, often implicitly.

Some of the claims made by proponents of CDA sound remarkably similar to things that Stebbing was saying about language half a century or more earlier. Firstly, there are similarities in terms of the types of texts studied. Roger Fowler identifies the most appropriate type of data for analysis in CDA as: 'Contemporary popular newspapers, advertisements, political speeches of the current scene, classroom discourse, and so on' (Fowler, 2002, p. 353). Secondly, there are similarities in terms of the objectives of study. Michael Toolan outlines the specific agenda of CDA, which is strikingly similar to Stebbing's stated aim in writing *Thinking to Some Purpose* of enabling the voting public to recognize when language was being used persuasively rather than rationally:

CDA aims to make its users aware of, and able to describe and deconstruct, vectors and effects in texts and semiotic materials generally which might otherwise remain to wield power uncritiqued. In these respects CDA may be a kind of wake-up call, or consciousness-raising, about the coercive or anti-democratizing effects of the discourses we live by. (Toolan, 2002, p. xxii)

Thirdly, there are similarities in terms of the actual conclusions drawn. Discussions by Stebbing and in CDA of the devices used by advertisers to persuade and to sell products offer a case in point. In *Thinking to Some Purpose*, Stebbing summarizes for her readers the content of a contemporary newspaper advertisement:

An advertisement for a cure for a common chest complaint includes 'letters of gratitude selected from hundreds'. A woman writes that she had despaired of ever being well, but now she is 'a different woman'. Eminent medical men and well-known public persons (unspecified) are said to have praised the treatment. The reader is assured: 'Health is your right'. (Stebbing, 1939, p. 82)

Stebbing sums up the techniques, or the implicit argument, used by advertisers as follows:

Something is wrong with you and the advertisement tells you to trust the expert upon whom you must in the end rely. The advertiser reckons upon your not pausing to ask for evidence that 'they all' swear by the goods offered, nor for evidence of the credentials of 'the expert' who hides so modestly behind the description. The purpose of the whole lay-out of the advertisement is to persuade you that you have been offered reliable evidence, although, in fact, you have not. (Stebbing, 1939, pp. 82–3)

Working in a CDA framework, Guy Cook has noticed similar phenomena in the more recent genre of television advertisements:

The device of the framing journal, which gives fantastic events a setting of sober scientific authority, is echoed by toothpaste and disinfectant ads which begin and end with a scientist's report. Sometimes the white-coated boffin even appears, like the good angel of medieval drama, in the kitchen or bathroom, either invisible to all the characters or conversing with only one of them while unseen by all the others! (Cook, 2001, p. 187)

The anonymous expert to whom Stebbing drew attention continues to figure in present-day advertising, then, and to appear to confer credibility, without specific evidence, on a range of products.

During the course of her philosophical career, Stebbing was a contemporary proponent of mathematical logic, a leading practitioner of conceptual analysis, a pioneering advocate of the importance of ordinary language in philosophical discussion and an impassioned analyst of the hidden assumptions in persuasive uses of language. In many ways, her work foreshadowed later thinking in philosophy and in linguistics. But a philosopher's contribution should of course not be evaluated solely in relation to how her field of study has subsequently developed, and Stebbing's work should be read for its own merits as well as for any indications of foresight or prescience. Both in her own context, relevant to the philosophical, scientific and political issues of her day, and in our present-day context, aware of developments in the study of language since her death, Stebbing's work on logic, language and ideology deserves to be read and appreciated afresh.[1]

Further reading

There is not a great deal of recent introductory work specifically on Stebbing, but there are a number of useful encyclopaedia entries that cover the main aspects of her life and work, including Warnock (2004), Beaney (2006) and Beaney and Chapman (2017). Chapman (2013) is to date the only book-length study of Stebbing; it considers her philosophy as a whole in relation to her life, professional associations and historical context and in the light of subsequent developments in philosophy and linguistics. Stebbing's work on analysis and her response to logical positivism are considered in detail in Beaney (2003, 2016), Milkov (2003) and Janssen-Lauret

(2017). A reconsideration of her work on ideology and rationality can be found in Stanley (2015).

Note

1 I am grateful to Michael Beaney and to Barry Lee for their very constructive comments and helpful suggestions in relation to earlier versions of this chapter.

Bibliography

Ayer, A. J. (1936), *Language, Truth and Logic*. London: Victor Gollancz.

Beaney, Michael (2003), 'Susan Stebbing on Cambridge and Vienna Analysis', in Stadler (2003), pp. 339–50.

Beaney, Michael (2006), 'Stebbing, Lizzie Susan (1885–1943)', in A. C. Grayling, Andrew Pyle and Naomi Goulder (eds), *The Continuum Encyclopedia of British Philosophy*, 4 vols, IV, London: Thoemmes Continuum, pp. 3023–8.

Beaney, Michael (2016), 'Susan Stebbing and the Early Reception of Logical Empiricism in Britain', in Christian Damböck (ed.), *Influences on the Aufbau* (Vienna Circle Institute Yearbook 18), Switzerland: Springer, pp. 233–56.

Beaney, Michael and Chapman, Siobhan (2017), 'Susan Stebbing', in *Stanford Encyclopedia of Philosophy*, ed. Edward N. Zalta, <https://plato.stanford.edu/archives/sum2017/entries/stebbing/ (accessed 12 December 2018).

Chapman, Siobhan (2013), *Susan Stebbing and the Language of Common Sense*. Basingstoke: Palgrave Macmillan.

Cheng, Eugenia (2018), *The Art of Logic, How to Make Sense in a World That Doesn't*. London: Profile Books.

Cook, Guy (2001), *The Discourse of Advertising*. London: Routledge.

Eddington, Arthur (1935), *The Nature of the Physical World*, London: J. M. Dent and Sons.

Fowler, Roger (2002), 'On Critical Linguistics', in Michael Toolan (ed.), *Critical Discourse Analysis*, London: Routledge, pp. 346–57.

Grice, Paul (1975), 'Logic and Conversation', in Peter Cole and L. J. Morgan (eds), *Syntax and Semantics 3: Speech Acts*, New York: Academic Press. Reprinted in Paul Grice (1989), *Studies in the Way of Words*, Harvard: Harvard University Press, pp. 22–40.

Janssen-Lauret, Frederique (2017), 'Susan Stebbing, Incomplete Symbols, and Foundherentist Meta-ontology', *Journal for the History of Analytical Philosophy*, 5(2), pp. 6–17.

Milkov, Nikolay (2003), 'Susan Stebbing's Criticism of Wittgenstein's *Tractatus*', in Stadler, 2003, pp. 351–63.

Schlick, Moritz (1932), 'Positivism and Realism', *Erkenntnis* III. Reprinted in A. J. Ayer (ed.) (1959) *Logical Positivism*, Glencoe, Illinois: The Free Press, pp. 82–107.

Sinnott-Armstrong, Walter (2018), *Think Again: How to Reason and Argue*. London: Pelican.

Stadler, Friedrich (ed.) (2003), *The Vienna Circle and Logical Empiricism* (Vienna Circle Institute Yearbook 10). Netherlands: Springer.

Stanley, Jason (2015), *How Propaganda Works*. Princeton: Princeton University Press.

Stebbing, L. Susan (1930), *A Modern Introduction to Logic*. London: Methuen [2nd ed., revised, 1933].

Stebbing, L. Susan (1932a), 'Substances, Events and Facts', *The Journal of Philosophy*, 29, pp. 309–22.

Stebbing, L. Susan (1932b), 'The Method of Analysis in Metaphysics', *Proceedings of the Aristotelian Society*, 33, pp. 65–94.

Stebbing, L. Susan (1933), 'Logical Positivism and Analysis', *Proceedings of the British Academy*, 19, pp. 53–87.

Stebbing, L. Susan (1934), *Logic in Practice*. London: Methuen.

Stebbing, L. Susan (1937), *Philosophy and the Physicists*. London: Methuen.

Stebbing, L. Susan (1939), *Thinking to Some Purpose*. Harmondsworth: Penguin.

Stebbing, L. Susan (1941), *Ideals and Illusions*. London: Watts.

Stebbing, L. Susan (1943), *A Modern Elementary Logic*. London: Methuen [1961, London: Barnes and Noble].

Strawson, Peter (1950), 'On Referring', *Mind*, 59, pp. 320–44.

Toolan, Michael (2002), *Critical Discourse Analysis*, London: Routledge.

Urmson, J. O. (1953), 'Some Questions Concerning Validity', *Revue Internationale de Philosophie*, 7, pp. 217–29. Reprinted in Antony Flew (ed.) (1956), *Essays in Conceptual Analysis*, London: Macmillan, pp. 120–33.

Warnock, Mary (2004), 'Stebbing, (Lizzie) Susan (1885–1943)', in H. C. G. Matthew, Brian Harrison and Lawrence Goldman (eds), *Oxford Dictionary of National Biography*, Oxford: Oxford University Press. Accessed 12 December 2018.

Whitehead, A. N. and Russell, Bertrand (1910), *Principia Mathematica*, Vol. 1. Cambridge: Cambridge University Press.

CHAPTER SIX

AUSTIN

Guy Longworth

J. L. (John Langshaw) Austin dominated philosophy in Oxford from the end of the Second World War until death ended his tenure as White's Professor of Moral Philosophy in 1960. His work on speech acts has had a significant and lasting impact on the wider philosophical world. Another key aspect of his work, his views about the assessment of utterances as true and false, has been less well received. Recently, however, this aspect has assumed a central role in debates over the role of truth, or truth-conditions, in accounts of linguistic meaning. As will become apparent, Austin provides the bases for objections to accounts that view linguistic meaning as, or as determining, truth-conditions, and so to a major strand of contemporary thought. (See, for example, the chapter on Davidson.)

As a matter of principle, Austin published little.[1] He held that philosophers should go slowly and take care. Or, as Austin might have put it, philosophers should bite off no more than they can chew and then chew thoroughly. Two of his major works – *Sense and Sensibilia* (1962a) and *How to Do Things with Words* (1962b) – are posthumous and were assembled by colleagues from his lectures and notes for lectures. The historical record reflects only a fraction of Austin's work, much of which took place through personal engagements with students and other philosophers. Nevertheless, what we have contains a vein of insight that has not yet been exhausted.

In this chapter, I'll survey Austin's views in three areas: (i) language and philosophy; (ii) language and truth; and (iii) language and speech acts. The theme linking these views is Austin's rejection of any simple account of the assessment of utterances as true or false. I'll conclude by mentioning critical responses by some figures discussed in this volume. Since the historical record is slight, and space is short, exposition will involve some curve-fitting. This is especially risky when it comes to Austin, both because of the specificity of his claims and also his aversion to hasty generalization.

1. Language and philosophy

In this section, we'll look at Austin's views on the role of the study of language in philosophy more generally. Austin cared about language for two reasons. First, language-use is a central part of human activity, so it's an important topic in its own right. Second, the study of language is an aide – indeed, for many topics, a necessary preliminary – to the pursuit of philosophical topics. Many of Austin's most distinctive reflections on the use of language arise in the course of discussion of other topics.

One route to understanding Austin's approach is provided by reflection on the following comment by Stuart Hampshire:

> [Austin] was constitutionally unable to refrain from applying the same standards of truth and accuracy to a philosophical argument, sentence by sentence, as he would have applied to any other serious subject matter. He could not have adopted a special tone of voice, or attitude of mind, for philosophical questions. (Hampshire, 1960/1969, p. 34)

In short, it mattered to Austin that, in attempting to make out positions and arguments, philosophers should meet ordinary standards of truth, accuracy and so forth. And ordinary standards of truth, accuracy and so on, which apply to our utterances, can be sensitive to delicate nuances of linguistic meaning and use.

Among the risks associated with insensitivity to the nuances, two stand out. First, we are liable to miss distinctions that are made in our ordinary use of language and that are relevant to our concerns and claims. For example, failure to keep track of quite subtle differences in the uses of the expressions 'illusion' and 'delusion' might lead us to hold (a) that all illusions are delusions and so to infer (b) that all illusions have a property, F, in fact possessed by only some illusions, but by all delusions. F might be the property: making subjects think that they are presented with a thing of some type when they are not presented with any such thing. That might trick us into saying: this is an illusion (say, a straight stick appears bent); hence it is a delusion (because all illusions are); hence it instances F (we don't see a stick). Since we might at the same time see that it doesn't instance F (we do see a stick), we might fall into characteristically philosophical perplexity. Once we've confused ourselves in this way, it might seem that the only solution is to posit special non-material things that we see in such cases – 'sense data'. (See, for example, Austin, 1962a, pp. 8, 20–32.)

Second, failure to exploit fully the resources of ordinary language might make us susceptible to forced choices between unacceptable alternatives. Here Austin warns:

> It is worth bearing in mind ... the general rule that we must not expect to find simple labels for complicated cases ... however well-equipped our language, it can never be forearmed against all possible cases that may arise and call for description: fact is richer than diction. (1956a/1979, p. 195)

Language is likely to be well designed for the ends to which it is ordinarily put. But special, or especially complicated, cases may require special treatment. This is apt to be an especial liability when it comes to the question whether an expression applies, or fails to apply in a particular circumstance – that is, the question whether a sentence involving the expression can be used in that circumstance to state something true or false:

> We say, for example, that a certain statement is exaggerated or vague or bold, a description somewhat rough or misleading or not very good, an account rather general or too concise. In cases like these it is pointless to insist on deciding in simple terms whether the statement is 'true or false'. Is it true or false that Belfast is north of London? That the galaxy is the shape of a fried egg? That Beethoven was a drunkard? That Wellington won the battle of Waterloo? There are various *degrees and dimensions* of

success in making statements: the statements fit the facts always more or less loosely, in different ways on different occasions for different intents and purposes. (Austin, 1950/1979, pp. 129–30)

Austin makes two points here. First, when faced with a putative choice of this sort, we should not insist on deciding *in simple terms* whether a statement is true or false (or whether an expression applies or fails to apply to something). Some cases are complicated, and, in some of those cases, we are capable of meeting some of the complications by saying more: 'Well, it is true that Belfast is north of London if you understand that claim in the following way ...' Second, the complications can take different forms, and can matter in different ways, on different occasions. Given the prior course of our conversation, and our specific intents and purposes in discussing the issue, it might be manifest that, on that particular occasion, we will *understand* the complications, without a need for their articulation, so that the following is fine as it stands: 'Yes, it is true that Belfast is north of London.'

It's important to see that Austin's view here is based on what he takes to be our ordinary ways of assessing utterances, before we adopt the 'special tone of voice' philosophers are prone to use in talking of what is *strictly speaking* said by uses of 'Belfast is north of London'. Perhaps such special ways of talking also have their use, but that will only be apparent once we have a clear view of how we would ordinarily treat such claims.[2]

Austin summarized his view thus:

First, words are our tools, and, as a minimum, we should use clean tools: we should know what we mean and what we do not, and we must forearm ourselves against the traps that language sets us. Secondly, words are not (except in their own little corner) facts or things: we need therefore to prise them off the world, to hold them apart from and against it, so that we can realize their inadequacies and arbitrariness, and can re-look at the world without blinkers. Thirdly, and more hopefully, our common stock of words embodies all the distinctions men have found worth drawing, and the connexions they have found worth making, in the lifetimes of many generations: these surely are likely to be more sound, since they have stood up to the long test of the survival of the fittest, and more subtle, at least in all ordinary and reasonably practical matters, than any that you or I are likely to think up in our arm-chairs of an afternoon – the most favoured alternative method. (1956a/1979, pp. 181–2)

Austin holds, then, that a crucial preliminary to philosophizing on a topic – at least where the topic is 'ordinary and reasonably practical' – would be the detailed study of the language we use to speak on that topic, and of the way that we use it.

Austin met Noam Chomsky on a visit to Harvard in 1955, during which he gave the William James lectures (which were later to become his 1962b).[3] The meeting had a positive impact on both thinkers. Chomsky was immediately sympathetic to central aspects of Austin's thinking about language-use and truth. In particular, he found common cause with the view that ordinary assessment as to truth depends on specific features of the occasions on which we speak – for instance, our intents and purposes in speaking as we do.[4] Austin had long hoped (or, at least, wished) that the labour of philosophy would become more cooperative and (so) better distributed. But it may be that it was his meeting with Chomsky that induced him to consider whether the study of language that he envisaged might ultimately fall within the purview of science, rather than philosophy:

> In the history of human inquiry, philosophy has the place of the initial central sun, seminal and tumultuous: from time to time it throws off some portion of itself to take station as a science, a planet, cool and well regulated, progressing steadily towards a distant final state. This happened long ago at the birth of mathematics, and again at the birth of physics .... Is it not possible that the next century may see the birth, through the joint labours of philosophers, grammarians, and numerous other students of language, of a true and comprehensive *science of language*? Then we shall have rid ourselves of one more part of philosophy (there will still be plenty left) in the only way we ever can get rid of philosophy, by kicking it upstairs. (1956b/1979, p. 232)

It's important to see that Austin didn't think that the investigation of language was more than a preliminary to theorizing, either in philosophy or science. He wasn't averse to theory construction, even if its outcome was revisionary. His concern was only that such theorizing should be properly grounded, and not driven, for example, by any initial failure to keep track of distinctions marked in our ordinary use of language. As Hampshire alleged, Austin sought to use the same 'tone of voice' in doing philosophy that he would have used in discussing any serious subject matter.

2. Language and truth

I've already mentioned a central component of Austin's view about the relation between language and truth. This is his view that whether an utterance of ours is true or false, or involves the production of something that is true or false, is not decided solely by the linguistic expressions that we use in producing the utterance and the facts we speak about. In this section, we'll see how Austin argued for this view.

Austin viewed language as a sort of abstraction from the entire history of actions that involve speaking.[5] That is, linguistic expressions and their properties are aspects of repeatable patterns in some of the activities of speakers. In abstracting, we treat bits of language – including both words and the structures through which they combine into sentences – as repeatable types. We thereby allow that the same expressions can be used on a variety of different occasions – in and with respect to different circumstances and for various intents and purposes. On at least some of those occasions, we may use a bit of language to state something that is true or false. And a question then arises as to the role of the repeatable bit of language we use in facilitating our stating truth or falsehood: do the bits of language that we use bear properties that can determine which *statement* we make on an occasion of speaking and (so) determine, in conjunction with the facts, whether or not what we state is true? Austin gives a negative answer to this question, for two reasons. I'll deal with the first here and the second in the next section.

The first reason is that a sentence can be used to make different statements on different occasions. The way those statements depend for their truth or falsehood on the facts can vary with variation in specific features of the occasion, in particular with variation in our intents and purposes. As Austin puts it,

It seems to be fairly generally realized nowadays that, if you just take a bunch of sentences ... impeccably formulated in some language or other, there can be no question of sorting them out into those that are true and those that are false; for (leaving out of account so-called 'analytic' sentences) the question of truth and falsehood does not turn only on what a sentence *is*, nor yet on what it *means*, but on, speaking very broadly, the circumstances in which it is uttered. Sentences *as such* are not either true or false. (1962a, pp. 110–11)

We've already come across one ground that Austin offers for this striking claim. The assessment of a type of utterance as true or false can be bound up with the complications involved in particular cases in a way that may be understood, rather than articulated. And what is understood on one occasion may not be understood on another, so that it is right on one occasion, and not the other, to claim simply that an utterance of some type is true. A related ground is presented in the following passage:

... in the case of stating truly or falsely, just as in the case of advising well or badly, the intents and purposes of the utterance and its context are important; what is judged true in a school book may not be so judged in a work of historical research. Consider ... 'Lord Raglan won the battle of Alma', remembering that Alma was a soldier's battle if ever there was one and that Lord Raglan's orders were never transmitted to some of his subordinates. Did Lord Raglan then win the battle of Alma or did he not? Of course in some contexts, perhaps in a school book, it is perfectly justifiable to say so – it is something of an exaggeration, maybe, and there would be no question of giving Raglan a medal for it ... 'Lord Raglan won the battle of Alma' is exaggerated and suitable to some contexts and not to others; it would be pointless to insist on *its* [i.e. the *sentence's*] truth or falsehood. (1962b, pp. 143–4, my emphasis and interpolation)

It's important here to separate two questions. First, is the *sentence* 'Lord Raglan won the battle of Alma' true? Second, is any particular *statement*, made in using that sentence on a particular occasion, true? In order for the first question to get an affirmative answer, *every* use of the sentence would have to be – or issue in a statement that is – true.[6] But although the sentence can be used in a schoolbook to make a statement that is true, it might also be used in a work of historical research, or in support of Raglan's decoration, in making a false statement. Hence, the sentence doesn't take the same truth-value on *every* occasion: the sentence per se is neither true nor false. By contrast, there is no reason to deny that particular statements made on occasion in using the sentence are true: in particular, there is no reason to deny that the statement made by the schoolbook occurrence of the sentence is true. So, the second question can be given an affirmative answer, as long as we are willing to allow that a sentence can be used to make different statements on different occasions.[7]

We should avoid two possible misunderstandings of Austin here. First, his argument shows, at most, that whatever conspires with the facts to determine a particular truth-value varies from occasion to occasion. That does nothing to dislodge the natural view that a sentence can carry its meaning with it from occasion to occasion, and thus possess a literal meaning. However, if we wish to retain that idea, we must give up on the idea that sentence meaning simply conspires with the facts that are being spoken about to determine truth-value: we must reject the idea that sentence meanings determine truth-conditions. In taking this line, we would reject views of meaning according to which they are given by appeal to truth-conditions, as proposed, for example, by Donald Davidson (1967/2001; see the chapter on Davidson for further details). Second, the argument does not rule out that sentences can be used to state truths or falsehoods, as might be suggested by one reading of the following passage:

> Suppose that we confront 'France is hexagonal' with the facts, in this case, I suppose, with France, is it true or false? Well, if you like, up to a point; of course I can see what you mean by saying that it is true for certain intents and purposes. It is good enough for a top-ranking general, perhaps, but not for a geographer ... How can one answer this question, whether it is true or false that France is hexagonal? It is just rough, and that is the right and final answer to the question of the relation of 'France is hexagonal' to France. It is a rough description; it is not a true or a false one. (1962a, p. 143)

What Austin characterizes in his final denial is the *sentence* 'France is hexagonal', in relation to France. He needn't, and doesn't, deny that on occasion, for particular intents and purposes, one might use it to *state* a truth.

Now suppose that someone uttered 'France is hexagonal' out of the blue, without making manifest any intents and purposes. In that case, there would be nothing to go on, in seeking to establish whether the utterance was true or false, other than the words used, given their meanings. But those words might have been used to make a variety of statements, statements whose truth or falsehood depends on the facts in a variety of ways. Hence, unless we are willing to allow that the utterance is both true and false, we should withhold that mode of assessment: although such an utterance would involve a perfectly *meaningful* sentence, it would fail to be either true or false. Austin thought that our uses of words are always liable to that sort of failure, especially when we are doing philosophy. When used in cases that are out of the ordinary, or in the absence of the background required to sustain the statement of truths or falsehoods, words might literally fail us.

3. Language and speech acts

In this section, we'll consider the second reason that sentences, given their meanings, do not conspire with the facts to determine truth-values. The second reason is based on the fact that any sentence can be used in performing a variety of linguistic acts. Although in stating, we typically produce statements that are assessable as true or false, in performing other linguistic acts, we need not produce things that are assessable in that way. The second reason depends, then, on two sub-claims: first, that whether a sentence is used on an occasion to make a *statement* is dependent on more than just what it means; second, that some uses of sentences to perform linguistic acts other than the making of statements are not properly assessable as true or false.

Austin presents the second reason in considering whether there is a useful distinction to be drawn between (indicative) sentences that are used to make statements – which Austin labels *constatives* – and sentences that are useable in the performance of some act – which Austin labels *performatives* (or sometimes *performatory*).[8] Austin's opening list of examples of putative performatives includes: 'I take ... to be my lawfully wedded ...' – as uttered in the course of the marriage ceremony; 'I name this ship the *Queen Elizabeth*' – as uttered when smashing a bottle against the stern; 'I give and bequeath my watch to my brother' – as occurring in a will; 'I bet you sixpence it will rain tomorrow' (1962b, p. 5). About these examples, Austin writes:

> In these examples it seems clear that to utter the sentence (in, of course, the appropriate circumstances) is not to *describe* my doing of what I should be said in so uttering to be doing ... [fn. Still less anything that I have already done or have yet to do.] ... or to state that I am doing it. None of the utterances cited is either true or false: I assert this as obvious and do not argue it. (1962b, p. 6)

Austin is sometimes read as seeking to defend this view of performatives. However, four features of his presentation suggest that his view is not so straightforward. First, Austin presents the issue as concerning the classification by use of utterances of *types of sentence*, and we have already seen that he is in general sceptical about alleged associations between sentences and their occasional uses. Second, Austin fails here, and elsewhere, to offer serious arguments for his assertion that none of the cited utterances is either true or false. Third, Austin's assertion is made using the apparently performative form, 'I assert ...' – a form that appears, moreover, to falsify the generalization that performatives lack truth-values. Finally, Austin issues the following warning in a footnote, two pages earlier: 'Everything said in these sections is provisional, and subject to revision in the light of later sections' (1962b, p. 4, fn.1).

Austin goes on to discuss two apparently quite different modes of assessment for utterances of the two apparently different types. Constatives, as already noted, are assessed along the dimension of truth and falsehood. By contrast, performatives are assessed along dimensions of *happiness* and *unhappiness*, or *felicity* and *infelicity*. Taking the example of an utterance of 'I take ... to be my lawfully wedded ...', and simplifying Austin's discussion, there are two main sorts of unhappiness, or infelicity, to which this performative is liable. First, there are *misfires*:

... if we ... utter the formula incorrectly, or if ... we are not in a position to do the act because we are ... married already, or it is the purser and not the captain who is conducting the ceremony, then the act in question, ... marrying, is not successfully performed at all, ... [it] is not achieved. (1962b, pp. 15–16)

Second, there are *abuses*: in these cases, the act is performed, but insincerely – perhaps, for example, in instituting a marriage of convenience.

It's important to see that, even if it were true, in general, that some things done using performatives – for example, marrying, naming, bequeathing and betting – are neither true nor false, but rather are subject to assessment as happy or unhappy, it would not follow that truth is out of the picture. That would depend, not only on the basic claim that actions of those types per se are not true or false, but also on the claim that particular actions of those types are not also of other types that *are* assessable as true or false. And Austin recognized that actions can be of more than one type:

To say that I believe you 'is' on occasion to accept your statement; but it is also to make an assertion, which is not made by the strictly performatory utterance 'I accept your statement'. (1950/1979, p. 133)

In the examples that Austin cites, things are done that are not assessable as true or false – marrying, naming, betting and so forth. But as Austin points out, those examples might also involve other things being done – for example, the making of statements – that are, or involve things that are, assessable as true or false. However, even though this undermines Austin's provisional characterization of performatives, the possibility that we might sometimes do more than one thing in using a performative puts pressure on the idea that there is a simple connection between sentences and the various things we do in using them.

I've suggested that Austin's view of the putative distinction between performatives and constatives is less straightforward than it might at first seem. And the structure of Austin (1962b) bears out that assessment. Although much of the book seems to be devoted to pursuit of a distinction between performatives and constatives, none of the attempts succeeds. It is possible, but implausible, that in the course of the lectures Austin found that he was unable to draw a distinction that he thought should be drawn. A more plausible interpretation is that Austin's purpose is not to draw such a distinction. Rather it is to argue – through the failures of various attempts to draw the distinction – that there is no such simple distinction – no sorting of sentences into those apt for performative, and those apt for constative, use.

Austin argues against the distinction by appeal to the fact that the same forms of assessment are applicable to utterances apparently of both sorts:

> ... unhappiness ... seems to characterize both kinds of utterance, not merely the performative; and ... the requirement of conforming or bearing some relation to the facts, different in different cases, seems to characterize performatives .... (1962b, p. 91)

Attempts to make a statement are liable both to misfires and abuses. For example, an attempt to make a statement using 'France is hexagonal' might misfire if there were no such country as France, or (as discussed above) if no suitable intents and purposes were manifest (1962b, pp. 47–52). And an attempt might be an abuse if the speaker failed to believe that France was hexagonal. Attempts at performative utterance are liable to assessment either in terms of truth or falsehood, or in terms similarly dependent on conformity with the facts: my utterance of 'I warn you that the bull is about to charge' may be liable to criticism as *mistaken* rather than unhappy if the bull is not about to charge (1962b, p. 55). More generally, it is often impossible to decide, just from the words a speaker uses, whether their utterance is susceptible to one or another form of assessment. And there are cases like 'I state that ...' which seem to satisfy all formal and lexical requirements for being performative, and yet are used in utterances '... which surely are the making of statements, and surely are essentially true or false' (1962b, p. 91).

From the wreckage of the initial distinction, Austin assembles a new model. The new model is founded on distinctions among various kinds of thing speakers do – various *acts* they perform – when they produce an utterance.

The locutionary act: the production of an utterance that can be classified by its phonetic, grammatical, and lexical characteristics, up to sentence meaning (the *phatic* act). It is also the performance of an act that can be classified by its *content* (the *rhetic* act) – a feature distinctively of acts of speech. If I promise *that I'll be home for dinner* and then promise *that I'll work late*, my actions are instances of two different locutionary acts: one with the content that I'll be home for dinner, and one with the content that I'll work late. (See 1962b, pp. 94–8)

The illocutionary act: an act classifiable not only by its content – as with the locutionary act – but also by its *force* (stating, warning, promising etc.). If I *promise* that I'll be home for dinner and later *state* that I'll be home for dinner, my actions are instances of the same locutionary act: both actions involve the content that I'll be home for dinner. However, my actions are instances of different illocutionary acts: one has the force of a promise, while the other has the force of a statement. (See 1962b, pp. 98–101)

The perlocutionary act: an act classifiable by its '… consequential effects upon the feelings, thoughts, or actions of the audience, or of the speaker, or of other persons …'. If I warn that the ice is thin, and so perform one illocutionary act, I may thereby perform a variety of perlocutionary acts: I may *persuade* someone to avoid it, or *encourage* someone to take a risk, and so forth. (See 1962b, p. 101)

Austin's interest in the types of act so distinguished was '… essentially to fasten on the second, illocutionary act and contrast it with the other two …' (1962b, p. 103). What did Austin think was important about the illocutionary act? And what did he think were the dangers inherent in failing to mark it off from the other types?

Austin appears to have thought that the various modes of assessment that he discusses – for example, true/false, happy/unhappy – properly apply to the *illocutionary* act, rather than the locutionary or the perlocutionary act. One point is that Austin thought that philosophers have had a tendency to view some assessments as to happiness (or felicity) as really applying to perlocutionary acts, so as not bearing on the specifically linguistic things that speakers are up to. Another point – and perhaps the point of primary importance – is that Austin thought that philosophers have had a tendency to view assessments as to truth as really applying to locutionary acts. Moreover, he thought that philosophers had conceived locutionary acts, not as abstractions from illocutionary acts, but rather as things that might be done without any illocutionary purpose, just by virtue of the linguistic expressions employed or their meanings. By contrast, Austin held that locutionary acts are abstracted from instances of illocutionary acts, and that assessment as to truth is directed most fundamentally to the illocutionary act.

For Austin, then, assessment as to truth is of a piece with various forms of assessment as to happiness, and like those forms it is the assessment of an act with respect to its goodness or badness. Thus Austin's discussion of illocutionary acts is bound up with his other discussions of the ways in which assessment of utterances as to truth is dependent upon specific features of the circumstances of utterance. He writes:

> The truth or falsity of statements is affected by what they leave out or put in and by their being misleading, and so on. Thus, for example, descriptions, which are said to be true or false or, if you like, are 'statements', are surely liable to these criticisms, since they are selective and uttered for a purpose. *It is essential to realize that 'true' and false', like 'free' and 'unfree', do not stand for anything simple at all;* but only for a general dimension of being a right and proper thing to say as opposed to a wrong thing, in these circumstances, to this audience, for these purposes and with these intentions. (1962b, pp. 144–5, emphasis added)

According to Austin, there is more involved in any such assessment than a simple comparison of requirements imposed by linguistic meaning with the facts.

4. Responses to Austin

The reception of Austin's work has been mixed. On the one hand, distinctions between locutionary, illocutionary and perlocutionary acts have assumed something like canonical status in philosophy and linguistics – though largely detached from the argumentative purposes to which Austin had put them. On the other hand, Austin's purpose in drawing the distinctions in the way that he did, and his specific views on the role of occasion-specific intents and purposes in shaping the assessment of utterances as to truth, have not won widespread acceptance. It is beyond the scope of this chapter to examine fully the reasons for this pattern, but I shall briefly examine a partial explanation.

The two major critical responses to Austin's work in the philosophy of language pull in different directions. The first, and most important, is that it is – perhaps by nature of its target – insufficiently systematic. The second is that it aims for more discipline than the phenomena warrant. In part, the first response is bolstered and maintained by fear that there is something to the second.

In an early critical response, W. V. Quine raised two main concerns from the perspective of the systematizer. His first concern was broadly methodological:

> I suppose that before Einstein some astronomers pondered [the perturbations of Mercury] with an eager curiosity, hoping that they might be a key to important traits of nature hitherto undetected, while other astronomers saw in them a vexatious anomaly and longed to see how to explain them away in terms of instrumental error. Attitudes towards philosophical problems vary similarly, and Austin's was of the negative kind. (1965/1969, p. 89)[9]

A related complaint would be that Austin's eye for detail blinded him to systematic patterns that are only accessible through idealization. Quine's second concern can be seen as a particular application of that complaint:

> Tarski's paradigm ... works for evaluations ... as well as for statements of fact ... And it works equally well for performatives. ... 'I bid you good morning' is true of us on a given occasion if and only if, on that occasion, I bid you good morning. (1965/1969, p. 90)

'Tarski's paradigm' is that every instance of (T) is true, where 'S' is a sentence of English:

(T) 'S' is true if and only if S.[10]

So, for example, we have the instance in (1):

(1) 'France is hexagonal' is true if and only if France is hexagonal.

Quine's claim was that the paradigm supplies a simple model for the assessment of sentences as to truth. He thought that the simple model avoided the need to take into account the illocutionary forces with which sentences are uttered, or other features of the specific occasion of their utterance.

Well, we've seen that Austin's view of performatives is less clear-cut than Quine suggests. But Austin also provides grounds for a different response. Sentences can be used on different occasions with a variety of intents and purposes. Austin makes it plausible that, because of this, ordinary assessment as to truth of the illocutionary act performed through use of a sentence can vary from occasion to occasion. Consider an occasion, say a school lesson, on which 'France is hexagonal' is used to state something true. Now if we view that assessment as applying to the *sentence*, we will have that the sentence 'France is hexagonal' is true. And then, from (T), we will have that France *is* hexagonal. And now a geographer who denies that France is hexagonal will thereby be found, implausibly, to be in error. Except as an idealization – which may be useful or important for particular purposes – Austin provides reasons for rejecting instances of (T). Insofar as such idealization is inappropriate when it comes to accounting for the details of our linguistic activities and abilities, Austin would have rejected such accounts in which instances of (T) – or principles like it in forging close connections between meaning and truth-conditions – play a central role. (See the chapter on Davidson for discussion of one such account.)

Austin's student, Paul Grice, offered a related, and much more developed, response to Austin (Grice, 1989, from lectures given in 1967). Grice attempted to mark off a notion of what is said in utterances that is both assessable as to truth and also determined, more or less, by the sentence used in the utterance. Most importantly, he sought to explain apparent variation in assessment as to truth as due, not to variation in what is 'strictly and literally' *said* or *stated*, but rather to variation in what is *implicated* by its being said, what he called the utterance's *implicature*. Roughly, where Austin views speakers' intents and purposes as mediating a transition from the stable linguistic meanings of their words to (e.g.) what they state, Grice views their intents and purposes as mediating a transition from (e.g.) what they state to what they implicate. It has seemed to many philosophers that Grice's account provides a means of protecting views on which meaning is closely associated with truth and truth-conditions from the threat to those views implicit in Austin's account. Grice's work has played a central role in the negative reception of the core of Austin's work, and coming to grips with it is essential to a proper assessment of Austin's views. (See the chapter on Grice for further details and discussion.)

The second, opposing type of critical response is that Austin's account is *too* systematic. Jacques Derrida argued that Austin's account is skewed by his failure to take into account (what Austin refers to as) *non-serious* uses of language – for example, uses of language in making jokes, on the stage, speaking nonsense. Derrida suggests that, if we take all these uses of language into account, then it will be impossible to separate out the literal meanings of words and sentences from the clouds of associations that they carry. And those clouds will change shape with each new use of a word (Derrida, 1977/1982). Fear that an account more like Grice's than Austin's is required to preserve theoretical order in the face of the sort of chaos that Derrida depicts may have played a role in the comparative assessment of those accounts. (See the chapter on Derrida for further discussion.)

Derrida's suggestion points to a way in which the order contained in Austin's account may be *imposed* as much as it is discerned. If that is right, then a central question is whether – or rather, for what purposes – we should seek to simplify, or to make more complex, the sketch that Austin provides.

Further reading

In addition to Austin (1961/1979), (1962a) and (1962b), the reminiscences contained in Fann (1969), and Berlin et al. (1973), are worthwhile. Warnock (1991) is an excellent book length treatment of Austin's work. Longworth (2017a) provides a more concise overview of Austin's life and work. Hornsby (2006) provides a useful discussion of Austin's and others' work on speech acts and performatives. Travis (2008) is an important defence of

Austin's views about the relations between meaning and truth. Longworth (2017b), connects Austin's work on speech acts with his work on truth, and discusses both with reference to Grice's critical response. There is a recording of Austin's voice at: https://olponline. wordpress.com/2010/07/29/audio-j-l-austins-voice.

Notes

1   Austin on 'principle':

> How would one respond, say as an examiner, to the offer of a bribe? Hare (if memory serves) said that he would say 'I don't take bribes, on principle.' Austin said: 'Would you, Hare? I think I'd say "No, thanks".' (Warnock, 1973, p. 40, fn. 6)

2   Consider again Austin's reply to Hare (note 1, above). Austin would have viewed claims to the effect that 'Belfast is north of London' *strictly speaking* is always used to state the same thing about the cities' relation, and so to state something true on every use, or something false on every use, as out of the ordinary in the same way as Hare's suggested reply. That doesn't show that such claims aren't true, but only that they should be seen as special and in need of special motivation.

3   Chomsky (1957), was discussed at Austin's 'Saturday mornings' discussion group in the term before Austin's death (Warnock, 1963/1969, p. 15).

4   Chomsky (2000, p. 132), mentions Austin as an influence on Chomsky (1957).

5   See Austin (1962b, pp. 1 (fn.1), 20, 147, 148).

6   The requirement here would have to be made more complicated in order to cope with the different way that truth can vary across contexts due to indexicals (e.g. 'here', 'now') or demonstratives (e.g. 'this'). However, since the sentences we are considering do not (explicitly) involve indexicals or demonstratives, we can ignore that complication for present purposes.

7   The bases for an array of such examples can be found in Austin (1962a, pp. 62–77).

8   Austin (1962b). Austin first appeals to something like the distinction in 1946/1979, pp. 97–103, in discussing the function of claims to know.

9   Recall Austin's comment that one reason for taking care in our use of language is that we should ensure that our tools are clean.

10   Note that Tarski thought that analogues of (T) applied only to
     regimented formal languages and not to natural languages. See Tarski
     (1933/1983). So it's not clear that Tarski's view of (T) is in conflict
     with Austin's.

Bibliography

Austin, J. L. (1946/1979), 'Other Minds', *Proceedings of the Aristotelian
    Society*, Suppl. Vol., 20, pp. 148–87. Reprinted in Austin, 1979,
    pp. 76–116.

Austin, J. L. (1950/1979), 'Truth', *Proceedings of the Aristotelian Society*,
    suppl. vol., 24, pp. 111–28. Reprinted in Austin, 1979, pp. 117–33.

Austin, J. L. (1956a/1979), 'A Plea for Excuses', *Proceedings of
    the Aristotelian Society*, 57: 1–30. Reprinted in Austin, 1979,
    pp. 175–204.

Austin, J. L. (1956b/1979), 'Ifs and Cans', *Proceedings of the British
    Academy*, 42, pp. 109–32. Reprinted in Austin, 1979, pp. 205–32.

Austin, J. L. (1962a), *Sense and Sensibilia*, ed. G. J. Warnock.
    Oxford: Oxford University Press.

Austin, J. L. (1962b), *How to Do Things with Words*, ed. J. O. Urmson
    and Marina Sbisà. Oxford: Oxford University Press.

Austin, J. L. (1979), *Philosophical Papers*, 3rd edn. Oxford: Clarendon
    Press (1st edn, 1961).

Berlin, I. et al. (1973), *Essays on J. L. Austin*. Oxford: Clarendon Press.

Chomsky, N. (1957), *Syntactic Structures*. The Hague/Paris: Mouton.

Chomsky, N. (2000), *New Horizons in the Study of Language and Mind*.
    Cambridge: Cambridge University Press.

Davidson, D. (1967/2001), 'Truth and Meaning', *Synthese*, 17 (1), pp.
    304–23. Reprinted in his *Inquiries into Truth and Interpretation*.
    Oxford: Clarendon Press, pp. 17–42.

Derrida, J. (1977/1982), 'Signature, Event, Context', *Glyph*, 1. Baltimore,
    MD: Johns Hopkins Press, pp. 172–97. Reproduced in his *Margins of
    Philosophy*, trans. Alan Bass. Brighton: Harvester Press, pp. 307–30.

Fann, K. T. (ed.) (1969), *Symposium on J. L. Austin*. London: Routledge
    & Kegan Paul.

Grice, P. (1989), *Studies in the Way of Words*. Cambridge, MA: Harvard
    University Press.

Hampshire, S. (1960/1969), 'J. L. Austin, 1911–1960', *Proceedings of the
    Aristotelian Society*, 60, pp. i–xiv. Reprinted in Fann, 1969, pp. 33–46.

Hornsby, J. (2006), 'Speech Acts and Performatives', in E. Lepore and B.
    C. Smith (eds), *The Oxford Handbook of Philosophy of Language*.
    Oxford: Oxford University Press, pp. 893–909.

Longworth, G. (2017a), 'John Langshaw Austin', *The Stanford Encyclopedia of Philosophy* (Spring 2017 Edition), ed. Edward N. Zalta. https://plato.stanford.edu/archives/spr2017/entries/austin-jl/.

Longworth, G. (2017b), 'Semantics and Pragmatics', in B. Hale, C. Wright, and A. Miller (eds) *A Companion to the Philosophy of Language*. Oxford: John Wiley.

Quine, W. V. (1965/1969), 'J. L. Austin: Comment', *Journal of Philosophy*, 62 (19), pp. 509–10. Reprinted in full in Fann, 1969, pp. 86–90.

Tarski, A. (1933/1983), 'The Concept of Truth in the Languages of the Deductive Sciences'. Expanded English translation in his *Logic, Semantics, Metamathematics,* ed. John Corcoran. Indianapolis, IN: Hackett, pp. 152–278.

Travis, C. (2008), *Occasion-Sensitivity: Selected Essays*. Oxford: Oxford University Press.

Warnock, G. J. (1963/1969), 'John Langshaw Austin: A Biographical Sketch'. *Proceedings of the British Academy*. Reprinted in Fann, 1969, pp. 3–21.

Warnock, G. J. (1973), 'Saturday Mornings', in Berlin et al., 1973, pp. 31–45.

Warnock, G. J. (1991) *J. L. Austin*. London: Routledge.

CHAPTER SEVEN

WITTGENSTEIN: *PHILOSOPHICAL INVESTIGATIONS*

Arif Ahmed

1. Transition

Having completed the *Tractatus*, Wittgenstein left philosophy for a decade before returning to it, and Cambridge, in 1929. He sought at first to remedy what then appeared to be local defects in the *Tractatus*, for example, his treatment of chromatic exclusion.

The fundamental point of the *Tractatus* is that whatever can be said at all can be said clearly. In particular, any sentence of ordinary language should have an analysis that clearly displays just what demand it makes on reality: that is, in which possible circumstances it would be true and in which false. And if two sentences p and q make incompatible demands on reality, so that they *could* not be true at once, then their analyses should display this too. The analyses should show that in every possible circumstance that made p true, some proposition r was both true in that circumstance and such that its *negation* was true in every possible circumstance that made q true. This is the meaning of Wittgenstein's claim in the *Tractatus* that the only necessity that exists is logical necessity (*TLP* 6.37).

But if we consider the proposition p that a given point in the visual field is green, and the proposition q that that same point is red, it looks as though we have two propositions that cannot satisfy the demand. For whatever incompatibility there is between them isn't *logical*. In the *Tractatus* Wittgenstein had proposed to analyse these propositions into ones that *were* logically incompatible (*TLP* 6.3751). But his suggestions for such analyses – for instance, the proposition that a certain particle has some velocity and the proposition that it has some other velocity – looked no more *logically* incompatible than what they were analysing.

Whatever conviction this counterexample ultimately carries, its effect upon Wittgenstein was to encourage re-examination of not only the details but also the basic orientation of his earlier philosophy of language. The works of the consequent 'middle' period 1929–36 – now published as *Philosophical Remarks*, *Philosophical Grammar*, *The Big Typescript*, *The Blue Book* and *The Brown Book* – bear witness to a lengthy internal struggle between the intellectual spirit of the *Tractatus* and something quite new. *Philosophical Investigations* ('PI' below) is the monument of the new philosophy and of its victory over the old one.

The *Investigations* is not just a critique of Wittgenstein's earlier work; it also constitutes a forceful attack on a conception of language that continues to inform the philosophical study of it today. At the micro-level, Wittgenstein is expressly hostile to what remains today the dominant approach to sentential meaning, namely the approach that holds that it is best explained in terms of a given sentence's *truth-conditions*, as opposed to its *use-conditions*. And at the macro-level, he is implicitly sceptical of the idea that linguistic understanding can be construed as tacit grasp of a formal theory.

2. The Augustinian picture

Much of what lay behind that older doctrine as well as these more recent ones is also in the background of the Augustinian quotation with which PI opens.

> When they (my elders) named some object, and accordingly moved towards something, I saw this and I grasped that the thing was called by the sound they uttered when they meant to point

it out. Their intention was shewn by their bodily movements, as it were the natural language of all peoples: the expression of the face, the play of the eyes, the movement of the other parts of the body, and the tone of voice which expresses our state of mind in seeking, having, rejecting, or avoiding something. Thus, as I heard words repeatedly used in their proper places in various sentences, I gradually learnt to understand what objects they signified; and after I had trained my mouth to form these signs, I used them to express my own desires. (Augustine, *Confessions*, I. 8)

According to Wittgenstein, this Augustinian 'picture' includes three claims: (a) that names mean what they refer to (equivalently: what they *denote*); (b) that language consists of arrangements of names; (c) that names may be introduced into language by means of ostension. This last was not a doctrine of the *Tractatus* (though the first two were – see *TLP* 3.201, 4.0311), but it *was* at work in Russell's 'Principle of Acquaintance' (Russell, 2001, p. 32).

Let us focus for the moment on (a) and (b). Wittgenstein doesn't argue against these claims directly, in the sense, for example, of producing obvious counterexamples. Look at the 'grocer' example (PI, 1d).

Now think of the following use of language: I send someone shopping. I give him a slip marked "five red apples". He takes the slip to the shopkeeper, who opens the drawer marked "apples"; then he looks up the word "red" in a table and finds a colour sample opposite it; then he says the series of elementary number-words – I assume that he knows them by heart – up to the word "five", and for each number-word he takes an apple of the same colour as the sample out of the drawer. — It is in this and similar ways that one operates with words.

Here we are not told that 'five' or 'red' have meanings other than what they denote; the point is rather that our actual operations involving the words are indifferent to *what* they denote.

PI 2–4 expand upon the theme of PI 1c: that the Augustinian 'picture of language' that may be discerned in the opening quotation is more appropriate to some kinds of language than to others. Thus, compare the first 'builders' example (PI, 2b) with the 'grocer' example.

Let us imagine a language for which the description given by Augustine is right: the language is meant to serve for communication between a builder A and an assistant B. A is building with building stones: there are blocks, pillars, slabs and beams. B has to pass him the stones and to do so in the order in which A needs them. For this purpose they make use of a language consisting of the words "block", "pillar", "slab", "beam". A calls them out; B brings the stone which he has learnt to bring at such-and-such a call. — Conceive of this as a complete primitive language.

There is some sort of point in assigning to 'block' what the Augustinian picture represents as its meaning, that is, blocks; for it is blocks that the builder's assistant picks up when he hears 'Block!' Does any analogous point about the customer's operations with 'five' motivate us to say that it refers to whatever peculiar denoted object the Augustinian picture represents as *its* meaning?

Now this doesn't *compel* us to deny that the meaning of an expression is in all cases its reference. We could say that however it is used each word refers none the less to something (including the words 'five', 'not' and so on). But what would be the point? The question is not whether that doctrine can be defended through thick and thin (anything *can* be defended through thick and thin); the questions are rather: why one should want to defend it in the first place; and whether doing so leaves anything *worth* defending. Wittgenstein's answer to the first question is that we are misled: we take the uniformity in the form of our words to indicate a uniformity in what makes them meaningful (cf. the 'locomotive' example, PI, 12). And his answer to the second question is that if we insist that all words stand in a relation called 'reference' to some extraverbal bit of reality, then the notion of 'reference' becomes so thin that we have said *nothing*.

Wittgenstein then attacks the specific version of (a) and (b) that we find in the *Tractatus*. The two essential points of it are: (i) that ordinary English 'names' are not real names; (ii) that real names denote *simple* objects.

Doctrine (i) had been common to Wittgenstein (the general attitude is well expressed at *TLP* 4.002, 4.0031) and Russell (for whom the only real name was 'This'; see Russell, 1985, p. 62). In

PI, Wittgenstein considers an argument for it from the premise that real names are the *simple* elements of language.

(1) Real names are *not* further analysable

(2) Ordinary names *are* analysable

(3) Therefore ordinary names are not real names

What motivates (2) is the thought that ordinary names denote *complex* objects (e.g. a broom); it is supposed to follow that statements involving them can therefore be analysed into ones whose terms denote not these complex objects but their simpler constituents (e.g. the brush and the broomstick). Analysis thus conceived was prominent in the *Tractatus*, and it was supposed to terminate in names for simple objects (*TLP*, 2.0201; see also PI, 87a).

But Wittgenstein rejects that motivation for (2) at PI 60–4. Although he accepts (PI, 79) that ordinary names abbreviate definite descriptions (or clusters of them) that pick out physically complex objects, he denies that what one means by 'The broom is in the corner' is revealed more clearly by an analysis like 'The brush is in the corner and the broomstick is in the corner and the broomstick is fitted in the brush'. The point at PI 60 is that these sentences don't obviously mean the same; and while he concedes at PI 61 that they *may* mean the same, his view is that an aspect of meaning may also be *lost* in translation, for instance (PI, 63–4) because it is blind to the unity or gestalt of those experiences whose descriptions it dissects.

The most important argument that Wittgenstein considers for (ii) is from *Theaetetus* (PI, 46). Real names, being simple, cannot themselves describe any situation in reality; so:

(4) If 'A' is a real name then 'A exists' does not make sense

(5) If 'A' denotes a complex then 'A exists' makes sense

(6) Therefore real names don't denote complexes

Wittgenstein denies (5) for reasons that he presents by analogy with the standard metre rod (PI, 50). This is something of which it makes no sense to assert that it is, or that it is not, exactly one metre long. Why? Not because there is anything special about that rod, but simply because it plays a certain role in the practice of measurement, that is, as a final arbiter. Similarly those things of which, *in a given language*, it makes no sense to say that they exist or that they do not, have no special properties (such as 'simplicity'). It is just that they play a particular role *in that language*.

You might object that a language whose names denote complexes somehow fails to match reality, for it presents as simple what is really complex. Could we not at least say that (5) holds of *ideal* languages? But Wittgenstein denies any absolute notion of 'simplicity' or 'composition'; so there is no saying whether one language approaches more or less closely than another to that ideal:

> Is the colour of a square on a chessboard simple, or does it consist of pure white and pure yellow? And is white simple, or does it consist of the colours of the rainbow? – Is this length of 2 cm simple, or does it consist of two parts, each 1 cm long? But why not one bit 3 cm long and one bit 1 cm long measured in the opposite direction? (PI, 47)

Let us move on to (c): names can be introduced by ostensive definition. You point at the reference of a word, or otherwise bring it to a pupil's attention, and that is how he comes to understand it. Wittgenstein's point is not that ostension can *never* achieve that, but rather that ostension cannot be *all* that connects words to their referents. The reason is that the pupil has to know how to interpret the pointing gesture, and in particular how to identify its object. If I point at a man while saying his name, how is the pupil supposed to settle that I mean the *man* and not, for example, his *height* or his *demeanour*, or even a direction of the compass (PI, 28)?

Instead of directly answering this question Wittgenstein now asks another: what made it true about *me* that *I* meant that man and not his demeanour? Clearly my accompanying behaviour won't normally settle it: it isn't as though I screw up my eyes or move my fingers in some special way whenever I point to a man and not his demeanour. (Of course, it might happen that I usually say in such cases 'That *man* is called …'. But I will not say this if I am teaching the name to a pupil who does not understand 'man'.)

Now *because* no type of behaviour invariably distinguishes pointing at a man from pointing at his demeanour, there is a strong temptation to postulate a *mental process*: an inner experience 'behind' my behaviour that turns it from *mere* behaviour into a meaningful act.

> Where our language suggests a body and there is none: there, we should like to say, is a *spirit*. (PI, 36)

But this complicates our first question: if my meaning what I did by the ostension was some inner process that accompanied the 'mere' pointing, then we are going to have to credit my pupil with some sort of X-ray capacity to see into that realm.

Wittgenstein argues that no such inner experience is either necessary (PI, 35a) or sufficient (PI, 34, 35a) for my meaning what I did. Not necessary because there *is* no one experience of 'meaning this and not that': there are just different experiences on different occasions, and – though he does not say this here – on many occasions there are none (cf. PI, 171b). And not sufficient because even if the pupil *knew* my experiences or had them himself, he could still *understand* the name to mean something else:

> But suppose someone said "I always do the same thing when I attend to the shape: my eye follows the outline and I feel ..." And suppose this person to give someone else the ostensive definition "That is called a 'circle'", pointing to a circular object and having all those experiences——cannot his hearer still interpret the definition differently, even though he sees the other's eyes following the outline, and even though he feels what the other feels? (PI, 34)

But then what *does* make the difference between pointing at a man and pointing at his demeanour? – and how does the pupil tell? The answer to both questions lies not *behind* any bit of behaviour but in what *surrounds* it. This will become clearer when we discuss rule-following.

3. Family resemblance

The discussion so far has looked at many mini-languages, that is, relatively simple and localized activities with uses of words woven into them: languages whose terms do not refer (PI, 1), whose terms do refer (PI, 2), whose names can be meaningful without referring (PI, 41) or whose sentences combine names (PI, 48). Wittgenstein calls these mini-languages 'language-games' (PI, 7). And at PI 65 he raises an objection to this pluralistic conception of language: what do all of these language-games have in common that warrants their being called *languages*? Doesn't language have an essence? And isn't that what the *Tractatus* sought? (And, at *TLP* 4.5, what it found?)

Here we reach the famous comparison with games, implicit all along in the term 'language-game'. 'Game' emphasizes that language is a human activity: words only become language if they connect with our uses of them (PI, 23; PI, 43). But it also alludes to the fact that linguistic practices, like games, have *no one thing in common that makes us use the same word for all*. In attacking the idea that they do, Wittgenstein is disrupting a line of thought that goes back to Plato (*Euthyphro* 5d; for further discussion see Forster, 2010) and which had hitherto seemed almost irresistible to philosophers and non-philosophers alike.

For instance there are different similarities between different games. As Wittgenstein says (PI, 66) these can be criss-cross: some games resemble one another in virtue of being played with cards (like poker and snap), others in virtue of having a gambling element (poker and backgammon). And they may overlap: 'Snakes and Ladders' resembles backgammon in virtue of involving a board and also in virtue of involving dice. Wittgenstein calls these *family* resemblances; and we may say that concepts whose instances are so variously united, that no one common feature makes us use the same word for all, are *family resemblance concepts*.

But if no one thing is common to their instances – at least none that helps me distinguish, for example, games from non-games – then how did I *learn* enough of the meanings of 'game' or 'language' to judge of their application in new cases? Well, how do we explain the terms to someone else? '[W]e should describe games to him, and we might add: "This *and similar things* are called 'games' "' (PI, 69). And that is roughly how you and I learnt 'game' too.

But that leaves it wide open what the 'similar things' are. Everything is similar to anything else in *some* respect. So it can seem as though his grasp of 'game' is something lodged within the teacher's breast at which his merely verbal explanations can only *gesture*; as though the pupil has somehow to *guess* the essential thing – in this case how to take 'similar'.

At PI 72–3 Wittgenstein engages this doctrine on what is, so to speak, its home ground: the case of chromatic terms. Here it gets combined with the idea of understanding as a kind of inner *vision*. I can give you examples of green things: but in order to get what I mean, mustn't you *have in mind* what I do? And doesn't my 'having this in mind' consist in quasi-sensory contact with an inner object whose nature I must somehow impart to you?

So Locke thought: it was one basis for his doctrine of abstract ideas (*Essay*, III.iii.6–7). The 'inner idea' guides my use of 'green' by serving as a standard with which I compare *outer* candidates for greenness: those that match the inner sample themselves get to be called 'green'. At PI 73a Wittgenstein raises Berkeley's objection to this (*Principles*, Introduction s13): How can a single idea of green match *all* shades of green? Well, it can't; but this means that we *use* the inner sample in a way that *it* itself cannot dictate, for *we* have to settle what counts as *enough* of a match with it to justify applying 'green'. But then the inner sample is no *more* definitive a guide to applying 'green' in new cases than was 'and similar things' to applying '*game*' in new cases.

The point is not that some puzzle about how we understand 'game' also applies to our understanding of 'green'. The point is that the 'vague' verbal explanation of 'game' need not fall short of imparting a clarity of understanding that some 'inner' possession *could* help us to attain.

But there are sources for the idea that understanding is an inner state or process other than the felt need to compensate for vagueness in verbal explanation. It is upon these that Wittgenstein focuses in the material on rule-following. So let us now turn to that.

4. Following a rule

One of the things that can make understanding seem inescapably inner is an objection to Wittgenstein's rough equation of meaning with use (PI, 43). Surely the meaning that you attach to a word is not the use itself but something that *guides* the use. For it seems to be something that can be wholly present in an *instant*:

> But we understand the meaning of a word when we hear or say it; we grasp it in a flash, and what we grasp in a flash is surely something different from the 'use' which is extended in time! (PI, 138)

And this 'grasping in a flash' is something's coming before your mind. And *what* comes before your mind is the *meaning* that your subsequent use fits.

But what *does* come before your mind when you understand, say, 'cube'? Could it be a picture of a cube? But how can a *use* 'fit' that picture?

> Perhaps you say: "It's quite simple; – if that picture occurs to me and I point to a triangular prism or instance, and say it is a cube, then this use of the word doesn't fit the picture." (PI, 139)

But of course it *does* 'fit' the picture if you imagine the right lines of projection; and what in the picture settles *what* lines of projection you are *supposed* to imagine? And if you have the same picture before you but project from it differently on different occasions, then the correct thing to say is not that the *same* meaning came before your mind on each occasion but that you meant 'cube' *differently* on each occasion (PI, 140c).

Wittgenstein comments that he has so chosen the example that it is 'quite easy to imagine a *method of projection* according to which the picture [of a cube] does fit [the triangular prism] after all' (PI, 139). This alludes to *TLP* 3.11, where he had said that the 'method of projection' was the means whereby the thinking subject turned inert signs into meaningful symbols: one *meant* this or that object by one's meaningful use of a propositional sign containing its name. Now he is doubting whether there *is* any mental occurrence of 'meaning it'.

He next discusses another case where we naturally imagine meaning as a sort of mental reservoir from which the use flows. A learner is given initial elements of a numerical sequence (say, the sequence 1, 2, 4, 8, 16, ...) and asked to continue it. It seems obvious that for him to grasp the sequence is not *just* for him to continue it right: he must grasp a formula or other concise description of the series from which he then *derives* its later elements. Now by itself that gets us no further: if there is a problem with deriving a sequence from its initial elements then there is going to be the same problem with deriving it from the formula (PI, 146b).

But still, there is a difference between *deriving* the sequence and just writing down the right numbers willy-nilly. And isn't it just that *deriving* that distinguishes a use that is *informed by your understanding* from what you might call 'mere' use? – so there is after all a mental component of 'meaning it': it is whatever turns the 'mere' writing down of the sequence into a *derivation*.

Wittgenstein now considers deriving in connection with the simpler example of 'reading' (which covers: transcription, sight-reading, copying printed text in cursive etc.: PI, 156). Here too it is tempting to say that reading is not just, for example, making the right sounds when you see the right letters: there is a mental act of *deriving* sounds from letters. But consider a sequence of equally possible but increasingly convoluted ways to 'derive' an italic text from a roman one:

(i)   Somebody writes '*a*' when he sees 'a', '*b*' when he sees 'b' etc.
(ii) He writes '*b*' when he sees 'a', '*c*' when he sees 'b' ... '*a*' when he sees 'z'
(iii) He writes '*a*' the first time he sees 'a', '*b*' the second time, '*c*' the third time etc. – and so on with each letter of the alphabet
(iv) He alternates between rules (i), (ii) and (iii) ...

– and so on. Clearly a sufficiently tangled 'derivation' is indistinguishable from simply writing cursive letters at random – but what point in this sequence do we want to call the first case of non-reading? And, since any answer is arbitrary, what mental occurrence *is* common to all cases of derivation that distinguishes them from non-derivation (PI, 162)? Clearly the same goes for the 'derivation' of a numerical sequence from its first few members or from a formula.

Wittgenstein's inference is not that there is no such thing as reading, or derivation, or understanding; but that these are *family resemblance* concepts. We say that somebody is deriving if he responds in ways that resemble other kinds of deriving in the right respects; but no one thing, and in particular no one type of mental occurrence, distinguishes derivation from non-derivation. It is because of the behavioural *diversity* of 'derivations' that we felt compelled to postulate a mental *unity* behind them (PI, 36); but that is a mistake.

At PI 185 Wittgenstein introduces a learner of the sequence +2: 0, 2, 4, 6, ... So far he has written correct continuations of +2, but never beyond 1000. When we *do* ask him to go beyond 1000 he writes '1000, 1004, 1008, ...'. And when we protest that he was meant to do the *same* thing at each step, he says: 'But I *am* doing the "same" thing'. He has 'taken' the instructions or examples differently from the way that you or I would take those very instructions or examples; and yet he might well have experienced the *same* introspectible mental processes as us. And this imaginary character is deviant in just *one* of the many ways in which one might be deviant: in fact indefinitely many continuations of the sequence are inconsistent with one another and yet seemingly consistent with the very instructions and experiences from which you and I extrapolate with such confidence.

This undermines the idea that when I understand the series there is any mental act of meaning that as it were flies ahead and takes every step in the sequence before I actually write it down. 'But *when I gave the instruction* I meant that he was to write 1002 after 1000!' That is true, but it does not imply that any mental act of meaning it was going on at that time, any more than 'If he had fallen into the water then, I should have jumped in after him' implies that some mental act of jumping was going on at *that* time (PI, 187).

But then how am I supposed to tell, at any point in developing +2, what its correct continuation *is*? Even worse, what *makes* any continuation faithful to what I meant all along? It seems that the answer is *nothing*: any answer that I give – say, an inner image, or an instruction – might equally be something that the deviant of PI 185 could cite in *his* defence; so no candidate answer could possibly be right. The argument clearly generalizes, forcing the question: How can *any* rule determine *any* pattern of use, if it can't rule out indefinitely many others? This is the famous 'paradox' of PI 201:

This was our paradox: no course of action could be determined by a rule, because any course of action can be made out to accord with the rule. The answer was: if any action can be made out to accord with the rule, then it can be made out to conflict with it. And so there would be neither accord nor conflict here. (PI, 201a)

If it applies here then the semantic scepticism of PI 201a applies to all cases where some linguistic or mental item is supposed to mean something outside of itself. A wish can seem to cast a shadow upon what follows it: whatever *actually* happens after the wish is made, there is such a thing as what the wish *meant* all along, something with which actual events can either accord or fail to accord (PI, 437). But then what makes the wish a wish for *this* rather than for *that*? Or what makes a description of a situation a description of *that* situation; or what makes it true, when I speak of a particular person, that I am speaking of *him* (PI, 689)?

So we have a general threat to the possibility of meaning. And its *im*possibility is the conclusion that Kripke draws in his seminal monograph on PI. 'There can be no such thing as meaning anything by any word', he writes. 'Each new application we make is a leap in the dark; any present intention could be interpreted so as to accord with anything we may choose to do. So there can be neither accord, nor conflict' (Kripke, 1982, p. 55).

But that isn't what *Wittgenstein* thinks. *He* has no interest in denying that a meaning can occur to you, that you grasp it in a flash, that it reaches beyond the examples, and the rest (see, for example, PI, 141c; PI, 151b; PI, 208–10). What he denies is that what turns the mere hearing of an instruction, or the mere utterance of a sentence, into an occasion of *understanding* or *meaning* it, is some *inner* process that *accompanies* those outer occurrences.

But then what *does* make that difference? At PI 198 Wittgenstein writes:

Let me ask this: what has the expression of a rule – say a sign-post – got to do with my actions? What sort of connexion is there here? – Well, perhaps this one: I have been trained to react to the sign in a particular way, and now I do so react to it.

But that is only to give a causal connexion; to tell how it has come about that we now go by the sign-post; not what this going-by-the-sign really consists in. On the contrary; I have further indicated that a person goes by a sign-post only in so far as there exists a regular use of sign-posts, a custom.

It is belonging to a *customary* pattern of use that gives *your* use a significance that outruns what it makes explicit. The possibility of a deviant such as at PI 185 does not affect the fact that when *I* say '+2' or write down its initial elements, I *mean* a sequence whose correct continuation is '1000, 1002, 1004' and not one whose correct continuation is '1000, 1004, 1008'. And I mean it, not because of something going on inside me but because of something going on *outside* me: my belonging to a linguistic community to which the continuation '+2' comes naturally.

(Compare: a daub of paint on a canvas *is* a painted smile, but not because of anything intrinsic to it. That very daub might have been a frown – if, for instance, the painter had turned the canvas upside down before doing the rest of the face. What makes the daub a painted smile is the disposition of the painted features around it. This is not to say that *it* is not really a smile; it is to say *why* it really *is* one.)

There is much more to be said about this communitarian conception of meaning but I lack the space to say much more here.[1] Let me turn instead to ostensive definition. At the end of Section 2 I left hanging the question: If no accompanying process makes it true that you mean to point at, for example, a man, and not his demeanour, what *does* make it true? We can now appreciate Wittgenstein's answer that it is the *surroundings* of the activity. It is the fact that you yourself do, and that you live among people who do, customarily respond in one way rather than another to such episodes – that is, they take you to be pointing to a man; they use the name to call that man and to speak to him and so forth – that qualifies that episode as one of pointing at a man and not at any of the many other things that a Martian might reasonably have taken you to be indicating.[2]

5. Private language

But once we have *regularities* of linguistic usage the *community* that Wittgenstein seems to postulate looks gratuitous. *Given* my patterns of use, why should the existence and linguistic behaviour of *others* make any difference to *my* meaning?

Wittgenstein nowhere, to my knowledge, gives any reason for thinking that it should; but he does defend a slightly weaker anti-individualism. He contends that I cannot introduce expressions to refer to what is *in principle* inaccessible to others. Those empiricists, like Locke and Russell, who thought that we *could* speak of such 'private' items, usually thought of them as introspectible 'ideas' or 'sense data'. But if Wittgenstein's argument works then it works against terms for any 'inner' occurrence of which there is no 'outer' or publicly accessible sign. If it works, then although my speaking a language may not imply that other speakers of it *do* exist, it *does* imply that they *might* exist.

What Wittgenstein argues is that I could not *introduce* a term referring to a private type of occurrence. Such an act would be one of private ostensive definition; and that is his target at PI 258. (At this point I suggest that the reader get the passage in view as I lack the space to reproduce it here.)

Although its detail is controversial, its drift is clear enough. Wittgenstein thinks that the mental act of focusing on a sensation while uttering its name 'S' *does not suffice* to introduce 'S' into my language because it does not establish a standard for its use. But why not?

Three answers are popular. On the *verificationist* interpretation (Malcolm, 1954/1968, p. 68), inner ostension doesn't enable me to *check* whether I am using 'S' in accordance with its definition. Such a check requires external – that is, publicly available – criteria for the sensation. Ayer has replied that all language and all checking must ultimately be founded upon *some* expressions whose usage cannot be checked, so the demand that my use of 'S' be checkable is unmotivated (Ayer, 1954, p. 256). And Blackburn has replied that in any case nothing stands in the way of checking my use of 'S' against further *inner* regularities (Blackburn, 1984, pp. 299–300).

On the *meaning-check* interpretation (Kenny, 1975, p. 192) the difficulty is rather that I can't tell *what that original definition was*. For the definition was an 'inner' episode, that is, involving no external criteria: so it left no traces. So I have no way to settle a doubt about what I introduced 'S' to mean in the first place; so no way of knowing now what 'S' *does* mean.

But why should my current understanding of an expression require that I be able to check it *if* a doubt arises? So long as I *do in fact* use 'S' in accordance with what I meant all along, and so long as no doubts about this use of it *do in fact* arise, I know well enough what I meant by 'S' (cf. PI, 87b).

The *sortalist* reading (McGinn, 1997, pp. 131–4; Stroud, 2001) is that *there was never any original definition in the first place.* The 'definition' was a focusing upon a sensational event and the utterance of 'S'. That leaves it open *in what respects* any other event that is properly labelled 'S' is supposed to resemble the baptismal one. 'Quite simple', you reply: 'You are supposed to use "S" for the occurrences of the same *sensation* as made its appearance on that occasion.' But 'sensation' is a word of *public* language and there are *public* criteria for whether two inner occurrences are of the 'same sensation' (PI, 261).[3]

It remains unclear just what the problem is. Why couldn't a purely *private* criterion exist for whether two inner occurrences were the 'same sensation'? 'In that case "same sensation" would lose its everyday meaning.' But why? Couldn't we each attach the *same* private meaning to 'same sensation'; couldn't that determine our use of it? 'But then you could never *know* what anybody else means by "same sensation".' Maybe: but why must you *know*, and not just have a *true belief* about what another means for effective communication with him? Edward Craig has made it very plausible that you needn't know. He also makes it plausible that establishing the opposite with any conviction requires a verificationist premise that makes this whole argument otiose. Indeed his work on the subject constitutes a rock upon which, to my knowledge, *every* reading of PI 258 has foundered (see Craig, 1982 and 1997).

None of this affects the fact that PI establishes, with as much cogency as philosophy ever attains, the most important points on which Wittgenstein came to differ from his *Tractatus* position. These are (a) that linguistic meaning does not depend upon a substructure of purely referring terms; (b) that neither meaning a sentence nor understanding it requires some inner psychic event that accompanies its use; they depend only on that use. What it did *not* establish was that this 'use' demands the actual or even the possible involvement of a linguistic 'community'.

The real lessons of *Philosophical Investigations* are therefore consistent with a use-based but *purely* individualistic conception of meaning, one to which (and despite his assertion that language is a 'social art') the work of W. V. Quine is more plainly hospitable. And in my view it is in Quine's work on language that Wittgenstein's best insights into it have found clearest and fullest expression.

Further reading

Introductions to Wittgenstein's *Investigations* include:

Ahmed, A. (2010), *Wittgenstein's* Philosophical Investigations: *A Reader's Guide*. London: Continuum.
Fogelin, R. (1987), *Wittgenstein*, 2nd edn. London: Routledge.
McGinn, M. (1997), *Wittgenstein and the* Philosophical Investigations. London: Routledge.

The most thorough discussion is certainly that contained in Baker and Hacker's monumental four-volume commentary, of which the first two volumes have recently been republished (G. P. Baker and P. M. S. Hacker, *Wittgenstein: Understanding and Meaning*, Oxford: Wiley-Blackwell, 2009; G. P. Baker and P. M. S. Hacker, *Wittgenstein: Rules, Grammar and Necessity*, Oxford: Wiley-Blackwell, 2014).

The most philosophically engaging discussion (which is however quite dubious as an interpretation) is certainly Saul Kripke's *Wittgenstein on Rules and Private Language* (Oxford: Blackwell, 1981). Any philosopher who wants to know why there is so much fuss about Wittgenstein should read this book.

Notes

1 For further discussion see especially McDowell (1984).
2 Of course there are often cases where a *genuine* (and not merely 'philosophical') question arises about what you meant by a pointing gesture – and in these cases it cannot be what others customarily take you to mean that settles what you meant. There may not *be* any one thing that they customarily take you to mean. But it is still true that what you mean is settled not by some accompanying inner process but by additional outer ones: for instance, what you would say if asked what you meant. See PI, 210, 665ff. Of course one *might* raise further question about what you meant by these clarifications; but that I should be at a loss to answer them hardly shows that after all I meant nothing; rather, what makes it true that I mean something is that these doubts typically do *not* arise.
3 'Criteria' here denotes a kind of state that is defeasibly but essentially evidence for the state of which it is criterial; here it might include typical neurological causes and/or behavioural effects of a sensation. (This is just one side of a rich debate that has grown up around Wittgenstein's contrasting uses of 'criterion' and 'symptom'. See further: PI, 354; Baker [1975]; McDowell [1982].)

Bibliography

Ayer, A. J. (1954), 'Could There Be a Private Language?' *Proceedings of the Aristotelian Society*, Supplementary Vol. 28, pp. 63–76. Reprinted in G. Pitcher (ed.), *Wittgenstein: The Philosophical Investigations*. London: Macmillan, pp. 251–66.

Baker, G. P. (1975), 'Criteria: A New Foundation for Semantics', *Ratio*, 17, pp. 156–89.

Blackburn, S. (1984), 'The Individual Strikes Back', *Synthese*, 58, pp. 281–301.

Craig, E. J. (1982), 'Meaning, Use and Privacy', *Mind*, 91, pp. 541–64.

Craig, E. J. (1997), 'Meaning and Privacy', in R. Hale and C. Wright (eds), *Blackwell Companion to the Philosophy of Language*. Oxford: Blackwell, pp. 127–45.

Forster, M. (2010), 'Wittgenstein on Family Resemblance Concepts', in A. Ahmed (ed.), *Wittgenstein's Philosophical Investigations: A Critical Guide*. Cambridge: Cambridge University Press, pp. 66–87.

Kenny, A. (1975), *Wittgenstein*. Harmondsworth: Penguin.

Kripke, S. A. (1982), *Wittgenstein on Rules and Private Language*. Oxford: Blackwell.

Malcolm, N. (1954/1968), 'Wittgenstein's *Philosophical Investigations*'. *Philosophical Review*, 63, pp. 530–59. Reprinted in G. Pitcher (ed.), *Wittgenstein: The Philosophical Investigations*. London: Macmillan, 1968, pp. 65–103.

McDowell, J. (1982), 'Criteria, Defeasibility, and Knowledge', *Proceedings of the British Academy*, 68, pp. 456–79.

McDowell, J. (1984), 'Wittgenstein on Following a Rule', *Synthese*, 58, pp. 325–63.

McGinn, M. (1997), *Wittgenstein and the* Philosophical Investigations. London: Routledge.

Russell, B. ([1912] 2001), *The Problems of Philosophy*. Oxford: Oxford University Press.

Russell, B. ([1918] 1985), *The Philosophy of Logical Atomism*. La Salle, IL: Open Court.

Stroud, B. (2001), 'Private Objects, Physical Objects and Ostension', in D. Charles and W. Child (eds), *Wittgensteinian Themes: Essays in Honour of David Pears*. Oxford: Oxford University Press, pp. 143–62.

Wittgenstein, L. (1961 [1921]), *Tractatus Logico-Philosopicus*, trans. D. F. Pears and B. F. McGuinness. London: Routledge.

Wittgenstein, L. (2001 [1953]), *Philosophical Investigations*, trans. G. E. M. Anscombe, ed. G. E. M. Anscombe and R. Rhees. Oxford: Blackwell.

CHAPTER EIGHT

QUINE

Gary Kemp

W. V. Quine is routinely mentioned as one of the most important figures in post–Second World War philosophy of language. Yet on the face of it, his views were almost entirely negative, with few philosophers of language today subscribing to them. He dismisses almost everything that most philosophers of language assume as the basic tools with which to conduct their more specialized inquiries, including such staples as the positing of universals or attributes (to explain the meaning of predicates), modality and other departures from extensionality, propositions as the meanings of sentences, and even the notion of meaning itself. So why is Quine so famous, especially when the rejections just listed are thought, by most of those in the profession, to have been unsuccessful?

Much of Quine's popular fame in the philosophy of language is due to his enormously exciting early and early-middle-period works, especially 'Two Dogmas of Empiricism' from 1951 (FLPV, pp. 20–41), and chapter two of *Word and Object* from 1960 (WO, pp. 26–79).[1] In the first he challenged the orthodoxy of the day, namely that the notion of *analyticity* – truth by virtue of meaning alone – was a fundamental notion of epistemology. Some have found the argument frustratingly lacking in perspicuity, but most agree that it deserves a response; and many celebrate, even if they do not advocate, the alternative epistemological picture known as 'holism', which Quine sketched to take the place of analyticity-involving reductionism. In the second work he provided what is for many an object-lesson in the limits of strict empiricism: in arguing that empirical methods can never justify uniquely correct ascriptions of meaning, he merely displayed the limits of such methods – even if he himself took it the other way, holding that if the notion of meaning is impenetrable to empirical methods then so much the worse for it.

Thus the popular picture of Quine: a powerfully learned and clever sceptic, but one whose scepticism has long since been overcome, and indeed one who ignored the central challenges presented by language. But this picture drastically underestimates Quine. In later but less well-known writings – from about 1965 until his death in 2000 – it is abundantly clear that Quine's rejections flowed from a coherent position that is difficult to refute, once it is thoroughly understood – a position which dismisses as bogus many of the questions posed by mainstream philosophy of language. Furthermore, the position issues in a positive conception of what language is, of how it performs its principal functions, and what those functions are; it by no means leaves the main questions unaddressed.

Quine's name for the position – 'naturalism' – is suggestive, but care must be taken not to class Quine with others who call themselves naturalists; naturalism broadly speaking is probably the dominant world-view among philosophers – indeed Quine's own work is partly responsible for the rise of nationalism – but the proportion of out-and-out Quineans is much smaller. We shall try to see the negative by the light of the positive: we shall articulate Quine's naturalism, and then attempt to see how Quine not only rejects certain ideas but shows how he thinks we can get along without them. But first, it will be instructive to see the situation of 'Two Dogmas' as Quine saw it at the time of writing it, before he had gained the self-conscious conviction that followed later with his explicit avowal of naturalism.

1. Empiricism as Quine saw it

In 1933, while in his mid-20s and having just completed his doctoral thesis, Quine travelled to Prague to visit Rudolf Carnap.[2] Quine knew of Carnap's *Der Logische Aufbau der Welt* (1928; translated as *The Logical Structure of the World* in 1967), and knew that

Carnap was working on his *Logische Syntax der Sprache* (1934; translated as *The Logical Syntax of Language* in 1937). In science, these were the early years of Relativity Theory, Quantum Theory, and the breakthroughs in mathematical logic due to Frege, Russell and others.[3] New dawns seemed to be breaking in philosophy as well; this was the time of the *Vienna Circle*, a group including Carnap, known for proposing Logical Positivism (Logical Empiricism, as Carnap preferred). It is difficult to recapture the excitement that all of this occasioned in those involved. In the Foreword to the *Logical Syntax,* Carnap wrote:

> *Philosophy is to be replaced by the logic of science* – that is to say, by the logical analysis of the concepts and sentences of the science of the sciences, for *the logic of science is nothing other than the logical syntax of the language of science.* (Carnap, 1937, p. xiii)

Yes – philosophy is to be *replaced* by the logic of science. (Carnap was well aware of the hackles this would raise, applying his ideas to none other than Heidegger, for one, purporting to show that some of Heidegger's sentences were literally nonsense.) For Carnap, then, the key question for philosophy is just this: What does one have to assume in order to do science, to explain the ways of the world?

In particular, Carnap aimed to show that there is no need for the *synthetic* a priori, for Kantian a priori intuition. The idea of what Carnap called *phenomenological reductionism* was that sensory experience plus logic is all that required to account for genuine knowledge, namely science. It's an old idea, but the new and much more powerful symbolic logic of Russell and Frege promised that such a thesis might be demonstrated precisely rather than merely sketched in the manner of Hume. But – leaving sensory experience aside for the moment – of what exactly does knowledge of logic consist? Neither Russell nor Frege could answer that question satisfactorily; both held that the basic principles of logic must simply be assumed by science. Carnap's *Logical Syntax* provided a more sophisticated answer: by developing an exact method of constructing logic in the form of 'sentences about sentences', Carnap held that knowledge of logic is ultimately based upon our acceptance of certain *conventions* for the use of language. Just as one plays chess only if one follows the rules of chess, to speak a language is to be bound by certain rules, the analytic truths of the language. Our knowledge, for example, that *If it's raining and it's night time then it's raining*, depends simply on our decision to speak the language we do. The domain of the a priori is decided pragmatically, not theoretically.

Quine's doubts over Carnap's scheme surfaced as early as 1935 in 'Truth by Convention' (WP, pp. 77–106). First, especially in view of Carnap's toleration for different languages with different conventions, what exactly is the basis for distinguishing the conventional from the non-conventional? Why not declare the principles of thermodynamics, say, to be conventions? Second, it is hard to see how the truths of logic can themselves be matters of convention. If we say: 'It is a convention of language governing "if-then" that if we are given "if p then q" and "p" as premises, then we may infer "q"', we are still *using* a statement which *involves* if-then in order to state the supposed convention. One might say with Carnap that such things are stated from outside the language, in a 'metalanguage', but that only raises the same question with respect to the metalanguage.

After the Second World War, Quine generalized and sharpened his attack on Carnap's philosophy in his 'Two Dogmas of Empiricism'. It's vital to keep the foregoing background in mind in reading Quine's discussion; Quine's central criticism of the notion of analyticity was not that no such notion could be coherent – in fact he would later define his own notion of analyticity – *but analyticity has nothing like the epistemological importance claimed for it.*[4] Quine discusses various definitions, explanations or explications of the notion that might be advanced, making use of such notions as *synonymy, definitions, necessity, empirical content, verification conditions* and so on. We will pass over the details and instead highlight two fundamental points. First, Quine's most general claim as regards the list of possible explanations and analyticity itself is simply that the situation is 'like a closed curve is space' (FLPV, p. 30) – if one is dissatisfied with any of them, then that dissatisfaction will carry over to the rest. Carnap and others were trying to account for the a priori in terms of some such notions; they assumed that such a framework *must* be presupposed before any empirical discoveries can be made and interpreted. It is because of this that Quine's second main point is vital to the force of the first: Quine's crucial contention is that there is no need for such a presupposition.

In two pages at the middle of section 5 of 'Two Dogmas', Quine points out that in Carnap's scheme, at a critical stage of the reduction of statements about physical objects to statements about sensation, it is necessary to define the term 'is at' as it appears in statements of the form q is at $<x, y, z, t>$ where q is a sensory quality, x, y, z, are spatial coordinates and t is time. Such a definition is needed to effect the transition from inner sensory experience to statements about the external world as a matter of meaning. The trouble is that to be at all plausible, there has to be a certain looseness in that notion, for among other things we sometimes make mistakes in perception – about where q 'is at', for instance. Carnap's solution is to impose certain principles whereby sensory qualities are to be assigned to space-time in such a way as to maximize simplicity, continuity and other features. This presumably will take care of such cases as a referee's finding upon reflection that the ball could not possibly have crossed the line despite its having appeared to; the constraints tell him to rescind his original judgement. But those constraints do not tell us how to reduce a *single* statement of the form q is at $<x, y, z, t>$; at most they tell us how, given a whole *collection* of statements about immediate experience, we should assign truth-values to those statements so as to yield the right sort of overall world. In the case just described, an assignment of sense-qualities to space-time points may have accorded well with experience up to a point, but must now be revised in order best to satisfy the principles governing such assignments.

So the single greatest attempt to make out phenomenological reductionism failed. But now, memorably, Quine claims that there is no need for the key idea on which such an idea depends. Considerations of simplicity, continuity and the like are appealed to in generating theories of the world – even the most mundane ones – but they apply only *holistically*, that is, only to whole theories, or otherwise large collections of statements. Here then is the famous Quinean *web of belief*: rather than absolute rules telling us how to respond to particular experiences, we have various weightings of various factors leaving room for choice, and which may themselves be re-evaluated:

> The totality of our so-called knowledge or beliefs, from the most casual matters of geography and history to the profoundest laws of atomic physics or even of pure mathematics and logic,

is a man-made fabric which impinges on experience only along the edges. Or, to change the figure, total science is like a field of force whose boundary conditions are experience. A conflict with experience at the periphery occasions readjustments in the interior of the field. Truth values have to redistributed over some of our statements ... [T]he total field is so underdetermined by its boundary conditions, experience, that there is much latitude of choice as to what statements to reëvaluate in the light of any single contrary experience. No particular experiences are linked with any particular statements in the interior of the field, except indirectly through considerations of equilibrium affecting the field as a whole. (FLVP, pp. 42–3)

Crucially, the web includes the statements 'of pure mathematics and logic', hence obviating the clearest motivation for analyticity, convention or the a priori. All statements are in that sense 'revisable'. Quine himself came later to stress that the point is only 'legalistic': there is little real prospect of discarding what are the most central and certain principles of logic and mathematics. A supposition, say, of $1 + 1 = 5$, would reverberate intolerably throughout science, simply because it is logically related to the rest of arithmetic and other accepted statements. But this thoroughgoing entanglement with science explains not only why it has seemed tempting to suppose that their *necessity* explains the apparent irrevisability of statements of logic and mathematics, but why there is no such need for such a supposition. Our mastery of these statements need not be explained in terms of the cognition of special features not found to some degree in any other statement.

2. Naturalism

The web of belief metaphor needed, as Quine remarked later, considerable 'unpacking' (CE, p. 398). If sensory reductionism is not viable, the challenge now is to give a positive, detailed and explicit explanation of human knowledge *without* the bald assumption of the concept of analyticity or concepts in terms of which it might be defined, such as the concept of meaning. There are three very general points we should have before us in advance of seeing how Quine's scheme works.

First, Quine assumes that the main questions of epistemology are questions of language. Language is the very medium of theories, which collectively constitute the whole of human knowledge. Of course, some of what one knows doesn't seem to amount to a *theory*; one's knowledge that one has a neck, for example. All the same, one is *disposed to assent* to the sentence 'You have a neck'; although his focus is often on the higher flights of theory – physics, mathematics – Quine simply extends such words as 'theory' to cover the whole of a person's beliefs.

Secondly, Quine intends to remove from circulation what Carnap had identified as the last remaining realm of irreducibly a priori, philosophical concepts. *Only* genuinely scientific concepts – especially those pertaining to causal relations – remain. And as we shall see shortly, this means that an explanation of knowledge or language should not presuppose such ideas as immaterial referential ties between mind and things or word and object. And it will not be justifiable to suppose, as Frege did, that language is significant by virtue of the mind's 'grasping' those abstract entities known as thoughts or propositions; that psychological idea is from Quine's perspective unintelligible – how can abstract, immaterial objects explain human cognition, the stuff of axons and synapses? As Frege famously put it (Frege, 1984 [1919], p. 371), how can thoughts act? They can't, is Quine's answer.

Thirdly, Quine envisages a certain re-ordering of epistemology. Quine's principal aim is not to *prove* or *justify* our claims to knowledge, but to *explain* them (see RR, pp. 1–4; SS, pp. 15–16). Given that we have such and such knowledge, what precisely does it involve? What are its most general presuppositions? To take a striking example, Quine agrees with Hume about the principle of induction – the principle that if a certain proportion of a randomly chosen, large enough sample of a kind of thing has a certain feature, then that proportion may be generalized to the whole population of the kind. It is not a truth of logic – its negation is not self-contradictory – and it would be circular to try to establish it empirically: 'the Humean predicament', as Quine puts it, 'is the human predicament' (OR, p. 72). But for Quine, to show that the principle is presupposed by and systematically embedded in empirical science is all the justification that may be asked for, just as those things showed why we must accept the truths of arithmetic.

Naturalism sums all this up. There is, Quine proclaims, no 'first philosophy; it is only within science itself, and not in some prior philosophy, that reality is to be identified and described' (TT, p. 21) – meaning not that philosophy is doomed, but that it operates in the more abstract and general end of things, not in a totally separate sphere of concepts and principles. It is as if, as Quine quotes from Otto Neurath, we are aboard a ship at sea, having to make running repairs; philosophers look after the more abstract and fundamental things, but cannot deconstruct the whole thing on pain of sinking (WO, p. 3). The essential thing for our purposes is tolerably clear: Our aim is to explain the core use of language – linguistic competence as it is sometimes called – *strictly within the causal realm of scientific psychology.*

3. Dispositions, observation sentences and primitive theory

Quine's account of the kernel of knowledge-bearing language is one which, again, explains the most essential aspects of the mastery of language without appealing to an unanalysed notion of meaning or the like. Absolutely central to Quine's picture is the notion of a linguistic disposition: for Quine, the possession of language just is that of a forbiddingly complex set of interconnected linguistic dispositions. This is not to invoke unexplained explainers: by a linguistic disposition Quine always means some state of the nervous system, even though these are at least at present generally unknown, and their exact realization will presumably vary from person to person.

Empiricists generally, and the logical positivists in particular, have laid a good deal of stress on statements directly reporting sensory experiences, or statements about 'the given', or 'protocol statements'. Quine is in a sense part of that tradition, but with a critical difference attendant on his naturalism. In 'Two Dogmas' Quine spoke of 'immediate experience' (p. 20); but by the time of *Word and Object*, Quine 'stiffened up [his] flabby reference to "experience" by turning to our physical interface with the external world' (CE, p. 398). Thus what Quine calls an 'observation sentence' such as 'It's raining' is roughly one that a person has a disposition to assent to or dissent from *if and only if his neural receptors are triggered in a particular way.*

The notions of *assent* and *dissent* are in turn, for Quine, characterized behaviourally: if person is disposed to make a certain noise in response to say 'Gavagai?' if and only if a rabbit is visible, then it is very probable that 'Gavagai' plays a role like that of 'There's a rabbit' and the noise manifests assent; the probability that the noise does manifest assent approaches certainty the more that analogous behaviour is observed with respect to other sentences.

An observation sentence is correlated with the firing of certain sensory receptors. In *Word and Object* this was called the 'stimulus meaning' of the sentence, but Quine stopped calling it by that name, partly because of the presence of the word 'meaning'. A native observation sentence might be 'Gavagai!', which we might translate as 'There's a rabbit!' or just the one-word sentence 'Rabbit!', but neither sentence *means*, in the intuitive sense, that one has such-and-such sensory stimulations. Sensory stimulations are individual; you have yours and I have mine. Rather than use 'stimulus meaning', it's best just to speak plainly of correlations between dispositions to assent and sensory triggering.

'Language', says Quine, 'is a social art'; it is of the essence of language that we communicate through its use. And observation sentences are the means by which we communicate about the here and now. So far we have said nothing to explain how that is possible; since there is no reason to expect that different people will have their sensory receptors laid out in exactly the same way, a given observation sentence will normally be correlated with different sensory triggerings in different people. The missing piece is provided by the theory of natural selection. We each have sensory habits of 'locking onto' such objects in the environment as a rabbit because of the obvious survival value of such habits; what Quine calls the 'pre-established harmony' of perception is strictly a fact about our neural constitution; it is not a fact requiring semantics or the concept of intention for its expression (CE, pp. 473–6, 486–92). Thus each of us possesses a disposition to respond to the triggerings caused in us by passing rabbits and the like. Equally, we higher animals are susceptible to training; thus we can learn to be disposed to assent to 'There's a rabbit' if and only if we undergo the triggering. The association thus acquired is sufficient for learning the observation sentence; the sentence is jointly held yet its exact sensory component will be individual.

Observation sentences so described are what Quine calls 'holophrastic' – they admit of being learned as wholes, without internal structure. The next step is to see, if only very briefly and schematically, how one can go on to learn to think of them as structured, which is necessary for learning the non-observational parts of language.

Other observation sentences can be learned by chopping up those already learned and recombining; thus, for example, having learned 'There's a white dog' and 'There's a black cat', one might substitute 'white' for 'black' in the latter, venturing 'There's a white cat' in what one takes to be appropriate circumstances. The truth-functional logical particles such as 'not' and 'and' can be acquired by learning (1) to assent to a sentence S if only if one dissents from 'not-S' and vice-versa, and (2) to assent to 'S and S*' if and only if one assents to S and S* individually and to dissent from 'S and S*' if and only if one dissents from either S or S*. With these two devices learned, together with the idea of grouping – distinguishing, for example, '(Not-S) and S*' from 'Not-(S and S*)' – a subject has in principle mastered all of truth-functional logic, and hence other truth-functions such as 'or' and 'if-then' (for these can be defined in terms of 'not' and 'and').

With these devices on board, the subject can now formulate examples of the central notion of the *observation categorical*. For example, 'If it's snowing, then it's cold' is formed by combining two observation sentences by means of the conditional 'if-then'. It is not itself an observation sentence; it is a *standing* sentence – roughly, it is a sentence that is always assented to *whatever* the circumstances. Furthermore, a candidate for this status is *testable*: we wait for the situations in which we assent to the antecedent, and see if conditions prompt assent to the consequent. Observation categoricals, then, comprise the most primitive examples of theory; the *empirical content* of more sophisticated theories nevertheless consists simply in the observation categoricals entailed by them.

The example above of 'white cat' and 'black dog' gave a hint of what is meant by the notions of 'predication' and 'reference', but the full story emerges only with the introduction of *pronouns* and *quantifiers* – the stuff needed to express *generality* – to the discourse. Compare the sentence 'Every raven is black' with 'If there is a raven, there is a black raven'; in order to get the hang of the first generalization, more is required than is given by the devices discussed so far. For mastery of the second, it suffices to find that every time one assents to the observation sentence 'Raven!', one assents to the observation sentence 'Black Raven!'; still that would tolerate white ravens if for some reason they were always accompanied by a black one. For mastery of the first, one's dispositions have to be such as to distinguish the two cases – by dissenting from the first generalization in situations where one assents to the second. This is *equivalent* to saying that one has the capacity to see that *a thing* is a raven, and then to check whether *it* is black. Re-identification is of the essence of both reification – the assuming of objects – and reference, as shown by the function of the pronoun 'it' (the natural language analogue of the quantificational variables of formal logic).

Quine's exact story of how generality and reference emerge is too complex to enter into here, but we've seen enough to appreciate the following general point. To speak of *reference* is for Quine to speak of *referential language* of the sort just sketched, a language with pronouns (or their equivalent) and quantifiers. Mastery of that apparatus is sufficient for referential language, for reference. There is no mention of immaterial links between word and object in an adequate description of the apparatus; saying that one refers to objects is the same as saying that one has mastered such devices as pronouns and quantifiers. Environmental objects play a generative or causal role in explaining how, despite being associated with individual patterns of sensory stimulation, humans manage to learn the same observation sentences, but that is not reference; at that level the quantifiers and pronouns whose mastery constitute reference do not enter into the story at all. As we've seen, the abilities of a creature possessing only observation sentences and truth-functions can be explained without the concept of reference.

4. The inscrutability of reference and the indeterminacy of translation

Suppose you and I were each individually to attempt to devise translation manuals of a foreign tongue, where the language in view – call it 'Language X' – was previously untranslated. Since surely one expression correctly translates another if and only if it has the same meaning as the other, we should expect our respective manuals, insofar as they are successful, to converge; in particular, with respect to a given expression of Language X, we should expect them to deliver the same translation (allowing of course for discrepancies on points of emphasis, style, and other grammatical and lexical alternatives that, as we say, amount to the same thing).

Quine, however, famously claims that translation is 'indeterminate' – that even if you and I were to go about our respective tasks with impeccable correctness, there is no reason to deny that we could devise manuals that do not converge in this way. The two manuals could correctly translate one sentence of Language X into different sentences of English that 'stand in no plausible relation of equivalence, however loose' (WO, p. 27); there is thus no 'fact of the matter' as regards meaning. Meaning itself is not something objective; the assignment of particular meanings to expressions is irreducibly intuitive and interest-relative, not something that could be validated by the impersonal procedures of science. And as emphasized, the notion plays no role in Quine's account of language. Indeed from the naturalistic point of view, it is completely unclear what role such a notion *could* play. If we find that two inequivalent verdicts are respectively each part of a complete analysis of a given person's language – an analysis that painstakingly catalogues all the person's linguistic dispositions – then the only way to maintain that the two verdicts herald different ascriptions of meaning is to suppose that the differences of meaning are real but do not show up in the person's linguistic dispositions. That this is ruled out is part of what Quine meant by accepting 'linguistic behaviourism'; it is expressed succinctly in a piece from 1975:

... the fixed points are just the shared stimulus and the word; the ideas in between are as may be and may vary as they please, so long as the external stimulus in question stays paired up with the word in question for all concerned. The point is well dramatized by the familiar fantasy of complementary colour perception. Who knows but that I see things in colour opposite to those in which you see the thing? For communication it is a matter of indifference. (CE, p. 248)[5]

A simple argument for indeterminacy involves what Quine calls the *inscrutability of reference*. Observation sentences are, according to Quine, the 'entering wedge' into a language; since they are by definition the ones that a creature's disposition to assent to them varies with changes in the environment, we can think of a translator as beginning by observation of the native, looking out for environmental changes that go with changes in the native's disposition to assent to observation sentences. Suppose then that the native's 'Gavagai!' is found to correlate with the presence of rabbits, which presumably stimulate his visual nerves in certain distinctive ways. The observation sentences 'Rabbit!' and 'Rabbit-stage!' – a momentary stage of a rabbit – are associated with the same sensory receptors in a given individual (other 'stimulus-synonymous' sentences are 'Undetached rabbit-part!', 'Rabbithood manifestation!', and other more artificial things). Thus the fact that 'Rabbit!' and 'Gavagai!' are equivalent in this respect does not imply that 'rabbit' and 'gavagai' are synonymous or co-extensive *terms*.

To find out whether the term 'gavagai' has the same reference as 'rabbit' or 'rabbit-stage', we need to translate some native expression as 'is the same as' or equivalent. Suppose we have identified the native construction 'ipso' as a candidate for 'is the same as', and 'yo' as a demonstrative pronoun, like 'that' in English. The native, we find, affirms:

(1) Yo gavagai ipso yo gavagai.

He affirms this, we find, when and only when we point at the same rabbit the whole time. This would seem to confirm the hypothesis that 'gavagai' means rabbit rather than rabbit-stage. But it doesn't. Here are two translations of the sentence (1):

(2) That rabbit is the same as that rabbit.
(3) That rabbit-stage is part of the same animal-history as that rabbit-stage.

(2) and (3) are correlated with the same sensory receptors; indeed we have the same rabbit if and only if we have rabbit-stages that are part of the same animal-history (OR, p. 4). So the native's speech-dispositions will not fix the reference of the term 'gavagai'. Of course, the expressions involved in (1) – 'gavagai', 'ipso' – have

uses in the rest of Language X, so the translations of these will have ramifications for other translations. But just as the data left us with choices in assigning references to the parts of (1), so these choices can be compensated for where other choices emerge in connection with other parts of the translation manual (WO, pp. 71–2; see also OR, pp. 1–3, 30–5). This not to say we or the natives do not know the difference between rabbits and rabbit-stages – *within* a language such as English, 'rabbits = rabbit-stages' remains false – but all the same we can translate the word of Language X in either way, so long as corresponding adjustments are made elsewhere.

A more general and abstract version of this argument came swiftly after the initial presentation in *Word and Object*, called now 'Ontological Relativity' (and later still the 'Indeterminacy of Reference'). Suppose we imagine a language with all linguistic dispositions charted, plus a reference scheme. Formulate what Quine calls a proxy-function: a proxy-function assigns for each input x a unique correlate that is not x itself. Now formulate a new reference scheme: where the original had a given object in the set of things a given term is true of, then the new scheme has the proxy of that object in the new set (e.g. 'spatio-temporal complement of' – the universe minus the object – is a proxy-function with respect to physical objects). The two reference schemes are equivalent, in the sense that the new scheme leaves unaffected the truth-value of every sentence: for example 'Sally smokes' is equivalent to 'The proxy of Sally is the proxy of a smoker'. Furthermore, the set of sensory receptors associated with each sentence has not been altered. So there is nothing observable, nothing objective to decide between the two schemes; thus as a pair of hypotheses about the language in question, the difference is unreal.

Early on, Quine referred to this cluster of arguments as ones that 'press from below' to the general conclusion of the indeterminacy of translation or meaning. However he soon began to emphasize that these arguments deliver only the indeterminacy of reference of *terms*. This is not as radical as the purported indeterminacy of translation of *entire sentences*. (Of course 'There is a rabbit' and 'There is a rabbit-stage' do not intuitively mean the same thing, as they do not contain reference to the same objects, but in some sense they amount to the same thing.)[6]

It is difficult to imagine arguments for indeterminacy of translation of whole sentences, but there is one argument Quine gives, an argument that 'presses from above'. Like many philosophers of science, Quine holds that science is *underdetermined by its evidence*. More exactly, if we think of *all* the evidential statements – the observation categoricals – past, present and future, as having their truth-values determined, then the actual theory which implies them, A (our actual scientific theory), could be replaced by another, different theory, B, which nevertheless has the same exact set of observational implications. Of course that is very much an 'in principle' prospect, as it is vanishingly unlikely that such an alternative will actually be produced. But suppose that the possibility is real. The translator has no trouble with observation sentences and truth-functional connectives, and thus not with observation categoricals. But he has no direct evidence for standing sentences, and in particular not for theoretical sentences such as 'Light travels at 186,000 miles per second'. So in principle he could attribute either A or B to them. Thus undetermination of theory implies indeterminacy of translation.

In subsequent years, however, Quine tended not to cite this argument; partly because of various underlying complexities concerning the undetermination of theory thesis itself, and partly because those issues tend to obscure the main point. He tended rather to clarify and to refine the thesis itself, without providing arguments for it. In a late piece – 'Indeterminacy without Tears' – Quine wrote:

> The following ... is an aseptic restatement of the imagined conflict between the two impeccable manuals. We have a recording of a long native discourse, and we have smooth, clear English translation of it from the two manuals; but if we mesh the translations, alternating them sentence by sentence, the result is incoherent. (Quine, 2008a [1994], pp. 447–8)

This is rather vague, but its significance is that Quine wishes to enunciate a thesis which by his lights makes relative sense in terms of linguistic behaviour, which a thesis including the word 'meaning' would not.

If the more radical thesis is thus clarified, the argument for it is not. Yet – and this is crucial to understanding Quine – it is ultimately not so important whether the radical indeterminacy thesis is true. Quine takes it as quite reasonable to suppose that if a language can be translated one way, then it's likely that there will be other ways. But the fate of Quine's scheme does not rest on that of the indeterminacy thesis. The scheme as outlined in the last section says or implies nothing about it, and in fact Quine, in later years, after having discussed the thesis in print on number of occasions, said that the thesis is merely a 'conjecture', that is, with no knock-down reasons either for it or against it. That a scheme of language allows the *possibility* of such a thing is itself the important fact; it flies the face of our intuitive expectations. And if within the bounds of Quine's conception of language it so happened that there are no such cases, that would not threaten the conception; indeed it would benefit from the consonance with common sense. If there were no indeterminacy, then classes of translationally equivalent sentences could be called 'the meaning' of a sentence – but the explanation of why the classes are as they are would nevertheless be independent of and prior to the application of the concept of meaning.

Quine doesn't officially use the concept of meaning, but is well aware that the word 'meaning' is a part of language. He devotes several pages over the years to explaining how in fact the word is employed, not by philosophers or theoretical linguists but by lexicographers and ordinary persons, and finds rather a rag-bag of different uses that do not add up to anything like a systematic theory. And if they did, then perhaps the *conceivability* of indeterminacy shows that the intuitive notion of meaning is contradictory and so must be rejected from science, like the pre-Russell intuitive or naive notion of set, or the concept of absolute simultaneity in physics.

5. Ontological relativity, realism and truth

The argument to the inscrutability or indeterminacy of *reference* remains unscathed by the doubts one might have of indeterminacy generally. Indeed, the force of the point can be stated without mentioning meaning, reference, semantics, interpretation or translation. One could in principle re-cast the whole of one's theory – one's science or beliefs – explicitly into a theory of proxies. Thus the lesson is one of the *epistemology* of the relation between evidence and theory: no matter what our theory contains, it is always possible to reconfigure it as theory concerning different objects. There will typically be no reason to, but still the possibility is real and remains open. The upshot is that ontology is 'defused'; the question of what there is doesn't have quite the status that Quine thought it had early his career.[7] To invoke yet another Quineism: the ideology of a theory – its predicates and structure – and not its ontology – the particular things of which the predicates are true – is where the action is.

To be sure, the hold of the contrary thought, that reference is the key to the mind–world relation, can be powerful. For surely one speaker could have exactly the same linguistic dispositions as another, yet those two speakers refer to different things, as suggested by Hilary Putnam's twin-worlds and similar scenarios (two groups of speakers might be sensitive to just the same sorts of cat-like appearances, for instance, but one group be referring to things of the species *Felis catus*, while the others refer to cat-like things of a different kind – see Putnam, 1975). Quine is indeed committed to such creatures possessing exactly the same linguistic properties. The notion of a linguistic disposition is meant to provide for the explanation of language in terms of causal relevance; if two creatures have *all* the same precise dispositions then they have all the same causal propensities. But Quine feels that such possibilities as Putnam describes, besides being fanciful, are not so important that they refute his brand of naturalism.

The study of what philosophers call the relation between mind or language and the world or reality boils down to observation sentences and their causal interface. According to naturalism, the story takes place having *presupposed* the world. There is thus no question of deriving from such an account conclusions which might jeopardize the reality of objects. Quine is a realist, but a common-sense if not naive realist. He does not assert a more deep-going realism in terms of reference to the external world – not because he thinks such a doctrine false so much as spurious and ill-conceived; he simply sees no reason to accept that there is a queer relation between the mind and reality which is effected by reference. By the same token, he does not accept anti-realism: that dialectic is in play only if one accepts something that Quine rejects, namely that the reality of the world is something to be decided after the results of one's theory of reference are in.

Quine did say in 'Two Dogmas' that ordinary objects are 'posits, comparable epistemologically, to the gods of Homer' (FLPV, p. 44);

the language chosen was perhaps intemperate, but all that Quine meant is that an ancient Greek picks up a language with certain terms, just as we do words for ordinary objects. The Greek may have believed in the gods, but he was wrong, just as we sometimes errantly suppose something to exist. It is not that the difference on the score of certainty, or embeddedness in our conceptual scheme, between ordinary objects and the gods is not vast; but as vast as the difference is, it is not a difference of principle. To call something a posit, says Quine, 'is not to patronize it' (WO, p. 22).

Quine's naturalism also dovetails with his stance on *truth*. Just as reference played no role in articulating the relation between language and reality, neither does truth. We have a truth predicate because we sometimes must have recourse to what Quine calls 'semantic ascent'. The basic fact about truth is that we may assert, within our language, all such sentences as ' "Snow is white" is true if only if Snow is white'. Truth is at bottom *disquotational*: the effect of ascribing truth to a sentence is equivalent to asserting that same sentence shorn of quotation-marks, 'disquoted'. That in itself does not expand the expressiveness of our language, but what 'true' does make available is another *dimension of generalization*. We can generalize on 'This man is mortal' by writing 'Every man is mortal'. Similarly we can generalize on ' "1 + 2 = 2" is a theorem of arithmetic and 1 +1 = 2' by writing 'Every theorem of arithmetic is true' (PT, pp. 80–1). Such sentences are not equivalent to any sentence not containing the word 'true'; such is the irreducible dividend of 'true'.

Truth does not afford a detached, transcendent or otherwise categorically wider or deeper perspective on language, knowledge or the world. Truth does not consist in the existence of supernatural rays connecting sentences or mental states to reality, any more than reference does. By 'truth is immanent' (TT, pp. 21–2), Quine means that 'is true' is a device of English whose objects are sentences of English; the concern of ' "Snow is white" is true' is just the whiteness of snow, nothing more.

6. Quine's influence

Much of Quine's influence is a matter of provoking responses, but many of his would-be critics have filtered his views through assumptions he would not have endorsed and do not engage fully with his views or his naturalism. Hilary Putnam and David Lewis have been influenced more directly, though still they emerge with very different points of view.

Donald Davidson has been the most explicitly close to Quine, serving both as champion and critic. As champion he endorses Quine's emphasis on a careful accounting of the facts relevant to translation, though his use of the apparatus for handling truth invented by Alfred Tarski in the interpretation of speakers' linguistic behaviour is a novel element which introduces significant changes in outlook.[8] As critic, Davidson finds fault with Quine's views on both reference and truth (Davidson, 2005, pp. 47–62, and pp. 63–80). Rather than worry over how two people can learn the same observation sentence when their sensory constitutions differ, Davidson identifies the salient cause of the two responses as the object of reference. And Davidson urges that the concept of truth is transcendental, not immanent: according to his approach to interpretation, we must ascribe truth to utterances in advance of interpretation, which strictly speaking is not possible if truth is immanent as Quine claims. So although Davidson's view is promising even from Quine's point of view, it is debatable with how much of Quine's naturalism the view is consistent.

Further reading

The best and most comprehensive introduction to Quine is Hylton's book, listed below. Also recommended is *The Philosophy of W. V. Quine: An Expository Essay*, by Roger Gibson (Gainesville, FL: University of Florida Press, 1982), which has a slightly different emphasis; and the relatively short *Quine: A Guide for the Perplexed*, by Gary Kemp (London: Continuum, 2006). Of the many volumes of essays devoted to Quine, two of the best, not least because they contain Quine's responses, are *Words and Objections: Essays on the Work of W. V. Quine*, ed. D. Davidson and J. Hintikka (Dordrecht: Reidel, 1969) and *The Philosophy of W. V. Quine*, ed. Lewis Edwin Hahn and Paul Arthur Schilpp (Carbondale, IL: Open Court, 1986); also good and pitched at a more introductory level is *The Cambridge Companion to Quine*, ed. Roger F. Gibson, Jr (Cambridge: Cambridge University Press, 2004).

Notes

1   The first is at present the most cited article in the philosophy of
    language; it –registers over 8,000 citations in Google Scholar; the
    second is presently the second most cited book, just behind Saul
    Kripke's *Naming and Necessity.*
2   See the chapter on Carnap in this volume.
3   Frege's *Begriffsschrift* appeared in 1879 but to almost no notice;
    the first volume of Whitehead and Russell's *Principia Mathematica*
    appeared in 1910. See the chapters on Frege and Russell in this
    volume.
4   Quine's most considered treatment of the issue is in 'Two Dogmas in
    Retrospect' (CE, pp. 390–400). See also Hylton (2007, pp. 65–8).
5   Some perceive striking similarities to the Private Language Argument in
    Wittgenstein; see the chapter on the later Wittgenstein in this volume.
6   One characterization of indeterminacy is as follows. Suppose that
    you and I, in carrying out our respective translations of Language
    X, differed so radically that you translate a certain sentence as S
    and I translate the same sentence as not-S. Suppose further that the
    sentence of Language X were neither affirmed nor denied by the
    natives, and likewise we agree that 'S if and only if not-S' is a logical
    falsehood. That would amount to indeterminacy, expressible without
    using terms such as 'meaning'. But merely to describe it gives no reason
    to think it actually obtains.
7   Contrast FLPV, pp. 1–19, with CE, pp. 404–6, 458, and 469–71.
    Quine writes:

> In my youth I thought of the question of existence, or what there
> is, as perhaps the most basic question of philosophy and science. In
> the fullness of time the scales fell from my eyes. Any two ontologies
> are equally supported by all possible data if we can express a one-
> to-one correlation, what I call a proxy-function, between them.
> (Quine, CE, p. 189)

8   See the chapter on Davidson in this volume.

Bibliography

Works by W. V. Quine

Quine, W. V. (1960), *Word and Object* (noted in text as WO). Cambridge,
    MA: MIT Press.

Quine, W. V. (1961 [1953]), *From a Logical Point of View*, 2nd edn (noted
in text as FLPV). Cambridge, MA: Harvard University Press.
Quine, W. V. (1969), *Ontological Relativity and Other Essays* (noted in
text as OR). New York: Columbia University Press.
Quine, W. V. (1974), *The Roots of Reference* (noted in text as RR). La
Salle, IL: Open Court.
Quine, W. V. (1976), *Ways of Paradox*, revised edn (noted in text as WP).
Cambridge, MA: Harvard University Press.
Quine, W. V. (1981), *Theories and Things* (noted in text as TT).
Cambridge, MA: Harvard University Press.
Quine, W. V. (1992), *Pursuit of Truth* (noted in text as PT), 2nd edn.
Cambridge, MA: Harvard University Press.
Quine, W. V. (1995), *From Stimulus to Science* (noted in text as SS).
Cambridge, MA: Harvard University Press.
Quine, W. V. (2008a), *Confessions of a Confirmed Extensionalist and
Other Essays* (noted in text as CE), ed. D. Føllesdal and D. B. Quine.
Cambridge, MA: Harvard University Press.
Quine, W. V. (2008b), *Quine in Dialogue* (noted in text as QD), ed. D.
Føllesdal and D. B. Quine. Cambridge, MA: Harvard University
Press.

Works by others

Carnap, R. (1937 [1934]), *The Logical Syntax of Language*, trans.
Amethe Smeaton. London: Routledge and Kegan Paul.
Carnap, R. (1967 [1928]), *The Logical Structure of the World
and Pseudoproblems in Philosophy*, trans. R. George. Los
Angeles: University of California Press.
Davidson, D. (2005), *Truth, Language, and History*. Oxford: Oxford
University Press.
Frege, G. (1953 [1884]), *The Foundations of Arithmetic*, trans. J. Austin.
London: Basil Blackwell.
Frege, G. (1967 [1879]), *Begriffsschrift*. Reprinted in J. van
Heijenoort (ed.), *From Frege to Gödel: A Source Book in
Mathematical Logic, 1879–1931*. Cambridge, MA: Harvard
University Press, pp. 1–82.
Frege, G. (1984), *Collected Papers on Mathematics, Logic,
and Philosophy*, ed. B. McGuinness, trans. M. Black et al.
London: Blackwell.
Hylton, P. (2007), *Quine*. London: Routledge.
Kripke, S. (1972/1980) *Naming and Necessity*, revised edn. Cambridge,
MA: Harvard University Press.

Putnam, H. (1975), 'The Meaning of "Meaning"', in his *Mind, Language and Reality, Philosophical Papers, volume 2*. Cambridge: Cambridge University Press, pp. 215–71.

Russell, B. (1997 [1912]), *The Problems of Philosophy*, with an introduction by J. Perry. Oxford: Oxford University Press.

Whitehead, A. N. and Russell, B. (1910; 2nd edn, 1927), *Principia Mathematica*. Cambridge: Cambridge University Press.

Wittgenstein, L. (2001 [1953]), *Philosophical Investigations*, ed. and trans. E. Anscombe. London: Blackwell.

CHAPTER NINE

CHOMSKY
John Collins

1. Introduction

Noam Chomsky is in the lineage of philosopher-scientists, such as Descartes, Newton, Turing and Einstein. That is, he has not only offered great theoretical insights, but has also had a constant eye on the methodological and philosophical consequences of his empirical work. To be sure, unlike the other luminaries, the lasting significance of Chomsky's ideas is a matter for the future. What is beyond dispute is that his work has reconfigured two whole disciplines – linguistics and psychology – and has had a tremendous impact on current philosophy of language and mind, equal, I think, to any other contemporary thinker. Chomsky would perhaps not feature in a professional philosophers' Top 10 of the last century, but nor would Einstein.

In the following section, I shall briefly sketch Chomsky's general naturalistic orientation. The third section will elaborate an *internalism* about language that Chomsky takes to be a consequence of his naturalism. The remaining two sections will elaborate on Chomsky's remarks about semantics, and defend his semantic internalism against some objections.

2. Naturalism about language

Physicists say many strange things. For Newton, my waving my hand here on Earth has an instantaneous effect on Saturn. Faraday averred that things are never in contact. Eddington denied the existence of the table before him. Nowadays, string theorists claim that there are ten spatial dimensions, with seven of them wrapped up inside the remaining space-time dimensions. Some of these claims are perhaps simply unintelligible without the maths. Still, no one now, I think, would suggest that physicists are wrong to make such claims *because* they clash with common sense. Such licence to be counter-intuitive is granted, not simply on the basis of the great success physics has enjoyed, but primarily because it is understood that explanation of any depth must not be constrained to hold to the pre-theoretical concepts with which we readily carve up the world and, indeed, begin inquiry. Theories seek to be universal, to discover the hidden unities that tie together otherwise disparate phenomena. Such goals would be unthinkable if physics were constrained to employ the imprecise and perspective-bound concepts we unreflectively employ in our normal dealings with the world.

Throughout his career, Chomsky has championed such methodological freedom in an area closer to home than physics, namely, our knowledge, acquisition and use of language. Under his influence, what was a humanities discipline has transformed into something recognizable as a science.[1] In his first book, *The Logical Structure of Linguistic Theory* (written in the 1950s, but not published until 1975), Chomsky writes:

> [A] field of investigation cannot be clearly delimited in advance of the theory dealing with this subject matter; in fact, it is one of the functions of a theory to give such a precise delimitation. Before we have constructed a linguistic theory we can only have certain vaguely formulated questions to guide the development of the theory. A simple and natural theory, once established, determines the precise formulation of the questions that originally motivated it, and leads to the formulation and resolution of new problems that could not previously have been raised. (Chomsky, 1955–6/1975, p. 61)

As a description of inquiry in the physical sciences, these remarks are quite unremarkable. Pertaining to language, however, they mean that we must be unconstrained by any notion that languages are public 'objects' more or less known by divergent populations, or that languages must somehow be open to view, transparent to adults, who inculcate the young into their linguistic practices. Language and its acquisition are empirical phenomena that are as likely to elude our pre-theoretical conception as any other complex phenomena. What a theory must do, then, is target some apparently stable phenomena and progress from that basis, free from a priori views of what language *is*. Vague talk of language being public, social, transparent, essentially communicable, or being *for* this or that does not designate any kind of phenomenon at all, still less a stable one.

Two facts, however, seem eminently stable in advance of any theorizing:

Complex competence: Each speaker/hearer is continuously novel in their consumption and production of language and possesses a mass of 'feelings' and 'judgements' about their language that in part informs their competence with the language.

Universality: Each 'normal' human acquires at least one language with no conscious effort and no explicit tutelage. They could have acquired any other language, no matter how distinct, with equal alacrity. A Vietnamese baby, for example, is not fated to speak Vietnamese, or any other particular language.

So, we begin with two leading questions. The first is concerned with what we know such that we can be effortlessly competent with such an apparently complex thing as a language (we shall see how complex it is shortly). The second major question is concerned with what we all must share as humans, given the fact that we can acquire any given language with equal ease – a feat beyond any other species, no matter how much explicit tutelage is provided. The two questions, of course, are intimate, for only in light of some theoretical formulation of our mature competence is it possible seriously to inquire into how that competence develops within individual humans; simply put, if we don't know what language is, we shall hardly be in a position to understand its development. This explanatory order also holds for the question of the evolution of language. We cannot seriously inquire into the evolution of *anything* without having a solid conception of just what evolved.

There are, to be sure, many other fundamental questions to be asked about language apart from what it is and how it develops in individuals. How do we use language? How does language change? How did language evolve in the hominid line? How is linguistic knowledge realized in the human brain? Why is language the way it is and not some other way? Chomsky does not mean to ignore these questions; on the contrary, his idea is that only once we have some working answer to our two leading questions can we profitably think about the others (Chomsky, 1995, pp. 1–2). In fact, lines of inquiry are pursued simultaneously: the dependence I have in mind is explanatory or logical.

Let us look at some linguistic phenomena that exhibit both the complexity of normal linguistic competence and the demands such complexity imposes on an account of language acquisition.

Consider the following:

(1)   Who do you want to help?

Note that (1) is ambiguous between a reading where (i) you want to give help to someone, or (ii) someone is such that you want *them* to help with something; that is, we can take (1) to be related to either of the following sentences:

(2)   a.   You want WHO to help
      b.   You want to help WHO

In other words, (1) can be a questioning of the subject or object of *help*. Now, *want+to* is often contracted to *wanna*. So we can have:

(3)   Who do you wanna help?

(3) is not ambiguous. It only has a reading in which the object is questioned corresponding to (2b). For sure, the difference is subtle, but is generally witnessed (acknowledged by all speakers).[2] To see the difference clearly, consider:

(4) a. Who do you want to help Bill
    b. *Who do you wanna help Bill

Sentence (4a) is not ambiguous at all: it only has the reading where the helper of Bill is questioned; (4b), on the other hand, is not even acceptable, and is not generally witnessed. Try saying it out loud; 'Bill' is dangling, as if you were addressing Bill.

What's going on? One suggestion is that the phenomena turn on the presence of *empty categories* – elements of structures that are mentally represented in the understanding of the sentences, but which do not support any phonological properties (think of them as invisible words). So, (1) can roughly be represented in two ways:

(5) a. Who do you want <who> to help
    b. Who do you want PRO to help <who>

Here '<who>' and 'PRO' are empty categories. We may assume PRO to be a fixed pronoun-like element, which can either be 'free' or dependent on some other elements. For purposes of understanding the present examples, PRO can be read as a reflexive linked to the preceding subject. So, (5b) can be read as *Who do you want yourself to help.* (The status of PRO is currently controversial, but the theoretical interest of the contraction data remains unaffected by the various disagreements about PRO.) Copies like '<who>' are items that mark the presence of an element that has moved higher up the structure. In our example, for instance, *who* serves as both subject/object of an embedded verb and as a question-operator. We now have the means to frame a generalization in terms of contraction not being possible in the location of copied elements like <who>, but being possible in the location of PRO. That appears to capture the data. Sentence (3) is acceptable, and it's not ambiguous, because it only has a reading where *who* is not understood to be in the location of the contraction, whereas (4b) is not acceptable, because the contraction must be in the location of the copied *who*. Now, that is fairly elegant, but hardly convincing; after all, it seems extravagant to posit something like empty categories to explain something so trivial and seemingly parochial. The generalization, though, works more broadly.

Consider the following:

(6) a.   Bill is intending to arrive the same time as I am
         <intending to arrive>.
    b.   *Bill is intending to arrive the same time as I'm
         <intending to arrive>.
    c.   Do you know where the meeting is *<where>* tomorrow?
    d.   *Do you know where the meeting's *<where>*
         tomorrow?
    e.   Do you know why the meeting is tomorrow *<why>*?
    f.   Do you know why the meeting's tomorrow *<why>*?

Here we witness exactly the same pattern with other kinds of
contraction, which corroborates the initial hypothesis. The
significance of empty categories is also independently witnessed;
in fact, empty categories were initially proposed for theoretical
reasons entirely independent from contraction phenomena (see
Chomsky, 1975). Consider:

(7) a.   Mary wants to leave by herself
    b.   *Mary wants to leave by himself
    c.   Sarah wonders who Mary wants to leave by herself
    d.   Sarah wonders who Mary wants to leave by himself

Sentence (7a) is acceptable when non-embedded and when
embedded, as in (7c). On the other hand, (7b) is not acceptable
when non-embedded, but becomes acceptable when embedded. We
immediately recognize the difference, even though, for most readers,
I imagine such a pattern had never occurred to them, still less was it
taught them, no matter what school they went to.

Again, the pattern can be explained by the positing of empty
categories. Let the following representations hold:

(8) a.   Mary$_i$ wants PRO$_i$ to leave by herself/*himself
    b.   Sarah wonders who Mary wants *<who>* to leave by
         herself/himself

Here, we take PRO to be referentially dependent on *Mary* (as
marked by the indexes); hence, only (7a) is acceptable. Because *who*
is gender-neutral, it can serve as the antecedent of either *herself* or
himself.

The present point is not that these particular analyses are definitely correct; the point is only that we have *some* explanation of the data by way of positing structure that is wholly abstract, in no way recorded by the explicit means of linguistic expression. The data are not explained by vague appeals to communication or use or meaning or context or intentions or any number of other philosophical shibboleths; or rather, at least to my knowledge, no one has even attempted to explain such data and innumerable other such patterns witnessed in all of the world's languages without appeal to some abstract structure that far transcends what is publicly available. If, then, some such account as sketched above is correct, speaker/hearers understand sentences by way of abstract concepts, such as PRO and *copy*. Furthermore, such understanding is obviously not some kind of intellectual achievement, for children too must employ the same resources, for they understand the sentences equally, and no one has instructed them in their acceptability. In a very real sense, therefore, inquiry governed by our leading questions is internalist in that it targets a speaker/hearer's unconscious representational machinery. What there is to language, as an empirical phenomenon, is just what enters into our best theories.[3] It thus becomes moot what sense there is in appeals to public languages, at least if the topic is our linguistic competence and its development.

3. Internalism about language

From a philosophical perspective, the above reasoning can seem too quick, and potentially dubious, for '[i]t remains an open question whether the rules hypothesised by a grammar are psychologically real' (Devitt, 2006, p. 9). Devitt here echoes many other philosophers.[4] Devitt's underlying thought is true enough. If we begin with a collection of sentence types, as exemplified above, and then hypothesize various structures involving copies and PRO and much more besides, then it is surely extravagant to claim that such structure is somehow 'in the head' of the competent user of the language, even if the posited structures do reflect the pattern of our judgements about the exhibited sentences. The kind of worry Devitt voices, however, only makes sense if premised on the idea that we have no broader theoretical interests in developing syntactic notions of copy and PRO, as if we first have a grammar embodying copy and PRO and then are left wondering what the grammar could be true of, maybe languages understood in some non-cognitive, external sense, or maybe the speaker/hearer's psychology. As it is, Chomsky's very point is that we begin with our leading questions, which are squarely psychological, and develop theories as answers to them. In this respect, we are not in a neutral position, and it is the burden of those who would imagine grammars to be about an external language to say why such a conception of language enters into or is presupposed by our leading questions. Chomsky (1981a, p. 7) writes:

> The shift of focus from language (an obscure and I believe ultimately unimportant notion) to grammar [i.e. the cognitive states underlying our competence] is essential if we are to proceed towards assimilating the study of language to the natural sciences. It is a move from data collection and organization to the study of the real systems that actually exist (in the mind/brain) and that enter into an explanation of the phenomena we observe. Contrary to what is widely assumed, the notion 'language' (however characterized) is of a higher order of abstraction and idealization than grammar, and correspondingly, the study of 'language' introduces new and more difficult problems. One may ask whether there is any reason to try to clarify or define such a notion and whether any purpose is served in doing so. Perhaps so, but I am sceptical.

The reasoning here is methodological, not metaphysical. The idea of an external language might or might not receive a clear characterization. Whether it does or not is, without further ado, irrelevant to inquiry into the character and development of a speaker/hearer's linguistic competence. This is because, as Chomsky notes, the very idea of a public language is an abstraction from what particular members of a population understand; the idea of such a language, then, presupposes some linguistic cognition on the part of the users of that language, which is precisely the target of Chomsky's inquiry.

Responses can be made, for sure. One could entertain a Platonist position, under which a language is somehow a mind-independent, abstract object. In this sense, our linguistic cognition would be one thing; the language we represent would be something else entirely.[5] One can, to be sure, talk this way; it comes naturally to us to reify any abstract noun. The real problem with Platonism is not that it is inherently obscure or introduces a host of mysteries. (Are there languages in Plato's heaven no one uses? If not, why not? If so, how do we get to use one of them?) The problem is that Platonic languages are irrelevant, pointless. If languages are abstract objects, then the only way we could discover their properties would be to study the users of the language, an inquiry that does not presuppose or establish the language as an abstract object. That is, if there were no languages as abstract objects, the methodology and results of linguistics would be exactly as if there were. In essence, therefore, Platonism is merely a metaphysical thesis rather than the natural ontology of a theory that targets our linguistic competence. This reasoning, note, does not refute the very idea of Platonism; it simply tells us that the truth of the thesis is irrelevant to empirical inquiry.

One line of resistance to this reasoning goes as follows. We *know* a language; at any rate, we know lots of facts about the language we speak. If we know a language, then the language must somehow be external to us; otherwise, there would be no difference between the language *seeming* to us to be a certain way, and the language actually being that way. So, given that we do have linguistic knowledge, a thorough internalism about language is mistaken.

The distinction between how things seem and how things are is clearly correct, but the mere distinction does not create any trouble for Chomsky. Chomsky (1981b, p. 223) writes:

> [S]aying that a person knows his grammar and knows the rules and principles of his grammar ... does not imply that he has propositional knowledge that these are the rules and principles of his grammar. The linguist may develop such propositional knowledge, but that is quite a different matter.

This is not to say, of course, that competent speaker/hearers do not know a language, or that they don't know many details about it. The point is that when we speak this way, we have in mind the mass of feelings and intuitions that arise from competence; we don't have in mind the theorist's principles that are attributed to speaker/hearers in order to *explain* the feelings and intuitions.

4. Internalist semantics

According to Chomsky's methodological brand of naturalism, empirical inquiry into language is not constrained to cleave to any pre-theoretical conceptions of the relevant linguistic phenomena. In particular, on the basis of the leading questions that reflect perhaps the most stable and salient phenomena, we are led to eschew any public or external conception of language, not because such a conception cannot be consistently spelt out, but because it appears to be redundant. Naturalistic inquiry into language is therefore internalist, which means nothing more than that linguistics is conceived as a science of states theoretically individuated independently of factors external to the organism. Of course, many external factors enter into the possibility of a human mind/brain developing in such a way as to enable the subject's realization of a linguistic competence, not least the basic environmental factors that sustain the life of an organism. Internalism only claims that the generalizations that serve to explain linguistic phenomena do not factor in external kinds. For example, no one thinks that an isolated child will acquire language. The crucial point is that the input that suffices for the development of language varies massively, so much so that there is next to no prospect of generalizations framed over the states of mature linguistic competence and input kinds. In crude terms, independently of the linguistic mind, there is no kind at all that encompasses the varied sound waves, inscriptions and hand gestures that correspond to the sentence *The cat sat on the mat*.

Although Chomsky's ideas have proved to be highly controversial in philosophy, there is perhaps now broad acceptance of the general naturalistic approach to language in the area of syntax. In the area of semantics or meaning, however, Chomsky's views remain very much against the mainstream. In the remainder of the present section, I shall provide some background to Chomsky's views on semantics. In the following section, I shall briefly defend Chomsky's position against some objections.

4.1 Autonomy

Chomsky is celebrated for his work on syntax, but is much less noted as someone with developed views on semantics. In part, this is due to the common misconception that Chomsky's early 'autonomy thesis' (1955–6/1975, 1957) was somehow an anti-semantic thesis. Crudely put, the 'thesis' claims that syntactic hypotheses may be formulated without their prior grounding in semantic concepts. Such methodological advice, however, is not intended to denigrate semantic inquiry ('an essential task for linguistics' (Chomsky, 1955–6/1975, p. 97)), but only to suggest that the kind of structural phenomena revealed by syntactic inquiry have no clear rationale or explanation in terms of existing conceptions of meaning, a claim highly controversial in the 1950s (Chomsky, 1955).[6] For example, from the perspective of meaning, why on earth should contraction be limited in the ways detailed above? Thus, in the absence of a compelling argument that structural phenomena *must* be based on semantics, syntax can and should be studied on its own terms. From a naturalistic perspective, this advice is unobjectionable. Chomsky (1957, pp. 101–3) made a further claim which is much less discussed, although far more intriguing. He suggested that syntax may be happily construed as part of semantics, in the sense that one fruitful way of approaching meaning is to figure out how the 'vehicles' of meaning are structured. Such structural facts obviously affect and constrain what can be meant by a construction. Perhaps the best way of exhibiting the syntactic constraints on meaning is to consider the ambiguity of *minimal pairs*.

Take the following sentence:

(9)   The duck is easy to eat

This sentence is unambiguous; it has the single reading corresponding to the paraphrase: *It is easy for one to eat the duck*. That is to say, the duck itself is not easy in a *to eat*-kind of way; it is the eating of the duck that is easy. In abstract terms, *easy* modifies the event of the duck being eaten, not the duck itself. But compare (9) to (10), where we have just substituted one adjective for another:

(10)   The duck is ready to eat

One reading of (10) is immediately accessible: *The duck is ready for one to eat it*. Note that this reading is distinct from the sole reading of (9); here, *ready* does modify *the duck*, not its eating. Also unlike (9), (10) has a second reading, which is not so readily accessible: *The duck is ready for itself to eat something or other* (imagine a pet duck recovering from ill health). In short, *the duck* can be both subject or object of *eat* (the eater or the eaten) in (10), but may only be the object of *eat* in (9). This difference produces the difference in the number of readings between (9) and (10), but the only difference between the two sentences is the presence of the adjectives *easy* or *ready*. In some sense, therefore, a speaker's understanding of the adjectives involves a cognizance, albeit tacit, of the structural facts just sketched.

The difference between *easy* and *ready* manifests itself structurally in other ways, too. Consider the cases in (11):

(11) a.   *The duck is easy to be eaten
      b.   The duck is ready to be eaten

Now, (11a) 'feels' as if it should mean the same as (9), only in the passive: *It is easy for the duck to be eaten by one*. For all that, it fails to have the reading: *easy* forces its grammatical subject (*the duck*) to be distinct from the understood subject of the infinitive subordinate clause (*to be eaten*), but that subject position is the only one in which *the duck* may be understood relative to *eat* – that is, the duck is not eating, so it must be the thing being eaten. In distinction, (11b) is ambiguous. On one readily available meaning, it means the same as one reading of (10), where the duck is ready for someone or other to eat it. On another reading, one may say the duck is prepared to meet its maker, a reading which (10) lacks. The difference is between thinking of the duck being ready as a piece of meat or being ready as a cognitive agent. This subtle difference is easily explicable. The active *to eat* implies something eaten, whether stated or not, so when we construe (10) with *the duck* construed as the eater, the duck is an agent. With (11b), *the duck* as the subject of the passive *to be eaten* cannot be an agent (the eater), but there are two different ways in which one can be ready to be eaten simply because ready is ambiguous between a mental and physical state.

So, with just single changes of word without changes of grammatical category, we go from no ambiguity, to two-way ambiguity, to nonsense, back to two-way ambiguity, save different from the first pair of ambiguities. We may say that syntactic structure is somehow bound up in the meanings of words, but is not, in any straightforward sense, derivable from what we take the words to mean. The crucial point, for our purposes, is that such facts about meaning are syntactically grounded. The philosopher may offer a theory of propositions and correctly claim that (9) is associated with one of them, (10) is associated with two of them, (11a) is associated with none of them, and (11b), like (10), is associated with two of them, although not the same two. This advances not a jot, however, our understanding of why the association of meanings is different across the four cases.

So far so good, but granting that the structural conditions on meaning are syntactic, and so internalist by the lights of the above discussion, does not establish that meaning is similarly internalist. Content is one thing, its vehicle is quite another. I shall, here, only consider three principal reasons for the rejection of internalism: (i) the intimacy of truth and reference with meaning; (ii) the possibility of error; and (iii) externalist thought experiments. In his more recent writings, Chomsky (1996, 2000, 2004) has challenged the externalist reasoning in these three areas, although his criticisms go back much further (1975, 1980). In the following section, rather than present Chomsky's arguments in all their detail, I shall endeavour to distil the arguments against each of the considerations just mentioned.

5. Problems with externalism

5.1 Meaning and truth

In general terms, to specify the meaning of an expression is (at least) to specify its contribution to the truth-conditions of the constructions of which it is a possible constituent; but truth and reference are external relations; so, meaning essentially involves externalia. Chomsky (2000, p. 174) does not so much dispute the intimate connection, but rather suggests that semantic theorizing is really a part of syntax, in a broad sense. The basic point here is that the kind of semantic theorizing that assigns unique external 'semantic values' to linguistic material often does not reflect, and is not constrained by, our independent conceptions of the relevant objects. So, of course, truth and reference are external relations, but to specify linguistic meaning is not to specify independent externalia to which lexical items refer or are *true of*. To see the point here, consider an adaptation of one of Chomsky's examples:

(12)   Bill had the book in mind for four years, and was very pleased when it sold 1,000 copies in the first week, especially since it weighs two pounds.

If we take *book* to refer to books, (12) would appear to commit us to some *thing* that can be abstract/content (be in one's mind), be a type that can have copies, and be concrete (have weight). Now, the point here is *not* that the existence of such a thing is impossible or contradictory. The point, rather, is that understanding (12) hardly commits one to the possibility of such a thing, which flies in the face of our common-sense metaphysics that separates concrete from abstract objects. Of course, it would be madness to conclude that *book* does not refer to books (what else would it refer to? Cats?). The point of the example is only to highlight that it would be a mistake (a mistake we never make) to project from the semantic aspects of a word to a kind of object that independently exists. This being so, it is equally misguided to think that the semantic properties of our words are somehow answerable to or derivable from independently existing kinds of things. None of us really believe in such things as books, if by *book* one means things that realize all the properties *book* may be used to speak about.

Similar remarks apply to any noun one may care to consider (to say nothing of the abstractness of verbs and adjectives). Consider proper names.

It is standard in philosophical discussions to specify the meaning of a name disquotationally, which simply means that one specifies the referent of the name by using the name. For example:

(Dis-Name) 'Mary' refers to Mary

There is something right about such specifications, of course, but only in that the arbitrariness of the name–world relation is captured. What the disquotational method cannot explain, at least not without further ado, is how proper names may designate persons, concrete things, stuff or abstract objects, depending on the choice of verb, independently of whether we take the name to refer to any existent thing or not. Consider:

(13) a. After the steamroller was finished, Father Christmas was smeared across the road
       b. What this drama series needs is a Shakespeare

It doesn't matter if *Father Christmas* and *Shakespeare* are fiction names; they behave just like referring proper names in being able to serve as both mass nouns and abstract nouns. It is hardly for linguistics to decide or even care if there really was a playwright from Stratford, rather than one or more secret authors.

The problem for externalism in the cases rehearsed is *not* that names cannot be construed as labels for things in the world, and so cannot possess meanings specifiable merely by 'disquoting'. The problem is that such a conception of names does not appear to explain much of their content. Why on earth should names have such varied semantic aspects invariant over the existence and inexistence of their putative referents, if they are mere labels for things?

The bottom line, here, is that a name, just like any other lexical item, offers a complex set of perspectives with which we can speak about the world and fictions indifferently, but no one imagines that the perspectives at issue all reside in things out there anyhow. Chomsky (2004, p. 391) expresses the general point:

> We can, if we like, say that the word 'book' refers to books, 'sky' to the sky, 'health' to health, and so on. Such conventions basically express lack of interest in the semantic properties of words and how they are used to talk about things.

5.2 *Going right and wrong*

We can, it seems, go wrong about language, both semantically and syntactically. If, however, properties of language were in fact entirely determined by individual cognitive states, then how could we go wrong about language? Anything we thought was right, would be right, given that there would be, by hypothesis, no external language to which we are answerable. So, the very possibility of error appears to require externalism.

First off, internalism is not inconsistent with the possibility of linguistic error. All that internalism entails is that speakers do not go wrong about an external language/meaning. Internalism is perfectly consistent with the bare idea of speakers going wrong, deviating from their own criteria or standards, which might even be conceived by speakers as involving a public language or ways of speaking given a particular audience, say. So, what externalism requires is an argument that linguistic error actually involves the appropriate externalia, not the mere presumption that it does. It is not so easy to offer a relevant case in favour of externalism. Speakers are interested in converging, perhaps for general psychological reasons that have little intrinsic connection with language, but the convergence doesn't require or create anything that has an independent life to which speakers can go right or wrong about – they are interested in converging with each other, not on a language.

Secondly, as intimated, to grant the phenomenon of linguistic error is not to grant that a theory of language must explain it. Speakers' sensitivity to error appears to be a massive interaction effect, involving many cognitive capacities, including self-consciousness, above and beyond language. Acknowledging error is not constitutive of being linguistically competent, no more than not being crass or impolite is. We perhaps unreflectively consider being susceptible to correction to be central to language because that is how we learn language in the first place (Dummett, 1978; Quine, 1960; Wiggins, 1997; among many others). As it is, no empirical study has supported such 'common sense': children learn language with remarkably little negative feedback of any kind; they tend to ignore what feedback they do receive; and they make practically no mistakes, anyhow (Crain and Thornton, 1998; Roeper, 2007). As for adults, we might consider a speaker who persists in what we regard as an 'error' to be ignorant or obtuse, but we would be leery of describing him as linguistically incompetent.

5.3 Thought experiments

A pair of thought experiments has convinced many a philosopher of the truth of externalism as regards both linguistic and mental content. The thought experiments, due to Putnam (1975) and Burge (1979; 2007), are designed to show that we individuate a subject's thought or meaning relative to their environs, physical or social, not merely how things locally (internally) stand for the subject. Thus, imagine a Twin Earth exactly like Earth in every detail save that the stuff they call water has a chemical composition of XYZ, not H_2O. XYZ falls from the sky, quenches thirst, comes in snow and ice at winter time and so on, but is not the same stuff as H_2O. Putnam (1975) asks us to reflect on Oscar (on Earth) and Twin-Oscar (on Twin-Earth), who are physical *Doppelgangers*. Now, the intuition we are invited to accept is that while both may be equally ignorant of the respective chemistry of their planets, they possess distinct concepts, albeit homophonously expressed. The reason is that Oscar's thoughts are about (made true/false by) water (H_2O), whereas Twin-Oscar's thoughts are about some other stuff (XYZ). Burge offers a social variant of the same externalist intuition, where it is community agreement about word meaning (as opposed to the facts of chemistry) that is individuative of the concepts we linguistically express. The point of both 'experiments' is to trigger the intuition that we attribute thoughts partly on the basis of how things are in the world independently of how the thinker conceives of the world.

The issues arising from this pair of 'thought experiments' take up a good deal of the philosophy of language and mind of the past two decades. Space demands a brevity that I hope is not glib.

Putnam and Burge are clearly right that we individuate certain concepts in terms of 'essences' that are not exhausted by the surface properties of typical samples of the kind. So much defeats a traditional empiricist view of concepts and is in fact supported by much empirical work in developmental psychology (e.g. Carey, 2009; Keil, 1989). What is much less clear is why such anti-empiricist essentialism supports externalism (the view that lexical meaning is partly constituted by external factors, such as the presence of a natural kind out there in the world).

The Twin Earth 'experiment' turns, not on water *being* H_2O, but only upon our meaning by 'water' some stuff reference to which is not fixed by its *apparent* properties. Satisfying this condition does not involve there being any actual kinds at all. For example, we have lots of kind concepts that have no corresponding kinds (earth, air, fire etc.); as far as cognition is concerned, it would be an accident that a given kind term corresponds to an actual kind (Chomsky, 2000, p. 149). In other words, our conceptions of word meanings might be externalist, but that is no reason to think that externalism is true, only that it is an intuition that needs explaining.

Apart from such a general complaint, the intuitions themselves are less than clear-cut. We happily call stuff 'water', and would resist correction, even though we *know* what we happen to be referring to it isn't water by chemical standards (the contents of practically any river would do). So, even when we know the relevant chemistry, it appears not to anchor our referential use of language. Equally, we certainly don't call tea or coffee 'water', even if reflection would inform us that the cup of coffee is more water than the same amount of liquid drawn from the average river or lake. Burge (2003, p. 457) responds to such complaints by suggesting that 'We all recognize that tea, coffee, and Lake Erie are mostly water'. Well, 'we' who read Burge no doubt do, but externalism is supposed to be a thesis about human conceptuality, precisely not a thesis about the general knowledge of this or that population. Milk, orange juice, cucumbers, most of the organic world, and comets too, are 'mostly water', but not even someone included in Burge's 'we' is likely to think of themselves, *qua* being 'mostly water', to fall under the extension of 'water'. Coffee made with milk is still coffee, not water, even though milk is 'mostly water'. I do not think that any orange-coloured, citrus-flavoured sweet liquid is orange juice, but I don't think orange juice is water either. Water, water everywhere, but not a drop to refer to.

As it stands, inquiry into the constitutive, metaphysical conditions of the individuation of this or that property appears to be an inquiry into the distinctive human cognitive profile, which does not presuppose any external kinds 'out there' anyhow.

6. Concluding remarks

Most philosophers would perhaps be happy to concede that syntax is internal in the sense Chomsky means, but few have followed him regarding semantics. In large part, this is perhaps due to misunderstanding. When Chomsky speaks of 'internalism', he doesn't have in mind an 'inner theatre' or essential conscious access to content; rather; internalism is a thesis about states of the brain theoretically individuated to enter into an explanation of stable linguistic phenomena. This methodological stance is mistaken if there are significant linguistic phenomena whose explanation will essentially involve external kinds. This might be the case, but only empirical inquiry will give us the answer. It is not enough to appeal to common sense, or intuitions, or what we mean by 'language', or descriptions of communicative exchanges. All of this might be externalist, but it does not therefore contradict Chomsky's internalism.[7]

Further reading

Collins, J. (2008), *Chomsky: A Guide for the Perplexed.* London: Bloomsbury.

Pietroski, P. (2018), *Conjoining Meanings: Semantics without Truth Values.* Oxford: Oxford University Press.

Uriagereka, J. (1998), *Rhyme and Reason: An Introduction to Minimalist Syntax.* Cambridge, MA: MIT Press.

Notes

1 Of course, Chomsky was not alone. He was influential, in part, because of related work being conducted in psychology, engineering, early computer science, mathematics and so on. The development of these interdisciplinary relations is what we now call the 'cognitive revolution'.

2 See Crain and Thornton (1998, chapter 21).

3 Of course, our best theories might never be good enough – might never deal with all the data – but in the absence of a priori insight into the limits of inquiry, we shall always be best advised to follow our best theories.

4 See Katz (1981), George (1989), Higginbotham (1991), Soames (1984), among many others.

5 See Katz (1981) and Katz and Postal (1991). For responses, see Chomsky (1986, chapter 2) and Collins (2009).

6 See Collins (2008, pp. 39–45) for broader discussion of the 'autonomy thesis'.

7 My thanks go to Barry Lee for many useful suggestions on content and style.

Bibliography

Burge, T. (1979), 'Individualism and the Mental', *Midwest Studies in Philosophy*, 4, pp. 73–121.

Burge, T. (2003), 'Psychology and the Environment: A Reply to Chomsky', in M. Hahn and B. Ramberg (eds), *Reflections and Replies: Essays on the Philosophy of Tyler Burge*. Cambridge, MA: MIT Press, pp. 451–70.

Burge, T. (2007), *Foundations of Mind: Philosophical Essays*, vol. II. Oxford: Clarendon Press.

Carey, S. (2009), *The Origin of Concepts*. Oxford: Oxford University Press.

Chomsky, N. (1955), 'Logical Syntax and Semantics: Their Linguistic Relevance', *Language*, 31, pp. 36–45.

Chomsky, N. (1955–6/1975), *The Logical Structure of Linguistic Theory*. New York: Plenum.

Chomsky, N. (1957), *Syntactic Structures*. The Hague: Mouton.

Chomsky, N. (1975), *Reflections on Language*. London: Fontana.

Chomsky, N. (1980), *Rules and Representations*. New York: Columbia University Press.

Chomsky, N. (1981a), 'On the Representation of Form and Function', *Linguistic Review*, 1, pp. 3–40.

Chomsky, N. (1981b), 'Knowledge of Language: Its Elements and Origins', *Philosophical Transactions of the Royal Society*, B295, pp. 223–34.

Chomsky, N. (1986), *Knowledge of Language: Its Nature, Origin and Use*. Westport, CT: Praeger.

Chomsky, N. (1995), *The Minimalist Program*. Cambridge, MA: MIT Press.

Chomsky, N. (1996), *Powers and Prospects: Reflections on Human Nature and the Social Order*. London: Pluto Press.

Chomsky, N. (2000), *New Horizons in the Study of Language and Mind*. Cambridge: Cambridge University Press.

Chomsky, N. (2004), 'Language and Mind: Current Thoughts on Ancient Problems', in L. Jenkins (ed.), *Variation and Universals in Biolinguistics*. Oxford: Elsevier, pp. 379–406.

Collins, J. (2008), *Chomsky: A Guide for the Perplexed*. London: Continuum.

Collins, J. (2009), 'Naturalism in the Philosophy of Language; Or Why There Is No Such Thing as Language', in S. Sawyer (ed.), *New Waves in the Philosophy of Language*. London: Palgrave, pp. 41–59.

Crain, S. and Thornton, R. (1998), *Investigations in Universal Grammar: A Guide to Experiments on the Acquisition of Syntax and Semantics*. Cambridge, MA: MIT Press.

Devitt, M. (2006), *Ignorance of Language*. Oxford: Oxford University Press.

Dummett, M. (1978), *Truth and Other Enigmas*. London: Duckworth.

George, A. (1989), 'How Not to Become Confused about Linguistics', in A. George (ed.), *Reflections on Chomsky*. Oxford: Blackwell, pp. 90–110.

Higginbotham, J. (1991), 'Remarks on the Metaphysics of Linguistics', *Linguistics and Philosophy*, 14, pp. 555–66.

Katz, J. (1981), *Language and Other Abstract Objects*. Oxford: Blackwell.

Katz, J. and Postal, P. (1991), 'Realism vs Conceptualism in Linguistics', *Linguistics and Philosophy*, 14, pp. 515–54.

Keil, F. (1989), *Concepts, Kinds and Cognitive Development*. Cambridge, MA: MIT Press.

McGilvray, J. (1999), *Chomsky: Language, Mind and Politics*. Cambridge: Polity.

Putnam, H. (1975): 'The Meaning of "meaning"', in his *Mind, Language, and Reality: Philosophical Papers*, Vol. 2. Cambridge: Cambridge University Press, pp. 215–72.

Quine, W. V. O. (1960), *Word and Object*. Cambridge, MA: MIT Press.

Roeper, T. (2007), *The Prism of Grammar: How Child Language Illuminates Humanism*. Cambridge, MA: MIT Press.

Soames, S. (1984), 'Linguistics and Psychology', *Linguistics and Philosophy*, 7, pp. 155–79.

Wiggins, D. (1997), 'Languages as Social Objects', *Philosophy*, 72, pp. 499–524.

CHAPTER TEN

GRICE

Kent Bach

Paul Grice (1913–1988) took on various philosophical topics, including personal identity, perception and the senses, intention, reason, and value, but he was and is best known for his work on meaning. It has had lasting impact on debates about such questions as which kind of meaning, linguistic or speaker meaning, is more fundamental and on how and where to draw the line between semantics and pragmatics. Most influential are his analysis of speaker meaning and his account of conversational implicature. Grice's ingenious notion of reflexive intention was designed to capture what is distinctive about what we intend when we communicate, and his account of conversational implicature aimed to explain how we can say one thing and manage to communicate something else – how we can utter a sentence that has one meaning, and convey something different. As we will see, Grice's account effectively repudiated Wittgenstein's famous dictum, 'Don't look for the meaning, look for the use'. His emphasis on explanations in terms of *both* meaning (word and sentence meaning) *and* use undermined certain influential claims made during the heyday of ordinary language philosophy, and his views have affected debates on a wide range of philosophical issues within and beyond philosophy of language. Indeed, his work has had lasting impact on linguistics, psychology and even computer science. His legacy is encapsulated in such widely used phrases as 'Gricean intention', 'Gricean maxims', 'Gricean pragmatics' and 'Gricean reasoning'.

1. Meaning and use

To get an intuitive feel for Grice's basic ideas and the philosophical motivations behind them, we should begin with some simple examples. Compare what a speaker is likely to mean in uttering one or the other of these sentences:

(1) Lizzie felt lousy and ate some chicken soup.
(2) Lizzie ate some chicken soup and felt lousy.

A speaker is likely to use (1) to mean that Lizzie felt lousy and, then, in order to feel better, ate some chicken soup, but use (2) to mean that Lizzie ate some chicken soup and, because of something in the soup, later felt lousy. How should this difference in meaning be explained? The only relevant difference between the two sentences is the order of the two verb phrases. That might be enough to explain the difference in meaning if 'and' meant something like 'and then, as a result', but plausibly it does not mean that, even in this particular context. In 'Toledo is in Ohio and Memphis is in Tennessee', the question of order does not even arise.

Grice held that the meaning of 'and' is adequately captured by the '&' of formal logic, notwithstanding the fine-grained observations on everyday use made by the ordinary language philosophers of Oxford, notably Grice's former teacher J. L. Austin. Their 'linguistic botanizing' was a reaction to what they regarded as the excessive formalism characteristic of such philosophers as Frege, the early Wittgenstein, and the logical positivists, who abstracted from red-blooded speech to pursue their interest in language suitable for science. Austin and his followers evidently accepted the later Wittgenstein's view that, generally speaking, 'the meaning of a word is its use in the language' (1953, p. 20). Grice in contrast pressed the importance of distinguishing meaning and use, although he granted that meaning is grounded in use, as evident from his endorsement of the analytic–synthetic distinction (Grice and Strawson, 1956).

Ordinary language philosophers like Austin noted the intuitive differences between pairs of potential utterances like (1) and (2), and pointed out that systematic semantics seemed unable to account for these differences. If 'and' is just logical conjunction, then 'A and B' should be equivalent in meaning to 'B and A'; but this doesn't seem to be the case with pairs like (1) and (2). By identifying more and more cases like this, a sceptical view of the applicability of formal methods to natural language was supported. Grice argued that the differences found in cases like the one we're considering could be explained by theories which held on to the idea that words make constant (and relatively easily capturable) contributions to determining the meanings of the sentences in which they appear, in large part by distinguishing between sentence meaning (the meaning determined by constant word meanings) and speaker or occasion meaning (the meaning got across by the speaker using the sentence they did in the particular conversational context in which they spoke). Let's look at how this works in the current case in more detail.

In the case of (1) and (2), the difference in linguistic meaning (according to the sort of theory challenged by ordinary language philosophers) is minimal or nil, but the difference in *use* is considerable. According to Grice, it is the fact that the speaker *utters* (1) rather than (2) or, as the case may be, (2) rather than (1), presumably with a certain intention, that makes the difference. This difference derives from the order in which the speaker utters the two clauses and the presumption that this reflects the order of events described (assuming there is an order). Also, the speaker exploits the fact, and the hearer's knowledge of the fact, that it is folk wisdom that chicken soup can make one feel better or, alternatively, that any food can be contaminated, to convey something that goes well beyond the linguistic meaning of the sentence itself. Finally, notice that in uttering (1) or (2) the speaker could have cancelled the implication about the order of events (and about what caused what) by adding, 'but not in that order'. So this implication cannot be a matter of linguistic meaning.

Here is another kind of case, illustrating Grice's line of resistance to another ordinary language challenge to formal philosophy. Reacting to traditional philosophical worries, about such questions as what it is for an action to be voluntary and what it is for things in the world to be as they appear, Austin and his followers thought there was something wrong with the following (a)-sentences, in contrast to the very similar (b)-sentences:

(3) a. Sam scratched his head voluntarily.
    b. Sam handed over his car keys voluntarily.

(4) a. There appears to be a computer screen before me.
   b. There appears to be a dagger before me.

According to Austin's dictum, 'No modification without aberration' (1961, p. 137), the trouble with the (a)-sentences is that they are normally inappropriate to utter, since with (3a) there is no reason to think that Sam scratched his head involuntarily and with (4a) there is no reason (for me) to question whether there is a computer screen before me. However, surely this does not show that it is not *true* that Sam scratched his head voluntarily or that there appears to be a computer screen before me. Rather, it shows that there is normally no point in making such statements.

These examples illustrate how applying the distinction between linguistic meaning and language use can do justice both to traditional philosophical concerns and to niceties about everyday usage. Here are two more examples. One might argue that believing implies not knowing because to utter, say, 'I believe that bungee jumping is dangerous' implies that one does not know this, or argue that trying implies effort or difficulty because one would not say 'Harry tried to stand up' if Harry stood up with ease. However, as Grice would reply, what carries such implications is not what one is saying but that one is saying it – rather than the stronger 'I know that bungee jumping is dangerous' or 'Harry stood up'. Grice similarly objected to certain ambiguity claims, such as that the word 'or' has both an inclusive and an exclusive sense, by pointing out that it is not what 'or' means but its use that can carry the implication of exclusivity. Grice's *Modified Occam's Razor*, 'Senses are not to be multiplied beyond necessity' (1978/1989, p. 47), cut back on the growing philosophical conflation of language use with linguistic meaning. It has since helped linguists appreciate the importance of separating the domains of semantics and pragmatics.

2. Speaker meaning

In 'Meaning' Grice (1957) contrasted 'natural' meaning with the sort of meaning involved in language and communication. Whereas smoke means fire by virtue of being naturally correlated with fire, the word 'smoke' means smoke by virtue of being conventionally correlated with smoke. And, whereas smoke is correlated with fire in the sense of indicating the presence of fire, obviously the word 'smoke' is not correlated with the presence of smoke. It is a conventional means for talking about smoke, whether or not smoke is present. Its meaning is a matter of convention, since it could just as well have meant something else, and some other word could just as well have meant smoke. It means smoke because, and only because, speakers normally use it to mean that and expect others who use it to mean that as well.

Suppose a speaker utters the sentence, 'I smell smoke', using the pronoun 'I' to refer to herself, the verb 'smell' (in the present tense) for olfactory sensing, and the noun 'smoke' to refer to smoke, presumably some smoke in her vicinity. Presumably she means that she then smells smoke. Importantly, this is not a direct consequence of what her words mean, and of how their meanings are put together into the meaning of the sentence, given its grammatical structure. After all, she could have been speaking figuratively, and have meant, say in response to an explanation her husband just gave her, that she suspects that he is trying to divert her attention. So it is one thing for words to mean something and another for a speaker to mean something, even if it is the same thing, in uttering those words.

2.1 Communicative intentions

Grice held that speaker meaning is more basic than word meaning, on the grounds that the meanings of words ultimately come down to what people mean in uttering them (Grice, 1968). But what is it for a speaker to mean something, whether in uttering words or in doing something else?

It is not merely to cause some effect on one's audience. There are lots of ways of doing that. At the very least it must be intentional. But there are different ways in which one can intend to produce some effect on others, and most of them do not involve communication. In communicating something, one intends one's audience to identify what effect one is trying to produce in them. Indeed, as Grice (1957) argued, one intends to produce that effect precisely by way of their recognizing one's intention to produce it. This is the gist of Grice's ingenious idea that the special sort of intention involved in meaning something, in trying to communicate something, is in a certain sense *reflexive*.

Think about what is involved in communicating. You have a certain thought and you wish to 'get it across' to someone. So your intention to convey it must be overt. Your intention will not be communicative if you intend the hearer to think a certain thing without thinking you intend them to think it. Suppose, for example, you want the person to think you are modest, and you make some self-deprecating remarks. In this case your intention will *not* be fulfilled if it is recognized. The person will not think that you are modest but merely that you want them to think that. And even if your intention is overt, that doesn't by itself make it communicative. For example, by turning up the heater you could intend to get your guest to think that it is time to leave, but you would not have *communicated* that. If the person comes to think that it is time to leave, their awareness of this need not depend on their recognition of your intention for them to think that. If the room is hot enough, your intention will be fulfilled independently of their recognizing it.

Such examples suggested to Grice that for an intention to be communicative, it must be overt in a specific sort of way. His idea was that communicative intentions are intentionally overt and that this feature plays a special role in their fulfilment. That is, in trying to communicate something to others by saying something, a speaker intends the audience to recognize that intention partly by taking into account that they are so intended. Because this is part of what the speaker intends, communicative intentions are distinctively self-referential or 'reflexive'. A speaker means something by his utterance only if he intends his utterance 'to produce some effect in an audience by means of the recognition of this intention' (Grice, 1957/1989, p. 220). However, not just any sort of effect will do.

2.2 The intended 'effect'

If you are communicating something to someone, communicative success does not require that they respond as you wish – coming to believe you, obeying you, forgiving you, or whatever. As Searle pointed out, these are *perlocutionary* effects (Austin, 1962, pp. 101ff.), the production of which goes beyond communication (see Searle, 1969, p. 47). It is enough, as Strawson had argued, for the utterance to be understood (1964, p. 459). For that the hearer must identify the attitude (including its content) the speaker is expressing – believing, intending, regretting and so forth – whether or not the speaker actually possesses that attitude. This suggests that for a speaker to mean something is to intend just such an effect. If, as Bach and Harnish proposed, 'to express an attitude is reflexively to intend the hearer to take one's utterance as reason to think one has that attitude' (1979, p. 15), then communicating successfully, being understood, consists in having the expressed attitude recognized. It does not require the hearer to respond in any further way. For a communicative intention, 'its fulfillment consists in its recognition' (ibid.). This is the flip side of Grice's idea that communicative intentions are inherently reflexive.

2.3 Reflexive paradox?

Commenting on the notion of an intention 'to produce an effect in an audience by means of the recognition of this intention', Grice remarked, 'this seems to involve a reflexive paradox, but it does not really do so' (1957/1989, p. 219). It seems to involve paradox because the intention is self-referential. Indeed, this air of paradox may seem to imbue the hearer's inference with circularity, inasmuch as the hearer is to identify the speaker's intention partly on the supposition that he is intended to. Is there anything paradoxical about this?

It might seem paradoxical if one confuses iterative intentions with reflexive ones, as indeed Grice himself seems to have done. Indeed, earlier in the very paragraph just quoted from, Grice gives an alternate formulation, requiring that a speaker 'must also intend his utterance to be recognized as so intended' (1957/1989, p. 219). And, in his later attempt to improve upon his earlier formulation, Grice (1969) abandons reflexive intentions in favour of iterative intentions. Still later, in 'Meaning revisited', he rejects that idea and suggests that what is needed instead is the absence of 'sneaky intentions' (1982/1989, p. 302). However, Gilbert Harman thinks that Grice should have stuck with his original idea:

> Grice himself originally states his analysis as involving a self-referential intention ... but, because of worries about what he calls 'self-reflective paradox', he goes on to restate the analysis as involving a series of intentions, each about the preceding one.

This turns out to lead to tremendous complexity in the resulting theory. Much of this complexity is artificial and due to Grice's refusal to stick with the original analysis and its appeal to a self-referential intention. (Harman, 1986, pp. 87–8)

A reflexive intention is not a series of intentions, each referring to the previous one. A speaker does not have an intention to convey something and a further intention that the first be recognized, which itself must be accompanied by an intention that it in turn be recognized, and so on ad infinitum. Grice's move to iterative intentions led to increasingly complex formulations beginning with Strawson's (1964), followed by Grice's (1969) own, and culminating with Schiffer's (1972), each prompted by counterexamples to the previous one. However, as Harman pointed out, sticking with self-referential intentions avoids this complexity and the threat of an infinite regress. Bach (1987) argued similarly, responding also to other concerns, due to Recanati (1986), about reflexive intentions.

The semblance of reflexive paradox arises from Grice's key phrase 'by means of the recognition of this intention'. This might suggest that, to understand the speaker, the hearer must engage in some sort of circular reasoning. It sounds as though the hearer must already know what the speaker's communicative intention is in order to recognize it. However, that misconstrues what the hearer has to take into account in order to recognize the speaker's intention. The hearer does not infer that the speaker means a certain thing from the premise that the speaker intends to convey that very thing. Rather, operating on the presumption that the speaker, like any speaker, intends to communicate something or other, the hearer takes this general fact, not the content of the specific intention, into account in order to identify that intention.

3. Conversational implicature

Grice is best known, especially in linguistics, for his theory of conversational implicature. The basic idea was not new. What was new, aside from Grice's name for it, was his account of it, which incorporated his account of speaker meaning, along with his application of it to various philosophical questions. A speaker implicates something if what she means is distinct from what she says. In general, though not always, it is also distinct from what is logically implied by what she says. That is why Grice (1967) uses the verb 'implicate' rather than 'imply', and the neologism 'implicature' rather than 'implication'.

For example, suppose you are asked about a dinner you had at an expensive restaurant, and you reply, 'The meal didn't give me food poisoning'. Saying this implicates that it was mediocre at best. However, what you said obviously does *not* imply this. After all, even excellent meals need not cause food poisoning. Besides, as Grice points out, conversational implicatures are *cancellable*. You could have added, 'I don't mean to suggest that the meal wasn't great'. In fact, there are circumstances in which the implicature would not arise in the first place, say if there had been a recent outbreak of *E. coli*. According to Grice, most implicatures are also *non-detachable*, in the sense that the speaker could have said what she said in a different way and still implicated the same thing. The exception, as discussed below, is the case where how the speaker says what she says, the wording or the pronunciation, plays an essential role.

How can a speaker implicate something that is not implied by what she says? She can do this by exploiting the fact that the hearer presumes her to be cooperative, in particular, to be speaking truthfully, informatively, relevantly and otherwise appropriately (from now on we will use 'she' for the *s*peaker and '*h*e' for the *h*earer). If taking the utterance at face value is incompatible with this presumption, the hearer, still relying on this presumption, must find some plausible candidate for what else the speaker could have meant. In the above example, where the speaker is asked to evaluate a certain dinner, he must figure out what she meant, relying on the presumption that she intended it to be an accurate, informative and appropriate answer to the question. In effect what the hearer does is, on the presumption that the speaker is being cooperative, to find a plausible explanation for why she said what she said.

3.1 The Cooperative Principle and the maxims of conversation

Grice codified these ideas by formulating an overarching *Cooperative Principle* and four sets of subordinate *maxims of conversation* (Grice, 1975/1989, pp. 26–7):

COOPERATIVE PRINCIPLE: Make your conversational contribution such as is required, at the stage at which it occurs, by the accepted purpose or direction of the conversational exchange.

QUALITY: Try to make your contribution one that is true.
1. Do not say what you believe to be false.
2. Do not say that for which you lack evidence.

QUANTITY:
1. Make your contribution as informative as is required (for the current purposes of the exchange).
2. Do not make your contribution more informative than is required.

RELATION: Be relevant.

MANNER: Be perspicuous.
1. Avoid obscurity of expression.
2. Avoid ambiguity.
3. Be brief. (Avoid unnecessary prolixity.)
4. Be orderly.

We could dwell on the precise meanings of these maxims, on whether they are adequately formulated, and on whether the list can be simplified (for discussion see Harnish, 1976). One might wonder, for example, about what happens when applying different maxims gives different candidates for what a speaker might be implicating. A common objection to Grice's account is that it is not adequately predictive and, indeed, that different social situations or even cultural differences make for different norms. All these issues have been raised, as if an adequate account must explain precisely how a hearer figures out what the speaker is implicating and, for that matter, how a speaker, in choosing what to say, manages to anticipate how the hearer is going to do this. Surely, though, this is expecting too much of a philosophical theory. These difficult issues belong to psychology (the psychology of the future).

Philosophically, the important point is that, whatever the details, speakers commonly succeed in conveying things that are distinct from or go beyond what they say and that, unless communication is a kind of telepathy, there must be rational constraints on speakers' communicative intentions and on hearers' inferences about them. As the examples below will illustrate, Grice's maxims point to the sorts of considerations that speakers and hearers take into account if communication is to succeed, as surely it often does. With this mind, Bach and Harnish suggest that the maxims are better viewed as presumptions, which the hearer relies on to guide his inference to what the speaker means (1979, pp. 62–5). So, when a presumption seems not to be in force, he seeks an interpretation of the speaker's utterance such that it does apply after all. Indeed, Bach and Harnish propose to replace Grice's CP, the vague and rather unrealistic Cooperative Principle, with a *Communicative Presumption*: when people speak, presumably they do so with identifiable communicative intentions (1979, pp. 12–15).

The following examples illustrate how hearers accommodate (to borrow a term from Lewis, 1979) apparent violations of different maxims (or, if you will, apparent suspensions of different presumptions). If a speaker says something that is obviously false, thereby flouting the first maxim of quality, she could well mean something else. For example, with (5) she might mean the opposite of what she says, with (6) something less extreme, and with (7) something more down to earth.

(5) *The Aristocrats* is the most wholesome movie I've ever seen.

(6) I had so much fun I could have played D&D for a month without ever sleeping.

(7) He bungee-jumped from 85% approval down to 40%, up to 60%, and down to 15%.

In these cases, of irony (sarcasm), hyperbole and metaphor, respectively, it should be evident what a speaker is likely to mean. It is not what she says or, as Grice puts it, 'makes as if to say'. Notice, however, that not all quality implicatures depend on the obvious falsity of the literal content. John Donne's famous 'No man is an island' is a case in point.

Quantity implicatures are typified by the fact that speakers convey information not just by what they say but also by the stronger things they *don't* say. Consider these examples:

(8) Barry tried hard to lift the 300-lb bar-bell.

(9) He thought he was strong enough to lift it.

(10) He had lifted the 250-lb bar-bell three times.

(11) Barry finished his workout with a swim or a run.

Keeping in mind that speakers, not sentences, implicate things, we have to imagine uttering such sentences or hearing them uttered in particular contexts in order to get clear examples of implicatures, quantity implicatures in this case. In uttering (8) you might implicate that Barry failed to lift the 300-lb bar-bell. Otherwise, you would have said that he succeeded. Similarly, with (9) you might implicate that he wasn't sure that he could lift it. With (10) you would probably implicate that he didn't lift the 250-lb bar-bell more than three times. And, finally, in uttering (11) you would implicate that Barry went for either a swim or a run and not both and that you do not know which. In the case of (8) and (9), what the speaker implicates can be figured out on the presumption that if she was in a position to give stronger or more specific information, she would have. With (10), the presumption is that the speaker is in a position to know how many times Barry lifted the 250-lb bar-bell, whereas with (11) the presumption is just the opposite, since if she knew whether Barry went for a swim or a run (or both), she would have said so.

Relevance implicatures can also be cases of conveying information by saying one thing and leaving something else out. Grice's two best-known examples are of this type:

(12) There is a garage around the corner. [said in response to 'I am out of petrol']

(13) He is punctual, and his handwriting is excellent. [the entire body of a letter of recommendation]

An utterance of (12) is relevant, and a rational speaker would intend it as such, only if the speaker means also that the garage is open and has petrol for sale. So the hearer is to reason accordingly. Example (13) is rather different, on account of the speaker's reason for not being more explicit. In this case, the writer intends the reader to figure out that if she had anything more positive to say about the candidate, she would have said it.

Manner implicatures are probably the least common of the lot. They exploit not just the speaker's saying a certain thing but her saying it in a certain way. For that reason, they are exceptions to Grice's non-detachability test. Obviously, if there are different ways of saying the same thing and how the speaker says it affects what the hearer is likely to take into account in figuring out what the speaker means, the implicature is detachable. The following examples illustrate this.

(14) You have prepared what closely resembles a meal of outstanding quality.

(15) I would like to see more of you.

Imagine a culinary instructor uttering the longwinded (14). Her intention would likely be to convey that the meal is not nearly as good as it appears. A speaker of (15) could exploit its ambiguity to convey something besides wanting to spend more time with the hearer.

It should be understood that Grice does not suppose that speakers consciously exploit the maxims or that hearers consciously take them into account. However, this raises the interesting question of just what is involved psychologically in the process of communication. This includes not only how hearers manage to figure out what speakers mean given that they say what they say, but also how speakers choose what to say and thereby manage to make evident what they mean, even when they do not make it explicit. Grice did not address the latter question, and his account of implicature is commonly misconstrued as an answer to the former.

3.2 Common misunderstandings

Numerous common misconceptions about conversational implicature have arisen, based on misreading 'Logic and Conversation' or on reading things into it. Space does not permit highlighting more than a few (for more see Bach, 2006) or documenting instances of them. The following two are perhaps the most important.

First of all, the maxims (or presumptions) do not determine implicatures but, rather, facilitate their communication. They are considerations that speakers implicitly intend hearers to, and hearers do, take into account to figure out – determine in the inferential sense – what the speaker is implicating. Since that is a matter of speaker meaning, it is the speaker's communicative intention that determines, in the constitutive sense of that word, what is implicated. Moreover, because the maxims figure in Grice's account of conversational implicature, that is, of how implicatures get conveyed, it is commonly but mistakenly supposed that the maxims apply only to implicatures. In fact, they apply equally to completely literal utterances, where the speaker means just what she says. After all, the hearer still has to infer this. It is thus wrong to suppose that the maxims come into play only where linguistic meaning leaves off and speaker meaning and extra-linguistic, contextual information take over (for more on context and what it does and doesn't determine, see Bach, 2005).

Another misconception is that linguistic expressions (sentences or even individual words) can implicate things. Speakers do. To be sure, certain expressions are characteristically used (by speakers) to implicate things. When this occurs we have what Grice calls *generalized* conversational implicatures (as opposed to *particularized* ones). These have been investigated in great depth by Stephen Levinson (2000), who thinks they give rise to an intermediate level of meaning. In fact, they give rise to an intermediate kind of inference, but Levinson confusedly thinks of GCIs as inferences.

A related misunderstanding leads to the objection that Grice's account misrepresents the inference process involved in recognizing implicatures and that it cannot account for the putative phenomenon of *pragmatic intrusion*, as exemplified by embedded implicatures. Here is a typical formulation of that objection:

> Grice's account makes implicature dependent on a prior determination of 'the said'. The said in turn depends on disambiguation, indexical resolution, reference fixing, not to mention ellipsis unpacking and generality narrowing. But each of these processes, which are prerequisites to determining the proposition expressed, may themselves depend crucially on processes that look indistinguishable from implicatures. Thus what is said seems both to determine and to be determined by implicature. Let us call this *Grice's circle*. (Levinson, 2000, p. 186)

This objection is based on confusing the two sorts of determination mentioned above. In the relevant, constitutive sense, what is said neither determines nor is determined by what is implicated. Levinson and many others misconstrue Grice's account as a psychological model of the hearer's inference, indeed one according to which the hearer must ascertain what the speaker says before figuring out what the speaker is implicating (see Bach, 2001, pp. 24–5; Saul, 2002). But that is not how Grice intended his account. He required that 'the presence of a conversational implicature be capable of being worked out' (1975/1989, p. 31), but he did not say that it must be, much less in what sequence.

The confusion just mentioned leads to the widespread misconception, evident from an extensive literature, that some implicatures are 'embedded', as with utterances of sentences like these:

(16) It is better to get married and get pregnant than to get pregnant and get married.

(17) Michelle thinks that Barack has two children.

Since the two infinitival clauses of (16) are semantically equivalent, a speaker is likely to implicate that what is better is getting married and *then* getting pregnant. With (17) the implicature is not that Barack has exactly two children but that Michelle thinks that. In fact, such examples illustrate merely that the process of figuring out what is implicated does not require first ascertaining what is said. They do not show that the implicature is embedded in anything. Indeed, since speakers implicate, it does not even make sense to say that some implicatures are embedded.

3.3 Between saying and implicating

With his contrast between saying and implicating, Grice allowed both for cases in which the speaker means what she says and something else as well and for ones in which the speaker says one thing and means something else instead. He counted both as kinds of implicature, although the latter might better be described as speaking figuratively. And, of course, a speaker can say something and mean just that. Grice seems to have overlooked an intermediate phenomenon, one that has been investigated by many others (Bach, 1994; Carston, 2002; Recanati, 2004; Sperber and Wilson, 1986). As they have observed, there are many sentences whose standard uses go beyond their meanings (even with references fixed and ambiguities resolved) but are not implicatures or figurative uses either.

One way in which this can occur is when what the speaker means is a more elaborate proposition than what is expressly said, as with a likely utterance of (18):

(18) Sidney and Sally are engaged.

The speaker is likely to mean that they are engaged *to each other*, even though she does not make the last part explicit. Clearly that element is cancellable, since she could have added 'but not to each other' to her utterance of (18) without contradicting herself. Similarly, someone uttering (2),

(2)   Lizzie ate some chicken soup and felt lousy.

would likely mean that Lizzie ate some chicken soup and *as a result* felt lousy. Again, the inexplicit part is cancellable, for the speaker could have uttered (2) and added, 'not that she felt lousy as a result of eating the soup'. In both cases it is not the linguistic meaning of the uttered sentences but the fact that the speaker said what she said, presumably with maximal relevant informativeness, as per the first maxim of quantity, that provides the hearer with reason to think that the speaker intended to convey something more expansive.

In other cases, what the speaker says is not merely less expansive than what she means but does not explicitly comprise a proposition. Suppose a boy has just finished his ice cream and blurts out (19),

(19) I want more.

He can't just mean that he wants more, full stop. Rather, he probably means that he wants more ice cream. And if his mother yells back,

(20) You've had enough.

she means that he has had enough ice cream. In both cases the sentence falls short of fully expressing a proposition – it is *semantically incomplete*. Yet what the speaker means *is* a complete proposition. Sentences like (19) and (20) appear to violate the grammar school dictum that a sentence, unlike a mere word, phrase, or 'sentence fragment', always expresses a 'complete thought'. As with (17) and (18), though for a different reason (semantic incompleteness), what the speaker means is more specific than what the sentence means. We might say that whereas what a user of (17) or (18) means is an *expansion* of the sentence meaning, what a user of (19) or (20) means is a *completion* of it.

Several of Grice's critics have pointed out that expansions and completions are not related closely enough to conventional meaning to fall under Grice's notion of what is said but are too closely related to count as implicatures. Sperber and Wilson (1986, p. 182) coined the word *explicature* for this in-between category, since part of what is meant 'explicates' what is said. Bach (1994) proposed calling these cases of *impliciture*, since part of what is meant is communicated implicitly, by way of expansion or completion. Recanati (2004) suggests that the notion of what is said should be extended to cover these cases (in fact, he offers a series of progressively more liberal notions of saying), but clearly he is going beyond Grice's conception of what is said as corresponding to the meanings of the constituents of the sentence with its syntactic structure (Grice, 1969/1989, p. 87).

Going further

Grice's accounts of speaker meaning and conversational implicature have had lasting strategic impact on philosophy and linguistics. Despite disagreements about many particular cases, it is widely acknowledged that the Gricean strategy reduces the burden on semantics by seeking to account for diverse meaning phenomena with the help of general principles of rational language use rather than needlessly complex word meanings. It has been applied to a wide range of problems not only in philosophy of language, such as propositional attitude reports and referential uses of definite descriptions, but also in other areas of philosophy, notably epistemology and meta-ethics. It has been employed in linguistics and computer science to address such topics as the lexicon, anaphora, speech planning and discourse analysis. The notion of speaker meaning, broadly construed, is relevant to literary theory and aesthetics, in connection with questions about author or artist intention. The distinction between saying and implicating bears on legal theory, in particular in helping to explain the difference between lying and misleading, a difference clearly central to the law of perjury, libel and fraud.

We have focused on Grice's most important and influential ideas, speaker meaning and conversational implicature. Stephen Neale (1992) presents a much fuller discussion of these and related ideas, Siobhan Chapman (2005) provides a full-length intellectual biography, which covers Grice's views beyond philosophy of language, Larry Horn (2009) offers a 40-year retrospective on implicature in particular, and Bart Geurts (2010) gives an in-depth study of quantity implicatures. A fuller treatment here would go into more detail on Grice's attempts to improve upon his analysis of speaker meaning (Grice, 1969, 1982), to reduce linguistic meaning to speaker meaning (1968), to justify complicating his account with the controversial hybrid notion of conventional implicature (for the controversy see Bach, 1999), and to give a pragmatic treatment of the notion of presupposition (Grice, 1981); and, as most recently illustrated by the papers collected in Petrus (2010), it would document the extent of the influence of his ideas in philosophy and beyond.

Bibliography

Austin, J. L. (1961), 'A Plea for Excuses', in J. L. Austin, *Philosophical Papers*, ed. J. O. Urmson and G. J. Warnock. Oxford: Oxford University Press, pp. 123–52.

Austin, J. L. (1962), *How to Do Things with Words*. Oxford: Oxford University Press.

Bach, K. (1987), 'On Communicative Intentions: A Reply to Recanati', *Mind & Language*, 2, pp. 141–54.

Bach, K. (1994), 'Conversational Impliciture', *Mind & Language*, 9, pp. 124–62.

Bach, K. (1999), 'The Myth of Conventional Implicature', *Linguistics and Philosophy*, 22, pp. 327–66.

Bach, K. (2001), 'You Don't Say?' *Synthese*, 128, pp. 15–44.

Bach, K. (2005), 'Context *ex machina*', in Z. Szabó (ed.), *Semantics versus Pragmatics*. Oxford: Oxford University Press, pp. 15–44.

Bach, K. (2006), 'The Top 10 Misconceptions about Implicature', in
B. Birner and G. Ward (eds), *Drawing the Boundaries of Meaning*.
Amsterdam: John Benjamins, pp. 21–30.

Bach, K. and Harnish, R. M. (1979), *Linguistic Communication and Speech Acts*. Cambridge, MA: MIT Press.

Carston, R. (2002), *Thoughts and Utterances*. Oxford: Blackwell.

Chapman, S. (2005), *Paul Grice: Philosopher and Linguist*. Basingstoke, UK: Palgrave Macmillan.

Geurts, B. (2010), *Quantity Implicatures*. Cambridge, UK: Cambridge University Press.

Grice, H. P. (1957), 'Meaning'. *The Philosophical Review*, 66, pp. 377–88. Reprinted in Grice, 1989, pp. 213–23.

Grice, H. P. (1968), 'Utterer's Meaning, Sentence-Meaning, and Word Meaning', *Foundations of Language*, 4, pp. 225–42. Reprinted in Grice, 1989, pp. 117–37.

Grice, H. P. (1969), 'Utterer's Meaning and Intentions', *The Philosophical Review*, 78, pp. 147–77. Reprinted in Grice, 1989, pp. 86–116.

Grice, H. P. (1975), 'Logic and Conversation', in P. Cole and J. Morgan (eds), *Syntax and Semantics, Vol. 3, Speech Acts*. New York: Academic Press, pp. 41–58. Reprinted in Grice, 1989, pp. 22–40.

Grice, H. P. (1978), 'Further Notes on Logic and Conversation', in P. Cole (ed.), *Syntax and Semantics, Vol. 9, Pragmatics*. New York: Academic Press, pp. 113–27. Reprinted in Grice, 1989, pp. 41–57.

Grice, H. P. (1981), 'Presupposition and Conversational Implicature', in P. Cole (ed.), *Radical Pragmatics*. New York: Academic Press, pp. 183–97. Reprinted abridged in Grice, 1989, pp. 269–82.

Grice, H. P. (1982), 'Meaning Revisited', in N. Smith (ed.), *Mutual Knowledge*. London: Academic Press, pp. 223–43. Reprinted in Grice, 1989, pp. 283–303.

Grice, H. P. (1989), *Studies in the Way of Words*. Cambridge, MA: Harvard University Press.

Grice, H. P. and Strawson, P. F. (1956), 'In Defense of a Dogma', *Philosophical Review*, 65, pp. 141–58. Reprinted in Grice, 1989, pp. 196–212.

Harman, G. (1986), *Change in View*. Cambridge, MA: MIT Press.

Harnish, R. M. (1976), 'Logical Form and Implicature', in T. Bever, J. Katz and T. Langendoen (eds), *An Integrated Theory of Linguistic Ability*. New York: Crowell, pp. 313–92.

Horn, L. (2009), 'WJ-40: Implicature, Truth, and Meaning', *International Review of Pragmatics*, 1, pp. 3–34.

Levinson, S. (2000), *Presumptive Meanings: The Theory of Generalized Conversational Implicature*. Cambridge, MA: MIT Press.

Lewis, D. (1979), 'Scorekeeping in a Language Game', *Journal of Philosophical Logic*, 8, pp. 339–59.

Neale, S. (1992), 'Paul Grice and the Philosophy of Language', *Linguistics and Philosophy*, 15, pp. 509–59.

Petrus, K. (ed.) (2010), *Meaning and Analysis: New Essays on Grice.* Basingstoke, UK: Palgrave Macmillan.

Recanati, F. (1986), 'On Defining Communicative Intentions'. *Mind & Language*, 1, pp. 213–42.

Recanati, F. (2004), *Literal Meaning.* Cambridge, UK: Cambridge University Press.

Saul, J. (2002), 'What Is Said and Psychological Reality, Grice's Project and Relevance Theorists' Criticisms', *Linguistics and Philosophy*, 25, pp. 347–72.

Schiffer, S. (1972), *Meaning.* Oxford: Oxford University Press.

Searle, J. (1969), *Speech Acts, An Essay in the Philosophy of Language.* Cambridge: Cambridge University Press.

Sperber, D. and Wilson, D. (1986), *Relevance.* Cambridge, MA: Harvard University Press.

Strawson, P. F. (1964), 'Intention and Convention in Speech Acts', *Philosophical Review*, 73, pp. 439–60.

Wittgenstein, L. (1953), *Philosophical Investigations*, trans. G. E. M. Anscombe, ed. G. E. M. Anscombe and R. Rhees. New York: Macmillan.

CHAPTER ELEVEN

DAVIDSON

Kirk Ludwig

1. Introduction

Donald Davidson was one of the most influential philosophers working in the theory of meaning in the latter half of the twentieth century. He can be credited with one of the few genuinely novel approaches to the theory of meaning that emerged in that period, namely, the programme of truth-theoretic semantics and its integration into the theory of radical interpretation.

The first of Davidson's two sub-projects is his famous though controversial proposal, advanced originally in 'Truth and Meaning' (1967), to use a Tarski-style truth theory (a theory that determines truth-conditions for all of the sentences in a language on the basis of axioms for each semantically primitive expression in it) to do the work of a compositional meaning theory (one that gives the meaning of each of a language's sentences on the basis of the meanings of its parts and their mode of combination). We will call this *the initial project*. This builds on Tarski's pioneering work on how to define a truth predicate for a formal language[1] (Tarski, 1944, 1983). Central to this was Tarski's Convention T, which requires that an adequate truth theory have as theorems all sentences of the form (T)

(T) s is T iff p

in which (i) 'is T' is a truth predicate in the metalanguage (the language in which the theory is expressed) for the object language (the language the theory is about), (ii) 's' is replaced by a description of an object language sentence as composed out of its significant parts (a structural description, for short) and (iii) 'p' is replaced by a metalanguage sentence that translates it. In contrast to Tarski, Davidson was not interested in formal but in natural languages, and he was not interested in defining a truth predicate but in adapting the kind of truth theory Tarski showed how to construct to natural languages, and in using a predicate known antecedently to express the concept of truth, in order to further the goals of a compositional meaning theory. Davidson's second sub-project is his proposal, inspired by Quine's project of radical translation (1960), to investigate the concepts of the theory of meaning by reflection on how a radical interpreter could confirm a truth theory for a speaker's language ('Radical Interpretation' (1973)). We will call this *the extended project,* since it embeds the first. The sub-projects represent two parts of a single enterprise: that of explaining what it is for words to mean what they do (2001b, p. xiii). The first aims to help explain how we understand complex expressions on the basis of their significant parts. The second aims to shed light on meaning more generally by showing how one can understand another speaker with whom one does not (initially) share a language, on the basis of his behaviour in relation to others and his environment. This relates facts about meaning to the context of communication in which they get their purpose, and to the evidence on the basis of which we must perforce interpret others, and so relates meaning to the more fundamental facts upon which it supervenes.

The suggestion that a truth theory can be used as a meaning theory has sometimes been met with incredulity. Ostensibly, a truth theory states only conditions under which a sentence is true, and though truth is determined by meaning and how the world is, specifying conditions under which a sentence is true seems to guarantee no insight into its meaning. For example, while (S)

(S) 'Snow is white' is true iff grass is green

specifies a condition under which 'Snow is white' is true, this yields no insight into the meaning of 'Snow is white'. It has therefore been suggested that Davidson must really have intended either the reduction of meaning to some (perhaps special, 'strong') notion of truth-conditions (Burge, 1992, pp. 20–1; Horwich, 2005, p. 4 and chapter 8) or the replacement of the traditional pursuit of a meaning theory with a successor project on the grounds that the notion of meaning is too confused for systematic investigation (Chihara, 1975; Cummins, 2002; Glock, 2003, pp. 142ff.; Katz, 1982, pp. 183–5; Soames, 1992, 2008; Stich, 1976). We'll see that each of these suggestions rests on a misunderstanding of how Davidson intends a truth theory to aid pursuit of a meaning theory.

In the following, we approach the twin themes of Davidson's work in the theory of meaning by looking at the motivations for the introduction of a truth theory as a vehicle for a meaning theory, and the influences on Davidson's choice of the position of the radical interpreter as the most fundamental from which to investigate the concepts of the theory of meaning.

2. Compositionality

Davidson's work in the theory of meaning starts with the observation that natural languages are compositional in the sense that they admit of a division into semantically primitive expressions and semantically complex expressions that are understood on the basis their primitive constituents and mode of combination. For example, the two sentences 'John loves Mary' and 'Mary loves John' are different in meaning but are understood on the basis of the same primitive vocabulary items and rules for their combination.

Davidson argued that natural languages are compositional because they have an infinity of non-synonymous sentences but are mastered by finite beings. As Davidson puts it (1965, p. 9 – all citations to page numbers are to reprints of articles in Davidson's collected papers, as indicated in the references), 'we do not at some point suddenly acquire an ability to intuit the meanings of sentences on no rule at all' and 'each new item of vocabulary, or new grammatical rule, takes some [minimum] finite time to be learned'. On this basis, Davidson introduces a requirement on an acceptable meaning theory for a natural language:

I propose what seems to me clearly to be a necessary feature of a learnable language: it must be possible to give a constructive account of the meaning of the sentences in the language. Such an account I call a theory of meaning for the language, and I suggest that a theory of meaning that conflicts with this condition ... cannot be a theory of a natural language; and if it ignores this condition, it fails to deal with something central to the concept of a language. (1965, p. 3)

The observation that natural languages are compositional seems straightforward, but places important constraints on meaning theories for natural languages. An adequate theory must exhibit expressions as falling into two classes and show how expressions falling into the category of semantically complex expressions are understood on the basis of understanding primitives and rules for their combination. A piecemeal approach that does not take into account the full range of uses of expressions in sentences will not meet the adequacy condition. And an account of any range of discourse that requires an infinite number of semantical primitives cannot be a correct account of a natural language.[2]

3. Criticism of the appeal to meanings as entities

A venerable tradition in accounting for the compositionality of natural languages, one that stretches back to Frege (see the chapter on Frege in this volume), involves assigning to every expression in the language a meaning that is grasped by anyone who understands it, and which determines the expression's extensional properties (relative to the way the world is), that is, its referent, its extension or its truth-value (as it is a name, predicate or sentence). The compositionality of natural languages then is expressed as the thesis that the meanings of complex expressions are functions of the meanings of their components.

Davidson took a dim view of this, and understanding why is crucial to understanding how he thought of the role of a truth theory in a meaning theory. To see the difficulty, suppose we associate a meaning with 'Theatetus', say, Theatetus, and with the predicate 'flies', say, the property of flying. The trouble is that by itself this gives us no insight into the meaning of 'Theatetus flies'. So far as anything we have said goes, it might as well be a list: Theatetus, the property of flying. It is natural to say that concatenation is itself semantically significant and that it means *instantiates*. Consistency requires we assign concatenation a meaning, the relation of instantiation. Now we simply have a longer list: Theatetus, the relation of instantiation, the property of flying. We want to say that 'Theatetus' and 'flies' do not both function as proper names. But this can't be determined by what object each term is associated with. We need a rule that shows how to interpret their concatenation as signalling their each making a different contribution to the formation of an expression of a different semantic type than either of them, which is evaluable as true or false.

Davidson illustrates the point with a simple reference theory.[3] Take a language fragment L whose primitive vocabulary consists of the names 'Marie' and 'Jean', which refer to Mary and to John, and the functor 'La mère de'. A singular term in the language consists of a name or the concatenation of 'La mère de' with any singular term. This generates an infinite set of referring terms. We want a theory that gives the reference of any expression in this infinite language fragment. Suppose we assign a function f to 'La mère de' and say that for any singular term α, the referent of 'La mère de'$^\frown\alpha$ is the value of f given the referent of α as argument (where '$\frown$' is the concatenation symbol). This yields *no insight* into the referent of any complex expression. To make the function scrutable, we must add that the value of f for any x is the mother of x. But then it is clear that the assignment of the function is not what is doing the work, but the use of 'the mother of' in saying what the combination of 'La mère de' with a singular term refers to. We might as well eliminate the middleman: for any singular term α, the referent of 'La mère de'$^\frown\alpha$ is the mother of the referent of α.

There are two points to take away from this. The first is that in explaining the semantic function of a complex expression on the basis of its parts one must give a rule. The second is that it is neither sufficient nor necessary for this that we assign an entity to every expression. For in our simple theory, we found that assigning an entity to 'La mère de' did not help with the work of the theory and that the work of the theory could be done without assigning any entity to it. So even in the context just of a reference theory, it is clear that it is misguided to think that the work of the theory is either advanced by, or requires, assigning an entity to every component expression of a complex term. This point, as we will see, extends to developing a meaning theory for a full language.

A simple extension turns our reference theory into a meaning theory. Although Davidson did not take this step with the example, it parallels the step he takes later with the truth theory. Seeing it in this simplified context will help us to appreciate how it works for the truth theory. We start by stating a criterion of adequacy on a reference theory: it should entail, for each object language singular term, a theorem of the form '*s* refers to *t*' where '*s*' is a structural description of an object language singular term and '*t*' is replaced by a metalanguage term that translates it. Call this Convention R. For our sample theory,

1. 'Marie' refers in L to Mary
2. 'Jean' refers in L to John
3. For any singular term α in L, 'La mère de'⌒α refers in L to the mother of what α refers to in L.

Convention R is satisfied because in the first two axioms the referents of the object language names are given using metalanguage names that translate them, and in the third axiom a metalanguage functor the same in meaning as the object language functor is used to give the rule. Any theory that satisfies this kind of constraint on its *axioms* satisfies (we will say) Convention A. The point of introducing Convention A is that it applies at the level of axioms, unlike R, which applies at the level of theorems, and this is important to a point we will make in a moment. Satisfying Convention A (relative to an appropriate class of proofs) suffices for the theory to satisfy Convention R, though not in general vice versa. If the theory satisfies Convention R, then – and this is the payoff – from a theorem of the form [r] we can infer a corresponding instance of [m],

[r] *s* refers in L to *t*
[m] *s* means in L *t*

because [m] is true if '*t*' translates *s*. Thus, we specify the meaning of each expression in our infinite language fragment on the basis of a finite number of rules attaching to its primitive expressions. Moreover, a step-by-step proof of a reference theorem shows how the meaning of each expression contributes to fixing the referent of the complex expression, for given that the theory meets Convention A (this is why Convention A turns out to be important), we reflect in the axioms the meanings of the primitive expressions and in the proofs their contributions in virtue of meaning to fixing the referents of complex referring terms. And as noted in the previous paragraph, this is accomplished without the need to assign an entity to every expression, and, specifically, our complex term forming device, 'La mère de'.

We identify a theory of meaning for a language with *the body of knowledge that puts us in a position to understand each expression in it*. The meaning theory then is not identical with the reference theory. For we have to know more than what the reference theory states to interpret each object language expression. We have to know (i) what the axioms are; (ii) what they state so-specified; (iii) that the theory satisfies Convention A, and so Convention R; (iv) a canonical proof procedure from axioms to the canonical theorems in virtue of which the theory satisfies Convention R; and (v) the inference rule that takes us from canonical theorems of the form [r] to [m].

Before extending these ideas to a whole language, we should review a final proposal Davidson considers for a compositional meaning theory that does not assign meanings to every expression, but does assign meanings to sentences. The rejection of this proposal is important for understanding what he does next. The proposal is to extend the idea in the reference theory sketched to a whole language by treating sentences as referring to their meanings and predicate expressions like 'x is red' as functioning like 'the mother of x'. For example, we might give the following axiom for 'est rouge':

For any singular term α, α⌢'est rouge' refers to *the referent of α is red*.

Instantiated to 'Marie', we can infer

'Marie est rouge' refers to *Mary is red*.

We may replace 'refers to' if we like with 'means'. Davidson seeks to scotch this proposal with a famous argument, dubbed the Slingshot by Barwise and Perry (1981), which he attributes to Frege. It is too involved to go into here. Its conclusion is that if sentences are treated as singular terms referring to their meanings, on plausible assumptions, it follows that all sentences alike in truth-value refer to the same thing, and hence have the same meaning – an intolerable result. The argument, though, is unsuccessful, for it either equivocates or begs the question (Lepore and Ludwig, 2005, pp. 49–55). Despite this, there is little to recommend the view that sentences refer to anything, let alone what they mean, and the obstacles in the way to a workable theory along the lines sketched are non-trivial. If there is any other way to get the desired result, it would be preferable.

4. The proposal to use a truth theory in pursuit of a meaning theory

Davidson concludes:

> [a] What analogy [with the reference theory] demands is a theory that has as consequences all sentences of the form 's means m' where 's' is replaced by a structural description of a sentence and 'm' is replaced by a singular term that refers to the meaning of that sentence; a theory, moreover, that provides an effective method for arriving at the meaning of an arbitrary sentence structurally described ... Paradoxically, the one thing that meanings do not seem to do is oil the wheels of a theory of meaning – at least as long as we require of such a theory that it non-trivially give the meaning of every sentence in the language. (1967, pp. 20–1)

However, this leave us with the problem of proving theorems of the form 's means that p' from axioms attaching to primitives where we treat neither 'p' nor 'that p' as a referring term. Davidson suggests that, 'in wrestling with the logic of the apparently non-extensional "means that" we will encounter problems as hard as, or perhaps identical with, the problems our theory is out to solve' (p. 22). For we can substitute after 'means that' only on the basis of synonymy, which looks to require us to already have a meaning theory (for the metalanguage) of the sort we want to develop for the object language, which would force a regress. It is in the face of this that Davidson makes the proposal to use a truth theory (1967, pp. 22–3):

[b] The only way I know to deal with this difficulty is simple, and radical ... The theory will have done its work if it provides, for every sentence *s* of the language under study, a matching sentence (to replace '*p*') that, in some way yet to be made clear, 'gives the meaning' of *s*. One obvious candidate for matching sentence is just *s* itself, if the object language is contained in the metalanguage; otherwise a translation of *s* in the metalanguage. As a final bold step, let us try treating the position occupied by '*p*' extensionally: to implement this, sweep away the obscure 'means that', provide the sentence that replaces '*p*' with a proper sentential connective, and supply the description that replaces '*s*' with its own predicate. The plausible result is

(*T*) s is *T* iff *p*.

What we require of a theory of meaning for a language *L* is that without appeal to any (further) semantical notions it place enough restrictions on the predicate 'is *T*' to entail all sentences got from schema *T* when '*s*' is replaced by a structural description of a sentence of *L* and '*p*' by that sentence.

[c] ... it is clear that the sentences to which the predicate 'is *T*' applies will be just the true sentences of *L*, for the condition we have placed on satisfactory theories of meaning is in essence Tarski's Convention *T* that tests the adequacy of a formal semantical definition of truth.

To see how this is a clever pursuit of the initial project by indirect means, we can rephrase the design problem for an adequate meaning theory described in [a] in a more general way:

formulate a theory that has as consequences all sentences of the form '*s* ... *p*', where '*s*' is replaced by a structural description of sentence and '*p*' by a metalanguage sentence that *gives the meaning* of that sentence; a theory, moreover, that provides an effective method for arriving at the meaning of an arbitrary sentence structurally described.

If a theory issued in true theorems of the form (M)

(M) *s* means that *p*

on the basis of axioms for primitive expressions in the language, then it would satisfy this criterion. This essentially comes to matching an object language sentence *s* with a metalanguage sentence '*p*' in use that translates *s*. The difficulties in formulating such a theory appear formidable. Davidson's insight was to see that a truth theory that meets Convention T would in effect satisfy the criterion because it requires the truth theory to entail every instance of the (T)-schema in which '*s*' is replaced by a structural description of an object language sentence and '*p*' by a metalanguage sentence that translates it. This is the same relation that must hold between *s* and '*p*' for true instances of (M). We could, then, restate Convention T as the requirement that the truth theory entail all instances of (T) for which the corresponding instances of (M) are true. Thus, if an instance of (T) is one of the theorems of a truth theory in virtue of which it meets Convention T, then the corresponding instance of (M) yields an explicit statement of the meaning of the object language sentence.

To see this in more detail, consider a simple truth theory [T] for a fragment of a language L without quantifiers or context sensitivity. (A language is context sensitive if it contains elements whose contribution to truth-conditions is determined relative to a context of utterance, as in the case of tense, whose contribution is relative to the time of utterance, and pronouns like 'I', which refers to the person using it, and 'that', which refers to what the user demonstrates in using it. 'I like that', for example, expresses the speaker's partiality at the time of utterance towards what he demonstrates in using 'that'.)

1. 'Marie' refers in L to Mary.
2. 'Jean' refers in L to John.
3. For any name α, $\alpha^\frown$'dort' is true in L iff what α refers to is sleeping.
4. For any names α, β, $\alpha^\frown$'aime'$^\frown\beta$ is true in L iff what α refers to loves what β refers to.
5. For any sentence φ, 'Ce n'est pas le cas que'$^\frown\varphi$ is true in L iff it is not the case that φ is true in L.
6. For any sentences φ, ψ, $\varphi^\frown$'et'$^\frown\psi$ is true in L iff φ is true in L and ψ is true in L.

Suppose we know, as for the reference theory, that each axiom uses a metalanguage term that translates the object language expression. So 'Mary' translates 'Marie', 'John' translates 'Jean', 'is sleeping' translates 'dort' and so forth. If a truth theory meets this condition, then (parallel to the reference theory) it meets Convention A[4] and is *interpretative*. If it meets Convention A, it meets Convention T. For example, a theorem of this theory is (T*), from which we can infer (M*).

(T*) 'Ce n'est pas le cas que Jean aime Marie' is true in L iff it is not the case that John loves Mary.
(M*) 'Ce n'est pas le cas que Jean aime Marie' means in L that it is not the case that John loves Mary.

Call a T-sentence like (T*), where the metalanguage sentence on the right translates the sentence for which it gives truth-conditions, *interpretative*. Importantly, the theory does more than issue in interpretative theorems. Because it satisfies Convention A, the proofs of the relevant theorems reveal at each stage the contribution of each primitive object language term, by way of the contribution that invoking the axiom for it makes, to fixing the interpretative truth-conditions for the object language sentence, in virtue of the meaning of the object language term. That is, the theorem's proof reveals the compositional structure of the object language sentence for which interpretative truth-conditions are given. We have, thus, 'a constructive account of the meaning of the sentences in the language', which provides, in Dummett's apt phrase, 'a theoretical representation of a practical ability' (1993, p. 36).[5]

As for our sample reference theory, what enables us to interpret object language sentences includes more than the truth theory itself. To infer (M)-sentences from (T)-sentences we have to know that the theory satisfies Convention T; to use the proofs to reveal compositional structure we have to know that the axioms satisfy Convention A and know a canonical proof procedure that will terminate in the appropriate canonical theorems. Thus, the meaning theory is not the truth theory per se but an appropriate body of knowledge about it.

We have illustrated the idea with respect to a small fragment of a language without quantifiers or context sensitivity. Convention

A and Convention T can be modified to suit a context-sensitive language with quantifiers, and the conceptual points carry over straightforwardly.[6]

5. The extended project and the reduction and replacement interpretations

The project as presented is an enlightened pursuit of a compositional meaning theory for natural language without the expedient of assigning meanings as entities to every expression. Why has Davidson sometimes been taken, then, to have been aiming to reduce meaning to truth-conditions or to reject giving a meaning theory, on the grounds that it is irremediably confused, in favour of a best successor project? The answer lies in a proposal that he makes after proposing that a truth theory can be used as a vehicle for a compositional meaning theory, which represents his pursuit of what we called the extended project, in contrast with the initial project of providing a compositional meaning theory. The idea of the extended project is to place substantive constraints on a truth theory that ensure that it satisfies Convention T. The point of this extended project is to reveal connections between meaning facts and facts that are not about meaning as such. If we could place non-semantic constraints on a truth theory that sufficed for it to satisfy Convention T, we could claim to have shown something important about what grounds facts about meaning. Given the goal, it is clear that this is not a rejection of giving a meaning theory but an attempt to give one in an illuminating way.

Why should this give rise to a misinterpretation of Davidson? The two primary reasons are, first, that in his earliest presentation of the idea Davidson had not cleanly drawn the distinction between the truth theory and the meaning theory and, second, that at precisely the point at which Davidson suggests a truth theory can be used to get around the problems facing the direct approach, he likewise shifts, without explicitly indicating that he is doing so, his attention from the initial to the extended project. For he thought that he saw an opportunity, once we transition to a truth theory for a language with context-sensitive expressions, and especially demonstratives, to place a simple substantive constraint on a truth theory that would suffice for it to satisfy Convention T, namely, that it be extensionally adequate – that is, that it simply be a true theory. Thus, it can seem that Davidson was suggesting that a correct truth theory is on its own a theory of meaning. But since a truth theory does not say anything about meaning, and merely matching a mentioned object language sentence with a used metalanguage sentence correlated in truth-value does not give the meaning of the object language sentence, it can seem that what he says cannot be taken at face value. Surely he must be suggesting that meanings can be reduced to truth-conditions, or that talk of meaning is so obscure that it must be replaced in serious discussions by a theory that deals with more tractable concepts and offers the prospect of systematic investigation, much as explanations of illness in terms of evil spirits have given way to the germ theory of disease. By now it is clear that both of these interpretations involve serious mistakes about how the truth theory is supposed to play its role. First, the meaning theory is not the truth theory per se, but a certain body of knowledge about the truth theory. Second, the suggestion that an extensionally adequate truth theory would serve as a meaning theory, Davidson's first suggestion, was conditional on the supposition that extensional adequacy would suffice for the theory to meet Convention T.

Why did Davidson think extensional adequacy was enough? For example, as we noted earlier, although (S) is true, it hardly helps us understand 'Snow is white'.

(S) 'Snow is white' is true iff grass is green

There were two connected ideas. The first was that once we had moved to a context-sensitive language, we would have a very fine-grained test for the adequacy of a theory in the need to accommodate the truth-conditions of sentences containing demonstratives and other context-sensitive expressions. The second was that we would treat the theory as an empirical theory, which would then be responsible for all actual and potential utterances of speakers of the language, and so would be responsible for getting right anything anyone might say about any object. Thus, it would have to issue in the right truth-conditions for sentences such as 'That is grass', 'That is snow', 'That is white' and 'That is green' in application to any object. (S) would not survive this test, for the theory that generated it would also predict for example that an utterance of 'that is white' would be true of something iff 'that is green' was.

However, this initial case for taking extensional adequacy to be enough was found to be inadequate (Foster, 1976; Loar, 1976). Accommodating demonstratives would rule out such T-sentences as (S), but would not rule out *all* non-interpretative T-sentences. We could modify any predicate axiom of a truth theory by adding to the truth-conditions for it an eternally true sentence, such as 'the earth moves' or '2 + 2 = 4'. For example,

> For any speaker s, time t, for any name α, $\alpha\frown$'dort' is true as used by s at t in L iff the referent of α as used by s at t is sleeping at t and the earth moves.

This would generate a non-interpretative canonical theorem when instantiated to, for example, 'Marie' because the corresponding M-sentence is false. When this objection was raised, Davidson returned to the problem of specifying a substantive constraint on a truth theory that would enable it to be used to interpret object language sentences in the context of the project of radical interpretation, which is the subject of the next section. That Davidson tried to improve on his initial suggestion shows decisively that the reduction and replacement interpretations are incorrect, for on either account he would have had no reason to change is his view about the adequacy of his proposal.

6. What is the project of radical interpretation?

Radical interpretation is a successor to Quine's project of radical translation (see the chapter on Quine in this volume). The radical translator approaches the task of understanding another speaker without any prior knowledge of the speaker's meanings or attitudes. He restricts himself to the speaker's dispositions to verbal behaviour in response to stimulus in constructing a translation manual for the speaker's language, and thus isolates the empirical content of a theory of translation. According to Quine, the empirical content thus isolated exhausts the meaning facts. From this it follows that empirically indistinguishable translation manuals capture the meaning facts equally well. In 'Epistemology Naturalized' (1969), Quine explains the ground for this conclusion as follows:

> The sort of meaning that is basic to translation, and to the learning of one's own language, is necessarily empirical meaning ... Language is socially inculcated and controlled; the inculcation and control turn strictly on keying of sentences to shared stimulation ... Surely one has no choice but to be an empiricist so far as one's theory of linguistic meaning is concerned. (p. 81)

The idea is that since language is a tool for interpersonal communication the facts about meaning must be recoverable from intersubjective data. This conception of the ground of meaning facts had an enormous impact on Davidson. Davidson 'thought it was terrific' and reported: 'I sort of slowly put what I thought was good in Quine with what I had found in Tarski. And that's where my general approach to the subject came from' (2004, p. 258).

Radical interpretation is similar to radical translation. For each, the evidence ultimately available consists in a speaker's dispositions to verbal behaviour. But whereas the radical translator aims to produce a translation manual, the radical interpreter seeks to confirm an interpretative truth theory. And whereas the radical translator keys his translations to responses to patterns of stimulus at the sensory surfaces, the radical interpreter rather keys his interpretation to the speaker's responses to distal events – events in the shared environment.

Central to the radical interpreter's project is the confirmation of a Tarski-style axiomatic truth theory for the speaker's language. But this is not all that the interpreter aims to do. He must also fill in the picture of the speaker as a rational agent responding to his environment and others. Speaking is an activity embedded in a form of life appropriate for rational agents. As Davidson puts it at one point, '[a]ny attempt to understand verbal communication must view it in its natural setting as part of a larger enterprise' (2004, p. 151). This means that understanding what people mean by what they say must be fit into and be made coherent with a larger theory of them as rational beings.[7] Thus, in contrast to Quine's behaviourist approach, which eschewed any explicit appeal to psychological vocabulary, Davidson saw the framework of propositional attitude psychology and the explanation in its terms of behaviour generally as the essential setting for understanding language.

Davidson characterizes the project of radical interpretation in terms of two questions. First, what could we know that would enable us to interpret another speaker? Second, how could we come to know it? A straightforward answer to the first question would seem to be an interpretative truth theory as characterized above. The answer to the second then would be a description of how a radical interpreter could come to confirm one for a speaker. Davidson does not answer the first question in this way, but rather suggests that if a theory has met certain empirical constraints, it is interpretative: 'The present idea is that what Tarski assumes outright for each T-sentence can be indirectly elicited by a holistic constraint', namely, 'that the totality of T-sentences should (in the sense described above [i.e. by way of the procedure of the radical interpreter]) optimally fit evidence about sentences held true by native speakers' (1973, p. 139).

This gives rise to a puzzle, however. Suppose that the answer to the first question (what we could know that would enable us to interpret another) is that a truth theory (of such and such a sort) has been confirmed by a radical interpreter. Then the answer to the second question (how could we confirm what we could know) should be a description of how to confirm *that a theory has been confirmed by a radical interpreter* (Lepore and Ludwig, 2005, pp. 151–66). But the answer to the second question was *supposed* to be a description of *radical interpretation itself*. What we get instead is a description of how to confirm that a radical interpreter has confirmed a truth theory. Something has gone wrong.

To avoid this problem, we can advert to another idea Davidson has identified as important, namely, that the theory be lawlike in the sense that it be projectable to instances that have not yet been observed, that is, that it make the correct predictions for future and counter-factual utterances. Then the revised answer to the first question would be: the simplest lawlike theory that accommodates the behavioural evidence. The problem, however, is that we have seen already that being lawlike is *not* sufficient for interpretativeness, and it is not easy to see why being the *simplest* lawlike theory, if there is one, guarantees interpretativeness if lawlikeness does not.

Our problem is that, on the one hand, taking the proposal Davidson makes literally, given his questions, directs attention at the wrong thing, while retreating to the requirement that we confirm a lawlike truth theory clearly falls short of what is needed for interpretativeness. What is the solution to these difficulties? To have a clear target for the radical interpreter to aim at, we should answer the *first* question by citing something *uncontroversially* sufficient for interpretation, namely, an interpretative truth theory (and that it is interpretative and so on, as above). We beg no questions by specifying that as the interpreter's aim, for to say that is his aim is not to say what the correct theory is for any given speaker. This has the added benefit that it gives us a clear standard by which to judge whether the interpreter's evidential base and constraints suffice for confirming something sufficient for interpretation.

To return to the radical interpreter's procedure, although the radical interpreter's evidential base is ultimately purely behavioural evidence, Davidson helps himself 'at an intermediate stage' (1975, p. 161) to knowledge of a speaker's hold-true attitudes towards sentences. A speaker holds true a sentence *s* iff he believes *s* to be true. Davidson assumes that hold-true attitudes can be identified on the basis of more primitive behavioural evidence and that, by and large, for each of his beliefs a speaker holds true a sentence that expresses it. A speaker holds true a sentence *s* if *s* means that *p* and he believes that *p*. The point of focusing on hold-true attitudes then is that one can know someone holds a sentence true without knowing what it means or what belief it is based on. This helps to focus the question of how the radical interpreter is to marshal his evidence in order to assign meanings to sentences and detailed contents to attitudes. The ultimate aim of this is to illuminate the concept of meaning and related concepts, which Davidson treats as theoretical relative to the interpreter's evidence, by showing what the empirical content of a theory deploying them is. The empirical content is revealed in the implications any given theory has for what behaviour should be expected assuming the theory is true. This shows what patterns in the data the theoretical concepts pick out, that is, how they organize the data into patterns intelligible in their terms.

If we can identify hold-true attitudes, then we can correlate them with what is going on in the speaker's environment. We will look for those hold-true attitudes which vary with variation in the environment and aim to identify lawlike correlations expressible in sentences of the form (L).

(L) x holds true φ at t iff p

How do we get from data in this form to an assignment of meaning to the sentence held true and content to the belief on the basis of which it is held true? If we knew either, we could solve for the other, but we don't start out with knowledge of either.

To break into the circle of meaning and belief we need to bring to bear a theoretical principle. Davidson proposed the Principle of Charity, according to which a speaker is largely rational and mostly right about his environment.[8] The Principle of Charity fixes belief to solve for meaning. If a speaker's beliefs about his environment are largely correct, then we can tentatively read the content of his beliefs off from the conditions correlated with the corresponding hold-true attitudes. The sentences that the speaker holds true can then be taken to express the conditions correlated with them. For those conditions may be taken to give the contents of the beliefs on the basis of which he holds the sentences true. From correlations of the form (L) we can infer tentatively, where 'L' designates the subject's language, that (T) is a target theorem for an interpretative truth theory for L.

(T) For any speaker x, and time t, s is true in L at t for x iff p

Once the interpreter has identified target theorems of an interpretative truth theory, the interpreter formulates axioms that entail those theorems. These are used to make further predictions about behaviour. Since people make mistakes, some of the beliefs that were initially treated as true may come to be treated as false, if that makes better overall sense of the speaker. In this way, the theory is adjusted until it achieves, within the theoretical constraints, an optimal fit with the evidence.

The Principle of Charity is the single most important theoretical upshot of taking the position of the radical interpreter as conceptually basic in understanding language. Davidson assumes that, as it is necessary for interpretation, being largely right about one's environment is constitutive of being a speaker. This entails that massive error in our empirical beliefs is incompatible with our possessing a language and that as language-speakers our thoughts are relationally individuated: for with the same internal physical states, a creature interpretable in a radically different environment will have radically different thoughts. Seeing the interpreter's standpoint as conceptually basic represents a complete reorientation of thinking about the relation of the mind to the world that is profoundly anti-Cartesian in the sense that it represents our epistemic and conceptual starting point as being, not the first-person point of view of introspection, but instead the third-person point of view of the interpreter of another.

7. Indeterminacy and the measurement analogy

A startling consequence of taking the radical interpreter's evidential position to be conceptually basic might be thought to call into question this fundamental assumption of the project. For after all the data is in, there will remain a range of incompatible interpretation theories which are empirically equivalent. One way this can happen is by making different choices about when to suppose someone is mistaken about something in the environment, as opposed to meaning something different than we do by his words. A more fundamental source of the underdetermination of theory by evidence is the fact that it seems in principle possible to start with very different sets of (L) sentences. For if there is a correlation of a hold-true attitude with one condition in the environment, there will be many others. To use Quine's example, rabbits co-occur with undetached rabbit parts, the instantiation of rabbithood, and time slices of rabbits. Beyond this, typically when one thing is causally responsible for another it is so only relative to background conditions. Our (L) sentences must be taken to hold only relative to those conditions – we do not *always* hold-true 'There is a rabbit' when there are rabbits around. But by focusing on something that is in the background relative to one (L) sentence, and bringing it to the foreground, while letting the previously correlated condition recede into the background, we can formulate a different (L) sentence. And if we do this systematically, we may arrive at very different interpretation theories for the speaker's language.

This is a serious difficulty. From the point of view of the interpreter himself, the theories do not assign the same interpretations to object language sentences, because they represent them as being about different conditions in the environment. Prima facie, the conclusion should be that the radical interpreter's evidential base is inadequate to confirm an interpretative truth theory and that it cannot exhaust the relevant evidence. This would undermine the view that the concepts of the theory of interpretation are theoretical concepts whose content is exhausted by the organization they impose on the behavioural data and likewise the conclusions that follow from treating the Principle of Charity as constitutive of the interpreter's subject matter, since it could no longer be justified by holding it is necessary in order for radical interpretation to succeed.

However, Davidson held, following Quine's lead, that since the meaning facts are exhausted by the facts available to the radical interpreter, if different interpretation theories work equally well after all the evidence is in, they all capture the facts of the matter equally well. This is not underdetermination of theory by evidence, but *indeterminacy* of interpretation, in the sense that there is no determinate fact of the matter as to which of the range of empirically adequate theories is correct. Davidson aimed to render indeterminacy non-threatening. It is no more a problem, he maintained, than the fact that we can use either the Fahrenheit or Centigrade scales in keeping track of temperatures. We do not contradict each other when you say that it is 50 degrees Fahrenheit and I say that it is 10 degrees Celsius. We use relations among numbers to keep track of relations among temperatures by giving a physical interpretation to the use of numerals, for example, in terms of the height of a column of mercury. The numbers have more structure than what we use them to keep track of, so the choice of the mapping is only partly constrained by the phenomena. We must make some initial, arbitrary choices, such as to what temperature to assign 0 and what difference in temperature corresponds to the interval between 0 and 1. Relative to those choices, we can recover the empirical content of the use of a number to specify a temperature. So it is, Davidson claims, for different interpretation theories which are confirmable from the radical interpreter's standpoint. We use our sentences with their properties to keep track of other speakers' behaviour. The semantic structure of our language is richer than the behaviour. As an analogy, think of our practice of attributing attitudes to animals.

Rover wags his tail upon hearing a car pull into the driveway. We keep track of his behaviour equally well by saying that he thinks his master is home, or that he thinks his provider is home. The behavioural evidence won't distinguish between these. Each attribution will work to track Rover's behaviour, provided we are systematic. This renders innocent the differences between schemes we might use in keeping track of Rover's behaviour.[9] So also, the thought is, in the case of an interpreter of another speaker. We make certain arbitrary choices at the outset. Then we make further assignments of our words and sentences to those of the speaker we are interpreting in light of initial choices. As long as we keep track of the initial arbitrary choices, we can see how the different elaborations keep track of the same underlying phenomena.

It is far from clear that the measurement analogy is an adequate response to the difficulty. For it requires the interpreter to suppose that his own language has a richer semantic structure than that of the speaker he is interpreting. But the interpreter himself speaks a language. And the argument for underdetermination applies as well for any speaker of his language who attempts to interpret him from the standpoint of the radical interpreter. Since by hypothesis such a speaker has as rich a language, and since it must be possible for another to speak the interpreter's language, we have to conclude that the position of the radical interpreter is not after all adequate to confirm an interpretation theory for any language. For here the supposition required by the analogy is false.

It is natural to search for additional constraints. In later work, Davidson suggested that factoring in another speaker would help to narrow down choices. For we can, he says, identify the object of a speaker's thought with the common cause of a common response of the speaker and another with whom he is interacting (Davidson, 1991a, 1991b). They triangulate on an object, which is identified as what each is thinking about. It is doubtful that this gets us much traction, however. If two people sit in front of a television watching the news, for example, there will be many common causes of their common responses: events at the screen, in the television, in the signal from the TV station, in the news room, in satellites in orbit and in distant trouble spots around the world. Another natural response would be to appeal to others being conspecifics and so very much like us in basic interests and in what they find salient. This would radically narrow down what to correlate their attitudes with. This way out, however, gives up on taking the standpoint of the radical interpreter, which takes the third-person behavioural facts to determine the meaning facts, to be the fundamental standpoint from which to investigate meaning, for it allows that the first person stance on our own thoughts plays a fundamental role in interpretation.

Thus, in the end, it is not clear that the austere starting point of the radical interpreter puts one in a position to confirm something sufficient for interpreting another speaker's utterances, and to that extent it is not clear that the pure third-person point of view suffices for understanding thought and language.

8. Davidson's place in twentieth-century philosophy

Davidson sought to revolutionize the theory of meaning by effecting three reorientations in our thinking about it. The first is the introduction of the truth theory as the vehicle for the meaning theory, which aims to recover from the resources of the theory of reference all that we want from a compositional meaning theory. The second is the rejection of reductive analysis of 'is meaningful' in favour of a looser and more holistic form of conceptual illumination as represented by the application of an interpretation theory as a whole to the evidence as a whole. The third is the restriction of the evidence for the theory to what is available from the third-person point of view without any presuppositions about meaning or the psychology of the speaker. Though still often misunderstood, Davidson's proposal that insight into meaning in natural languages can be obtained by reflection on how to construct and to confirm axiomatic truth theories for them has been hugely influential, both as a framework for doing natural language semantics and as a foil for critical discussion of foundational issues in the theory of meaning. Truth-theoretic semantics now is one of the paradigms for doing natural language semantics: its philosophical foundations and implications continue to attract debate; it has helped to clarify the distinction between investigations of logical form and lexical analysis; and a great deal of detailed and fruitful work on natural language semantics has been undertaken within the framework, including important contributions by Davidson. Radical interpretation and the lessons Davidson drew from it have been more controversial, as it deals with a fundamental issue in thinking about the relation of thought and language to the word, namely, whether the concepts we use to describe these are properly thought of as deployed in the first instance from the third-person point of view. Though there are difficulties in seeing how to make good on the idea, it would be hard to overemphasize its importance.

Davidson's project can be seen, ironically, as a development of the broadly empiricist arc of analytic philosophy in the twentieth century. Quine was the greatest influence on Davidson, as Carnap was on Quine. Carnap's outlook was structured by acceptance of the analytic–synthetic distinction and the view that the meaning of synthetic statements lies in their implications for sensory experience. This underwent two transformations in Quine. The first was his rejection of the analytic–synthetic distinction. The investigation of meaning then becomes a broadly empirical enterprise continuous with science and subject to considerations of fit with the rest of our empirical theory of the world. This gave rise to the second transformation, motivated by the view that language is a social art, which makes sensory experience appear an unsuitable basis for meaning, namely, the keying of meaning not to sensory experience but to stimulation of sensory surfaces. This represents a conservative modification of empiricist doctrine. Davidson takes over the third-person stance from Quine, but the basis of meaning takes another step towards objectivity in being keyed to distal stimuli in the environment of speaker and interpreter. In this final step, the last vestiges of the traditional role of sensory experience in empiricism, as the basis of meaning and knowledge of the external world, are relinquished. Traditional empiricism, with its emphasis on the foundational role of experience in understanding meaning and knowledge, is turned on its head through a series of internal changes by which the third-person point of view becomes conceptually, epistemically and ontically basic. In this, Davidson completes the transformation of a fundamental philosophical view into something so remote from its progenitor that its provenance can only be determined by tracing out the incremental steps by which it was accomplished.

Further reading

In addition to the items cited already in this chapter, you'll find the following useful in developing a deeper understanding of Davidson's work.

Davidson, Donald (2006), *The Essential Davidson*. Oxford: Oxford University Press.
Glüer, Kathrin (2011), *Donald Davidson: A Short Introduction*. Oxford: Oxford University Press.
Hahn, L. (ed.) (1999), *The Philosophy of Donald Davidson*. Chicago, IL: Open Court.
Lepore, Ernest (ed.) (1986), *Truth and Interpretation: Perspectives on the Philosophy of Donald Davidson*. Cambridge: Blackwell.
Ludwig, Kirk (ed.) (2003), *Donald Davidson*. Cambridge: Cambridge University Press.
Ludwig, Kirk (2015), 'Was Davidson's Project a Carnapian Explication of Meaning?' *The Journal of the History of Analytic Philosophy*, 4, pp. 7–15.
Ludwig, Kirk (2017), 'Truth-theoretic Semantics and Its Limits', *Argumenta*, 3, pp. 21–38.

Notes

1   A formal language has a precisely defined set of well-formed formulas generated recursively with formation rules operating over a set of primitive symbols, as for the languages of symbolic logic. It may be partially or fully interpreted.
2   Davidson thought, for example, that both Frege's and Carnap's treatment of belief sentences violated this constraint. Davidson's interest in the problems of compositionality was sparked initially by reflection on Carnap's treatment of belief sentences (Davidson, 1963).
3   I change the example to a fragment of French to set the stage for generalizing and extending the point.
4   As in the case of the reference theory, placing this requirement on the axioms goes beyond anything Davidson said, but it is implicit in the goal of providing a compositional meaning theory by way of a truth theory. See Lepore and Ludwig (2005, pp. 71–4; 2007, pp. 34–9).
5   This is not to claim that competence is realized by propositional knowledge of the theory. In 'A Nice Derangement of Epitaphs' (1986, p. 438), for example, Davidson says, 'To say that an explicit theory for interpreting a speaker is a model of the interpreter's linguistic

competence is not to suggest that the interpreter knows any such
theory ... They are rather claims about what must be said to give a
satisfactory description of the competence of the interpreter.'
6 See Lepore and Ludwig (2005, chapter 5), for a basic discussion of
the modifications needed to accommodate context sensitivity, and
see Lepore and Ludwig (2007, chapters 2–3), for a discussion of
quantifiers, and chapters 4–11 for a discussion of context-sensitive
referring terms and tense.
7 Davidson's (2001a) influential work in the philosophy of action bears
on the framework of rational agency invoked here.
8 The idea and the label are inspired by Quine's Principle of Charity,
'[A]ssertions startlingly false on the face of them are likely to turn
on hidden differences of languages' (1960, p. 59). Davidson later
distinguished the two elements mentioned here into the Principle of
Correspondence and the Principle of Coherence, the first of which
moves towards Richard Grandy's (1973) Principle of Humanity in
urging the interpreter to 'take the speaker to be responding to the same
features of the world that he (the interpreter) would be responding to
under similar circumstances' (see Davidson [2001c], p. 211).
9 Davidson held that animals do not have propositional attitudes,
so this is not an illustration of the idea he would have endorsed
himself.

Bibliography

Barwise, J. and Perry, J. (1981), 'Semantic Innocence and Uncompromising
Situations', *Midwest Studies in Philosophy*, 6 (1),
pp. 387–403.
Burge, T. (1992), 'Philosophy of Language and Mind: 1950–1990', *The
Philosophical Review*, 101 (1), pp. 3–51.
Chihara, C. S. (1975), 'Davidson's Extensional Theory of Meaning',
Philosophical Studies, 28 (1), pp. 1–15.
Cummins, R. (2002), 'Truth and Meaning', in J. K. Campbell, M.
O'Rourke and D. Shier (eds), *Meaning and Truth: Investigations
in Philosophical Semantics*. New York: Seven Bridges Press,
pp. 175–93.
Davidson, D. (1963), 'The Method of Extension and Intension', in P. A.
Schilpp (ed.), *The Philosophy of Rudolf Carnap*. La Salle, IL: Open
Court, pp. 311–50.
Davidson, D. (1965), 'Theories of Meaning and Learnable Languages', in
Y. Bar-Hillel (ed.), *Proceedings of the 1964 International Congress for*

Logic, Methodology and Philosophy of Science. Amsterdam: North
Holland Publishing Co., pp. 383–94. Reprinted in Davidson, 2001b.
Davidson, D. (1967), 'Truth and Meaning', *Synthese*, 17 (1), pp. 304–23.
Reprinted in Davidson, 2001b.
Davidson, D. (1973), 'Radical Interpretation', *Dialectica*, 27 (3–4),
pp. 314–28. Reprinted in Davidson, 2001b.
Davidson, D. (1975), 'Thought and Talk', in S. Guttenplan (ed.), *Mind
and Language.* Oxford: Oxford University Press. Reprinted in in
Davidson, 2001b.
Davidson, D. (1986), 'A Nice Derangement of Epitaphs', in E. Lepore
(ed.), *Truth and Interpretation: Perspectives on the Philosophy of
Donald Davidson.* Cambridge: Blackwell, pp. 433–46.
Davidson, D. (1991a), 'Epistemology Externalized', *Dialectica*, 45 (2–3),
pp. 191–202. Reprinted in Davidson, 2001c.
Davidson, D. (1991b), 'Three Varieties of Knowledge', *Philosophy*, 30,
(Supp), pp. 153–66. Reprinted in Davidson, 2001c.
Davidson, D. (2001a), *Essays on Actions and Events*, 2nd edn.
Oxford: Clarendon.
Davidson, D. (2001b), *Inquiries into Truth and Interpretation*, 2nd edn.
New York: Clarendon Press.
Davidson, D. (2001c), *Subjective, Intersubjective, Objective.*
New York: Clarendon Press.
Davidson, D. (2004), *Problems of Rationality.* Oxford: Oxford
University Press.
Dummett, M. (1993), *The Seas of Language.* Oxford: Oxford
University Press.
Foster, J. A. (1976), 'Meaning and Truth Theory', in G. Evans and
J. McDowell (eds), *Truth and Meaning: Essays in Semantics.*
Oxford: Clarendon Press, pp. 1–32.
Glock, H.-J. (2003), *Quine and Davidson on Language, Thought and
Reality.* Cambridge: Cambridge University Press.
Grandy, R. (1973), 'Reference, Meaning and Belief', *The Journal of
Philosophy*, 70 (14), pp. 439–52.
Horwich, P. (2005), *Reflections on Meaning.* Oxford: Oxford
University Press.
Katz, J. (1982), 'Common Sense in Semantics', *Notre Dame Journal of
Formal Logic*, 23 (2), pp. 174–218.
Lepore, E. and Ludwig, K. (2005), *Donald Davidson: Meaning, Truth,
Language, and Reality.* Oxford: Clarendon Press.
Lepore, E. and Ludwig, K. (2007), *Donald Davidson: Truth-Theoretic
Semantics.* New York: Oxford University Press.

Loar, B. (1976), 'Two Theories of Meaning', in G. Evans and J. McDowell (eds), *Truth and Meaning: Essays in Semantics*. Oxford: Clarendon Press, pp. 138–61.

Quine, W. V. O. (1960), *Word and Object*. Cambridge: MIT Press.

Quine, W. V. O. (1969), 'Epistemology Naturalized', in his *Ontological Relativity and Other Essays*. New York: Columbia University Press, pp. 69–90.

Soames, S. (1992), 'Truth, Meaning and Understanding', *Philosophical Studies*, 65, (1–2), pp. 17–35.

Soames, S. (2008), 'Truth and Meaning: In Perspective', *Midwest Studies in Philosophy*, 32 (1), pp. 1–19.

Stich, S. (1976), 'Davidson's Semantic Program', *Canadian Journal of Philosophy*, 6 (2), pp. 201–27.

Tarski, A. (1944), 'The Semantic Conception of Truth and the Foundations of Semantics', *Philosophy and Phenomenological Research*, 4 (3), pp. 341–76.

Tarski, A. (1983), 'The Concept of Truth in Formalized Languages', in *Logic, Semantics, Metamathematics* (2nd edn), trans. J. H. Woodger, ed. and with an introduction by John Corcoran. Indianapolis, IN: Hackett, pp. 152–278.

CHAPTER TWELVE

DUMMETT

Bernhard Weiss

One way of getting a sense of Dummett's distinctive contribution to the philosophy of language is to look at what he accepts and rejects in the writings of some of his major influences. First, and perhaps most importantly, Frege: from Frege, Dummett learns about the foundational role that the philosophy of language plays in analytic philosophy and the central roles played in the philosophy of language by a semantic theory detailing the relations of linguistic items to their worldly subject matter and a theory of sense explaining speakers' grasp of the semantic theory. But he rejects the underlying realism that permeates Frege's thinking. His rejection of Frege's realism is, in part, the application of a Wittgensteinian lesson. Frege makes senses objective by fiat – he reifies senses and places them in an objective third realm – Dummett rejects this and insists rather that we must see senses as established through speakers' use of terms in a publicly accessible realm; senses are intersubjective. Wittgenstein is wont to appeal to the conception of meaning in terms of use to buttress his rejection of systematic theorizing in philosophy. In contrast, language for Dummett is itself a mysterious phenomenon; it is not rendered so by philosophical misconceptions; and we illuminate its mystery by attempting to understand it systematically. Finally, the logical positivists: Dummett's interest in verificationist accounts of meaning has often led to false assimilations of his ideas to those of the logical positivists. But, while the latter advocate rejection of certain claims as meaningless, Dummett never does; rather he is revisionary of our conception of how we confer content on a claim. Dummett, like the positivists, is however suspicious of the easy assumption that philosophical and, in particular, metaphysical claims have clear content. But, rather than dismissing such claims as unscientific and meaningless, he taxes himself to determine their content.

In short, Dummett's writings offer many particular insights into the nature of language but do so from a clear and committed perspective about how to approach the philosophy of language and about how the philosophy of language relates to other areas of philosophy and, indeed, to philosophy itself.

1. Philosophy and the philosophy of language

Let us begin with a bold and striking claim: 'the philosophy of language is the foundation of all other philosophy' (1978, p. 442). Though bold and striking, it is far from clear what the content of the claim is; nor why we should accept it. Let's tackle these questions in tandem. Dummett provides the following support:

(1) 'the goal of philosophy is the analysis of the structure of *thought*'

(2) 'the study of *thought* is to be sharply distinguished from the psychological process of thinking'

(3) 'the only proper method for analysing thought consists in the analysis of *language*' (ibid., p. 458)[1]

Clearly the original claim gains some support and a little definiteness from the legitimacy of those of (1) and (3) and, as we shall see, (3) in turn depends, in part, on (2). I want to look first at claim (1) and then at (3).

For ease of exposition I'll assume for the moment that claim (3) is granted and thus shall not carefully distinguish the analysis of thought from the analysis of language, the philosophy of thought from the philosophy of language. I'll thus speak about a semantics or semantic theory for a region of inquiry; leaving it unclear for the moment whether the semantics applies to thought or to language. At base, Dummett's thought here has a Kantian inspiration: the philosopher should investigate the character of reality by investigating our representation of reality. Once we take that step, many branches of philosophy are seen to relate to semantic theory as species to genus. The philosopher of mathematics is interested in the analysis of thought/language in a particular area; likewise the philosopher of science or of one of the special sciences. So such philosophers are working *within* the realm of semantic theorizing and thus should defer in their practice to general principles securable by semantic theory itself. Thus the latter is foundational in two senses: (i) as the encompassing arena within which other philosophical enterprise takes place – every branch of philosophy is a branch of semantic theory; and (ii) as being the arbiter of successful endeavour in those specific arenas.

For semantic theory to play these foundational roles it would have to possess a kind of exhaustiveness – provision of an acceptable semantics for a region of inquiry should exhaust our philosophical interest in it – and a kind of autonomy – provision of an acceptable semantics for a region of inquiry should be possible independently of settling metaphysical, epistemological and perhaps other philosophical questions relating to it. Neither of these claims is particularly persuasive.

Take as an example the philosophy of mathematics. It is far from obvious that having a semantic theory for a mathematical theory exhausts our philosophical interest in it. We may still want to answer questions about the applicability of the theory. Just such an interest motivates Hartry Field's fictionalist philosophy of mathematics.[2] Though he accepts a platonic *construal* of mathematical statements – mathematics is to be understood as purporting to refer to a range of abstract objects – he rejects Platonism *as a philosophy of mathematics* by explaining the applicability of mathematics without assuming that its claims are true. Whether or not one is attracted to Field's programme the possibility of pursuing it testifies to the existence of an open question – how to explain the applicability of the theory – even granted a resolution of the semantic question. Nor is it clear that the acceptability of the semantic theory can be gauged without tackling epistemological or metaphysical questions. A Platonist semantics for mathematics may be found suspect precisely because of metaphysical or epistemological concerns about abstract objects.

In addition, there may well be concerns about whether general semantic principles can be arrived at independently of one's stance in the philosophy of mind, epistemology or metaphysics. In due course we shall find grounds for such concerns in the detail of Dummett's programme.

Let us move on to claim (3), namely, that the analysis of language is the method for analysing thought. The claim encapsulates Dummett's prioritizing of language over thought; it is a claim of explanatory priority. There are a number of strands in Dummett's thought here. He never denies that there may be thought independent of language: unverbalized thought and the thought of non-linguistic creatures. But such thought can play no role in the explanation of language precisely because any verbal formulation of the thought will deploy concepts which are alien to the thought itself; the thought thus cannot be accurately expressed in language and cannot explain linguistic thought. (See 1991a, pp. 323–4.)

Nor can we suppose that sentences are codes for thought, or that words are codes for concepts. How, on such a view, is the mind to forge a connection between word and concept? One might attempt an explanation by detailing how the ability to use the word appropriately amounts to grasp of the concept; but then a prior grasp of concepts would play no role in explaining one's understanding. Alternatively, since there's no content to the notion of simply having a concept before one's mind, we must presuppose an ability to *represent* the concept by means of mental items, that is, items which we suppose unproblematically *can* come before one's mind. However no such item is intrinsically representative, so how do they gain their representative capacity? We have made no progress. (See, e.g., 1993, pp. 97–8.)

Given this rejection of the code conception, we must view sentences as *expressions* of thoughts; rather than as encoding them. The structure of the sentence must thus reflect the structure of the thought, in the sense that a proper analysis of the semantic structure of the sentence must reveal the structure of the thought; it is after all *this* structure that enables it to express the thought.[3] Conversely there is no clear content to the notion of the structure of the thought independently of the structure of the sentence which expresses it. Thus, according to Dummett, we need to think of the analysis of the thought and of the sentence as proceeding in tandem; the structure of the thought is approached through the semantic analysis of the sentence, which is that structuring of the sentence which enables it to express a certain thought. So the analysis of thought cannot neglect the analysis of language. However, the analysis of language need make no appeal to the analysis of thought, since the semantic analysis of language is not the analysis of language in terms of its expression of thoughts or their components; rather it is the analysis of the semantic properties of complex expressions in terms of the semantic properties of their parts. In other words, the semantic analysis of sentences will display how the sentence is determined as true or false in accordance with its structure; it isn't a report of correlations between linguistic items and components of thoughts (see 1993a, p. 7).

A final argument for the priority of language proceeds as follows:

Thought requires a vehicle: we entertain a thought only in virtue of some mental activity.

Thought cannot be *identified* with that activity: claim (2).

So that activity constitutes the entertaining of the thought only against a certain background: uttering a sentence only counts as entertaining the thought against the background of a certain linguistic practice (so juxtaposing images, for instance, whether mental or physical, would do so only against a background of using those images in certain ways or the elaboration of specific details of a particular case and so on).

The background in a given case might be indefinitely various but is relatively uniform when the vehicle is linguistic; it is the background constituting linguistic competence.

Dummett concludes that 'our only hope' of analysing thought is thus via an analysis of language. (See 1991a, p. 323)

However the argument clearly doesn't establish the impossibility of approaching thought directly; rather it speaks to the methodological power of the linguistic approach. Let us, therefore, reserve judgement on the question of just how much the analysis of thought depends on the analysis of language; but concede that there are good reasons for deploying the analysis of language in attempting to analyse thought.

2. The philosophy of language and its method

The central question in the philosophy of language is that of the nature of linguistic meaning. So the philosophy of language aims primarily at a theory of (linguistic) meaning. Call a systematic specification of the meanings of expressions in a language a *meaning theory* for that language. Then Dummett's recommendation is that the method in the philosophy of language is that we pursue the theory of meaning by attempting to construct a meaning theory. He credits Davidson with having done most to teach us this lesson (1993, pp. viii–ix).

Briefly, Dummett's thought, in advocating the meaning-theoretic approach, is that our explicit use of the concept of meaning (in our everyday remarks about meaning) is, in general, not sufficiently robust to support a rewarding investigation into its character. The character of an expression's meaning is largely revealed implicitly in such things as our practices of illustrating and explaining that meaning through examples of use, through monitoring one another's use as correct or incorrect or through what we count as adequate displays of understanding; far less is revealed in explicit discussion of the expression's meaning and, since such discussion presupposes linguistic meaning, it could not provide an informative means of investigating linguistic meaning itself. To put the point more vividly, we might imagine a community which used a language lacking in a term for meaning. Though they would certainly have a concept of meaning, implicitly implicated in their practices of learning and teaching language, it obviously could not be accessed by looking at their use of a certain term (see 1993, pp. 1–3).

This account might make it seem that Dummett is interested in a wholly theoretical approach to the concept of meaning; that is, we investigate the concept of meaning by investigating the form of a *theorist's* attempt systematically to specify the meanings of terms in a language. And, in turn, it might now appear that there is a sharp discontinuity between the theorist's conception of meaning and that of the practitioners. On the one hand, this is correct: the upshot of the investigation is a reflective understanding of the workings of a linguistic practice which is unavailable to mere practitioners. On the other hand, we shouldn't over-exaggerate the discontinuity here. For, first, the theorist's enterprise is constrained by the nature of the practice itself and, second, the meaning theory itself will be a systematization and regimentation of the sort of explanations of meaning that will be offered by practitioners. Thus it is not wholly distinct from what practitioners do in monitoring one another's practice; rather it is an extension of that reflective enterprise in a systematic manner (see 1978, p. 451).

Let us now turn to the question of what the key characteristics of a meaning theory should be. Dummett's conception can be summarized in the following claims:

(1) A meaning theory is a theory of understanding: a meaning theory must contain or must deliver an account of what speakers know when they know how to speak a language.

(2) A meaning theory should deliver an account of the meanings of each expression which doesn't presuppose conceptual expertise which equates to an understanding of that expression; in Dummettian terms the theory should be robust not modest.[4]

(3) A meaning theory should account for the meaning of an expression in terms of the meanings of a proper fragment of the language and the relation of presupposition that is thus established should approach a partial order (roughly, for each expression, the meaning of that expression should presuppose a part of the language smaller than all of it); in Dummettian terms the theory should be molecular not holist.[5]

Obviously each of these claims stands in need of some clarification and wants some justification. We'll take each in turn.

2.1 A meaning theory is a theory of understanding

Comparatively little can be said in justification or explication of this claim. Dummett insists that the meaning theory must make it clear how the language functions and, if it fails to deliver an account of speakers' competence, then it fails to give an account of that which enables speakers to deploy language, primarily, in communicating with one another. So any such account fails to deliver an answer to our philosophical perplexity about language.

This seems fair enough, but it's worth noting as an aside that Dummett also thinks that any such account will *exhaust* our philosophical interest in language. And this additional claim is by no means obvious; take the following case. Many read the lessons of semantic externalism[6] as precisely revealing that an account of the competencies constitutive of understanding fail to determine the semantic facts concerning the relations of linguistic to worldly items.[7] Thus one might have an account which delivered or constituted a theory of understanding but which failed to issue in a semantics for the language. There is little reason to suppose that such an account would, in these circumstances, satisfy our philosophical curiosity about language. An implicit assumption seems to be at play in Dummett's thinking here, one he borrows from his luminary, Frege. Dummett assumes that the semantic properties of terms will be determined by the character of speakers' understanding of them. In Fregean terms, he assumes that sense determines reference. Though he defends this Fregean position from attacks based on semantic externalist arguments, he ought not to prejudge the issue against such theorists. The assumption – that the theory of understanding exhausts our philosophical interest in language – fortunately plays very little role in Dummett's thought. The converse assumption that a meaning theory must deliver an account of understanding is, however, basic to his thinking.

2.2 Robust and modest meaning theories

The goal of the meaning theory includes that of delivering an account of linguistic competence. No such account could be complete if it were to presuppose a conceptual accomplishment which is equivalent to that of understanding the basic expressions of the language. As we have mentioned, Dummett thinks that we cannot exploit a prior account of conceptual expertise in explaining an understanding of such primitive expressions; so any such account would fail to deliver an informative account of the competence involved in mastering the use of such terms and thus accepting it as final would simply be to renounce our goal.

Dummett makes this point by focusing on the basic clauses of a Davidsonian truth theory, deployed as a meaning theory. The Davidsonian truth theory will be based on clauses such as the following:

(AxT) 'Cape Town' denotes Cape Town.

From which we infer theorems of the form:

(ThT) 'Cape Town is a city' is true iff Cape Town is a city.

From which, if we are entitled to use the truth theory as a meaning theory, we derive clauses of the form:

(ThM) 'Cape Town is a city' means that Cape Town is a city.

Thus we suppose that competent speakers know clauses of the form (ThM). Dummett notes that one might well know that a clause of the form (ThM) is true, without knowing the proposition it expresses. How might one come to know this further thing? A plausible answer is to say that when the speaker knows the further thing she knows (ThM) to be true on the basis of having inferred it from clauses of the form (AxT). But then Dummett's question arises here too: What differentiates one who merely knows the truth of (AxT) from one who knows what (AxT) expresses? And here there seems no answer other than the obvious one: the latter person, but not the former, understands the meaning of 'Cape Town'. And thus the poverty of the approach is revealed: at base it has nothing to say about the nature of certain linguistic competencies but simply takes these as given (see 1991a, pp. 13–15).

Nonetheless the requirement of robustness might seem excessive and under-motivated; indeed, McDowell (1987 and 1997) has argued that it forces us to adopt a perspective from which the phenomenon of linguistic meaning is not rendered philosophically comprehensible, rather it becomes fugitive: Dummett's robust theorist will be unable to discern the phenomenon of meaning. The lesson for McDowell is that we should embrace modesty in the theory of meaning and should simultaneously deflate our explanatory ambitions in philosophy. I shall return to the debate between robust and modest theorists below.

2.3 *Molecularity and holism*

Though the task of the meaning theory is to deliver an account of linguistic competence, there are a number of ways in which it might make this delivery. Rarely will it be permissible simply to present a meaning theory and to take it as obvious how the theory represents speakers' capacities, their knowledge of meaning. In general, the theory will have to detail what knowledge of the theory consists in. We shall delve more deeply into this issue soon but the nub of it is that speakers will not know the theory explicitly – if they did then the business of the philosophy of language would be much easier than it is, since every competent speaker would be able to furnish a meaning theory for her language – rather the theory will be an explicit representation of merely implicit knowledge. This develops an obligation on the theorist, namely, to say what capacities constitute implicit knowledge of the theory. She might discharge that obligation in various ways: she may, somewhat implausibly, take each clause of the theory in isolation and explain what constitutes knowledge of it; she may take sets of interacting clauses together and say what constitutes knowledge of them; or, at the limit, she may eschew an interesting answer here and simply claim that knowledge of the entire theory is constituted by the ability to speak the language. Dummett is suspicious of the first atomistic position and castigates the latter holistic position as simply an abnegation of our responsibilities as theorists of language. He advocates the second molecular position, which, if it is not to explode into the holist one, requires that the selection of chunks of the theory imposes something close to a partial order on sentences in the language. The effect of this is that grasp of any piece of language is seen to depend only on grasp of a circumscribed region of language, which can therefore be seen as less complex. Three sorts of motivation for the view can be found in Dummett's writings.

The first motivation is based on our acquisition of linguistic mastery in a gradual, stage-by-stage fashion. The thought is that each stage provides a stable base for one's passage to the next stage. Thus the order in which we gain linguistic understanding imposes something close to a partial order on sentences in the language. If the account of meaning is to display language as perspicuously learnable then it had better adopt a molecular approach.

The second motivation focuses on the phenomenon of linguistic creativity. We are able to understand an indefinite number of novel expressions and we apparently do so on the basis of an understanding of their parts and the significance of so combining them. For this to be the case, the meaning of the complex must be explicable in terms of the meaning of its parts and, once again, we generate something like a partial order on expressions based on their complexity.[8]

The final motivation is quite different. A consequence of holism is that the meaning of any expression can only be given in relation to the meanings of expressions in the entire language or, at least, in relation to the meanings of expressions in some uncircumscribed region of language. But if this is to be so then the meaning of an expression is unsurveyable, in the sense that it cannot be an object of awareness; no speaker grasps the entire language (unless we consider the language to be an idiolect) and, even if she did, no speaker could bring to mind the meaning of an expression if that meaning were to be determined by the meanings of an uncircumscribed fragment of language. Moreover, Dummett thinks that in order to conceive of language use as rational we need to see speakers as deliberately using expressions on the basis of their meaning. Thus if language use is to be construed as rational, meanings must be surveyable and holism must be rejected. The conception of language use as rational is a crucial feature of Dummett's philosophy of language; he goes as far as to say that language use is 'the rational activity *par excellence*' (1993, p. 104; see also Taylor, 1987, p. 256). And maintaining this conception requires that we cannot see the ability to use language as a purely practical capacity; it involves awareness of meanings.

The first two motivations suffer from making the same assumption. Though we might grant that each thought justifies holding that the capacities constitutive of linguistic competence must be partially ordered – else they couldn't be acquired or deployed in novel ways to yield new capacities – there's no reason to suppose that these capacities each amount to grasp of meaning. We might, for instance, be able to think of there being a partially ordered set of capacities constitutive of understanding a language but be able to think too that those capacities can't be recognized as understanding portions of the language less than the whole of the language. Robert Brandom seems to suggest just such a possibility in his claim that language is fully recursive but not compositional (2008, pp. 133–6).

The third motivation evades this problem because what it requires to be surveyable is precisely the meaning of the expression. Where it might be questioned is in its assumption that if the character of an item is determined in some unsurveyable fashion then the item itself is unsurveyable. No doubt, in general, the assumption is surely questionable. But when it is so, this is surely because we suppose that we have access to the item concerned independently of the unsurveyable relations which constitute it. That, however, is a hard supposition to maintain in the case of meaning: how could we access meanings independently of the sorts of relations which bring them about? We'd either have to reify meanings and suppose we have a capacity to intuit them or we'd have to think of a medium for the representation of meanings. Neither is a palatable option.

3. The publicity of meaning

Like Frege, Dummett rejects any conception of meaning and understanding which makes meanings unshareable and agreement in understanding at best a hypothesis. But, while Frege attempts to secure these rejections by locating meanings in an objective realm, Dummett demurs. With Wittgenstein, Dummett sees meanings as established within communal practices of using language; thus meanings belong to an intersubjective realm in which we can be sure that we share meanings. Meanings, for Dummett, are publicly available.

Another formulation of Dummett's position is to say that agreement in use is agreement in meaning. This formulation is, as yet, quite vague, primarily because we haven't clarified how use is to be characterized. We shall return to this question, but for now we can push on simply by taking it that use is publicly available use – the sort of use that other speakers are able to scrutinize. But why should we take it that agreement in use is agreement in meaning? Well, to suppose otherwise is to suppose that there is an ingredient to the meaning one confers on a term which transcends the use one is able to make of it. But then, asks Dummett, how are speakers to settle that they do indeed share meanings and thus succeed in communicating? They could *infer* to the hypothesis that they do so. But what would justify the inference? One might argue that the hypothesis of shared meanings provides the simplest explanation of agreement in use. But since this justification would *always* be available, if it ever is, the supposition that meaning transcends use would be otiose. And, if agreement in use does not itself justify the inference then it is thoroughly mysterious what we might add so as to legitimate the inference, at least on certain occasions. In effect we are faced with a dilemma: either agreement in use never justifies claiming shared meanings, in which case, that we communicate must be a mere article of faith, or agreement in use always justifies claiming shared meanings, in which case meanings transcend use in no important sense.[9]

We now need to think more carefully about the nature of use of language. As we remarked above Dummett insists on seeing use of language as a rational activity and thus rejects any attempt to view linguistic mastery as a mere practical capacity (1991b, pp. 88–100). Knowledge or awareness of meaning is thus ineliminable in our conception of understanding. A good model for how linguistic knowledge figures in our rational use of language is to take this knowledge to be propositional in form; and, as such, it might enter into a reconstruction of intentional use of language as a product of rational deliberation. But equally, rigid adherence to this model would distort the nature of linguistic mastery – speakers cannot offer informative accounts of meaning for many expressions of their language – and would also render it inexplicable – knowledge of language would be explained only in terms of knowledge of language. Thus it is clear that there is a practical aspect to our knowledge of language. How are we to straddle these seemingly competing requirements?

Dummett's suggestion is as follows. We rightly represent speakers' knowledge of language as knowledge of a deductively articulated meaning theory (i.e. one where meaning specifications for complex expressions are deductively derived from the meaning specifications for their components), but in the main we are to think of this as implicit knowledge. What is implicit knowledge? Sometimes Dummett characterizes it as knowledge which the possessor is unable to articulate but of which she is able to recognize a correct formulation. And though this may capture a feature of implicit knowledge it obviously cannot exhaust its nature since then implicit knowledge would be explicable only in terms of a grasp of language and thus couldn't be foundational for our grasp of language. Rather there must be an aspect to possessing implicit knowledge which is displayed in one's capacity to use an expression; one must be able to manifest one's implicit knowledge (1978, pp. 216–17).

Dummett sometimes argues for this conclusion in the following manner (1991b, pp. 103–5). Grant that understanding is an epistemic state: it is knowledge of meaning. It follows that ascription of understanding is ascription of knowledge. An ascription of knowledge is only meaningful if one can say what distinguishes someone who possesses the knowledge from someone who lacks it. On occasion, the distinction will be made out in terms of the possessor's ability to give an account of the knowledge. But in the linguistic case, for reasons we've just outlined, this cannot be the global story; the knowledge will thus be possessed implicitly and the distinctive mark of someone who possesses the knowledge will be her ability to *do* something – to manifest her knowledge in use.

We thus develop what is often termed 'the manifestation constraint' on accounts of understanding. Dummett reads the constraint in a very strong sense; it must be possible for speakers who share an understanding to manifest this fact in their use. More weakly, one might argue that where speakers *differ* in their understanding then it must be possible for them to manifest this fact in their use. Dummett insists on the stronger reading because the weaker reading allows there to be an ingredient of one's understanding which, in principle, forever evades one's fellow speakers and to suppose this is to suppose that there is a purely private ingredient to one's understanding (see 1993, pp. xii–xv). Thus underlying Dummett's thought here is, as he admits, a conviction that Wittgenstein's prosecution of the private language argument is successful.

I want now to begin to connect these thoughts with the terms in which use is described and thus to the debate between the robust and modest theorists. Note that the manifestation constraint simply requires that speakers are able to manifest their understanding to other speakers. It thus allows that we might be able to describe that use which manifests understanding in terms that are only accessible to other speakers. And thus it would appear to motivate nothing stronger than a modest theory of meaning. Dummett, however, introduces a further element into his conception of publicity: he requires that the account of understanding make it clear how mastery of language is possible on the basis of *witnessing exhibitions of understanding*. This constraint is often termed the acquisition constraint. Discussion of the relations between the constraints abounds in the literature. Though there is insufficient space here to lay out the argument, it seems plausible to claim that the acquisition constraint adds something absent from the manifestation constraint, namely, that the use which manifests one's understanding be available to the learner and thus to someone innocent of the language. Thus it should be possible to describe that use in terms which don't presuppose grasp of the language. If this is right then fully to do justice to the acquisition constraint requires a robust rather than a modest theory of meaning.[10]

4. The form of a meaning theory

The main pillars of Dummett's conception of a meaning theory have now been erected: a meaning theory is a theory of understanding; the theory should be robust and molecular; and it should account for the publicity of meaning. With these elements in place we can begin to probe the likely form of a meaning theory. The first question we shall tackle is whether the meaning of a sentence can be conceived as given by its truth-conditions.

4.1 The viability of truth-conditional meaning theories

The dominant approach to systematic theorizing about meaning is the truth-conditional approach. On such an account we construct a meaning theory by adopting a favoured means of systematically generating specifications of the truth-conditions for every sentence in the language, or better, for utterances of such sentences. Putting to one side difficult semantic phenomena such as vagueness, one assumes that every sentence of the language is either true or false, or better, an utterance of any such sentence is either true or false; in other words we assume that the truth-conditions are determinately either fulfilled or are not fulfilled and truth thus applies bivalently. Dummett argues that no such theory can be reconciled with his conception of an adequate meaning theory. The argument proceeds as follows.

Many sentences of our language are undecidable in this sense: we have no method which is guaranteed to put us in touch with the best possible evidence either in favour of the sentence's truth or in favour of its falsity. Possible examples are sentences about the past, about the remote future, about unsurveyable domains such as large or distant regions of space or the natural numbers, or sentences which are – or are explained in terms of – subjunctive and counter-factual conditionals (conditionals which concern what *would* happen in certain sorts of circumstance, for example, 'If I were to be in a battle, I would behave bravely'). Many sentences of these particular types are, of course, known to be true or known to be false; the point is not that we *cannot* come to know their truth-value but simply that we have no sure-fire method for achieving this knowledge in all cases. On the truth-conditional account of meaning an understanding of such a sentence consists in knowledge of its bivalent truth-condition. Dummett's challenge is this: *what capacities manifest knowledge of the bivalent truth-conditions of an undecidable sentence?*

In general, one displays one's grasp of a sentence's meaning through an ability to investigate the truth-value of the sentence – to generate evidential situations – and then to exercise a capacity to recognize whether or not a given evidential situation warrants assertion of the sentence or not. When the sentence is decidable we can take this to constitute knowledge of truth-conditions; for, in such cases, the speaker will be able to institute a procedure whose upshot is to put her in an evidential situation in which she can either recognize the sentence to be true or to be false. But, in the case of undecidable sentences, nothing analogous is possible. By hypothesis, *any* investigation the speaker is able to perform may leave her in an evidential situation which fails to warrant assertion or denial of the sentence. Thus nothing the speaker is able to do entitles the claim that the sentence is determinately either true or false; in other words, no manifestable capacity of the speaker is able to show that what she grasps are bivalent truth-conditions. The cost of retaining a conception of understanding as grasp of bivalent truth-conditions is, in such cases, to allow that there is an ingredient of understanding which is not available to public scrutiny; and this is a cost Dummett, for reasons noted above, takes to be exorbitant.[11]

Let us note some of the assumptions of the argument. First, the speaker is required to possess a manifestable capacity with respect to *each* sentence. Second, attributing a semantic property to the sentence must be justified in terms of this capacity. Third, Dummett conceives of this capacity as a recognitional capacity. Although it doesn't affect the form of the argument, note that what constitutes a plausible recognitional capacity is surely an epistemological question. Thus the construction of a meaning theory will be beholden to results in epistemology. The first assumption is justified by Dummett's molecularism; the second by his Fregean view that sense determines reference; and the third by his adherence to robust theorizing. Consider how one might reply to the argument were one to reject each of these assumptions in turn.

First: molecularity. It is a striking feature of Dummett's philosophy that it is potentially revisionary; that is, Dummett has no qualms about the claim that we may have distinctively philosophical reasons for requiring a change in our ordinary, everyday linguistic practice. His thought is that if an aspect of our linguistic practice cannot be reconciled with our best philosophical theory of language, then it should be revised. Now, our usual practices of reasoning permit reasoning by dilemma, even when the sentence concerned is undecidable. The justification we give for this is that the sentence is determinately either true or false and thus whatever follows from both its truth and its falsity must be so. However, if Dummett's challenge is unanswerable, then we cannot offer this justification because we cannot assume that the sentence is determinately either true or false. Dummett's conclusion: we should reject such modes of reasoning.[12] How does this relate to the molecularity requirement? Well, if one were prepared to renounce molecularism then the following reply seems, at first sight anyway, plausible. A speaker's understanding of a sentence in her language cannot be extracted from her understanding of the language as a whole. We cannot thus think of her understanding of a sentence, *s*, as explicable purely in terms of her use of *s* in asserting that *s*; rather we need to consider her overall use of the sentence, which includes its use in sentences of the form '*s* or not-*s*'. A feature of her use of the latter sentence is that it can form a premise in an argument from dilemma. Since all of these uses manifest her understanding of the sentence, one now might claim that the best explanation of these capacities consists in attributing to her grasp of bivalent truth-conditions; else her acceptance of reasoning by dilemma will be mysterious. Thus, for the holist there are obvious potential responses to Dummett's challenge.

Second: the Fregean view of sense. Dummett takes it that we need to be able to justify attribution of a semantic property to an expression by appeal to the character of speakers' understanding of it. Certain (but not all) semantic externalists might disagree, claiming instead that the semantics of a term brings in worldly features of a speaker's use which transcend the character of her understanding of it. Thus, prosecuting Dummett's case against bivalent truth-conditions will involve engagement with arguments for semantic externalism.[13] We cannot enter into that terrain here.

Third: adherence to robust theories. Dummett's thought is that one can only manifest one's understanding of the sentence 'Fra Filippo Lippi was partial to boiled eggs' by exercising a capacity to recognize whether or not a piece of evidence warrants assertion (or, perhaps, also denial) of the sentence. Since that display does not justify the claim that, in grasping the sentence, one grasps a truth-condition which has a determinate truth-value, we are not entitled to assume that the sentence is determinately either true or false. Dummett's way of construing the nature of one's understanding is premised on his robust leanings: if one thinks that understanding should ultimately be explicable in terms which don't presuppose linguistic or conceptual competence then understanding will be a capacity for use characterized in some manner akin to Dummett's. More importantly, if one doesn't share Dummett's leanings then one might characterize use quite differently. One might, for instance claim, that one manifests one's understanding of 'Fra Filippo Lippi was partial to boiled eggs' as meaning that Fra Filippo Lippi was partial to boiled eggs by using the sentence to assert that Fra Filippo Lippi was partial to boiled eggs.[14] The fact that one was so using the sentence would be publicly available to suitably qualified observers of one's linguistic doings, namely, to those who understand the language one is using. The position is thus distinctly modest; no account of the nature of understanding is possible from a perspective which alienates itself from linguistic understanding. This modest view doesn't establish that speakers do indeed grasp bivalent truth-conditions; quite the reverse, the project of attempting to provide such a justification from either a pretended or genuine scepticism of this fact is rejected because it would be an attempt to justify such an attribution by appeal to more primitive capacities possessed by speakers. That is, it would be a descent into robust theorizing. But, as far as the modest theorist is concerned, Dummett's challenge is answered albeit only on her own terms.

4.2 Alternatives to truth-conditional accounts

Clearly, gauging the efficacy of Dummett's challenge is a matter of deciding where one stands with respect to a range of debates about the character of meaning theories, none of which will be settled here. But let us suppose that the challenge *is* effective. Where does that leave the semantic theorist? What alternatives are there to bivalent truth-conditional meaning theories? It is possible that one might revise one's conception of truth to a non-bivalent conception and then persist in offering a truth-conditional meaning theory. Crispin Wright has advocated this approach, attempting to understand truth as an enduring[15] warrant to assert, as, what he calls, superassertibility. Dummett has tended to read the lesson as requiring an entirely novel approach to the construction of meaning theories. The idea for such accounts is that we attempt to explain meaning in terms of some epistemic feature such as conditions warranting assertion, or conditions warranting denial. Such theories are not easily arrived at because, in general, such conditions provide only defeasible epistemic rights. For instance, the best warrant one may have for asserting our sentence about Lippi's partiality to eggs is compatible with the sentence's falsity; rarely is a piece of evidence guaranteed not to be deceptive. It is thus difficult to contemplate how the meaning of a sentence can be captured in some one set of such conditions. And Dummett argues that we must restrict our attention to some one set and derive other aspects of use from that set, else we violate the constraint of molecularity. Others have recommended looking to more than one set of use conditions, say, assertion *and* denial conditions, in characterizing meaning.[16] But whether any such attempt can be made workable and whether it can be reconciled with molecularity are open questions.[17]

5. Realism

Think of a subject matter and the likelihood is that whatever it is, whether it is mathematics, morality, talk about non-actual possibilities, the past, or other minds, it is possible to imagine either being a realist about it or of denying realism. But what is realism?[18] The realist about one or another thing holds that it is, in some sense, objective, or that how it is with that region of the world is independent of our thought, talk and knowledge of it, and that it is, in some sense, a genuine feature of the world. Dummett argues that realism should be construed as a semantic thesis, that disputes about realism and its denial are disputes about the correct semantics for a region of language. Such a construal of these debates has a threefold advantage: (i) it enables us to see commonalities between a variety of disputes across different subject matters; (ii) the semantic approach eschews metaphorical elucidations of metaphysical positions such as appeals to notions of independence or of construction;[19] (iii) the philosophy of language provides a neutral arbiter of the various debates – an instance of the foundational role of the philosophy of language.

A paradigm realist about a subject matter, for Dummett, is someone who adopts a semantics for the relevant region of language which uses a bivalent notion of truth based on a notion of reference. There are thus a variety of ways of departing from realism, each of which involves questioning a different aspect of the realist's semantic theory. Whether or not a particular semantics counts as realist or not – in some broader sense of the term – will depend on whether there is a plausible competitor which is closer to the paradigm realist position. A product of this conception of realism is that we also gain a better understanding of ways of departing from realism and, indeed, many such departures can be seen to gain in plausibility. For instance the anti-realist need not oppose the realist's conception of mind-independence with a conception of how an aspect of the world depends on the mind; rather she may simply cease to assume that truth applies bivalently. Moreover, the argument outlined in the last section against a theory of understanding which exploits a bivalent conception of truth is entirely general; that is, we have a novel argument which aims to move us away from *any* adoption of a realist semantic theory.

A final word on the issue of realism: many have contrasted a realist view with a reductionist view. So for instance one might reject realism about mental states by claiming that these are no more than, can, in some way, be reduced to dispositions to behave. Dummett does not deny the metaphysical relevance of reductive views; rather all such views involve a rejection of the paradigm realist position, since each fails to base its notion of truth on a notion of reference for terms in that arena. However in each case we need to go on to ask what consequence this rejection of realism at the level of reference has for the relevant notion of truth. And here different answers are possible; sometimes it may buttress a bivalent or realist conception of truth at other times it may undermine it. It all depends on the particulars of the case.

6. Prospects

Dummett's philosophy is programmatic in that he initiates a research enterprise, namely, that of constructing a theory of meaning which meets his requirements of molecularity, robustness and publicity. The value in his philosophy lies, at least partially, in the questions raised within and about the research programme: Are these requirements well motivated? Can one reconcile a truth-conditional meaning theory with these requirements? And, if not, how should we attempt to construct a meaning theory based on some set of use conditions? Though it is now some forty years or more since Dummett put these questions firmly on the philosophical agenda, they remain the subject of fascinating debate. And rightly so; for they provide a focused way of pursuing the question of how we gain a fully satisfying view of ourselves as rational beings who use language.[20]

Further reading

Useful book-length treatments of Dummett's work include: Green (2001); Matar (1997); and Weiss (2002a). Essays commenting on and responding to Dummett's views can be found in: Auxier and Hahn (2007); Brandl and Sullivan (1998); Heck (1997); Taylor (1987); and Weiss (2015a). Alex Miller has produced three targeted expository pieces which are worth investigating: 'What is the manifestation argument?' (2003a), 'What is the acquisition argument?' (2003b), and 'Realism' (2010). Additional brief overviews of Dummett's philosophy are: Green (2013); Murphy (2005); and Weiss (2002b). Weiss (2015b) is a useful guide to works by or on Dummett.

Notes

1   Dummett enunciates these claims as distinctive of analytical
    philosophy but, in addition, endorses them. Here I sidestep questions
    about his conception of analytical philosophy; I am solely concerned
    with Dummett's conception of philosophy and of the philosophy of
    language.
2   See his 1980.
3   Take as an example a case where syntactic and semantic structure
    might be taken to come apart. Let's suppose Russell was right
    about definite descriptions then the (underlying) semantic structure
    of the sentence – 'The F is G' – is seen to be that of an existential
    generalization and it is *this* feature of it which enables it to express
    the thought which it actually expresses.
4   In later work (e.g. 1991b) Dummett seems to prefer the term 'robust'
    to 'full-blooded', which he introduces in the earlier writings (see,
    e.g., the two 'What is a Theory of Meaning?' papers reprinted in
    Dummett, 1993). I've followed the later preference.
5   For elaboration of these claims see essays 1–4 in his 1993, and
    chapters 4 and 5 in his 1991b.
6   Semantic externalists argue that the causal, social or historical
    context of one's use needs to be factored into the account of how the
    reference of an expression is determined. Thus, one interpretation
    of the view, is that no individualistic set of factors can determine
    reference: retain the individualistic features but alter the contextual
    ones and the reference of a term may well be affected.
7   I don't say that the lessons need to be read this way nor that they are
    right to be read in this way, just that some do so read them.
8   For hints at both sorts of argument, see: his 1991b (pp. 224–5);
    Taylor (1987, p. 251); Auxier and Hahn (2007, pp. 617–21).
9   See, among others, 1993 (pp. 101–2); 1991b (pp. 83–6); 1978
    (pp. 216–18).
10 For fuller discussion see my 2010 (chapter 10).
11 See 1978 (pp. 16 and 224–6); 1993 (pp. 44–62); 2000
    (pp. 250–69).
12 This is an important feature of Dummett's philosophy; he
    advocates the rejection of classical logic in favour of intuitionistic
    logic. Intuitionism is an established position in the philosophy
    of mathematics and, in that context, intuitionistic mathematical
    theories and intuitionistic semantic theories are comparatively
    well-understood. One lesson of Dummett's philosophy of language
    may well be that we ought to generalize the intuitionistic account
    to empirical discourse; but since empirical warrants for assertion

are, unlike warrants provided by proofs, in general defeasible the difficulties are formidable.

13 See his 1981 (appendix to chapter 5); 1991a (pp. 144–8).
14 McDowell argues for just such a modest view.
15 Enduring no matter how extensive is one's investigation – see essay 14 in Wright (1993).
16 See Brandom (2000, 1994, 1976), and Rumfitt (2000).
17 Dummett provides a sustained study of intuitionistic mathematics in his 2000; his 1991a is an examination of the extension of intuitionism to natural language; and 'What is a Theory of Meaning? II' (1993, pp. 34–93) includes an examination of what he calls verificationist and pragmatist meaning theories; for recent modifications of his position see his 2004 and 2006.
18 See the preface and essays 1 and 10 in his 1978; essays 11 and 20 in his 1993; and his 2006.
19 What do we mean when we say that the world is independent of minds? In what sense is it claimed that minds construct the world?
20 Many thanks to the editor for inviting this contribution and for his helpful comments on an earlier draft.

Bibliography

Works by Dummett

Dummett, Michael A. E. (1978), *Truth and Other Enigmas*. London: Duckworth.

Dummett, Michael A. E. (1981), *Frege: Philosophy of Language*, 2nd edn. London: Duckworth.

Dummett, Michael A. E. (1991a), *Frege and Other Philosophers*. Oxford; New York: Clarendon Press/Oxford University Press.

Dummett, Michael A. E. (1991b), *The Logical Basis of Metaphysics*. London: Duckworth.

Dummett, Michael A. E. (1993), *Origins of Analytical Philosophy*. London: Duckworth.

Dummett, Michael A. E. (2000), *Elements of Intuitionism* (Oxford Logic Guides; 39), 2nd edn. Oxford: Clarendon.

Dummett, Michael A. E. (2004), *Truth and the Past*. New York: Columbia.

Dummett, Michael A. E. (2006), *Thought and Reality*. Oxford: Clarendon.

Dummett, Michael A. E. (2010), *The Nature and Future of Philosophy*. New York: Columbia.

Works by other writers

Auxier, Randall E. and Hahn, Lewis Edwin (eds) (2007), *The Philosophy of Michael Dummett* (Library of Living Philosophers series, vol. 31). Chicago, IL: Open Court.

Brandl, Johannes L and Sullivan, Peter (eds) (1998), *New Essays on the Philosophy of Michael Dummett*. Atlanta, GA: Rodopi.

Brandom, Robert (1976), 'Truth and Assertibility', *Journal of Philosophy*, 73, (03/25), pp. 137–49.

Brandom, Robert (1994), *Making It Explicit: Reasoning, Representing, and Discursive Commitment*. Cambridge, MA; London: Harvard University Press.

Brandom, Robert (2000), *Articulating Reasons: An Introduction to Inferentialism*. Cambridge, MA; London: Harvard University Press.

Brandom, Robert (2008), *Between Saying and Doing: Towards an Analytic Pragmatism*. Oxford: Oxford University Press.

Field, Hartry (1980), *Science without Numbers: A Defense of Nominalism*. Oxford: Blackwell.

Green, K. (2001), *Dummett: Philosophy of Language*. Oxford: Polity/ Blackwell.

Green, K. (2013), 'Introduction', *Teorema*, Vol. XXXII/1, pp. 5–17.

Gunson, D. (1998), *Michael Dummett and the Theory of Meaning*. Aldershot: Ashgate.

Heck, Richard G. (ed.) (1997), *Language, Thought, and Logic: Essays in Honour of Michael Dummett*. Oxford: Oxford University Press.

Luntley, M. (1988), *Language, Logic and Experience: The Case for Anti-realism*. London: Duckworth.

Matar, A. (1997), *From Dummett's Philosophical Perspective*. Berlin: de Gruyter.

McDowell, John (1976), 'Truth Conditions, Bivalence, and Verificationism', in G. Evans and J. McDowell (eds), *Truth and Meaning*. Oxford: Clarendon Press, pp. 42–66.

McDowell, John (1981), 'Anti-realism and the Epistemology of Understanding', in H. Parret and J. Bouveresse (eds), *Meaning and Understanding*. Berlin: de Gruyter, pp. 225–48.

McDowell, John (1987), 'In Defence of Modesty', in Taylor, 1987, pp. 59–80.

McDowell, John (1992), 'Meaning and Intentionality in Wittgenstein's Later Philosophy', *Midwest Studies in Philosophy*, 17 (01/01), pp. 40–52.

McDowell, John (1994), *Mind and World*. Cambridge, MA; London: Harvard University Press.

McDowell, John (1997), 'Another Plea for Modesty', in Heck, 1997, pp. 105–29.

McDowell, John (2004), 'Criteria, Defeasibility, and Knowledge', in T. R. Baldwin and T. J. Smiley (eds), *Studies in the Philosophy of Logic and Knowledge*. Oxford: Oxford University Press, pp. 7–30.

McGinn, Colin (1982), 'Realist Semantics and Content Ascription', *Synthese*, 52 (07/01), pp. 113–34.

McGuinness, B. and Oliveri, G. (eds) (1994), *The Philosophy of Michael Dummett*. Dordrecht: Kluwer.

Miller, A. (2003a), 'What is the Manifestation Argument?' *Pacific Philosophical Quarterly*, 83, pp. 352–83.

Miller, A. (2003b), 'What Is the Acquisition Argument?' in A. Barber (ed.), *Epistemology of Language*. Oxford: Oxford University Press, pp. 459–95.

Miller, A. (2010), 'Realism', at *The Stanford Encyclopedia of Philosophy* [online encyclopedia] (Summer 2010 Edition), ed. Edward N. Zalta, available at: http://plato.stanford.edu/archives/sum2010/entries/realism/.

Murphy, B. (2005) 'Michael Dummett', at *The Internet Encyclopedia of Philosophy*, available at: http://www.iep.utm.edu/dummett/.

Rumfitt, I. (2000), ' "Yes" and "No" ', *Mind*, 109, pp. 781–824.

Taylor, Barry (ed.) (1987), *Michael Dummett: Contributions to Philosophy*. Dordrecht, Holland: Nijhoff.

Tennant, N. (1987), *Anti-realism and Logic: Truth as Eternal*. Oxford: Clarendon.

Tennant, N. (1997), *The Taming of the True*. Oxford: Oxford University Press.

Weiss, Bernhard (1996), 'Anti-realism, Truth-value Links, and Tensed Truth Predicates', *Mind*, 105, pp. 577–602.

Weiss, Bernhard (2002a), *Michael Dummett* (Philosophy Now series). Chesham: Acumen.

Weiss, Bernhard (2002b), 'Dummett', in P. B. Dematteis, P. S. Fosl and L. B. McHenry (eds), *Dictionary of Literary Biography, vol. 262: British Philosophers 1800–2000*. Detroit: Gale, pp. 80–7.

Weiss, Bernhard (2004), 'Knowledge of Meaning', *Proceedings of the Aristotelian Society*, 104, pp. 75–94.

Weiss, Bernhard (2010), *How to Understand Language*. Durham: Acumen.

Weiss, Bernhard (2015a), *Dummett on Analytical Philosophy*. Basingstoke: Palgrave Macmillan.

Weiss, Bernhard (2015b), 'Michael Dummett' in the Oxford Bibliographies, Oxford University Press, http://www.

oxfordbibliographies.com/view/document/obo-9780195396577/obo-9780195396577-0294.xml (accessed December 2010).

Wright, Crispin (1980), *Wittgenstein on the Foundations of Mathematics*. Cambridge, MA: Harvard University Press.

Wright, Crispin (1992), *Truth and Objectivity*. Cambridge, MA: Harvard University Press.

Wright, Crispin (1993), *Realism, Meaning and Truth*, 2nd edn. Oxford: Blackwell.

Wright, Crispin (2003), *Saving the Differences: Essays on Themes from Truth and Objectivity*. Cambridge, MA: Harvard University Press.

CHAPTER THIRTEEN

KRIPKE

Bryan Frances

We are concerned with two main issues: meaning and linguistic understanding. Saul Kripke has investigated several fundamental philosophical questions concerning these, but in this chapter I will focus on just two themes of his work: what he said regarding the paradigm set up by Gottlob Frege (which touches on both meaning and linguistic understanding), and what he said about the metaphysics of meaning. I will concentrate on his 'A Puzzle about Belief' and *Wittgenstein on Rules and Private Language* more than on his *Naming and Necessity*, as the latter has already received much competent treatment at introductory and intermediate levels.[1]

By the late 1960s Fregean views dominated the philosophy of language, and with good reason. But in the 1970s Saul Kripke reduced that dominance and repositioned research into meaning and linguistic understanding. I begin below by reconstructing key elements of the Fregean paradigm, ones relevant to belief sentences. Then I explain how Kripke challenged those elements. I'll finish my discussion of the Kripkean challenges to the Fregean paradigm by sketching some of Kripke's positive theses regarding meaning and reference.

Then I move to Kripke's work on the *metaphysics* of meaning. In order to have anything like a systematic theoretical account of meaning it will probably be helpful to have an idea as to what meaning *is*. Kripke is interested in the underlying basis of facts such as 'Jones, like many of us, means addition by his use of "+" '. What facts about Jones make it true that when he uses '+' he is using it to express addition rather than something else (e.g. some other mathematical function)? Are there facts about Jones' mind or brain or linguistic behaviour that determine that he means addition by '+'? Kripke has no published answers to these questions, but in his landmark book *Wittgenstein on Rules and Private Language* he presents (without endorsement) an argument inspired by his study of Wittgenstein that has the shocking thesis that '[t]here can be no fact as to what I mean by "plus", or any other word at any time' (1982, p. 21). As we will see below, what this claim amounts to, even in the context of Kripke's discussion, is a difficult matter. We will also see that he provides the beginnings of a positive account of how to understand putative truths such as 'Jones means addition by "+" ' without running afoul of the previous thesis.

1. A reconstruction of some Fregean views concerning meaning

In this section, I outline a few key views on meaning that came out of Frege's work. You might want to read or re-read the Frege chapter before going on. When I was a graduate student I had a philosopher of language tell me that to say one needs to read Frege is like saying one needs to breathe; Kripke is not far behind Frege in that respect. However, a reading of Frege isn't *strictly* necessary here, as my goal is not to elucidate what Frege thought but rather to describe just five important ideas that in the 1960s were commonly endorsed by philosophers of language *inspired* by Frege.

The Fregeans we have in mind start with the innocent observation that there is more to the meaning of a proper name than its referent – at least, this is true for one important sense of 'meaning'. The two names 'Superman' and 'Clark Kent', for instance, differ in many psychologically relevant ways: we associate different notions with the two names. With 'Superman' we associate 'Superhuman powers', 'Can bend steel in his bare hands' and 'Wears a brightly coloured cape'. With 'Kent' people associate 'mild mannered', 'unassuming' and 'clumsy'. Even today just about everyone agrees that in a suitably broad sense of 'meaning', the two names differ in meaning despite having the same referent (for the purposes of this chapter I am pretending that they have the same real referent – pretending, that is, that the Superman/Kent story is true).

The Fregean's second step is to observe that it's intuitive that 'Lois Lane believes that Superman flies' is true while 'Lois Lane believes that Kent flies' is false. After all, if you ask her to evaluate 'Superman flies' and 'Kent flies' she will understand you and say that the first is true and the second is false.

The Fregean didn't leave it to pure intuition that (A) 'Lois believes Superman flies' is true while (B) 'Lois believes that Kent flies' is false. On my reconstruction, the third Fregean step is an *argument* that backs up the intuition mentioned in the second step. The argument could be articulated in various ways, but here is a particularly clear and perspicuous formulation of the argument for (A):

(A1) *Disquotation*: If a normal English speaker assents to a sentence 'p', then she believes p.
(A2) Lois satisfies the antecedent of (A1) when the sentence in question is 'Superman flies'.
(A3) Thus, by (A1) and (A2) Lois believes that Superman flies.
(A4) If Lois believes that Superman flies, then 'Lois believes that Superman flies' is true.
(A5) Therefore, by (A3) and (A4) 'Lois believes that Superman flies' is true.

As it is formulated in premise (A1), Disquotation is implausible, since one needs to add all sorts of qualifications to it to make it reasonable. For instance, I might assent to 'Dogs are insane' while acting in a play even though I don't believe that dogs are insane. Since Lois is an ordinary English speaker who is assenting to 'Superman flies' in the ordinary kind of circumstance where those qualifications don't matter (e.g. she isn't acting in a play or being insincere or anything like that), we can omit the qualifications.

Now here's the Fregean argument for (B):

(B1) *Disquotation*: If a normal English speaker assents to 'p', then she believes p.
(B2) Lois satisfies the antecedent of (B1) when the sentence in question is 'Kent doesn't fly'.
(B3) Thus, by (B1) and (B2) Lois believes that Kent doesn't fly.

(B4) *Consistency*: If someone has the belief p and the belief not-p, then she is irrational. Any pair of beliefs of the form p and *not-p* are called *contradictory* beliefs.

(B5) Lois is rational. (She is *confused* about 'Superman' and 'Kent', thinking that they pick out different men, but that doesn't mean she's *irrational*.)

(B6) Thus, by (B4) and (B5) Lois doesn't have the belief Kent flies as well as the belief Kent doesn't fly.

(B7) Thus, by (B3) and (B6) Lois does not have the belief that Kent flies.

(B8) If Lois doesn't believe that Kent flies, then 'Lois believes that Kent flies' is not true.

(B9) Thus, by (B7) and (B8) 'Lois believes that Kent flies' is not true.

As with Disquotation, the principle Consistency in premise (B4) would need to include a bunch of qualifications in order to be plausible. For instance, I could be rational in having beliefs p and not-p if I have them at different times. More interestingly, I could have multiple personality disorder and have those beliefs 'in' different personalities. Or, I could have the pair of contradictory beliefs deep in my subconscious but have never reflected on them; in such a case the charge of irrationality might be a bit too extreme. But just as before, none of those qualifications will matter to Lois's case.

By arguing that 'Lois believes Superman flies' is true while 'Lois believes that Kent flies' is false, the Fregean has argued against the principle *Substitutivity* for belief sentences, which says that when coreferential names are interchanged (substituted for one another) in the 'p' part of 'S believes p' no change in truth-value results.

The Fregean's fourth step is to notice that the phenomenon of associated notions mentioned earlier can be used to give an *account* of the alleged fact that 'Lois believes that Superman flies' is true while 'Lois believes that Kent flies' is false. The main idea here is that if the two names differ in 'Superman' and 'Kent' had the same meaning, as they would if the entire meaning of a name was its referent, then the two 'Lois' sentences would attribute the same belief to Lois, and so they couldn't differ in truth-value. But they do differ in truth-value. If the two names differ in meaning, as they would if the associated notions were parts of their meanings, then we can see how the two sentences can have different meanings and truth-values.

Thus, the Fregean is saying that this difference in notions associated with two names makes for a *truth-conditional* difference: a difference that generates a difference in the truth-conditions for sentences like 'Lois Lane thinks that Superman/Kent flies', so that the 'Superman' sentence is true while the 'Kent' sentence is false. This goes beyond the 'innocent observation' noted in the first Fregean step that we associate different notions with different names: the Fregean is saying that these associative differences make a *semantic* difference, since (she claims) they cause differences in *truth-conditions*. For instance, I personally associate different ideas with 'I love catsup' and 'I love ketchup', but I don't think that this difference affects the aspects of the meanings of 'catsup' and 'ketchup' that matter to truth-conditions. It's just a quirk of mine that has no semantic significance. The Fregean has argued that in cases of the kind we've been looking at the differences in associated notions *do* make semantic differences.

The fifth step is the observation that the difference in notions associated with the two names can also be used to account for how names refer to things. Fregeans called the truth-conditionally relevant notions we associate with names *senses*. They also typically thought that senses were the meanings of *definite descriptions*, or perhaps clusters of such descriptions. For instance, Kripke noted that just about the only thing some philosophers know about Giuseppe Peano is that he was a nineteenth-century mathematician who was the first person to come up with the axioms for arithmetic. They associate both the indefinite description 'a nineteenth-century mathematician' and the definite description 'the first person to come up with the axioms for arithmetic' with the name 'Giuseppe Peano'. But if the definite description gives part of the meaning of the name, as the Fregean hypothesized in the fourth step, then we can see how the name refers to the person: since the name 'Giuseppe Peano' has a meaning that includes what is expressed by 'the first person to come up with the axioms for arithmetic', and the latter refers to Peano in virtue of the fact that he alone satisfies that description, the name must refer to Peano. So, the name does its referring job via the description we associate with it.

In sum, the Fregean had several good points regarding the meanings of proper names (as well as some other terms):

(1) We often associate different notions with different names, even when the names are coreferential.

(2) It is intuitive that 'Lois believes Superman flies' is true while 'Lois believes that Kent flies' is false.

(3) There is a good argument backing up that anti-Substitutivity intuition in (2), relying on Disquotation and Consistency.

(4) We can use the differences in associated notions in order to indicate the facts in virtue of which the sentences in (2) have different truth-values.

(5) Since the associated notions are the meanings of definite descriptions, then we can also account for how names get linked to their referents. (The referent is just the one and only thing that is picked out by the description.)

All in all, it was a nice package of views. But as we are about to see, Kripke challenged the Fregean on (2)–(5).

2. Kripke's challenge to the Fregean argument against substitutivity

I start with Kripke's alleged refutation of the conjunction of Disquotation and Consistency. Kripke's Paderewski story (1988, pp. 130–1) seems to prove that if Disquotation is true, then Consistency is false. And if he is right about that, then of course the Fregean argument for (A) and (B) fails due to at least one false premise.

In the Paderewski story the protagonist Peter has for a long time thought that there are two famous people named 'Paderewski,' one a pianist with musical talent and one a politician without musical talent. In reality the politician is the pianist: there's just one relevant person named 'Paderewski' and Peter is just plain confused, although understandably so, since Paderewski keeps his two lives largely separate in the public eye. Here is a reconstruction of Kripke's main argument.[2]

(P1) Assume for the sake of argument that Disquotation is true: if a normal English speaker assents to 'p', then she believes p.

(P2) Peter is a normal English speaker who assents to both 'Paderewski is musical' and 'Paderewski isn't musical'. (He assents to the first on many occasions, such as when listening to a recording of Paderewski; he assents to the second on many occasions as well, such as when discussing how politicians are usually liars without any interesting talents.)

(P3) So by (P1) and (P2) Peter believes that Paderewski is musical and that Paderewski isn't musical.

(P4) Peter is rational (like Lois Lane he is confused but still rational).

(P5) Therefore, by (P3) and (P4) someone is rational and has beliefs p and *not-p*.

(P6) Thus, by (P5) Consistency is false.

(P7) Thus, by (P1)–(P6) if Disquotation is true, then Consistency is false. Alternatively, if Consistency is true then Disquotation is false. In any case, they can't *both* be true.

At this point in the dialectic the Fregean can try to adjust his arguments for (A) and (B) by slightly revising Disquotation and Consistency. The alleged problem with this move is that the Kripkean argument (P1)–(P7) can be revised in response to refute the revised Fregean principles. I won't go through these moves here.

Although Kripke claims to have undermined the Fregean argument against Substitutivity for belief sentences, Kripke holds that Substitutivity fails for other kinds of sentences. For instance, Kripke would probably accept that 'It is a priori known that if Superman exists, then Superman is Superman' is true while 'It is a priori known that if Superman exists, then Superman is Kent' is false (he argues for this in *Naming and Necessity*). So Kripke rejects Substitutivity for certain *epistemic* sentences (i.e. sentences about epistemological matters like a priori knowledge). However, he never explained *how* Substitutivity fails for such sentences; that is, he didn't tell us how the differences in 'Superman' and 'Kent' could create different truth-conditions for the two sentences 'It is a priori known that if Superman exists, then Superman is Superman/Kent'.

3. Kripke's challenge to semantic intuitions

In his essay 'A Puzzle about Belief' Kripke did not merely attempt to refute the Fregean argument against Substitutivity for belief sentences. He also argued that the Paderewski story presents us with a deep philosophical puzzle: although both Disquotation and Consistency are very reasonable (when the qualifications are added on), at least one of them is false (even with the qualifications added on).

Just because we might not be sure how to solve the puzzle (i.e. figure out which principle is false and why) doesn't mean that we can't draw any interesting conclusions from it. Although Kripke didn't go on to state it explicitly, I think he would say that the *main* lesson of the puzzle, before we proceed to any solution, is that we should put much less trust in our intuitions about semantic matters. The idea here would be that Disquotation and Consistency were about as intuitive as semantic principles ever get; so if we're wrong about *them*, well, then we need to take seriously the idea that our intuition could be wrong concerning just about any semantic principle. Thus, Kripke took the puzzle to have sceptical consequences for intuition-based theorizing in the philosophy of language.

This lesson is important when addressing a typical Fregean reply to Kripke's apparent refutation of the conjunction of Consistency and Disquotation. The Fregean might say that although the Fregean argument has failed, we're still left with the *highly intuitive* judgement that Substitutivity is false for belief sentences: just because (3) (from the end of section 1) is out doesn't mean that (2) is gone too. Since (2) is still in place, we should still reject Substitutivity for belief sentences. Thus, Kripke's refutation of (3) has only limited consequences.

However, this Fregean reply neglects the primary lesson of Kripke's puzzle: the point about semantic intuitions. Once we have seen that the extremely intuitive Disquotation and Consistency can't both be true, why on earth should we trust our intuition that Substitutivity is false for belief sentences? The puzzle's sceptical lesson undermines (2) just as much as the refutation undermines (3), or so I think Kripke would argue.

It's worth noting that the anti-Fregean typically *accepts* the Fregean argument (A1)–(A5) for the claim that 'Lois believes Superman flies' is true. And of course that means accepting its first premise, Disquotation. As Kripke noted, 'Taken in its obvious intent [i.e. with the qualifications added on], after all, the principle appears to be a self-evident truth' (1988, p. 113). Thus, many anti-Fregeans have gone on to reject Consistency.

Let me try to give a brief idea of why some philosophers have rejected Consistency (other than the reason that Disquotation seems true and at least one of the two principles has to be false). You understand the name 'Aristotle' because you've read some philosophy. You may also recall that US President John F. Kennedy's widow Jackie married a rich Greek guy, Aristotle Onassis. So there are two people named 'Aristotle' that you know about. In some contexts you will happily assent to 'Aristotle was a philosophical genius', as you know of great works of his; and on other occasions you will happily assent to 'Aristotle was not a philosophical genius', as you have no reason to think that Onassis was any good at philosophy, let alone a genius at it. You have something like two 'files' in your mind, both with the label 'Aristotle'. In one of them you have things like 'wicked smart philosopher' and in the other you have things like 'rich guy who married Jackie'. Naturally, you think that when you say 'Aristotle was a philosophical genius' and 'Aristotle was not a philosophical genius', in appropriate contexts, you are not contradicting yourself.

Ahh, but did you know this: the rich shipping guy just is the ancient Greek philosopher! The philosopher found the secret to eternal life eons ago, and has been around for thousands of years. Just for fun, he uses the name 'Aristotle' in some centuries before faking his death and taking on a new identity. (Just pretend with me here.)

When you say things like 'Aristotle once taught Alexander the Great' you refer to the very same person you refer to when you say things like 'Aristotle once was married to JFK's widow'. Now it seems as though your two beliefs ascribed with 'Aristotle was a philosophical genius' and 'Aristotle was not a philosophical genius' really do contradict each other – even though you are rational and couldn't discover the inconsistency without empirical help. If that's right, then Consistency is false.

When a philosopher tells you that a highly intuitive principle is false, she usually goes on to try to account for the intuitiveness of the principle – often by arguing that what we are finding intuitive isn't the false principle in question but a closely related true one that we are confusing with it. That's the case here: the philosophers who reject Consistency sometimes say that a principle closely related to Consistency is untouched by these considerations. This might be such a principle: elementary reflection and memory are sufficient to know whether you attach different notions to two uses of a name. But the thesis that elementary reflection and memory are sufficient to know whether you attach different *truth-conditionally relevant* notions to two uses of a name – notions that effect the truth-conditions of belief sentences – is a different and more ambitious thesis, one that might have to be rejected along with Consistency.

It's hard to quarrel with the premises that your many assents in normal philosophical contexts to 'Aristotle was a philosophical genius' show that you do indeed believe that Aristotle was a philosophical genius, and that your many assents in normal political gossip contexts to 'Aristotle was not a philosophical genius' show that you do indeed believe that Aristotle was not a philosophical genius. Notice that when *I* write 'You believed that Aristotle was a philosophical genius and you believed that Aristotle was not a philosophical genius' I am the one using 'Aristotle' and since I know perfectly well of the identity of the philosopher and the rich shipping guy, my use is univocal. So Disquotation really is being used to attribute contradictory yet rational beliefs.

A Fregean has the resources to say that the two beliefs don't really contradict each other even though only one of them is true: the real content of the belief you have with 'Aristotle was a philosophical genius' is given by 'The guy who wrote the *Nicomachean Ethics*, taught Alexander the Great, etc. was a philosophical genius' whereas the content of the belief you express with 'Aristotle was not a philosophical genius' is given by 'The rich guy who married JFK's widow Jackie, etc. was not a philosophical genius', and those two meanings don't contradict each other in the sense of logical contradiction relevant to Consistency. One problem with this approach is that it doesn't look as though we have a decent argument or trustworthy intuition that senses are truth-conditionally relevant to belief sentences.

Now for a potential lesson regarding not meaning but linguistic understanding. If we give up on Consistency, then we are saying that a rational person could 'gaze' at two of her occurrent thoughts, perhaps expressed with 'Superman flies' and 'Kent doesn't fly', and not be able to tell by reflection alone that they contradict one another. That has consequences for our view of the nature of linguistic understanding. After all, now we are saying that a person can *understand* two sentences that express her beliefs and yet she doesn't know that one is the negation of the other. Thus, understanding a sentence – or grasping a thought – has serious limitations: just because you have a thought and express it with a sentence doesn't mean that you understand its truth-conditional structure, as Lois understands 'Superman flies and Kent doesn't fly' and she thinks it has structure 'a is F and b isn't F' but really it has the structure 'a is F and a isn't F'. The truth-conditional structure of the thought is not immediately open to view – even though, as we noted above, we do seem to know, without any empirical investigation, the notions we associate with various concepts and words.

In the wake of Kripke's work on belief sentences philosophers of language have tried to figure out the logical structure of belief sentences. Often, although not always, they have accepted Substitutivity for belief sentences. For additional thoughts on this topic first study Salmon (1986) and Salmon and Soames (1988).

4. Kripke's challenges to the Fregean theory of truth-conditional senses

Kripke's work in this area has already been competently and thoroughly presented and evaluated in many places in the literature, so I will have little to say about it. For in-depth treatment see Devitt (1981) and Soames (2002).

The central Fregean idea, which is the basis for themes (4) and (5) (from the end of Section 1), is this:

(*) The meaning of a name as used by a specific person is expressed by a definite description (or perhaps a group of such descriptions) in the person's mind.

Thesis (*) has a couple of interesting consequences:

(**) Since a person uses 'Superman' with the meaning expressed by a definite description such as 'The superhero who flies and has x-ray vision', it follows that the meaning of 'If Superman exists, then Superman is the superhero who flies and has x-ray vision' should have the meaning had by 'If the superhero who flies and has x-ray vision exists, then the superhero who flies and has x-ray vision is the superhero who flies and has x-ray vision'. And the latter is both a necessary truth and knowable a priori. So the former is as well, as they have the same meaning.

(***) Since a person uses 'Superman' with the meaning expressed by a definite description such as 'The superhero who flies and has x-ray vision', it follows that 'Superman' in their mouth refers to whatever is referred to by 'The superhero who flies and has x-ray vision'.

Kripke offered several arguments against (*)–(***) and thus (4) and (5).

First, in many cases people understand a name and use it to refer to its standard referent even though they have no definite description in their minds that picks out the referent. For instance, many people know that Richard Feynman was a famous physicist, but they might not know of any description that picks him out uniquely. They know he is *a* famous physicist, but they don't know anything that picks him out *uniquely*. Thus, it's not the case that each person who uses a name to refer to something has in her mind a definite description that picks that person out uniquely. Thus, (*) is false.

Second, in some cases people understand a name and use it to refer to its standard referent even though the definite descriptions they associate with the name pick out some other entity or nothing at all. Earlier in this essay I mentioned that some people associate both the indefinite description 'a nineteenth-century mathematician' and the definite description 'the first person to come up with the axioms for arithmetic' with the name 'Giuseppe Peano'. But although Peano did come up with those axioms, he was not the *first* person to do so. That was an honest mistake people made, as it was later discovered that Richard Dedekind found the axioms first. Thus, I might use a name to refer to X even though the definite descriptions I associate with the name might actually pick out not X but Y. Thus, (***) is false. In addition, if someone uses 'the first person to come up the axioms for arithmetic' to give the meaning of 'Peano', then 'If Peano exists, then Peano is the first person to come up with the axioms for arithmetic' would have to be both necessarily true and knowable a priori, as per (**). But it's not even true, let alone necessary and a priori! Thus, (**) is false.

For the most part philosophers of language have tended to agree with Kripke that the truth-conditional part of the meaning of a name is not also expressed by a definite description (or group of such descriptions). Even so, philosophers of language have explored various Fregean options in response to Kripke's challenges. For instance, there is the question of whether the Fregean can repair matters by appealing to more clever definite descriptions, perhaps even ones that the user of the name doesn't know about consciously; alternatively, perhaps senses for proper names aren't expressed by definite descriptions but some other means (for these ideas see: Chalmers [2002]; Evans [1973, 1982]; Jackson [1998]; and McDowell [1977]).

5. Kripke's positive theses regarding names

Kripke has a positive view regarding names: they are 'rigid designators'. In order to understand how rigid and non-rigid designation works it is helpful to start with a non-rigid definite description (and then we'll move back to names). Consider 'The best male tennis player in the world in the 1990s'. As a matter of fact, this definite description denotes Pete Sampras. We can put it this way: *when evaluated at the actual world*, the bit of our language 'The best male tennis player in the world in the 1990s' refers to Sampras because he *actually is* the best male tennis player in the world in the 1990s. Now consider three possible scenarios.

Possible world W1: Pete Sampras breaks his arm at tennis camp as a kid. This makes him hate tennis so he plays baseball instead. He's no good at it and ends up an investment banker.

Possible world W2: Pete Sampras starts out as a fantastic tennis player. Then at 17 he first reads Hume's *Dialogues on Natural Religion*. He becomes a highly intelligent plumber.

Possible world W3: Pete Sampras wins every Grand Slam tennis tournament in the 1990s.

When *evaluated at* W1 or W2, 'The best male tennis player in the world in the 1990s' doesn't designate Sampras (perhaps it designates Andre Agassi if he's the best male tennis player in the 1990s in those worlds); when evaluated at W3 or the actual world it does designate Sampras. That is, when we consider W1–W3 and ask who would be picked out by the meaning we actually attach to 'the best ...' we don't get the same person every time. That's what we mean in saying that the definite description designates different things 'in' or, perhaps better, 'when evaluated at' those possible worlds; the description is non-rigid. On the other hand, 'the positive square root of nine' designates the very same thing when evaluated at every possible world; so it's rigid. And according to Kripke 'Pete Sampras' designates the very same thing in each world (e.g. it never designates Agassi); so it's rigid.

Kripke also had a positive view about how the reference of a name is transmitted from one person to the next, sometimes a bit misleadingly called the 'causal theory of reference' (it's misleading because it's not a theory of reference – it's a theory of reference *transmission* from person to person – and it relies on a lot more than causality). He never developed the view into a fully fledged theory that one can rigorously evaluate. Perhaps the best that can be said by way of introducing his view is what he said himself (for evaluation, first study Stanford and Kitcher, 2000, and chapter 4 of Devitt and Sterelny, 1999):

> Someone, let's say, a baby, is born; his parents call him by a certain name. They talk about him to their friends. Other people meet him. Through various sorts of talk the name is spread from link to link as if by a chain. A speaker who is on the far end of this chain, who has heard about, say Richard Feynman, in the market place or elsewhere, may be referring to Richard Feynman even though he can't remember from whom he first heard of Feynman or from whom he ever heard of Feynman. He knows that Feynman is a famous physicist. A certain passage of communication reaching ultimately to the man himself does reach the speaker ... [A] chain of communication going back to Feynman himself has been established, by virtue of his membership in a community which passed the name on from link to link .... (1980, p. 91)

6. Kripke's thoughts on the metaphysics of meaning

Kripke's book on Ludwig Wittgenstein is meant to be an *exposition* of some of Wittgenstein's primary thoughts on rules and private language. It may strike you as surprising that most philosophers have not bothered to figure out if Kripke's exposition is accurate – whether it really fits what Wittgenstein said. This lack of interest makes sense though for several reasons, the most important of which is that Kripke's Wittgenstein – often called 'Kripkenstein' – is interesting regardless of whether he's the real Wittgenstein. (Another reason: Wittgensteinians tend to be very picky, even prickly, about what Wittgenstein 'really said'.)

We tend to think that some facts are at a 'higher level' than other facts; and the 'low level' facts somehow determine the 'high level' facts. For instance, the water in my tea-kettle just started boiling. This happened in virtue of, or because of, a whole bunch of facts about what was happening to the individual water molecules in the kettle. The high-level and macroscopic fact that my kettle started boiling right then is determined or fixed by the various low-level and microscopic facts about the water molecules in the kettle.

It's natural to think that facts about meaning are high-level. Suppose we visit an alien culture and we are trying to figure out what meanings their words have. We pick an individual alien, call him Odd, and ask ourselves 'What does Odd mean when he uses the symbol "*"?', where '*' is a symbol from his language. One would think that the answer to our question might be found in a number of places. Perhaps what he means by '*' is determined by what is going on in his brain, the various physical facts about his brain. So the low-level determining facts are facts about his brain. Or maybe the facts about how he *uses* '*' – what he applies it to, what he refuses to apply it to – fix the meaning of his uses of '*'. Or maybe some combination of those and other low-level facts fix the meaning of his uses of '*'. Let's say that Odd uses '*' to pick out property or substance P (e.g. P might be the property red, so his '*' and our 'red' are synonymous, or the substance water, in which case his '*' and our 'water' are synonyms).

Kripke's, or should I say Kripkenstein's, answer to 'What facts make it true that Odd uses "*" to express P?' seems to be 'None at all'. But interpretation is difficult here. On the one hand, Kripke writes in many places things like '[t]here can be no fact as to what I mean by "plus", or any other word at any time' (1982, p. 21). He writes that there is no 'condition in either the "internal" or the "external" world' that 'constitutes my meaning addition by "plus"' (1982, p. 69). Again, 'no facts, no truth-conditions, correspond to statements such as "Jones means addition by '+'"' (1982, p. 77). Passages like those seem to make it clear that Kripkenstein is saying that *it's not a fact and not true* that I mean addition by 'plus' (or that Odd means P by '*'). And yet there are all sorts of passages that prove that such an interpretation of Kripkenstein is superficial at best:

> We do not even wish to deny the propriety of an ordinary use of the phrase 'the fact that Jones meant addition by such-and-such a symbol', and indeed such expressions do have perfectly ordinary uses. We merely wish to deny the existence of the 'superlative fact' that philosophers misleadingly attach to such ordinary forms of words, not the propriety of the forms of words themselves. (1982, p. 69)

> Do we not call assertions [such as 'Jones, like many of us, means addition by "+"'] 'true' or 'false'? Can we not with propriety precede such assertions with 'It is a fact that' or 'It is not a fact that'? [Wittgenstein's way with these challenges is this: we] *call* something a proposition, and hence true or false, when in our language we apply the calculus of truth functions to it. That is, it is just a primitive part of our language game, not susceptible of deeper explanation, that truth functions are applied to certain sentences. (1982, p. 86)

These crucial passages require us to take great care in figuring out what Kripkenstein's thesis is. For he now seems to be admitting that it really is *true* that Jones means addition by 'plus'; it's a *fact* that he means addition by 'plus' – which is precisely what it looked like he was denying above.

Perhaps Kripkenstein's thesis is something along this line: although it's true that Jones means addition by 'plus', there is nothing that *makes* that truth true. There are no underlying or low-level facts ('condition[s] in either the "internal" or the "external" world', 'superlative fact[s]') in virtue of which the Jones truth is true (that 'constitute' the Jones truth). This is unlike the teakettle case in which various facts about the water molecules underlie the high-level fact that the water is boiling. It's also inconsistent with various popular and influential theories of meaning determination put forward by Fred Dretske, Jerry Fodor and others.

This interpretation has the merit of making a good deal of Kripke's discussion make sense, as most of his energy in the book seems to be spent arguing why various candidate lower-level facts cannot be the truthmakers for truths such as 'Odd means redness by "*"'. For instance, it might be thought that what makes it the case that Odd means redness by '*' is some special mental state that he instantiates when and only when he grasps the concept of redness. But how did that mental state get the property of being a grasp of *that* concept instead of some other concept? Again, we are looking for some lower-level facts in virtue of which the mental state in question gets its specific meaning. But there is nothing in Odd's mind or brain that shows that he meant redness rather than some closely related property such as scarlet or crimson.

There is a great deal to say about Kripke's arguments, but I want to close with an analogy meant to give a rough idea of Kripkenstein's *positive* view about the metaphysics of meaning.[3] We agree on 'Cats have four feet' because we see that it's true: the agreement *follows* the truth. But 'Bishops move diagonally in chess' is true because we agree on it: the truth *follows* the agreement. So the relation between social agreement and truth is reversed. Roughly put, Kripkenstein would put meaning facts in with the chess fact and not with the cat fact. In some sense, we just decide to adopt a rule that bishops move diagonally; similarly, we just decide to adopt a certain rule regarding meaning 'Jones will mean addition by "+"'. The latter case is much more complicated, and Kripke attempts to flesh it out in his Wittgenstein book.

I think Kripkenstein would agree that there are underlying facts in virtue of which 'Jones means addition by "+"' is judged by us as true: we see that certain conditions are met, and then we think that that means that the Jones sentence is true. We could discover the same thing about Odd and his linguistic community. But Kripkenstein would say that such facts aren't what *make* the 'S means X by Y' sentences true. Instead, those lower-level conditions are what we go by in *attributing* various meanings to Odd.

Further reading

On Fregean sense and substitutivity

Devitt, Michael and Sterelny, Kim (1999), *Language and Reality: An Introduction to the Philosophy of Language*, 2nd edn. Cambridge, MA: MIT Press.
Salmon, Nathan (1986), *Frege's Puzzle*. Atascadero, CA: Ridgeview.
Salmon, Nathan and Soames, Scott (eds) (1988), *Propositions and Attitudes*. New York: Oxford University Press.
Soames, Scott (2002), *Beyond Rigidity: The Unfinished Semantic Agenda of Naming and Necessity*. New York: Oxford University Press.

On the causal theory of reference transmission

Kyle, P. and Kitcher, Philip (2000), 'Refining the Causal Theory of Reference for Natural Kind Terms', *Philosophical Studies*, 97, 97–127.

On the metaphysics of meaning

Miller, Alexander and Wright, Crispin (eds) (2002), *Rule Following and Meaning*. Montreal: McGill-Queen's University Press.

Notes

1 In the philosophy of language Kripke has also done significant work on theories of truth (1975), speaker's reference versus semantic reference (1977), logical form and Russell's theory of descriptions (1976, 2005), presupposition and anaphora (2009), the social character of naming (1986), and the interpretation of Frege's philosophy of language (2008). Most of these essays demand more of the reader than the works examined in this chapter. A number of his unpublished essays will soon be published in several volumes under the title *Collected Papers* by Oxford University Press.

2 It should be noted that Kripke didn't set out the argument this precisely; neither did he make Consistency explicit anywhere in his long and detailed article. Nevertheless, most philosophers think Consistency did figure in his arguments in an essential way.

3 Boghossian (1989); Byrne (1996); Soames (1998a) and Soames
   (1998b) are central articles devoted to working through Kripkenstein's
   arguments and theses; additional central essays are collected in Miller
   and Wright (2002). I recommend the Soames articles as the best for an
   initial study.

Bibliography

Boghossian, Paul (1989), 'The Rule-following Considerations', *Mind*, 98,
   pp. 507–49.
Byrne, Alex (1996), 'On Misinterpreting Kripke's Wittgenstein',
   Philosophy and Phenomenological Research, 56, pp. 339–43.
Chalmers, David (2002), 'On Sense and Intension', in James Tomberlin
   (ed.), *Philosophical Perspectives 16: Language and Mind*.
   Oxford: Blackwell, pp. 135–82.
Devitt, Michael (1981), *Designation*. New York: Columbia
   University Press.
Devitt, Michael and Sterelny, Kim (1999), *Language and Reality: An
   Introduction to the Philosophy of Language*, 2nd edn. Cambridge,
   MA: MIT Press.
Evans, Gareth (1973), 'The Causal Theory of Names', *Proceedings of the
   Aristotelian Society, Supplementary Volume 47*, pp. 187–208.
Evans, Gareth (1982), *The Varieties of Reference*, ed. John McDowell.
   Oxford: Clarendon Press.
Jackson, Frank (1998), 'Reference and Descriptions Revisited', in James
   Tomberlin (ed.), *Philosophical Perspectives 12: Language, Mind, and
   Ontology*. Oxford: Blackwell, pp. 201–18.
Kripke, Saul (1972/1980), 'Naming and Necessity', in Davidson and
   Harman (eds), *Semantics of Natural Language*. Dordrecht: Reidel, pp.
   253–355 and 763–9. Reprinted in 1980 with a new preface as *Naming
   and Necessity*. Cambridge, MA: Harvard University Press.
Kripke, Saul (1975), 'Outline of a Theory of Truth', *Journal of
   Philosophy*, 72, pp. 690–716.
Kripke, Saul (1976), 'Is There a Problem about Substitutional
   Quantification?' in G. Evans and J. McDowell (eds), *Truth and
   Meaning; Essays in Semantics*. Oxford: Oxford University Press, pp.
   324–419.
Kripke, Saul (1977). 'Speaker Reference and Semantic Reference', in P.
   French, T. Uehling, and H. Wettstein (eds), *Contemporary Perspectives
   in the Philosophy of Language*. Minneapolis: University of Minnesota
   Press, pp. 6–27.

Kripke, Saul (1979/1988), 'A Puzzle about Belief', in A. Margalit (ed.), *Meaning and Use*. Dordrecht: Reidel, pp. 239–83. Reprinted in 1988 in Salmon and Soames (eds), *Propositions and Attitudes*. New York: Oxford University Press, pp. 102–48.

Kripke, Saul (1982), *Wittgenstein On Rules and Private Language*. Cambridge, MA: Harvard University Press.

Kripke, Saul (1986), 'A Problem in the Theory of Reference: The Linguistic Division of Labor and the Social Character of Naming', in *Philosophy and Culture (Proceedings of the XVIIth World Congress of Philosophy)*. Montreal: Editions du Beffroi, Editions Montmorency, pp. 241–7.

Kripke, Saul (2005), 'Russell's Notion of Scope', *Mind*, 114, pp. 1005–37.

Kripke, Saul (2008), 'Frege's Theory of Sense and Reference: Some Exegetical Notes', *Theoria*, 74, pp. 181–218.

Kripke, Saul (2009), 'Presupposition and Anaphora: Remarks on the Formulation of the Projection Problem', *Linguistic Inquiry*, 40, pp. 367–86.

McDowell, John (1977), 'On the Sense and Reference of a Proper Name', *Mind*, 84, pp. 159–85.

Miller, Alexander and Wright, Crispin (eds) (2002), *Rule Following and Meaning*. Montreal: McGill-Queen's University Press.

Salmon, Nathan (1986), *Frege's Puzzle*. Atascadero, CA: Ridgeview.

Salmon, Nathan and Soames, Scott (eds) (1988), *Propositions and Attitudes*. New York: Oxford University Press.

Soames, Scott (1998a), 'Facts, Truth Conditions, and the Skeptical Solution to the Rule-Following Paradox', in James Tomberlin (ed.), *Philosophical Perspectives, 12, Language, Mind and Ontology*. Oxford: Blackwell, pp. 313–48.

Soames, Scott (1998b), 'Skepticism about Meaning: Indeterminacy, Normativity, and the Rule Following Paradox', *Canadian Journal of Philosophy, Supplementary Volume 23 (Meaning and Reference)*, ed. Ali A. Kazmi, pp. 211–49.

Soames, Scott (2002), *Beyond Rigidity: The Unfinished Semantic Agenda of Naming and Necessity*. New York: Oxford University Press.

Stanford, P. Kyle and Kitcher, Philip (2000), 'Refining the Causal Theory of Reference for Natural Kind Terms', *Philosophical Studies*, 97, pp. 97–127.

CHAPTER FOURTEEN

DERRIDA

Thomas Baldwin

Derrida was born and grew up in Algeria. He was excluded from school as a Jew in the period 1942–44, but in 1948 he gained a place at a lycée in Paris and he was admitted to the École Normale Supérieure in 1952. After passing the *agrégation* in 1956 he taught in Le Mans and at the Sorbonne, and also spent a year at Harvard, before securing a position as 'mâitre-assistant' at the École Normale in 1964. His seminars there soon became renowned in France, and this reputation was maintained when he moved in 1984 to the École des Hautes Études en Sciences Sociales.

During the 1950s when Derrida was studying at the École Normale, academic philosophy in France was much influenced by the phenomenology of Husserl and Heidegger; and Derrida's philosophical work starts off from a critical engagement with their writings, especially where they concern language. Language had long been an important theme of the phenomenological movement. Heidegger starts off his 1946 'Letter on Humanism' with the bold claim that 'Language is the house of being. In its home human beings dwell' (Heidegger, 1998, p. 239); and Husserl discussed language throughout his work, from his early *Logical Investigations* of 1900 (Husserl, 1970) to his late essay 'The Origin of Geometry' of 1936 (Husserl, 1989). As we shall see, it is in fact these discussions of language by Husserl which provide Derrida with his starting point. Thus what is distinctive about Derrida's approach to philosophy is not the attention that he gives to language but the account of language he advances, which he uses to criticize, first, the philosophical programme of transcendental phenomenology initiated by Husserl, and then, much more ambitiously, '*the* philosophy and history of the West' (Derrida, 1973, p. 51). In this short chapter I shall concentrate on the development of Derrida's distinctive philosophy of language in his early writings without attempting to address the issues raised by his subsequent massive *oeuvre*.

1. On Husserl's 'The Origin of Geometry'

Derrida's first significant philosophical work was his introduction to his translation of Husserl's 1936 essay 'The Origin of Geometry' (Derrida's introduction and translation were published in 1962; the introduction is translated in Derrida, 1989). In this essay Husserl sought to elucidate the relationship between our subjective experience of the geometry of space as self-evident and the conception of geometry as a body of objective truths concerning ideal objects. Husserl's account of this relationship starts from the thesis that language provides the 'living body', the vehicle, for the content of subjective experience, and the initial connection with objectivity is then dealt with by the thesis that language and objectivity are fundamentally 'intertwined':

> The objective world is from the start the world for all, the world which 'everyone' has as world-horizon. Its objective being presupposes men, understood as men with a common language ... Thus men as men, fellow men, world – the world of which men, of which we, always talk and can talk – and, on the other hand, language, are inseparably intertwined. (Husserl, 1989, p. 162)

These two points show clearly the central place that language holds in Husserl's philosophy at this time, both as vehicle for the content of subjective experience and as essentially 'intertwined' with the world in such a way that the world is thought of as objective. The resulting position is similar to that later developed by Davidson in his discussions of 'triangulation', according to which it is in virtue of sharing a language that speakers are able to appreciate that they share a world (see Davidson, 2001). For Husserl, however, this line of thought does not fully elucidate the status of geometry with its theorems and ideal objects since these are not parts of the world-horizon of ordinary language. To deal with this, Husserl introduces a thesis reminiscent of Plato's theory of recollection: this aspect of geometry, he suggests, is dependent upon the existence of *written* constructions, especially diagrams, which exhibit ideal geometrical objects in such a way that it is possible to 'reactivate' the subjective self-evidence of the experience of geometrical truth (Husserl, 1989, p. 164).

Derrida's introduction to his translation of Husserl's essay is about a hundred pages longer than the translation itself, and his main aim is to elucidate what he calls the 'exemplary significance' of Husserl's essay by pointing to the emphasis Husserl places on language as the intertwining of thought and objectivity and to the role of writing in the account of geometrical truth. But Derrida also picks out two issues which he will later take up. First, while endorsing Husserl's emphasis on the connection between a language shared with others and the objectivity of the world described in this language, Derrida suggests that language has a yet more fundamental role in enabling an individual to identify and recognize objects at different times:

> Before the 'same' is recognized and communicated among several individuals, it is recognized and communicated within the individual consciousness ...
>
> In a certain way, therefore, intersubjectivity is first the non-empirical relation of Ego to Ego, of my present present to other presents as such; i.e., as others and as presents (as past presents). (Derrida, 1989, pp. 85–6)

The issue here is one that often arises in the context of discussions of linguistic rule-following and the situation of an isolated subject such as Robinson Crusoe. Wittgenstein briefly alludes to Crusoe in his 1935 'Notes for Lectures on "Private Experience" and "Sense Data"' (see Wittgenstein, 1993, p. 237); and Otto Neurath, one of the central members of the Vienna Circle, defended Crusoe's capacity for language in his 1933 paper 'Protocol Sentences' (see Ayer, 1959, p. 205). Derrida follows, and indeed extends Neurath's position: he holds that the intertemporal relationship between Crusoe yesterday and Crusoe today which sustains his capacity for objective thought is fundamental to the possibility of an intersubjective relationship between Crusoe and Man Friday. Second, Derrida suggests that the role of writing in language is more far-reaching than Husserl recognized. Whereas for Husserl the importance of written geometrical demonstrations is primarily that they provide an enduring basis for reactivating the construction of ideal geometrical objects which exhibit the self-evidence of geometrical truth, Derrida suggests that the existence of writing indicates a much more striking possibility, the possibility of a meaningful text that becomes separated from the intentions of individual speakers:

> Without the ultimate objectification that writing permits, all language would as yet remain captive of the de facto and actual intentionality of a speaking subject or community of speaking subjects. By absolutely virtualizing dialogue, writing creates a kind of autonomous transcendental field from which every present subject can be absent. (Derrida, 1989, pp. 87–8)

This conception of language as an 'autonomous transcendental field' that can be considered without immediate reference to a speaking subject is alien to Husserl. Derrida does not here press the point – he leaves his line of thought just as a suggestion, but one with an implication that would certainly be unsettling for Husserl (who thought that subjective experience is the primary phenomenon for philosophy), namely that 'a subjectless transcendental field is one of the "conditions" of transcendental subjectivity' (Derrida, 1989, p. 88).

2. Speech and Phenomena

In his next, short, book *Speech and Phenomena* (published in 1967; English translation in Derrida, 1973) Derrida returned to Husserl, but now with a different purpose. Going back to the account of language Husserl had set out in his early *Logical Investigations* (Husserl, 1970) and relied on thereafter, Derrida argues that Husserl's account is both characteristic of his phenomenological approach to philosophy and untenable. Hence, as Derrida makes clear (Derrida, 1973, pp. 45–6, n. 4), the message of his book is not just that Husserl's account of language is flawed, but also that it is necessary to rethink the conception of phenomenology as an inquiry which seeks to make explicit the way in which the a priori structure of ordinary experience is grounded in fundamental 'sense-bestowing' acts of consciousness which make sense of what is presented (given) in perception. Derrida's critique of Husserl is comparable to Sellars' attack on the 'Myth of the Given' (Sellars, 1963, p. 140), but it is developed in a different way via the claim that all forms of intentionality, including perception, have a structure comparable to that of language; and since language depends upon the fact that signs are used, and *re*used, with the same meaning in different contexts, this structure is to be found within all forms of intentionality. Hence perception depends upon the ability to *re*cognize perceptual 'signs' that recur in different contexts and thereby *re*present the perceived world; it is inescapably meaningful rather than dependent on the 'presence' of contents given in 'pure' perceptions to a subject who makes sense of them *ex nihilo*.

Husserl begins his discussion of language in the first of his 'Logical Investigations' by introducing a distinction between two types of sign somewhat comparable to Grice's later distinction between 'non-natural' and 'natural' meaning (see Grice, 1989, p. 214). Generally, according to Husserl, we think of a sign as an 'expression' (*Ausdruck*) which expresses thoughts and feelings in virtue of its conventional (non-natural) meaning, and it is expressive signs of this kind that Husserl had in mind in his later account of language as the 'body' of geometrical experience. But, Husserl observes, there are also signs which are merely indications (*Anzeichen*) without being meaningful expressions at all: 'We say the Martian canals are signs of the existence of intelligent beings on Mars' (Husserl, 1970, vol. I, p. 270 – old pictures of Mars taken through telescopes showed patterns on its surface which some interpreted as 'canals'). Phenomena which are taken to be natural signs of this latter kind are associated, typically causally, with the object or state of affairs of which they are signs and they function as indicative signs when attention is drawn to them in order to indicate this object or state to someone. Since expressive signs are also often used to indicate things, one might suppose that they too are indicative signs, albeit of a different kind. But Husserl makes it clear that this is not his position: although expressive signs often have an indicative role, this is not essential to them: for 'Expressions function meaningfully even in isolated mental life, where they no longer serve to indicate anything' (Husserl, 1970, vol. I, p. 269). Husserl infers from this that the meaning of an expressive sign is not dependent upon its indicative potential; instead expressive signs acquire their meaning from 'meaning-conferring acts' (Husserl, 1970, vol. I, p. 281) in which a thinker confers meaning on a sign by defining it through a 'directly intuitive presentation' which 'fulfils' the meaning thus conferred by presenting the object meant by means of the content of the intuitive presentation. We can think of this as an idealized form of ostensive definition which a thinker carries out for herself.

Derrida's objection to this account of the meaning of expressive signs starts off from Husserl's later thesis that written signs such as geometrical diagrams facilitate the reactivation of the self-evidence of earlier experiences. Derrida, however, does not take over this thesis; on the contrary he holds that past experiences cannot be brought back to life at all. Nonetheless he takes it to be characteristic of all expressive signs that they involve the 'reactivation', not of past experiences, but of the sign itself. For he holds that the meaning of expressive signs is dependent upon their repeated use, that is, the use of distinct token signs which are representative of one and the same sign type:

> When in fact I *actually* use words, and whether or not I do it for communicative ends, ... I must from the outset operate (within) a structure of repetition whose basic element can only be representative. A sign is never an event, if by event we mean an irreplaceable and irreversible empirical particular. (Derrida, 1973, p. 50)

Derrida goes on to infer that Husserl's account of the meaning of expressive signs is fundamentally mistaken; where Husserl holds that this meaning is based upon isolated, non-communicative, mental acts, Derrida maintains that it is essentially dependent on communicative practices in which signs are repeated.

Husserl might reply that he too holds that expressive signs are essentially repeatable since the meaning conferred by the initial act can be carried forward into later repetitions of the sign in virtue of the ability of a subject to recall the way in which her original meaning-conferring act was fulfilled by a direct intuitive presentation of an object. In response, Derrida need not deny that we often rely on memory to recall the meaning of the words we use; but he can argue that this common-sense point, so far from supporting Husserl's position, undermines it; for in using memory in this way we rely on our ability to recapture the content of earlier experiences that cannot now be literally brought back to life and this ability requires the use now of expressive signs whose meaning represents the earlier experience. But this dependence of memory upon the occurrence of meaningful signs undermines the suggestion that, fundamentally, the use of signs depends upon memory of original meaning-conferring acts. Instead, according to Derrida, meaning accrues to sign types through the regular practice of using tokens of them to signify objects, properties, acts or whatever, and each particular use of a token sign, therefore, 'can only be representative' of a sign type whose meaning is dependent upon this practice.

In expounding Derrida's position I have imported type/token terminology which he does not use. But he clearly acknowledges what is in effect the type/token distinction (Derrida, 1973, p. 50) and emphasizes that our capacity to produce and recognize linguistic tokens of sign types is absolutely fundamental to language; he puts this point by saying that 'this representative structure is signification itself' (Derrida, 1973, p. 50). The conclusion he draws is not simply that Husserl's account of meaning is flawed. He takes it that there is a whole philosophical tradition ('the philosophy and history of the West' – Derrida, 1973, p. 51) which grounds meaning, and thus conceptual content, in privileged meaning-conferring acts in which an object or property meant is wholly 'present' to consciousness. This is exaggeration: as recent discussions of Kant's philosophy by McDowell indicate (see McDowell, 2009) Kant's critical philosophy does not exemplify the 'metaphysics of presence' which Derrida opposes, since Kant takes it that experience is inherently conceptual and provides substantive arguments concerning the significance of the a priori intuitions, concepts and principles that are at the core of his philosophy. But it is not necessary to enter into detailed debates here about the justice or not of Derrida's characterization of the history of philosophy. It is sufficient for the moment to pursue further the way in which Derrida applies his critical line of thought to Husserl's phenomenology.

Derrida's claim is that what sustains Husserl's position is an illusion about the way in which we can use inner speech to capture our thoughts and experiences. The key concept Derrida deploys here is '*voix*' ('voice') whose translation as 'speech' (as in the translation of Derrida's title *La voix et le phénomène* as *Speech and Phenomena*) does not quite capture Derrida's meaning, which is that the 'voice' of inner speech is so very close to the thinker's experience whose content it signifies that for the thinker it seems to merge with that experience itself. This inner voice is, as Derrida puts it, diaphanous – effacing itself as such so that it becomes 'the very form of the immediate presence of the signified' (Derrida, 1973, p. 77). Hence this self-consciousness strikes the thinker as a pure self-consciousness inherent in experience itself:

> When I speak it belongs to the phenomenological essence of this operation that *I hear myself at the same time* that I speak. The signifier, animated by my breath and by the meaning-intention ... is in absolute proximity to me. The living act, the life-giving act, the *Lebendigkeit*, which animates the body of the signifier and transforms it into a meaningful expression, the soul of language, seems not to separate itself from itself, from its own self-presence. (Derrida, 1973, p. 77)

As such, Derrida suggests, 'the operation of "hearing oneself speak" is an auto-affection of a unique kind' (Derrida, 1973, p. 78; 'auto-affection' is a term Derrida uses to characterize ways of affecting, or experiencing, oneself). For this voice of inner speech brings us, as it seems, into the immediate presence of our own thought and experience:

> As pure auto-affection, the operation of hearing oneself speak seems to reduce even the inward surface of one's own body; in its phenomenal being it seems capable of dispensing with this exteriority within interiority ... for the voice meets no obstacle to its emission in the world precisely because it is produced *as pure auto-affection*. This auto-affection is no doubt the possibility for what is called *subjectivity* or the *for-itself* .... (Derrida, 1973, p. 79)

So the diaphaneity of the voice of inner speech generates the illusion that the contents of thought and experience are directly available to a thinker in self-consciousness without any conceptual mediation;

and according to Derrida it is this illusion which sustains the promise of a 'pure phenomenology'; hence the connection between 'voice' ('*La voix*') and phenomena ('*le phénomène*').

This illusion is, however, broken when 'instead of hearing myself speak, I see myself write or gesture' (Derrida, 1973, p. 80). For written symbols and gestures do not carry their meaning on the very surface of their form; they are inescapably spatial, and thus external to consciousness. A self-consciousness that expresses itself with signs of these types cannot sustain the illusion that the reflecting, second-order, consciousness immediately presents the reflected, first-order, consciousness; instead it draws upon the established meaning of these signs to represent a first-order consciousness that is not itself constituted by the signs. But it is especially written symbols and gestures that make evident the fact that meaningful signs are sustained through practices in which their meaning depends upon their use, upon repetition at different times and in different contexts. The voice of inner speech seemed to offer a form of signification which is not dependent upon the future repetition of tokens which represent a type of sign. But that was an illusion, the illusion that there is a fundamental form of signification that can be fixed by 'direct intuitive presentation'. Once that illusion is discarded, speech has to be seen as no different in kind from writing.

So far the discussion has been largely critical – a rejection of Husserl's 'metaphysics of presence'. What positive story does Derrida have to put in its place? The key concept here is 'differance': this neologism is invented by Derrida to characterize as a unified phenomenon two aspects of language, one synchronic, the other diachronic, which can be separately described as types of 'différence' in French. For the French verb 'différer' means both to differ and to defer (in a temporal sense): thus 'différence' means both difference and deferral. At the start of the twentieth century, the Swiss linguist Ferdinand de Saussure had advanced a holistic conception of language as a system of differences, in which the meaning of any one sign is connected with the meanings of the other, different, signs which together characterize an area of discourse (Saussure, 1916). Saussure's position became orthodoxy in the 'structuralist' movement which was dominant in French intellectual life in the 1960s, and Derrida incorporated it into his approach as the synchronic dimension of 'differance'. What was novel in his approach is the other, diachronic, dimension of differance as 'deferral'. This is an allusion to the point already encountered, that the definitive meaning of a sign is inherently 'deferred' insofar as it depends upon the future use, the repetition, of tokens which *re*present the sign. So to think of language as essentially the activity of differance is to think it as involving signs whose meaning is connected into a network of synchronic distinctions involving different signs and dependent upon the diachronic practice of using tokens which represent these signs in different contexts. Thus the meaning of any one particular token utterance is like the proverbial tip of an iceberg: the meanings of the words used are connected into a network of distinctions identified by different word types and precariously sustained through the continuing use of tokens of the same word types on different occasions in different contexts: as Derrida puts it himself, in the phrase cited earlier, 'this representative structure is signification itself'. A point that Derrida particularly likes to emphasize in this connection is that although there is an intelligible distinction between 'literal' and 'metaphorical' uses of a term, it is a mistake to think of the metaphorical as just a derivative extrapolation, parasitic upon a fundamental literal meaning; instead, it often turns out that there are aspects of what is supposed to be the literal meaning of a term which depend on metaphorical uses of it (Derrida, 1973, p. 56).

Derrida holds that because the meaning of an utterance, including those which purport to state objective truths, is in this way dependent on distinctions and practices that are not manifest in the utterance itself, the possibility of objective truth is itself dependent on the activity of differance. Hence, he infers, any attempt to provide a fully objective characterization of this activity by means of a systematic theory is bound to be unsatisfactory, since this very attempt will itself be dependent upon the unstated activity of differance. Whether this conclusion is really inescapable is a difficult issue, and I shall defer it to my discussion below of Derrida's next major work *Of Grammatology*; but before leaving *Speech and Phenomena* there is one further theme to pursue. I begin with a typically gnomic Derriderean passage:

> This movement of differance is not something that happens to a transcendental subject; it produces a subject. Auto-affection is not a modality of experience that characterizes a being that

would already be itself (*autos*). It produces sameness as a relation to oneself within a difference from oneself. (Derrida, 1973, p. 82, translation modified)

Let us take this slowly. The phrase 'the movement of differance' is explained in his 1968 essay 'Differance' (translated in Derrida, 1973) as 'the movement by which language, or any code, any system of reference in general, becomes "historically" constituted as a fabric of differences' (Derrida, 1973, p. 141). So the 'movement of differance' turns out to be the practice whereby a language develops with the synchronic dimension of covering a 'fabric of differences' and the 'historical', diachronic, dimension of being regularly used to describe these differences. Derrida now says of this 'movement' that it is 'not something that happens to a transcendental subject; it produces a subject'. I take it that the position rejected here is that such a language is something that a 'transcendental subject', a speaker who already understands the world and herself, just happens to practice; instead, for Derrida, it is only in virtue of participating in the practice of language that a speaker acquires the concepts which enables her to become a subject, someone who understands the world and herself. This is the thesis we encountered briefly before, in the context of Derrida's introduction to *The Origin of Geometry*, when Derrida was proposing that written language be thought of as 'a subjectless transcendental field' which is 'one of the "conditions" of transcendental subjectivity'; and it has an important presupposition, also noted above, that there is no pre-linguistic consciousness which provides an understanding of the world and oneself. Otherwise, as Derrida observes:

> We might be tempted by an objection: to be sure, the subject becomes a *speaking* subject only by dealing with the system of linguistic differences ... But can we not conceive of a presence and self-presence of the subject before speech and its signs, a subject's self-presence in a silent and intuitive consciousness? ('Differance', Derrida, 1973, p. 146)

This hypothesis – 'a subject's self-presence in a silent and intuitive consciousness' – has, however, been rejected. In the passage under discussion here, this rejection is expressed as the thesis that 'Auto-affection', that is, self-experience, 'is not a modality of experience that characterizes a being that would already be itself (*autos*)'. Instead, Derrida maintains, we gain self-consciousness from an understanding of ourselves (which is a 'relation to oneself') by using concepts which belong within a language that is not exclusively our own here and now (and is therefore 'different from oneself').

3. Of Grammatology

Like *Speech and Phenomena*, *Of Grammatology* (Derrida, 1974) was published in 1967. *Of Grammatology* is, however, more difficult to interpret. I think that it is best approached in a Kantian spirit, as an inquiry which aims to vindicate the conception of language as 'movement of differance' by showing how this explains the possibility of meaningful language, and then explores some of the implications of this thesis. But it can also be interpreted as propounding a quietist message, to the effect that there cannot be a substantial philosophy of language at all. Derrida himself announces his goal in the following way:

> To make enigmatic what one thinks one understands by the words 'proximity', 'immediacy', 'presence' ... is my final intention in this book. This deconstruction of presence accomplishes itself through the deconstruction of consciousness, and therefore through the irreducible notion of the trace. (Derrida, 1974, p. 70)

I shall come back to 'deconstruction' in the following section, but we shall here have to attend to 'the irreducible notion of the trace'.

Derrida's title indicates that he is concerned to study the significance of writing. Although he adverts briefly to different types of writing, including hieroglyphs, Chinese characters and the kind of phonetic writing characteristic of European languages, he mainly uses the term 'writing' to emphasize the essential exteriority of genuine linguistic signs. Derrida now describes the position rejected in *Speech and Phenomena* which invokes an inner 'voice' of consciousness as 'phonocentrism', and maintains that phonocentrism brings with it a cluster of doctrines which exemplify the metaphysics of presence:

> We already have a foreboding that phonocentrism merges with the historical determination of the meaning of being in general

as *presence*, with all the subdeterminations which depend on their general form and which organize within it their system and their historical sequence (presence of the thing to sight as *eidos*, presence as substance/essence/existence [*ousia*], temporal presence as point [*stigmè*], of the now or of the moment [*nun*], the self-presence of the cogito, consciousness, subjectivity, the co-presence of the other and of the self, intersubjectivity as the intentional phenomenon of the ego, and so forth). Logocentrism would thus support the determination of the being of the entity as presence. (Derrida, 1974, p. 12; words in square brackets in original)

On the face of it Derrida is here putting together issues that should be separated – debates about the cogito and consciousness, on the one hand, and, for example, debates about metaphysical issues such as 'substance/essence/existence' and the structure of time, on the other; but the final sentence here suggests that there is a thesis implicit in phonocentrism which connects these issues – 'logocentrism'. 'Logocentrism' is the thesis that there is a way of conceiving a 'logos', the fundamental principles of some subject-matter, according to which such principles are intuitively available to a thinker as truths of reason without being conditioned by the requirement that they be expressed in a language that speakers use and understand. Thus in the following passage Derrida contrasts the '"rationality"' (the scare quotes are in the original) implicit in his own non-logocentric position with the connections supposedly inherent in the 'logos' which determine 'the significance of *truth*' and its 'metaphysical determinations':

The 'rationality' … which governs a writing thus enlarged and radicalized, no longer issues from a logos. Further it inaugurates the destruction, not the demolition but the de-sedimentation, the de-construction, of all the significations that have their source in that of the logos. Particularly the significance of *truth*. All the metaphysical determinations of truth … are more or less immediately inseparable from the instance of the logos, or of a reason thought within the lineage of the logos, in whatever sense it is understood … Within this logos, the original and essential link to the *phonè* has never been broken … As has been more or less implicitly determined, the essence of the *phonè* would be immediately proximate to that which within 'thought' as logos relates to 'meaning', produces it, receives it, speaks it, 'composes' it. (Derrida, 1974, p. 11)

It has to be said, however, that this is all very impressionistic rhetoric which has no obvious application to arguments in metaphysics which, so far from drawing on intuitions of pure reason, are sensitive to the importance of language and our uses of it. Is Kripke's *Naming and Necessity* (Kripke, 1980) to be charged with 'logocentrism'? One would hope not, since Kripke's arguments make central use of a sensitive discussion of language. But Kripke certainly argues for substantive and controversial conclusions concerning 'substance/essence/existence'. So, on the face of it, it is only a naive and dogmatic metaphysics that could be guilty of logocentrism.

One way to attempt to substantiate Derrida's position would be to introduce a concept mentioned earlier – 'the irreducible notion of the trace' (Derrida, 1974, p. 70). Derrida holds that '*The trace is in fact the absolute origin of sense in general … The trace is the differance* which opens appearance and signification' (Derrida, 1974, p. 65; italics in the original); but he also holds that 'The concept of arche-trace … is in fact contradictory and not acceptable within the logic of identity' (Derrida, 1974, p. 61; the conception of an '*arche*-trace' is that of a fundamental trace). Hence if 'traces' are inherently contradictory and yet fundamental to 'differance' there can be no possibility of constructing a coherent metaphysics which takes account of language as the movement of differance. The trouble with this line of thought, however, is that the concept of a trace is not explained by Derrida in a way which makes this thought persuasive. Traces are token utterances or symbols whose use within a practice 'retraces' past uses of similar tokens in such a way that they constitute meaningful signs. Wittgenstein famously suggested that language is essentially a matter of 'blind' rule-following (Wittgenstein, 1953, §219) and Derrida's talk of traces is, I suggest, the similar claim that language is fundamentally a matter of utterances which blindly retrace past uses without being guided by explicit rules. Interpreted in this way the position is comprehensible though no doubt oversimplified; what is not warranted, however, is the thesis that traces are inherently contradictory and 'not acceptable within the logic of identity'. The closest I can approach this thesis is via the type/token distinction, whereby *different* traces are (tokens of) the *same* trace (type); but there is plainly no contradiction here. So although the conception of token utterances or symbols as traces of meaningful signs is in principle suggestive, it does not sustain the thought that there could not be a coherent, non-logocentric, metaphysics which takes into account the conception of language as the movement of differance.

A different line of thought starts from the claim that because differance is 'the formation of form', there cannot be a 'science of differance' (Derrida, 1974, p. 63). For although the movement of differance generates, within a given context, the possibility of objective knowledge, as Derrida makes clear in the 'Afterword' to his essay *Limited Inc*,

> What is called 'objectivity', scientific for instance (in which I firmly believe, in a given situation), imposes itself only within a context which is extremely vast, old, powerfully established, stabilised or rooted in a network of conventions. (Derrida, 1988, p. 136)

he takes it that there is no possibility of applying this model to the study of differance itself. The issue here, however, is just what this claim amounts to. There is certainly something challenging in the thought of a systematic inquiry into 'the formation of form', that is, into the possibility of systematic inquiry. And yet Kant's *Critique of Pure Reason* is very carefully constructed to provide a systematic inquiry of this kind, relying on its own distinctive form of transcendental argument which seeks to vindicate a priori categories as conditions for the possibility of empirical knowledge. So why could there not be a similar inquiry into the possibility of language which aims to vindicate the movement of differance? Indeed is not Derrida's 'grammatology' precisely such as inquiry?

It is here that the interpretation of Derrida's position is difficult and disputed. At one point he remarks that differance involves a 'play of presence or absence ... within which metaphysics can be produced but which metaphysics cannot think' (Derrida, 1974, p. 167). If 'metaphysics' is understood here to include all systematic philosophical theory, it will exclude a philosophy of language which takes the form of a Kantian transcendental inquiry. Hence, to use the idioms of Wittgenstein's *Tractatus* (Wittgenstein, 1921,

4.1212), all that would remain for philosophy is to explain the way in which the practice of language 'shows' the movement of differance while also explaining why this movement cannot be 'said', that is, critically expounded and defended. This, then, provides the 'quietist' interpretation of Derrida favoured by Rorty (Rorty, 1978), as opposed to the Kantian approach to it I have proposed. My reason for favouring this approach, even if it conflicts with some of the things Derrida says, is the weakness of the objections to it. Why cannot a philosophy of language, 'think', or state, this 'play of presence and absence'? It cannot be because this differance is transcendent in the manner of God's exercise of His grace, and for that reason ineffable; on the contrary, the play of differance is supposed to be manifest in the living use of language by speakers. Perhaps the objection will be that such a project inevitably leads to 'logocentrism' by treating differance, the open and precarious practice of language, as if it were susceptible of a precise definition in terms of necessary and sufficient conditions whose validity could be demonstrated by abstract arguments. But it is obvious that such a project is incoherent; if the movement of differance is fundamental then there can be no possibility of providing a detached account of it that does not tacitly employ it. But the fact that, say, one cannot reflect critically on the validity of disputed logical inferences without employing logic oneself in one's reflections does not undermine the possibility of constructing significant arguments on these issues, as is shown by the long-standing debates concerning bivalence and excluded middle. Essentially the same point applies to any fundamental philosophical discussion of meaning, and the transcendental method is precisely intended to avoid accusations of circularity by 'working from within' in identifying presuppositions and connections.

It is because these objections to the possibility of a transcendental approach are so weak that it seems to me preferable not to construe Derrida's remark about the way in which 'metaphysics' necessarily excludes the play of differance as implying that all discursive philosophy must likewise fail to recognize the way in which language is constituted by the movement of differance. There is, however, one stumbling-block that needs to be acknowledged: as was apparent in the remarks about 'traces' cited earlier, Derrida holds that differance is intrinsically antithetical to the ordinary canons of logic, and thus that any attempt to provide a coherent general account of it is bound to fail. So if the term 'metaphysics' is understood to import a definite commitment to the requirements of consistency, one can see why Derrida would indeed hold that metaphysics is antithetical to differance; but it also follows that the imputation to Derrida of a Kantian approach is not straightforward either since the requirement of consistency seems intrinsic to this too. This objection, however, is not decisive. I have argued that the thesis that differance involves contradiction is unconvincing; but one does not need to insist on this point. Graham Priest's work on dialethism and paraconsistent logic shows that it is possible to provide coherent discussions of these matters without falling into absurdity (Priest, 2002, esp. chapter 14), and it seems to me that in the first part of *Of Grammatology* Derrida himself aims to provide a coherent general account of language and differance which allows for it to be contradictory. So the Kantian interpretation of Derrida's approach can circumvent the issue of the contradictoriness of differance, whatever one thinks of it.

4. Deconstruction

'Deconstruction' is the one term from Derrida's vocabulary which has passed into common discourse. Although it is a kind of critique, deconstruction always works from within:

> The movements of deconstruction do not destroy structures from the outside. They are not possible and effective, nor can they take accurate aim, except by inhabiting these structures. (Derrida, 1974, p. 24)

Thus where deconstruction is employed as a method of philosophical dialectic, it implies that philosophical argument proceeds by a critical exploration of a position which is initially 'inhabited'. So, as we have seen, Derrida's exposition of language as movement of differance is arrived at via a deconstruction of presence as expressed in writings by Husserl which Derrida himself judges to be of exemplary significance. In undertaking this, although one borrows 'all the strategic and economic resources of subversion from the old structure' (Derrida, 1974, p. 24), the aim is generally to subvert the overt thesis of the position under discussion by calling attention to 'marginal' claims, claims made in the 'margins' of the text which turn out to reveal presumptions that are fundamental to the position being advanced while also conflicting with its overt thesis. Thus when, in the latter part of *Of Grammatology*, Derrida discusses Rousseau's 'Essay on the Origin of Languages' he argues that Rousseau himself subverts his contrast between the intrinsic goodness of nature and the corruption of society by characterizing the natural state as one whose value depends on the possibility of discourse which celebrates the joys of nature, without noticing that he thereby makes the value of nature depend on the social arts (Derrida, 1974, pp. 215–16).

For Derrida, deconstruction draws on the work of differance in constituting the meaning of a text. So although deconstruction works from inside, in pursuing synchronic distinctions and diachronic practices one is inevitably led to questions about the discursive context of the text. This point provides, I think, a solution to an issue which has been for many a source of difficulty concerning Derrida's position. In *Of Grammatology* he remarks that the 'axial proposition of this essay' is that 'there is nothing outside the text' [*il n'y a pas de hors-texte*] (Derrida, 1974, p. 163), a proposition which, he later acknowledges, 'has become a sort of slogan, in general so badly understood, of deconstruction' (Derrida, 1988, p. 136). On the face of it, this remark suggests a radical form of linguistic idealism which without reducing all aspects of the world to texts as familiarly conceived, expands the notion of a text so that all aspects of the world are 'texts' in this enlarged sense; and this is certainly a very problematic position to encounter. As Derrida's comment about how the way in which he has been 'so badly understood' indicates, however, one needs to be careful here. It seems to me that the way to interpret his proposition is as a claim concerning what can be meant or referred to, to the effect that there is no reference or meaning 'outside the text', outside the play of differance, for example, by means of the bare presence of an object or meaning to consciousness. This may seem too limited in scope; but this interpretation is confirmed when he later affirms the dependence of deconstruction upon context and says that his axial proposition 'means nothing else: there is nothing outside context' (Derrida, 1988, p. 136). For the notion of context which he has here been expounding is precisely that of a discursive context which makes reference possible. This interpretation removes the troubling thought that all aspects of the world are themselves texts, while retaining the thesis that reference to any such aspect is necessarily both enabled and constrained by the practices inherent in the use of texts. If there is any idealism here, it is a transcendental idealism concerning the movement of differance as a condition for the possibility of reference and truth. But that is just what, on my Kantian interpretation of Derrida, one should expect.

Further reading

Bennington, G. and Derrida, J. (1993), *Jacques Derrida*. Chicago, IL: University of Chicago Press, 1993. (Bennington's survey of Derrida's work comes with comments from Derrida himself.)

Chapter 7 of S. Glendinning's, *In the Name of Phenomenology* (London: Routledge, 2007) gives a very helpful introduction to Derrida's work which places it in the context of the phenomenological movement.

Bibliography

Ayer, A. J. (ed.) (1959), *Logical Positivism*. London: Allen & Unwin.

Davidson, D. (2001), 'Three Varieties of Knowledge', in his *Subjective, Intersubjective, Objective*. Oxford: Clarendon Press, pp. 205–20.

Derrida, J. (1973), *Speech and Phenomena, and Other Essays on Husserl's Theory of Signs*, trans. D. Allinson. Evanston, IL: Northwestern University Press.

Derrida, J. (1974), *Of Grammatology*, trans. G. Spivak. Baltimore, MD: Johns Hopkins University Press.

Derrida, J. (1988), *Limited Inc*, trans. S. Weber. Evanston, IL: Northwestern University Press.

Derrida, J. (1989), *Edmund Husserl's Origin of Geometry: An Introduction*, trans. J. P. Leavey. Lincoln, NE: University of Nebraska Press.

Grice, H. P. (1989), *Studies in the Way of Words*. Cambridge, MA: Harvard University Press.

Heidegger, M. (1998), *Pathmarks*, trans. W. McNeill. Cambridge: Cambridge University Press.

Husserl, E. (1970), *Logical Investigations*, 2 vols, trans. J. N. Findlay. London: Routledge.

Husserl, E. (1989), 'The Origin of Geometry', trans. D. Carr, in Derrida, 1989, pp. 155–80.

Kripke, S. (1980), *Naming and Necessity*. Oxford: Blackwell.

McDowell, J. (2009), *Having the World in View*. Cambridge, MA: Harvard University Press.

Priest, G. (2002), *Beyond the Limits of Thought*, 2nd edn. Oxford: Oxford University Press.

Rorty, R. (1978), 'Philosophy as a Kind of Writing: An Essay on Derrida', *New Literary History*, 10, pp. 141–60.

Saussure, F. de (1916), *Cours de linguistique generale*, ed. C. Bally and A. Scheehaye. Lausanne and Paris: Payot.

Sellars, W. (1963), *Science, Perception and Reality*. London: Routledge.

Wittgenstein, L. (1921), *Tractatus Logico-Philosophicus*, trans. C. K. Ogden. London: Routledge.

Wittgenstein, L. (1953), *Philosophical Investigations*, trans. G. E. M. Anscombe. Oxford: Blackwell.

Wittgenstein, L. (1993), *Philosophical Occasions*, ed. J. Klagge and A. Nordmann. Indianapolis, IN: Hackett.

CHAPTER FIFTEEN

FEMINIST PHILOSOPHY OF LANGUAGE
Maura Tumulty

1. Introduction: What is *feminist* about feminist philosophy of language?

You may have already thought about what particular topics within the philosophy of language you would most like to pursue – especially if you have already read several of the other chapters in this book. But you may also have thought about particular approaches to the philosophy of language. You might have found yourself drawn to Wittgensteinian or Austinian approaches, because of their emphasis on the social context of language use; or you might have felt the pull of Carnapian or Quinean approaches, because you appreciated the links each of those philosophers makes between the philosophical and the scientific study of language. Even so, the use of 'feminist' as an adjective modifying 'philosophy of language' may seem odd. What could a *feminist* – as opposed to a Wittgensteinian or Stebbingsian – approach to the philosophy of language be?

Puzzlement here might take two forms. We might be wondering quite generally, about any topic, what would make philosophy of *it* feminist. But we might also be wondering about the philosophy of language in particular, and having a harder time imagining how a feminist lens would be relevant to it. Gender (and so feminism) might seem obviously relevant to political philosophy, or ethics, or maybe – because of the role of testimony in most legal systems – to epistemology. But linking it to metaphysics or the philosophy of language might seem like a stretch.[1]

Taking up an expansive definition of 'feminist' will help with both forms of puzzlement. Consider, for example, the definition offered by the novelist and social critic Chimamanda Ngozi Adichie, who writes that a feminist is 'a man or a woman who says, yes, there's a problem with gender as it is today and we must fix it, we must do better' (Adichie, 2012, p. 48). The 'problem with gender' affects and even harms men as well as women. Nevertheless, Adichie argues, the name for any effort at 'doing better' in this domain should be *feminism* rather than, say, *humanism* or *human egalitarianism*. Using those labels would be 'a way of pretending that it was not women who have, for centuries, been excluded. It would be a way of denying that the problem of gender targets women' (p. 41). So we might say this: for any *x*, to do feminist philosophy of *x* is to proceed with a keen awareness that gender – as a not entirely happy phenomenon – has been relevant either to *x* or to traditional approaches to its study. We might see immediately that, for example, feminist philosophy of law and feminist political philosophy are plausible and important undertakings. We would also see that even when we approach these fields with an awareness of gender's unhappy role, we may disagree about which philosophical questions are most significant, as well as about which particular theories we think best solve them.

It might seem harder to see how an awareness of gender would enable progress in the philosophy of language. And it might seem harder to suppose that even if it did, a considerable diversity of opinion could exist about what best served that progress. And yet both claims are true – or so this chapter will argue. Just as feminist political philosophers disagree about the proper understanding of autonomy (see Stoljar, 2015), or feminist legal philosophers disagree about the proper way to understand difference and inequality (see Minow, 1990), feminist philosophers of language engage in vigorous and productive disagreement with one another.[2] Thus, for example, one can find theorists who put a good deal of emphasis on speakers' intentions in their accounts of communication (e.g. Jennifer Hornsby) and theorists who want to de-emphasize this (e.g. Rebecca Kukla).[3] One can find theorists who think modelling the understanding of a language on an individual's tacit knowledge of a theory of meaning is unlikely to be helpful, and those who find much to value in such an approach (see Antony, 2012). And of course one finds diversity, if not disagreement, in feminist philosophers' choice of topics. Some thinkers are especially interested in the reference of kind-terms like 'woman' (e.g. Sally Haslanger and Katherine Jenkins); some, following Austin or Grice or both, are especially interested in speech-act theory (e.g. Jennifer Hornsby, Rae Langton and Ishani Maitra); and some work at the border between epistemology and the philosophy of language to pursue questions about testimony (e.g. Kristie Dotson, Elizabeth Fricker and José Medina).

All the philosophers taking up these questions accept that with respect to gender, women have been (and in some ways still are) disadvantaged with respect to men. Their work shows, too, that they find this fact philosophically significant. Arguably, they agree on two additional commitments. First, they appear to agree that work in the philosophy of language is sometimes needed if we are to understand – let alone try to undo – some of the ways in which women's subordination is perpetuated. Consider this example. Think of the distinction between what a speaker might say ('Hazel is so patient and cheerful') and what she might imply (that Hazel is not worth hiring for this high-pressure job, if that is the best thing that can be said of her). Consider also the distinction between (1) a question ('Should we hire Hazel?') and its answer ('The boss *really* likes her') and (2) what both parties must presuppose to be true in order for *that* answer to count as a conversationally appropriate response to *that* question.[4] Figuring out how implication and presupposition work in such cases helps show how sexist stereotypes are kept in circulation. They circulate as part of the common conversational background not only when they are explicitly invoked but also whenever their relevance is implied and no one protests. And that, then, could help explain why prejudice is so easy to spread and so hard to defeat.[5]

Secondly, feminist philosophers of language take it that many general questions in the philosophy of language – such as the distinction between semantic meaning and speaker meaning (see the chapter on Grice in this volume), or between illocutionary and perlocutionary acts (see the chapter on Austin) – are thrown into sharper relief, or seen as requiring more nuanced responses, when we investigate them with reference to contexts in which gender (and/or sexism) is salient. Analytic philosophers of language, like analytic philosophers generally, use a stock of tricky cases to test their theories. Consider, for example, exonyms: the names for geographic features and languages that are not in common use among the people who now live near that feature or use that language. Kripke uses an exonym in his famous thought-experiment about the Francophone Pierre. Suppose Pierre doesn't know that 'London' and 'Londres' refer to the same city. Suppose he picks up a French-language book about London architecture and, after viewing several of the city's most striking buildings, forms the belief that he would express as 'Londres est belle', but visiting the city to work in a grim neighbourhood comes to think the place the locals call London is far from beautiful. In English, may we report Pierre's belief in the beauty of the city that houses Big Ben by saying 'Pierre believes London is beautiful', or must we say 'Pierre believes Londres is beautiful'?[6] As Kripke (and the many philosophers who were inspired by the puzzle of Pierre) realized, thinking about exonyms reveals important features of names, and complexities about the beliefs expressed (and reported) by means of those names.[7] It might be rare for a speaker's unexpected use of an exonym to produce serious confusion. Nevertheless, examining the contours of that confusion is valuable. We learn lessons not just about exonymns, but about referential communication and indirect discourse more generally.

Suppose we puzzle over why a female floor manager isn't heard as *ordering* but only *requesting* her employees to come back promptly from their break (Kukla, 2014); or why a woman's loudly saying 'No' isn't heard by a man as a refusal of his sexual advances; or why 'Humans nurse their young' doesn't sound as awkward as 'Humans have ovaries'. Feminist philosophers of language take it that we will thereby learn about more than the trials women face in factories and bars, and the difficulties of writing concise biology textbooks. We are likely to learn quite general facts about language and language users, and discover productive sites for philosophical reflection.

2. Methodology: When do we make more progress by focusing on failure?

That we can learn general lessons from these cases is perhaps explained by the utility of looking at failure and not just success. Theorists working in ethics, political philosophy and epistemology often distinguish two ways of navigating their respective fields along these lines. On the one hand, we might focus on, and try to construct a clear account of, a form of success: we try to describe, in detail, a virtuous person, a just society or an instance of knowledge. And we expect that failure – vice, injustice, false or absent belief – can be understood simply as the absence of success.

Now, of course, when we are trying to do something well – whether raising a child, organizing a labour union or speaking a language – we likely need to have in mind some sense of what that activity would look like in the best possible conditions. Otherwise, we might not set our goals high enough.

However, focusing only on our model of success may make it hard for us to see problems in our current situation. That's why some theorists prefer a second approach. These theorists emphasize what has been called 'non-ideal theory' (Mills, 2005, p. 168 – following Onora O'Neill). They argue that at least as 'ideal theory' (the 'envision success first' approach) has typically been practiced, it is likely to be insufficient. When we take that approach, we may assume, for example, that altruism, kindness and an interest in fairness (beyond the desire to 'get mine') are more widespread than they in fact are. We may not worry enough about what an individual should do to pursue success (in truth-telling, politics or child-rearing) when many of those around her aren't bothering to do such things well at all. Crucially, when we do discuss obstacles to success from within 'ideal theory', we are more likely to focus on individual deficiencies, or on factors – like the unpredictability of the weather – for which no one is to blame.[8] Mills (2007) brings these concerns to epistemology. He notes how often analytic philosophers have worried about barriers to knowledge that are faced by individuals on their own – such as being subject to an optical illusion or being afflicted with hallucinations. He also notes how comparatively little time they've spent reflecting on ways in which racism could interact with racial identity so as to all but ensure that certain people lack information about, or cling to false beliefs about, whole swathes of their nation's history. As noted above, the mere fact that something is statistically rare doesn't mean its philosophical investigation won't yield significant results. But looking broadly at human history, racism and other forms of group-based oppression are not rare at all; so it is surprising how little philosophical attention was paid to querying their possible epistemic effects.

When we turn to philosophy of language, we can pose similar questions. Have theorists focused too much on constructing models of successful communication and expression, and assumed that failure can then be theorized as the simple absence of success? Have theorists failed to pay adequate attention to social dynamics that could affect who succeeds and who faces difficulties in communication? Philosophy of language is often carried out at a high level of abstraction – stripping out much of the detail surrounding particular episodes of language use. Some abstraction is required if we are going to make progress at uncovering general patterns, but we should ask what it is that we regularly abstract from, and why. If we look critically at the philosophy of language up until the fairly recent past, we see how little attention was paid to certain kinds of communicative failure that are, in fact, incredibly common – especially when would-be communicators come from different social groups. Abstracting away from the gender, race, class and age of speakers sometimes makes sense.[9] It can even be productive, in approaching some topics, to abstract away from factors that affect the power relations between speakers in a conversation, and the identity-based background assumptions they carry. *But* for other topics, abstracting away from these features, or assuming without investigation that attention to one sub-set of them can substitute for attention to all, can lead us seriously astray. Feminist philosophers of language have helped call us back. When we are thinking about meaning and communicative force, for example, we can't ignore more literal forms of force, or we will miss part of what we were hoping to understand.

3. Topics: What kinds of questions have been taken up in this field?

As we've already seen, theorists working in feminist philosophy of language take up a number of questions, and pursue a variety of strategies for grappling with them. This brief section can give only a small sample of the breadth here.

Feminist philosophers of language have examined uses of 'man' or 'he' in contexts that ostensibly include women as well as men, but which reveal their gendered nature as the conversation progresses. (See, for example, the increasingly awkward phrases here: 'Man is a featherless biped ... he nurses his young ... using his mammary glands.') The complexities of such uses are connected to the question of when, and why, a generic attributing a sex-linked trait to whole kind ('Humans birth live young') is accepted as true, and when it is rejected as false ('Humans have ovaries'). These and other questions about generics (explored below) are interesting, and we could explore them without expecting to uncover anything pernicious. In that regard, they contrast with sentences like

> In the night, the villagers all left in canoes, leaving us behind with the women and children.[10]

The use of a term like 'villager' – whose literal meaning is not gender-restricted – in a gender-exclusive way raises a number of concerns. It expresses a conflation of 'a general category with some prominent subgroup of individuals belonging to the category', and repeated such uses 'help obscure [the] exclusion of certain kinds of people in various domains' (McConnell-Ginet, 2008, p. 503). If 'villager' or 'medical student' and so on are used in this way, we aren't marking the fact that women aren't thought of as important villagers, or that the medical school is shunting female applicants aside. That may make us less ready to complain about those facts. We may also become increasingly comfortable with the idea that the male subgroup is always the one that counts. That might be especially likely when the telling shift from a literally gender-neutral term to an obviously gender-exclusive term is delayed. Speakers and writers don't always betray their non-counting of women within the time-span of a single sentence. By the time they do, we might already have been lulled into complacent acceptance.

Feminist philosophers of language have also examined ways in which the male gender functions as the supposedly neutral standard against which female versions of pretty much anything are assessed, and verbally marked (e.g. 'novelist' vs 'woman novelist'; 'CEO' vs 'female CEO'). They've looked at the semantics and pragmatics of misogynist slurs (like the b-word and the c-word). They've proposed explanations for why 'You do that like a girl' can be pejorative when directed at either a girl or a boy, even though it is hard to come up with contexts in which 'You do that like a boy' could be pejoratively addressed to a child of either sex.[11] They've considered what happens when speakers lack easily available verbal tags for concepts or experiences that need to be discussed – especially when those speakers want to protest their own unjust treatment (see e.g. Fricker, 2007;Medina, 2013). They have thought about how to understand the reference of 'woman' and 'female' in connection with advocacy for the just treatment of transgender persons and of persons with intersex conditions; and about whether 'woman' includes the concept of oppression (so that in a world without gender oppression, there would be females but no women).[12] They've investigated how language, or specific uses of it by authoritative speakers (such as judges or university policy-makers), could constitute and not just cause oppression (see e.g. Langton, 1993; McGowan, 2009; Langton, Haslanger and Anderson, 2012). Crossing philosophical subfields into epistemology, they have also thought about what, beyond mere assertion, is involved in testimony (see, e.g. Dotson, 2011), and about the relation between prejudice and misinterpretation (see, e.g. Peet, 2017).

The interest in the reference and meaning of words like 'woman', and in the problem posed by a lack of a term to clearly label an experience one resents, is connected to long-standing philosophical questions about the relations between language, thought and the world about which we speak and think. Philosophers have tracked many versions of such word–world questions. Sometimes the primary aim is to understand language better (as with Wittgenstein's challenges to the assumption that ostensive naming could be, by itself, a foundational linguistic act). Sometimes instead a primary aim is to better understand the world. Recall, for example, Austin's methodological suggestion that philosophers get out of their armchairs and pay attention to common talk:

> our common stock of words embodies all the distinctions men have found worth drawing, and the connexions they have found worth making, in the lifetimes of many generations.[13]

Suppose we grant Austin a generous reading of his generic 'man'. We still aren't likely to want to accept what folks have taken gender to be, and so aren't likely to want to accept what they've assumed 'gender' must mean.[14] That is, there are distinctions around gender that we may not have been drawing well. Furthermore, it is likely that some distinctions actually worth drawing have not been taken to be worth the trouble – at least not by those with the most capacity to shape the common stock of words and the practices by which we interpret one another's uses of them. So we should look carefully at who has the easiest time speaking about his or her own concerns, and who commands the most attention when so speaking. Doing that careful looking is a key aim of feminist philosophy of language. In the remainder of this chapter, we will take up two topics that have received a good deal of careful attention: the silencing of women's speech, and the distinct role of generics in our conversation and, perhaps, our thought.

4. Silencing

There are obvious and literal ways in which a woman could be silenced: someone could hold a hand over her mouth and prevent her from uttering words; someone could command her at gunpoint to remain silent; or the state could pass and brutally enforce a law that prevented any woman from speaking – at least on certain topics, or in certain places.[15]

But there are less obvious ways to silence someone. Consider the fact that our aim in speaking is rarely, if ever, simply to produce noise. Nor is it simply to produce noises that others will recognize as words in some language or other. While theorists disagree about how best to characterize our various aims in speaking, it is widely agreed that speakers usually aim at being understood. Speakers aim to get themselves, or their attitudes, or some fact understood by their audience. (We sometimes have other aims, such as merely giving vent to anger or pain. But presumably our practice of using meaningful words – and not just moans or grunts – to fulfil that aim depends on our using words for more obviously communicative reasons most of the time.) So if silencing is what we do to *speakers*, not just noise-makers, then someone could silence you by forcibly re-locating you to a region inhabited by people with whom you share no common language. At least at first, there is nothing you could say that could be understood by them – and so you would likely (at least at first) see little point in speaking. You could still utter sentences like, 'I was kidnapped and brought here against my will' or 'I am a political prisoner'. You would likely be recognized by the locals as trying to verbally communicate with them. But (at least until some effort at mutual language-learning began) you wouldn't be much better off than someone wearing a gag she couldn't remove.

Now, consider the point – prominently and creatively defended by Austin – that the same words uttered in different contexts can be sayings of different kinds. Consider, for example, how the sentence 'I'll be back' could be uttered either as a reassurance or as a threat. To put things in Austinian terms, we can distinguish between *locutions* – the words and sentences uttered – and *illocutions* – the things done in locuting, or the communicative force of our utterances.[16] The locution 'I'll be back' could be used to *assert* a fact to a co-worker as I leave the office briefly; to *promise* a child worried he'll be left alone too long; or to *threaten* someone whose behaviour I hope to control even in my absence. Suppose it were possible to prevent someone from doing with an utterance what she wanted, and what she could do, absent that intervention. Suppose, for example, you could make it impossible for her to threaten or to promise. If so, that would be a form of silencing her. Like the gagging or the forced relocation, it illegitimately prevents her from exercising her agency in language.[17]

Austin introduced the terms *happy* and *felicitous* to describe successful illocutions. When a student complies with my request to please open a window in our stuffy classroom, or a server withdraws the grinder after I say 'No, thank you' to refuse the offer of fresh-ground pepper on my salad, we have what look like happy illocutions: felicitous requests and refusals. Austin used the terms *unhappy* and *infelicitous* to track situations in which a speaker utters a sentence, apparently with the intention of performing some particular illocutionary act, but the act is not fully successful. In examining the absence of success, he distinguished between *misfires* and *abuses*. In a misfire, the illocution at which the speaker aims doesn't quite come off, and sometimes the speaker herself has no idea that she has not achieved her illocutionary aim. Such a misfire could result when a speaker lacks the authority to do what she is trying to do with her words, but doesn't realize her deficiency. For example, suppose I say, 'You're fired!' to an employee over whom I have had full hire-and-fire authority. But I don't know that just five minutes ago, *my* supervisor fired me (by signing some papers I am about to have delivered to me) – and so, though I don't realize this, my utterance cannot be a firing. Or, to take another case, suppose that what I am trying to do with my words has already been done and that it isn't like complimenting – it isn't the sort of thing that can be done repeatedly. Thus I could not, by uttering some sentence that begins, 'I hereby inform you that ...', put someone on notice that there is a legal action against her if my law partner already did so; nor could I fire the secretary for our law firm if my partner already did so. As we see from these cases, speakers whose illocutions are unhappy or infelicitous due to misfires need not have misbehaved. They may have been quite responsible morally and epistemically; they need not even have breached any rules of common etiquette. Arguably, most misfires are non-culpable communicative failures.

Abuses are different. In an abuse, an agent knows what would be required for a particular illocution to be a happy one. And she is aware that at least one of the relevant conditions is not met, but proceeds with the illocution anyway. Perhaps she hopes that others will not realize the deficiencies of the context they are in. Consider, for example, a wedding ceremony, at which the officiant is endowed by the state with the power to effect a legally binding marriage. Suppose someone is deliberately insincere when answering 'I will' to the question 'Will you take so-and-so to be your lawful wedded spouse?' For 'I will' to be a felicitous illocution (a promising, or a contracting of marriage), the speaker must intend to be entering into marriage. It is therefore an abuse to speak those words, in that context, while knowing that key intention to be absent. Another type of abuse turns on a speaker's awareness that an institutional requirement for felicity has not been satisfied. For example, suppose an employee of a public university says, 'I give you a clean bill of health; you are now permitted to practice and compete with the diving team', while knowing full well that her medical license has expired. She knows that she lacks the legal qualification to certify athletes eligible to practice and compete. Her uttering such sentences in these conditions is an illocutionary abuse; unhappiness results.

When we consider the whole of our communicative lives, including not only formal institutional settings like weddings but also kitchen-table banter, we see that many illocutions have characteristic aims which may not be fully secured even in a happy case (Green, 2017). Thus, when I *testify* to a university safety officer that a student or colleague has threatened me, I intend for the officer to understand that I am so testifying.[18] But I also hope that the officer is *persuaded* by my testimony. I hope his attitudes shift: that he comes to believe my account of the facts, or at least comes to believe further investigation is appropriate.[19] I can do some things to make it more likely that I bring off what Austin called the *perlocutionary* effect of my testifying – persuading – but I cannot myself ensure that I do. Likewise, I can frame an invitation more or less attractively; but I cannot ensure that you will satisfy my perlocutionary aim and accept my invitation. I can affectionately tease you, yet fail to amuse you, and so on.

In certain contexts, women seem to have limited success in achieving such perlocutionary aims. They may say 'No' with the intention of refusing a man's aggressive sexual advances, but that illocution doesn't persuade him to stop. They may say, 'That night manager is harassing those of us who work on the north side of the building because it is out of sight of any other manager.' And they may say this with the intention of testifying to a pattern of abuse, but that illocution doesn't persuade the vice president to take any action. Of course, while we can influence our audiences, none of us can fully control others' responses to our communications (see Kukla, 2014). But it is worth separating two ways in which a speaker might fail to get the response she hoped (see Maitra, 2009). She might be heard as refusing, or as testifying (her audience might appreciate her illocutionary act as the distinctive kind it is) but the audience might not see her performance of that act as a reason for them to behave as she hoped – to stop roughly pushing for sex, or to start investigating the behaviour of that night manager. In this case, we might say, the speaker didn't suffer any *illocutionary* disadvantage. Her audience just chose not to respond in her preferred way to her successful speech. On the other hand, it might be that the audience's continuing to roughly push for sex, or refusing to open an investigation, is due in part to their failure to *hear* the speaker as refusing and testifying, respectively. Suppose a man believes women often say 'No' in order to consent to sex while preserving an apparent demure reluctance. In some contexts, then, he may not hear the locution 'No' as a refusing illocution. He may not understand that the woman was speaking with the perlocutionary aim of persuading him to stop.

The possibility that something – pornography, or sexist myths about women and sexual desire, or some other cultural baggage – has shaped some men's background beliefs so that they don't hear particular locutions of 'No' as refusals of their demands for sex was first raised in the analytic philosophy of language literature by Langton and Hornsby. Especially in their early work, they were interested in the possibility that pornography played a causal role in preventing women from being able to refuse sex by uttering 'No'. In some cases – such as legal debates over the United States' First Amendment protections of freedom of speech – establishing this thesis would have strategic implications. That's because it would show that one set of speakers – producers of violent pornography – were hampering the *speech* rights of another set – women at risk of sexual assault. It would then be possible to argue that restrictions on the production or distribution of certain kinds of pornography were not restrictions on speech as such, but rather efforts to balance free speech rights for all persons. If this causal thesis turns out to lack empirical support, the broader point might still be true: something about a particular culture could make it especially difficult for women to be understood as refusing demands for sex.

Of course, even those theorists who suggest illocutionary disablement can happen are careful about what lessons to draw. They may hold that a woman who is not heard as refusing has failed to perform the illocutionary act of refusal with her utterance of 'No', but they do not think that any sexual contact that follows such utterances of 'No' counts as consensual. Nor do they think that the man in question had good evidence for thinking that it did. (It can't be the case that the wrong of sexual assault becomes conceptually impossible once misogynistic beliefs are sufficiently widespread.[20]) The point, rather, is this: it seems the woman in this scenario cannot do with the locution 'No' what a man could do, or what a woman being pressed for sex by a woman could do, or what a woman being pressed by anyone for something other than sex could do: speak with the illocutionary force of refusal and be heard as doing so. In at least a relative sense, then, this woman's linguistic agency has been diminished.

This helps us see that there is a kind of communicative unhappiness that is captured neither by the notion of misfire nor the notion of abuse, as least not as each is usually understood. The woman who attempts to use the word 'No' to refuse has not abused any convention relevant to the illocution of refusal; if there is abuse here, it is not speaker-side. If we turn to the category of misfire, however, we find mechanisms for disrupting illocution that don't make much room for assessments of culpability. If they appear to make such room, it is likely because they are connected to speaker-side abuse – as when a speaker knowingly exploits an institutional hiccup to perform an illocution she has no right to perform. But thinking through cases like those of the woman who tries to refuse sexual advances in saying 'No', the women who try to testify to a pattern of workplace harassment, or the women who try to raise an objection to a paper at an academic conference but are heard only as expressing confusion or requesting clarification shows us additional ways things can go awry. When someone is unable to speak and be understood as she intends, it turns out this can be due to no epistemic or moral deficiency on her part. She is disadvantaged, perhaps severely, and not through her own fault.[21]

Examinations of such disadvantage and the mechanisms that produce it have been philosophically productive. As one would expect, there are ongoing disagreements about exactly how to analyse such disadvantage. When a woman fails to achieve her perlocutionary aim and persuade the man pushing her for sex to respect her refusal, should we say she has been illocutionarily silenced? Or was she instead able to perform the illocutionary act of refusal – though her intended audience was unable to appreciate her speech act for what it was? This and related questions become even more complicated as theorists branch out to consider cases beyond the case of sexual refusal. For example, there is continuing debate about the exact ways in which speakers are vulnerable to their audiences. Certainly, one rarely achieves all one's aims in speaking without some cooperation from one's audience. So most theorists agree that *fully* successful illocution requires an audience to appreciate the type of illocution performed by the speaker.[22] But we often think we can characterize an action – properly take it to be a token of a particular type – even if it fails to be a fully successful action, or fails to help the agent reach the goal with reference to which she performed it. (Suppose you detest the socks I buy you for your birthday. Presumably, I failed in my aim to please you – but I still gave you a present.) I might want to warn you that the bus is coming, but you, my intended audience, are absorbed in the podcast you are hearing through earbuds I don't see, and so you don't hear me. My utterance of 'Yikes! Here comes the bus!' might still count as an illocutionary act of warning nevertheless (a passer-by would hear it as such, after all). Things are trickier if no potential audience would take my utterance as warning. In such a case, would I have performed the illocutionary act I intended? Some theorists do argue that speakers can refuse, or assert and so on, even if no one understands them as doing so – even if no one in the local context *would* understand them as doing so. What matters is that speakers fulfil their portion of conditions for success (see, e.g. Bird, 2002). But other theorists argue that we cannot neatly carve out separate 'speaker-side' and 'audience-side' contributions to successful communication (for different reasons, each of Anderson, 2018; Hornsby, 2000; and Kukla, 2014 makes this case). On these views, any answer to the question 'What did S try to do?' may involve facts about what happened after S spoke.

Further complicating matters is that agents use aims in forming intentions. We think there is a difference between my intending to bake bread and my intending to bake crackers. We allow that I could have either intention even if something (like a sudden power outage) prevented me from succeeding in my aim of producing bread (or crackers) to eat. But if I know that my oven cannot get hot enough to bake crackers, it is hard to see how to credit me with the intention to bake *them* – as opposed to an intention to bake something else (like flatbread). What could make it crackers I intend to bake if I know crackers – crisp and brittle – can't be what will come out of the oven? Compare the case of refusal. I surely can intend, now, to refuse – even if (as it turns out) my refusal will fail to persuade. I also can intend, now, to refuse – even if, as it turns out, my refusal won't be heard as a refusal. (Whether I in fact *did* refuse in that case is debated.) But suppose I know my refusal will not persuade, perhaps because I know, to my horror, that my audience has no interest in respecting any of my wishes. Can I still intend to refuse? If I know my (illocutionary) act will fail to achieve its characteristic (perlocutionary) aim, can I still sufficiently individuate the act and intend to perform it (rather than some other)? Perhaps I can. Perhaps I can intend that my audience hears that I refuse, even if I know they will disregard my refusal. But what if I know my act will fail to achieve its characteristic aim – persuasion – *because* it will fail to be seen as the act I intend (refusal)? Can I intend *then* to refuse?[23] Perhaps not. In refusing sexual contact, one is aiming to persuade a particular person. One's audience is particular, rather than the general, anyone-within-earshot audience for a warning like 'Fire!' That an eavesdropper hearing my 'No' would understand I was aiming to refuse may not – even if I know this – be enough to make up for the fact that my intended audience would not.

Investigations of these cases have spurred renewed interest in Austin and Grice, and in general questions about the roles played in communication by speakers' intentions and audiences' background assumptions. Debate continues over whether true illocutionary silencing is possible, or whether instead a speaker with the right intentions can always succeed at meaning as she wishes – even if she is not understood or believed. But even without a final resolution of this and related questions, we can see something crucial: communicative success runs in grooves that track other kinds of advantage and disadvantage.[24] We see that there are communicative disruptions that are neither non-culpable misfires nor speaker-side abuses. And we can then go on to ask: Who is most likely to suffer from those? Who worries most about such disruptions, and so sometimes decides not to speak at all (Dotson, 2011)? Remembering that such *self*-silencing is possible helps answer a question about what rides on these debates. When we focus narrowly on the case of attempted refusals of sexual contact, it is true that the harms are, sadly, more or less the same whether they are due to silencing (because women are unable to perform the illocution of refusal), to audience incapacity (because particular men are unable to hear particular women as refusing) or to failure of perlocutionary aim (because women refuse, but the relevant men are not persuaded to stop). And in any of those cases, there is culpability, but never with the woman in question. So why worry over whether a woman can perform the illocutionary act of refusal in such a case? Because thinking through the conditions required for her to do so helps illuminate the conditions for certain kinds of communicative success; and because it helps us see how certain kinds of disadvantage can affect what people are heard as saying, what people are willing to say and what people can say. And we can then investigate cases where this might indeed make a difference to the harms they suffer.

Thinking these questions through, of course, requires that we not abstract from the race, gender, class, age and health characteristics of speakers. Keeping those particulars in mind also helps illuminate another facet of communicative success. Consider a situation in which speaker S could do act A with locution L, and yet speaker M cannot. Knowing this is not sufficient for concluding that M has anything of which to complain. Even adding that the social identities of S and M are relevant to this difference in capacity is not sufficient. Suppose, for example, that S can affectionately address a fellow member of S's racial group with a re-appropriated slur against that group, while M – who is not a member of that group – cannot use that word to address that person (Anderson, 2018). Or, suppose, M cannot flirtatiously invite S with locution L, but only creepily proposition S with locution L. And suppose this is because S is younger than M, S is female and M is male, and they are co-workers (Kukla, 2014). In neither case is it obvious that M has been wronged, even though there is an illocution M cannot – not merely should not, but actually cannot – perform. Thinking through these kinds of cases helps us probe more thoroughly what, beyond speaker intention, is required for successful communication. Considering the potential failures of some women's illocutions helped reveal that there are socially variant obstacles to communicative success. Intrusive background noise, or auditory hallucinations or a speaker's dishonest exploitation of linguistic convention can all derail communicative success, but so also can sexism and its complicated social, cultural and psychological effects.

5. Generics

The case of illocutionary silencing continues to draw interest, in part, because of questions it raises about how audiences' background beliefs shape what they hear and understand, and how speakers and audiences together establish and maintain the common assumptions on which smooth communication depends. Consider, for example, how an audience's failure to protest a speaker's introduction of the descriptor 'slut' into a conversation will shape what is now permissible in the rest of that conversation – and what prejudices and stereotypes may be strengthened as a result (McGowan, 2009). Generics – generalizations such as 'Humans are mortal' or 'Cats are cunning' – likewise draw interest because their use may correlate with, and even cause, certain forms of prejudicial thinking. But even if that empirical hypothesis turned out to be false, generics would still present puzzles.[25] Reflecting especially on those generics we use to express generalizations about social kinds (like *woman* or *Muslim*) forces us to think very carefully about truth-conditions for generics across the board. Identifying the truth-conditions for generics that *are* true (assuming some are) is not easy. Nor is it easy to answer questions about how speakers signal and audiences grasp the relevant interpretation of utterances deploying generics.

Members of a key class of generics attribute properties to members of kinds. Crucially, such generics are often accepted as true even when many – or most – members of the kind lack the predicated property. So the truth-conditions of such generics must involve more than the statistical frequency with which a property is found among members of the kind. Consider, for example, 'Ducks lay eggs' (discussed in Leslie, 2008, 2017). That generalization is accepted as true even though no male duck can lay eggs, and only the sexually mature females are likely to be doing so in any given time frame. The difficulty is this: what account of why 'Ducks lay eggs' is true will be compatible with our treating 'Ducks have ovaries' as false? After all, since female ducks have ovaries at birth, *more ducks* (at any given time) have the property 'having ovaries' than have the property 'lay eggs'.

Consider also generics that are counted as true even though *very* few of the members of the relevant kind have the property predicated in the generic expression, such as 'Mosquitoes carry the West Nile virus' and 'Sharks attack bathers'.[26] There is widespread agreement that generic-containing expressions don't function like sentences containing standard quantifiers such as 'all' and 'some', nor even like sentences containing quantificational adverbs such as 'usually'.[27] What is disputed is what positive account of their truth-conditions to give.

One approach – and we are skating very lightly here over a good deal of complexity – is to emphasize the perspective of the relevant linguistic community and its explanatory interests. Sarah-Jane Leslie has argued for this approach on both conceptual and empirical grounds. She argues that generics express a cognitively primitive form of generalization, mastered early on in our development. This primitive capacity tracks what we find interesting, and meshes with some of the background assumptions to which we appeal as we build our basic theories about the world. Thus, for example, we accept 'Ducks lay eggs' because we see reproduction as characteristic of animal kinds; we expect ducks to have some method of reproduction, and note their egg-laying rather than the live-young-birthing method. No duck has a method of reproduction other than egg-laying. So we accept 'Ducks lay eggs' even though male ducks *don't* lay eggs. What about 'Ducks have ovaries', though? Male ducks don't – no more than they lay eggs. But those same male ducks have reproduction-relevant organs that are not ovaries. They have their own way of filling in the property of having reproduction-relevant organs. So 'Ducks have ovaries' is rejected, because having testicles is a positive, and equally relevant (to reproductive anatomy), property in the context.

Acceptance patterns for generics may also be sensitive to other features of the properties being generalized about. Leslie suggests we are more likely to accept as true those generic claims that predicate a property that is striking and/or dangerous. And properties are striking and/or dangerous with respect, of course, to us: with respect to our perceptual systems, and our survival needs. Thus, 'sharks attack bathers' is accepted as true because 'attacking bathers' is the kind of property it is important for us to know about and avoid. When we are generalizing about properties less relevant to our needs, we perhaps require a more frequent instantiation of the property among members of the kind before we treat a generic concerning it as true.

Given the way our social world is shaped, we might expect that versions of these accounts would apply to generics about human kinds. It may be that the explanation for our acceptance of 'Sharks attack bathers' and 'Mosquitoes carry the West Nile virus' will work to explain why some people are willing to accept 'Muslims are violent' despite the very low statistical frequency of the predicated property among members of that kind. Perhaps, that is, we find it easy to use the primitive generalizations expressed with generics whenever we find striking or dangerous properties – which is to say no more than: we find it easy to use them whenever we are struck, or fearful. (And we aren't always fearful for good reasons.) We could override that default tendency, and issue a more exact quantified statement ('Some sharks attack bathers'). But perhaps only in the case of generalizations about human social groups, especially human social groups subject to prejudice, is there anything approaching an obligation to do so.

Not all accounts of generic generalizations foreground human interests. One option (proposed in Nickel, 2016) focuses instead on whether a relevant causal mechanism can explain why members of a kind have the feature predicated in the generic. Suppressing some detail, we can lay out the shape of the account. Nickel argues that generics track properties that are characteristic of kinds.[28] A generic is true, on his account, when the property in question is characteristic of the kind in question. Characteristicness is cashed out in terms of whether there is an explanation, available in the relevant context, for why that property is normally instantiated by members of that kind. Which explanatory strategies are relevant to the assessment of a generic is determined by both the subject matter (are we discussing dolphin biology or tractors?) and speakers' interests (are we marine biologists or zookeepers?). But whether there *is* an explanation depends on whether there is a causal mechanism linking the kind members to the property – and that is a matter of fact about which speakers may be in the dark.[29]

Nickel's view can explain why some social-kind generics – say, 'Women are timid' – are true: there may be coercive social mechanisms that inculcate the relevant property into members of the kind. It can also, he suggests, explain why people might mistakenly believe that certain generics referring to social kinds are true. As he puts it, if 'our lives are theoretical through and through', then it is unsurprising that in the social domain, we would encounter stereotypes: 'symptoms of bad theories that cannot be shown to be worthy of rejection by showing that they have counterexamples or countervailing evidence' (p. 245). With a reference to Kuhn, Nickel suggests stereotypes – or, better, the bad theories underlying them – will fall out of use not because of an accumulation of counter-examples, but because 'they lead to degenerating research programmes' (p. 245). Presumably we realize we'd like to 'do better' than the folk-theories of gender and race on which we've been drawing, and the generic claims that were spun off by them will gradually disappear.

To some extent, the final analysis of generics will have to wait on some empirical questions – such as just what cognitive mechanisms spur our capacity to generalize, and how exactly those mechanisms are reflected in our language. If generics express a primitive generalizing capacity – as Leslie thinks and Nickel doubts – it is likely hard for us to override or redirect that mechanism, especially when we are stressed or under some other cognitive load. And yet if Leslie is correct that we often take the presence of properties predicated by generics to be explained by a kind's essence, we may have reason to want to redirect that mechanism. Viewing the behaviour and condition of disadvantaged groups in terms of traits it is part of their essence to display tends to be correlated with some problematic attitudes. It predicts, for example, a lack of interest in investigating how social structures might be working to disadvantage members of those groups.[30] For that reason, Leslie (2017) and Langton, Haslanger, and Anderson (2012) suggest we be cautious about generics. Langton, Haslanger and Anderson recommend they be avoided; Leslie is somewhat more equivocal, acknowledging that their use by members of subordinated groups may at times be politically useful (2017, p. 421). In any event, thoughtfulness about how we speak about social groups – both those to which we belong, and those with respect to which we are outsiders – seems warranted.

6. Conclusion

Philosophers have, at different times and places, drawn the boundaries around and within their discipline in different ways. At present, it is very common for us to draw a distinction between value theory – aesthetics, ethics and political philosophy – on the one hand, and the 'LEMM' fields – language, epistemology, metaphysics and mind – on the other. We expect to meet normative questions in value theory, but they arise elsewhere, too. Epistemologists sometimes advise us on when we could permissibly believe, and when instead we ought to withhold judgment; but similar recommendations might initially seem less at home in the philosophy of language.

Philosophers of language do rely on speakers' sense of the correct and the permissible in order to analyse patterns of use, notions of assertability and so on. And they may offer theories about what 'correct use' amounts to. But it would be unusual for them to recommend correct use to us in anything like the way normative or applied ethics might recommend a course of action. If a speaker violates important rules for correct use, she is usually met with some level of blank incomprehension. Her violation isn't analogous to the violation of a moral norm by someone who seeks to gratify some private temptation. It isn't surprising that warnings against it wouldn't look the same.

However, if the more psychological account of generics is correct, then we have a case where we might want to consider *not* using a form of expression, precisely because it works too well. The recommendation to avoid generics would then look more like the recommendation of a normative ethicist, and less like a grammarian's reminder. And if communicative success requires more from speakers and audiences than we might have thought when we focused only on standard kinds of misfires and abuses, and if those communicative resources are distributed in ways that track unjust social arrangements, then philosophy of language may face questions of distributive or reparative justice that are more familiar from political philosophy. Thinking about the questions feminist philosophers have raised could reshape how the boundaries around philosophy of language are drawn.[31]

Further reading

The first two items suggested here have not yet been mentioned previously, but all the rest have. The first article, Noëlle McAffee's 'Feminist Philosophy' in the *Stanford Encyclopedia of Philosophy*, provides a helpful overview of feminist work in philosophy generally. The second, Ann Garry's article 'Analytic Feminism' (also in the *Stanford Encyclopedia of Philosophy*), helpfully lays out an approach within which many of the theorists cited in this chapter would likely locate themselves. Saul and Diaz-Leon's 'Feminist Philosophy of Language' (2017) discusses work not only on silencing and generics but also on other topics – such as metaphor – which this chapter did not have space to address. For a trio of papers that will acquaint you with very distinct positions on the silencing question, I would recommend Bird (2002), Hornsby (1995) and Kukla (2014). Leslie (2017) combines clear discussion of puzzles about generics with an argument for why we should care about them.

Notes

1 For a trenchant criticism of the idea that gender is not a proper topic for metaphysical investigation, see Barnes (2014). For a general discussion of feminist approaches to metaphysics, see Haslanger and Ásta (2017).

2 The phrase 'feminist philosophers of x' is ambiguous. It could mean people with feminist political commitments who happen to study the philosophy of x – but without bringing any special attention to gender to that philosophical work. Alternatively, it could mean people who take some sort of feminist approach to the philosophical study of x. It is in that latter sense that I will be using the phrase.

3 Languages are not individual property, and yet of course individuals can make novel, even idiosyncratic, linguistic utterances. Philosophers vary in how they weight social and individual contributions to meaning. Kukla, for example, emphasizes the changes in social status that utterances can effect (Kukla, 2014). (Think of how a parental 'You may' changes the facts about what a child can – without penalty – do.) She argues that the identity of a speech act – whether or not it is a command, for example – is partially determined by the material changes it effects in social space. For Kukla, audiences' recognition of speakers' intentions need not play any role in the account of those material changes. Hornsby, like Kukla, believes that audience response is partially determinative of what force a speech act has. But unlike Kukla's, Hornsby's unpacking of communicative reciprocity between speaker and audience appeals to speakers' intentions, and audiences' recognition of them (see, e.g. 1995, pp. 129–34).

4 Consider common exchanges between friends like this: 'Are you coming out with us to the movie?' 'I have a test tomorrow.' If that answer satisfies the questioner, it would appear both parties presuppose that tests need to be studied for, and that studying and movie-going aren't compatible this evening. Depending on the context, that response to the question might also imply – though it doesn't say – that but for the test, the speaker would indeed come out to the movie.

5 See, for example, work by McConnell-Ginet (especially her 2008 discussion of 'conceptual baggage') and McGowan (especially her 2009 analysis of covert exercertives).

6   Sections 2, 3 and 4 of the Kripke chapter (this volume) discuss
    Kripke's work on names, but refer to other puzzles (not Pierre) from
    Kripke's 'A puzzle about belief' (1979).

7   Typically, exonyms are used by speakers of a language other than the
    one in common use around a geographic place. Thus, the people who
    work and live in Vienna are not the ones calling that city 'Vienna'.
    Some exonyms are such that one can easily guess the matching
    endonym. 'London' and 'Londres', and 'Vienna' and 'Wien', aren't all
    that dissimilar. But some pairs make such guessing harder. Consider,
    for example, 'Dubrovnik' and 'Ragusa'.

8   As Mills puts it, there has been a tendency in ethics and political
    philosophy to minimize 'cognitive obstacles [to virtue and just
    action]' by focusing either on individual 'biases of self-interest' or
    on 'the intrinsic difficulties of understanding the world' – with 'little
    or no attention paid to the distinctive role of hegemonic ideologies
    and group-specific experience in distorting our perceptions and
    conceptions of the social order' (2005, p. 169).

9   However, as feminist philosophy of language has helped to make
    clear, it wasn't often that, e.g. gender or race were being *fully*
    abstracted away. Rather, quite commonly, a particular race (white)
    and/or a particular gender (men) was treated as capable of standing
    in for all the others as we investigated language's function. See
    section 1 of Saul and Diaz-Leon (2017) for a useful survey.

10 McConnell-Ginet uses this example in both her 2008 and her 2012
    works. It is a quotation from Levi-Strauss, and she acknowledges
    the possibility that *he* was presenting it with tongue firmly in cheek.
    However, she notes that at least through the 1980s, she regularly
    saw sentences like this in textbooks. We ourselves can likely think of
    contemporary examples from conversations, even if the appearance
    of such ersatz gender-neutrality in published, well-edited texts is
    becoming less common. There is a related question, too, about when
    a gender-neutral term should not be used for an all-male group.
    Think of captions one often sees on newspaper photographs that
    use a gender-neutral term for a crowd that, to all appearances, is all
    male: 'Alt-right marchers gathered in Charlottesville, Virginia' or
    'Demonstrators protest in Karachi'. In some of those cases, the all-
    male nature of the group is worthy of recognition, but is not being
    remarked upon.

11 For helpful discussion of this asymmetry, see McConnell-Ginet
    (2010, pp. 177–8; 2012, p. 743). Hom (2010) gives a useful survey of
    different approaches to pejorative language. For a recent selection of
    work on slurs and pejoratives that draws on philosophy of language,
    epistemology and political philosophy – and that considers both race
    and gender – see the essays collected in Sosa (2018).

12 A background assumption in much of this work is that, with the possible exception of our classification of some natural kinds (such as elements like lead or arsenic), classification will involve choices. In particular, we will be making some choices about how to understand the intension of a concept – the rule or template for counting an object as falling under it (i.e. for falling within its extension). But choosing to sharpen our understandings of a concept's intension in one way or another should involve attention to our aims in using the concept in the first place. For example, are we trying primarily to observe and record certain facts about those people to whom 'woman' is taken to apply? Or are we trying to identify certain facts about those people in order to make their situation in some way better? Haslanger (2012a) urges that we consider ameliorative purposes in refining – and perhaps redefining – concepts. We should ask: What work should the concept 'woman' do, and which people should fall in its extension *if* we want to do better about gender (in Adichie's sense)? (See Jenkins, 2016, for the concern that Haslanger's proposal doesn't deal adequately with transgender individuals; see Bettcher, 2014, especially §7.3 and §8, for further discussion of some broader issues relating to transgender identity that are relevant here. For a poignant example of competing aims of classification, see Karkazis et al., 2012, and Karkazis and Carpenter, 2018, which critique the understanding of 'woman' being used by the International Association of Athletics Associations to regulate access to certain women's track and field events for women with intersex characteristics.)

13 A fuller quotation of the paragraph from which this snippet is taken can be found in Section 1 of the chapter on Austin in this volume; it is the passage that begins 'First, words are our tools'.

14 See Barnes (2014) and Haslanger (2012a).

15 There are, of course, non-speech-dependent forms of linguistic communication. I'm assuming for the sake of argument that the gag or the hand over the mouth suffices to eliminate the possibility of speech (in the broad sense) because the victim doesn't know, for example, British Sign Language.

16 Even sympathetic interpreters of Austin don't always agree on some of the relevant terminology. Sometimes, for example, 'illocutionary act' is used quite narrowly to cover cases like marrying and baptizing; sometimes 'illocutionary act' or 'illocution' is used more broadly to cover the notion of 'communicative force'. (This latter use would then include, e.g. acts in the former sense as a subset.) I am using the broader sense.

17 To silence someone is to prevent them from doing something they otherwise could do. And when we say that someone was silenced,

we imply that this interference was somehow inappropriate. So in the relevant sense I don't silence a toddler by singing her to sleep; nor does the state silence those who are not yet legal adults by maintaining laws mandating a minimum age for officiating at a wedding. My daughter cannot marry anyone in uttering, 'I now pronounce you married', because she is not yet eighteen – but she has not been illocutionarily silenced by the jurisdiction in which we reside. See below for another case when a speaker is unable to perform certain illocutions, but where this does not seem to be due to her having been wronged.

18   There are complex questions about when speakers' illocutionary intentions are necessary for successful illocution; when (if ever) they might be sufficient; and also about how explicit the relevant intentions need to be to the speaker herself. I am abstracting from these questions for now, and pursuing an example in which it seems plausible to suppose a speaker's intention plays *some* important role.

19   Even when we are aiming to shift audience attitudes, *belief* is not the only attitude we target; for helpful discussion, see Langton (2012).

20   For discussion of this worry, and responses to it, see pp. 219–21 (and accompanying notes) of Tumulty (2012).

21   Hornsby (1995, p. 143) emphasizes that as we track forms of women's disadvantage, we must take care not to mistake imposed disadvantage for innate deficiency. Women may often be misunderstood or not fully heard. But this is not, or certainly not only, because they are not responsible users of common linguistic resources. See Fricker (2007) and Medina (2013) for discussions (which bleed into epistemology) of the way women can be assigned such low credibility in various domains that it is hard for audiences to hear them as *testifying* as opposed to (say) merely venting. The mechanisms by which silencing could operate are likely varied; it may not be possible to subsume all of them under one model.

22   This requirement can be developed in different ways; for an Austinian approach, see Hornsby (1995, 2000); for a Gricean approach, see Maitra (2009).

23   For the suggestion that the answer to all these questions is 'No', see McConnell-Ginet (2010, p. 179).

24   When we take a suitably wide-angle lens here, we can also see that there are patterns of (dis)advantage around how likely one is to have one's *locutions* understood; see Peet (2017) for the argument that assumptions about speakers' racial and gender identities may affect the literal words we hear them as saying.

25   There has been a relatively recent explosion of interest in generics, generating a correspondingly large and complex literature. See Leslie

and Lerner (2016) for an overview. This section will follow only a few threads in this conversation.

26 These examples are Leslie's. Nickel critiques her treatment of them by distinguishing between occurrent, habitual and capacity readings of the relevant properties (2016, pp. 84–6).

27 Nickel (2016) does offer a quantificational account, but it introduces several technicalities and relies on a complicated notion of normality. This differentiates it from the kind of accounts of the universal and existential quantifier you might have covered in a logic module, and so does not present an exception to the claim that generics don't function as typical quantifier-containing sentences do. As we shall see, those (like Leslie, Langton, Haslanger, and Anderson) who are concerned about the role played by generics in the entrenchment of prejudice suggest avoiding them in favour of explicitly quantified statements using 'some' or 'a few'. This is precisely because the use of the generic implies commitments (about, e.g. how one's gender determines one's talents and interests) whose re-inscription they want us to avoid. But some of the information conveyed by the generic is simply true, and can be expressed via the quantifier instead. (Some girls do dislike math. But these authors suggest that 'girls dislike math' should be avoided, especially by parents and primary school teachers.) These proscriptions will be further discussed below.

28 Nickel can account for how the truth of a generic is sensitive to the distribution of a property over different subgroups of a kind's members, but I am suppressing this detail for now.

29 Nickel explicitly draws an analogy between his approach here, and the externalism about natural kinds familiar from Putnam's discussion of water (2016, pp. 187–8). See Section 5 of the chapter on Quine in this volume for a brief discussion of Putnam's 'twin earth' thought-experiment, and Section 5.3 of the Chomsky chapter for a longer one.

30 See, for example, the studies presented in pp. 289–90 of Fine (2012).

31 I am grateful to Barry Lee for very helpful comments on an earlier draft of this chapter.

Bibliography

Adichie, Chimamanda Ngozi (2012), *We Should All Be Feminists*. New York: Anchor Books.

Anderson, Luvell (2018), 'Calling, Addressing, and Appropriation', in Sosa, 2018, pp. 6–28.

Antony, Louise (2012), 'Is There a "Feminist" Philosophy of Language?' in Crasnow and Superson, 2012, pp. 245–85.

Barnes, Elizabeth (2014), 'Going Beyond the Fundamental: Feminism in Contemporary Metaphysics', *Proceedings of the Aristotelian Society*, 114 (3), pp. 335–51.

Bettcher, Talia (2014), 'Feminist Perspectives on Trans Issues', *The Stanford Encyclopedia of Philosophy*, ed. Edward N. Zalta, https://plato.stanford.edu/archives/fall2017/entries/feminism-trans (accessed 8 July 2019).

Bird, Alexander (2002), 'Illocutionary Silencing', *Pacific Philosophical Quarterly*, 83, pp. 1–15.

Crasnow, Sharon L. and Superson, Anita M. (2012), *Out from the Shadows: Analytical Feminist Contributions to Traditional Philosophy*. New York: Oxford University Press.

Dotson, Kristie (2011), 'Tracking Epistemic Violence, Tracking Practices of Silencing', *Hypatia*, 26 (2), pp. 236–57.

Fine, Cordelia (2012), 'Explaining, or Sustaining, the Status Quo? The Potentially Self-Fulfilling Effects of "Hardwired" Accounts of Sex Differences', *Neuroethics*, 5, pp. 285–94.

Fricker, Miranda (2007), *Epistemic Injustice: Power and the Ethics of Knowing*. New York: Oxford University Press.

Fricker, Miranda and Hornsby, Jennifer (eds) (2000), *The Cambridge Companion to Feminism in Philosophy*. Cambridge: Cambridge University Press.

Garry, Ann (2018), 'Analytic Feminism'. *The Stanford Encyclopedia of Philosophy*, ed. Edward N. Zalta, https://plato.stanford.edu/archives/fall2018/entries/femapproach-analytic/ (accessed 8 July 2019).

Green, Mitchell (2017), 'Speech Acts'. *Stanford Encyclopedia of Philosophy*, ed. Edward N. Zalta, https://plato.stanford.edu/archives/win2017/entries/speech-acts/ (accessed 8 July 2019).

Haslanger, Sally (2012a), 'Gender and Race: (What) Are They? (What) Do We Want Them to Be?' in Haslanger, 2012c, pp. 221–47.

Haslanger, Sally (2012b), 'What Knowledge Is and What It Ought to Be: Feminist Values and Normative Epistemology', in Haslanger, 2012c, pp. 341–64.

Haslanger, Sally (2012c), *Resisting Reality: Social Construction and Social Critique*. New York: Oxford University Press.

Haslanger, Sally and Ásta (2017), 'Feminist Metaphysics'. *The Stanford Encyclopedia of Philosophy*, ed. Edward N. Zalta, https://plato.stanford.edu/archives/fall2017/entries/feminism-metaphysics (accessed 8 July 2019).

Hom, Christopher (2010), 'Pejoratives', *Philosophy Compass*, 5 (2), pp. 164–85.

Hornsby, Jennifer (1995), 'Disempowered Speech', *Philosophical Topics*, 23 (2), pp. 127–47.

Hornsby, Jennifer (2000), 'Feminism in Philosophy of Language: Communicative Speech Acts', in Fricker and Hornsby, 2000, pp. 87–106.

Jenkins, Katharine (2016), 'Amelioration and Inclusion: Gender Identity and the Concept of *Woman*', *Ethics*, 126, pp. 394–421.

Karkazis, Katrina and Carpenter, Morgan (2018), 'Impossible "Choices": The Inherent Harms of Regulating Women's Testosterone in Sport'. *Bioethical Inquiry*, https://doi.org/10.1007/s11673-018-9876-3 (accessed 8 July 2019).

Karkazis, Katrina, Jordan-Young, Rebecca, Davis, Georgiann and Camporesi, Silvia (2012), 'Out of Bounds? A Critique of the New Policies on Hyperandrogenism in Elite Female Athletes', *The American Journal of Bioethics*, 12 (7), pp. 3–16.

Kripke, Saul (1979), 'A Puzzle About Belief', in Margalit, 1979, pp. 239–83.

Kukla, Rebecca (2014), 'Performative Force, Convention, and Discursive Injustice', *Hypatia*, 29 (2), pp. 440–57.

Langton, Rae (1993), 'Speech Acts and Unspeakable Acts', *Philosophy and Public Affairs*, 22, pp. 305–30.

Langton, Rae (2012), 'Beyond Belief: Pragmatics in Hate Speech and Pornography', in Maitra and McGowan, 2012, pp. 72–93.

Langton, Rae, Haslanger, Sally and Anderson, Luvell (2012), 'Language and Race', in Russell and Fara, 2012, pp. 753–67.

Leslie, Sarah-Jane (2008), 'Generics: Cognition and Acquisition', *Philosophical Review*, 117 (1), pp. 1–47.

Leslie, Sarah-Jane (2017), 'The Original Sin of Cognition: Fear, Prejudice, and Generalization', *The Journal of Philosophy*, 114 (8), pp. 393–421.

Leslie, Sarah-Jane and Lerner, Adam (2016), 'Generic Generalizations'. *The Stanford Encyclopedia of Philosophy*, ed. Edward N. Zalta, https://plato.stanford.edu/archives/win2016/entries/generics/ (accessed 8 July 2019).

Mackenzie, Catriona and Stoljar, Natalie (eds) (2000), *Relational Autonomy: Feminist Perspectives on Autonomy, Agency and the Social Self*. New York: Oxford University Press.

Maitra, Ishani (2009), 'Silencing Speech', *Canadian Journal of Philosophy*, 39 (2), pp. 309–38.

Maitra, Ishani and McGowan, Mary Kate (eds) (2012), *Speech and Harm: Controversies over Free Speech*. New York: Oxford University Press.

Margalit, Avishai (ed.) (1979), *Meaning and Use*. Dordrecht: D. Reidel.

McAfee, Noëlle (2018), 'Feminist Philosophy'. *The Stanford Encyclopedia of Philosophy*, ed. Edward N. Zalta, https://plato.stanford.edu/ archives/fall2018/entries/feminist-philosophy (accessed 8 July 2019).

McConnell-Ginet, Sally (2008), 'Words in the World: How and Why Meanings Can Matter', *Language*, 84 (3), pp. 497–527.

McConnell-Ginet, Sally (2010), *Gender, Sexuality, and Linguistic Practice: Linguistic Practice and Politics*. New York: Oxford University Press.

McConnell-Ginet, Sally (2012), 'Language, Gender, and Sexuality', in Russell and Fara, *The Routledge Companion to Philosophy of Language*, New York: Routledge, pp. 741–52.

McGowan, Mary Kate (2009), 'Oppressive Speech', *Australasian Journal of Philosophy*, 87 (3), pp. 389–407.

Medina, José (2013), *The Epistemology of Resistance: Gender and Racial Oppression, Epistemic Injustice, and Resistant Imaginations*. New York: Oxford University Press.

Mills, Charles W. (2005), '"Ideal theory" as Ideology', *Hypatia*, 20 (3), pp. 165–84.

Mills, Charles W. (2007), 'White Ignorance', in Sullivan and Tuana, 2007, pp. 13–38.

Minow, Martha (1990), *Making All the Difference: Inclusion, Exclusion, and American Law*. Ithaca, NY: Cornell University Press.

Nickel, Bernhard (2016), *Between Logic and the World: An Integrated Theory of Generics*. New York: Oxford University Press.

Peet, Andrew (2017), 'Epistemic Injustice in Utterance Interpretation', *Synthese*, 194, pp. 3421–43.

Russell, Gillian and Fara, Delia Graff (2012), *The Routledge Companion to Philosophy of Language*. New York: Routledge.

Saul, Jennifer and Diaz-Leon, Esa (2017), 'Feminist Philosophy of Language'. *The Stanford Encyclopedia of Philosophy*, ed. Edward N. Zalta, https://plato.stanford.edu/archives/fall2017/entries/ feminism-language.

Sosa, David (ed.) (2018), *Bad Words*. New York: Oxford University Press.

Stoljar, Natalie (2015), 'Feminist Perspectives on Autonomy'. *The Stanford Encyclopedia of Philosophy*, ed. Edward N. Zalta, https:// plato.stanford.edu/archives/fall2015/entries/feminism-autonomy (accessed 8 July 2019).

Sullivan, Shannon and Tuana, Nancy (eds) (2007), *Race and Epistemologies of Ignorance*. Albany: State University of New York Press.

Tumulty, Maura (2012), 'Illocution and Expectations of Being Heard', in Crasnow and Superson, pp. 217–44.

INDEX